MW00720366

Elena Calandri is Associate Professor of the History of International Relations at the University of Padua. She has published on the political history of the Mediterranean during the Cold War, European integration, and Italian foreign policy.

Daniele Caviglia is Associate Professor at the Università degli studi internazionali of Rome.

Antonio Varsori is Professor of the History of International Relations at the University of Padua.

DÉTENTE IN COLD WAR EUROPE

Politics and Diplomacy in the Mediterranean and the Middle East

EDITED BY
ELENA CALANDRI, DANIELE CAVIGLIA
AND ANTONIO VARSORI

I.B. TAURIS
LONDON · NEW YORK

Published in 2016 by
I.B.Tauris & Co. Ltd
London • New York
www.ibtauris.com

International Library of Twentieth Century History 49

ISBN 978 1 78076 108 4
eISBN: 978 0 85772 877 7

A full CIP record for this book is available from the British Library
A full CIP record for this book is available from the Library of Congress

Library of Congress catalog card: available

Printed and bound by CPI Group (UK) Ltd, Croydon, CR0 4YY
Camera-ready copy edited and supplied by the author

Contents

List of Authors

Jan Asmussen is a political scientist and historian at the Institute of Social Sciences at the University of Kiel, and Visiting Research Fellow at the School of Politics, International Studies and Philosophy at Queens University Belfast. His research focuses on state-building, reconciliation, and political developments in Europe and the Middle East. He previously served as head of the conflict and security cluster at the European Centre for Minority Studies, Flensburg, and worked at various universities in Cyprus.

Nicolas Badalassi is Associate Professor of Contemporary History at the University of South Brittany. He holds a PhD from the University of Paris, Sorbonne Nouvelle. In 2012–13, he administrated the Sorbonne Cold War Studies Project. He is the author of *En finir avec la guerre froide: la France, l'Europe et le processus d'Helsinki, 1965–1975* (2014). He has published various articles concerning French foreign policy in the Cold War era and the Helsinki Process. He has also co-edited the publication *Les pays d'Europe orientale et la Méditerranée: relations et regards croisés, 1967–1989* (2013).

Houda Ben Hamouda is a final year doctoral candidate in the history of international relations at the University of Paris, Panthéon-Sorbonne. Her research focuses on the policy of European cooperation towards the Mediterranean area during the Cold War, post-colonial relations between France and the countries of the Maghreb, and the political and economic history of the Maghreb region. She is, since September 2015, a postdoctoral within the Finnish Academy research project 'Supra- and Transnational Foreign Policy versus National Parliamentary Government' and is a member of the Pierre Renouvin Institute. Recent publications include 'L'accès aux fonds contemporains des archives nationales de la Tunisie: un état des lieux' (2014) and, co-edited with Nicolas Badalassi, *Les pays d'Europe orientale et la Méditerranée: relations et regards croisés, 1967–1989* (2013).

Elena Calandri is Associate Professor of the History of International Relations at the University of Padua. She has published on the political history of the Mediterranean during the Cold War, European integration, and Italian foreign policy. Her publications include *L'Occidente e la difesa del Mediterraneo 1947–1956* (1997), *Il primato sfuggente: l'Europa e l'intervento per lo sviluppo 1957–2007* (2009), 'Understanding the EEC Mediterranean Policy: Trade, security, development and the redrafting of Mediterranean boundaries', in C. Hiepel, *European Integration in a Globalizing World 1970–1985* (2014), *Prima della globalizzazione: L'Italia, la cooperazione allo sviluppo e la Guerra fredda 1955–1995* (2013), and, with M. E. Guasconi and R. Ranieri, *Storia politica e economica dell'integrazione europea* (2015).

Daniele Caviglia is Associate Professor at Università degli studi internazionali in Rome. Among his recent publications are *La diplomazia italiana e gli equilibri mediterranei: la politica mediorientale dell'Italia dalla guerra dei Sei Giorni al conflitto del Kippur (1967–1970)* (with M. Cricco and Soveria Mannelli, 2006), *Dollari, petrolio e aiuti allo sviluppo: le relazioni Nord-Sud negli anni '60 e '70* (edited with A. Varsori, 2008), and *Aldo Moro nell'Italia contemporanea* (edited with F. Perfetti, A. Ungari and D. De Luca, 2011).

Massimiliano Cricco currently teaches history of the European Union at the University of Urbino and previously taught international history at the University of Perugia, Tuscia and EMUNI (Euro-Mediterranean University of Slovenia). He is the author or co-author of four books, including *Il petrolio dei Senussi: Stati Uniti e Gran Bretagna dall'indipendenza a Gheddafi (1949–1973)* (2005) and with Federico Cresti, *Gheddafi: I volti del potere* (2011). He has also authored and co-authored many articles and chapters on Libya and the history of the Mediterranean countries.

Daniele De Luca is Associate Professor of the History of International Relations at the University of Salento. He has studied American Middle East policy during the Eisenhower and Kennedy administrations, writing essays and books on the subject (*La difficile amicizia: alle radici dell'alleanza israelo-americana, 1956–1963*, 2001). In 2011 he edited (with others) and published a volume on foreign and domestic Italian politics during the 1960s and 70s (*Aldo Moro nell'Italia contemporanea*, 2011).

Antonio Donno is Professor of the History of International Relations at the University of Salento. He has also lectured at LUISS, Rome. His studies are mainly focused on the relations of the United States with Middle Eastern countries, particularly Israel. He has recently edited (with Giuliana Iurlano) the volume *Nixon, Kissinger e il Medio Oriente (1969–1973)* (2010) and written *Una relazione speciale: Stati Uniti e Israele dal 1948 al 2009* (2013).

Mehmet Dosemeci is Assistant Professor of History at Bucknell University. His research interests include Turkish–EEC/EU relations, the history of European integration, national planning, and the vagaries of Turkish nationalism and Westernization in the twentieth century. He is the author of *Debating Turkish Modernity Civilization, Nationalism, and the EEC* (2013).

Marco Galeazzi († 2011) was a specialist of the History of European Communism and a member of the Fondazione Istituto Gramsci. Among his publications are *Togliatti e Tito: tra identità nazionale e internazionalismo* (2005) and *Il PCI e il movimento dei paesi non allineati 1955–1975* (2011).

Isabella Ginor (formerly Soviet/Russian affairs specialist for Israel's leading newspaper, *Ha'aretz*) and **Gideon Remez** (formerly head of foreign news, Israel Radio) are research fellows of the Truman Institute, Hebrew University of Jerusalem, specializing in the Soviet military and intelligence involvement in the Arab–Israeli conflict. Their book *Foxbats over Dimona: The Soviets' Nuclear Gamble in the Six-Day War* (2007) won the Washington Institute for Near East Policy's Book Prize silver medal.

Valentine Lomellini is Researcher at the Department of Political Science, Law and International Studies, University of Padua. She earned a PhD in Political Systems and Institutional Changes at the Institute of Advanced Studies IMT. She was awarded the Medal of the Presidency of the Italian Republic for her PhD dissertation. Her publications include *L'appuntamento mancato: la sinistra italiana ed il dissenso nei regimi comunisti, 1968–1989* (2010), *Les relations dangereuses: The French Communists and Socialists and the Human Rights Issue in the Eastern Countries* (2012).

Guia Migani is Lecturer at François Rabelais University, with a PhD in history, and works on relations between Europe and Africa, decolonization and EEC development policy, the Cold War and European integration. She is the author of *La France et l'Afrique sub-saharienne* (2008), co-editor with A. Varsori of *Europe in the International Arena during the 1970s* (2011), and with E. Bussière of *Les années Barroso* (2014).

Effie G. H. Pedaliu is a fellow at LSE IDEAS and Visiting Associate Professor at the University of Nottingham. She held posts previously at the London School of Economics, King's College London and University of the West of England. She is the author of *Britain, Italy and the Origins of the Cold War* (2003) and co-editor of *Britain in Global Politics Volume 2: From Churchill to Blair* (2013). Routledge will publish her book *The Contemporary Mediterranean World* in 2016. Pedaliu is a co-editor with John W. Young of the Palgrave Macmillan book series *Security Conflict and Cooperation in the Contemporary World*. She is a member of the Arts and Humanities Research Council's Peer Review College, a co-convenor of the International History Seminar (IHR) and reviews editor for *H-Diplo*.

Oliver Rathkolb is a professor at the Institute for Contemporary History and head of the Department of Contemporary History at the University of Vienna. He was Schumpeter Fellow at the Minda de Gunzburg Center for European Studies, Harvard University and a visiting professor at the University of Chicago and has published widely on Austrian and European contemporary political and cultural history, international affairs and on business history. He is the managing editor of *Zeitgeschichte* and member of the advisory board of the House of European History (European Parliament, Brussels). His prize-winning study *The Paradoxical Republic: Austria 1945–2005* was published by Berghahn Books in 2010.

John Sakkas is Professor of Modern History in the Department of Mediterranean Studies, University of the Aegean. His research focuses on Cold War history with an emphasis on the Mediterranean and the Middle East. He is the author of *Britain and the Greek Civil War, 1944–49: British Imperialism, Public Opinion and the Coming of the Cold War* (2013) and of articles in the *Journal of the Hellenic Diaspora, Journal of Southern Europe and the Balkans, Études Helléniques/Hellenic Studies* and *Thetis*.

Massimiliano Trentin is Assistant Professor at the Department of Political and Social Sciences, University of Bologna. He focuses on the history and international relations of the Middle East and Mediterranean, particularly on the interplay between Cold War, development and post-colonial politics. His publications include *La guerra fredda tedesca in Siria: diplomazia, economia e politica, 1963–1970* (2015), *Engineers of Modern Development: East German Experts in Ba'thist Syria* (2010), with M. Gerlini (eds) *The Middle East and the Cold War* (2012), and several articles in international journals including *Diplomatic History, Cold War History, Foro Internacional* and *Afriche e Orienti*.

Antonio Varsori is Professor of the History of International Relations at the University of Padua. His most recent publications include *L'Italia e la fine della guerra fredda: la politica estera dei governi Andreotti (1989-1992)* (2013), *Storia internazionale: dal 1919 a oggi* (2015) and *Radioso maggio: come l'Italia entrò in guerra* (2015).

Introduction

For a long time historical studies of the Cold War have viewed the 1970s as the climax in détente between East and West. During the first half of the decade in particular, owing mainly to the policies pursued by the Nixon administration and Kissinger's diplomatic skill, the USA and the Soviet Union achieved a series of significant diplomatic results which at the time were heralded as the end of open confrontation between the two superpowers. In 1972, the Strategic Arms Limitation Treaty (SALT 1) was signed and several minor agreements paved the way for close forms of economic and cultural cooperation between Washington and Moscow. In the Far East too, a peaceful approach seemed to characterize Washington's foreign policy; the traditional hostility between the United States and communist China was replaced by friendly 'ping-pong' diplomacy and Nixon's historic visit to the People's Republic of China. Moreover in 1973, peace agreements in Vietnam closed the long and bloody experience of America's military involvement in Indochina. Last but not least, Europe was portrayed as the area where détente reached its peak. The softening of tensions between Western Europe and the Soviet bloc originated in the 1960s with Khrushchev, and continued under his successors. During the second half of the decade, de Gaulle's France started dialogue with Moscow and some of Russia's more important satellites, especially Poland. In 1967, West German Foreign Minister, Willy Brandt, began to develop his *Ostpolitik*, which took on a new and bolder momentum when the Social Democrats won the German elections and Brandt became Chancellor in 1969. The invasion of Czechoslovakia in 1968 was regarded as a brief parenthesis, which did not put an end to dialogue between the two parts of a divided Europe. In 1975, the signing of the Helsinki Agreements was interpreted by most international opinion-makers as the end of the Cold War in Europe and the start of a new era in relations between Western Europe and the Soviet Union.

Some recent studies, however, have pointed out that although relations between the two superpowers definitely improved during the first half of the 1970s, and the 'old continent' experienced a period of peaceful relations and close political, economic and cultural cooperation between East and West, the Cold War was continuing in the Third World. Recent studies have thus begun to broaden the geographical perspective of the Cold War and have investigated how the bipolar conflict affected different regions, how it was affected by regional dynamics and how this conflict fuelled hidden relationships and forces that conditioned the post-Cold War age. These studies often focus almost exclusively on the superpowers. This book aims to offer a comprehensive historical assessment of the détente period in the Mediterranean in the light of a broad approach which includes the wider geographical awareness, a medium-term perspective, and a large range of actors.

In fact, even a cursory analysis of events along Europe's southern borders offers a contradictory image. From the late 1960s, southern Europe and the 'Mediterranean' – a geopolitical concept covering part of the Middle East – were characterized by turmoil, war, economic crisis and political instability. Western European nations had to confront new problems and challenges in relations with their Arab neighbours and with a changing balance in the Mediterranean, where both the US and Soviet military presence had become stronger. Peace in Europe was threatened by growing instability in the Middle East and the Arab–Israeli conflict. An increasing number of Palestinian groups decided that terrorism was the only instrument for giving a voice to the plight of their people. The hijacking of Western planes became quite a common feature in the skies of the eastern Mediterranean, and Europe was not immune from terrorist attacks, such as the tragic events during the 1972 Munich Olympic Games. Also in 1973, the Yom Kippur War marked a deep crisis, not only between the state of Israel and its traditional enemies, Egypt and Syria, but also by prompting several days of dangerous confrontation between Moscow and Washington and a deep crisis in Atlantic relations. As far as the European continent was concerned, in April 1974 the Carnation Revolution in Portugal opened the possibility of a communist-led regime in Western Europe. In July 1974, the failed coup d'état in Cyprus almost led to open military confrontation between Greece and Turkey, while the island was invaded by Turkish troops and then divided in two opposing entities. Ankara's decision led to a deterioration in relations between Turkey and its Western partners. The Cyprus crisis also led to the fall of the Greek military dictatorship. Although this event favoured the return of Athens to a democratic regime, nobody could foresee whether the new government led by Karamanlis would be able to create a stable democratic system. In 1975, another pillar in the Western defence system in southern Europe appeared to be being jeopardized by internal instability and growing turmoil. Franco's regime in Spain seemed to be coming to an end as the aged dictator was slowly dying. Last but not least, one of the more important southern European countries, Italy, was threatened with a serious economic, social and political crisis, which in the mid-1970s appeared to pave the way for the Italian Communist Party to come to power.

At the same time, the Soviet Union was exerting a growing influence in this area, whose strategic importance was underlined by the energy crisis. Regional actors and non-governmental entities grew increasingly active, as a consequence of the general cultural transformation of the time, and as a product of local conditions. Therefore, although détente was the key word in Western Europe, its southern border was characterized by trouble of a domestic nature and fears of a changing balance that many seemed to observe through the lens of the Cold War, although, in fact, it contained seeds of global and epochal transformation. The conceptual framework based on détente is therefore of little use when dealing with southern Europe and the Mediterranean. The events and dynamics which shaped these areas need further investigation and reassessment to elaborate a new conceptual framework for regions in which détente did not mean an easing of tensions and stabilization, but new tectonic and creative destabilization.

The first section of this book presents new evidences and interpretations of the role and politics of the Mediterranean as a whole as seen by various actors in international politics in the global context of the Cold War, and shows how they understood détente in the Mediterranean context. After being an 'American lake' in the 1950s and becoming a scenario for USA–USSR confrontation in the 1960s, in the 1970s the Mediterranean experienced a transition as a consequence of the interaction of super-power détente, détente in Europe, European integration and political and economic changes on the southern and eastern shores. In principle, multipolarism as a component of détente should favour a transformation of the power dynamics in the area, and this section presents an analysis of European governmental and non-governmental actors and their attempts to foster new regional assets.

The second section presents a broad analysis of the Middle Eastern and Cyprus crises. The years 1967–75 witnessed a period of extreme tension in the Arab–Israeli conflict, in which it overlapped with the East–West conflict. The re-explosion of the Cyprus issue in 1974, and the permanent

consequences it produced on Greco-Turkish relations and on both countries' relations with the West, had a multifaceted regional impact. The
chapters in this section offer new narratives and interpretations of regional
events and dynamics within a broader global context.

The third section is based on the Mediterranean as home to different
actors who were willing to elaborate personal views on (or also to reject)
the constraints of bipolarism and the Cold War (France, Turkey and the
Arab countries), and to whom détente meant the opportunity to recover
flexibility, independence and the chance to reflect on a different future.

Effie Pedaliu's broad interpretative framework analyses the transformation of the Mediterranean as a geopolitical and geocultural unitary reality,
which disappeared during the second half of the twentieth century as a
consequence of superpower influence. By the end of the 1950s, the process
of decolonization and the consequences of Cold War dynamics marked
the collapse of the era when heterogeneous Mediterranean populations
of different religions, and from both shores, peacefully shared an identity. During the following decade, security in the area was further unsettled by Moscow's naval build-up, increasing Arab–Israeli tensions, and
Washington's concern about Vietnam and its 'proto-détente' policy. The
aftermath of the Six-Day War led to a more complex and polarized region.
In order to guarantee maximum flexibility towards each other, the two
superpowers seemed rather reluctant to agree on parameters of behaviour
outside Europe. This led to greater American control over political developments in its client states through increasing support for the dictatorships
in order to avoid a vacuum of power emerging in the Mediterranean. The
exclusion of this region from détente stimulated many centrifugal forces
that resulted in a series of upheavals on the northern Mediterranean shores.
Within this framework, transition to democracy in Portugal, Greece and
Spain was interpreted by the USA as being more of a threat than an opportunity. At the same time, among the Nine there was a gradual shift towards
the priority of strengthening southern Europe by integrating the new
democracies into the EEC. The impact of bipolarism on the geopolitical
unity of the Mediterranean is further analysed in Elena Calandri's study of
the political meaning of EEC Mediterranean policy and changing US reactions to it. After the Eisenhower administration encouraged the wealthier
European states to 'share the burden' of the development of southern Europe
as European recovery proved successful, Washington grew uneasy with
EEC initiatives toward the Mediterranean states, showing a very limited,
hegemonic idea of the role of the European pillar in the Mediterranean.
Therefore, the launch of a Global Mediterranean Policy concerned the

USA, which overlooked any possible political advantage of an EEC initiative for the West. Although initially it urged the European Commission to focus on financial and technical assistance, rather than the trade sector, the European understanding of détente as an opportunity for the emergence of a European pole was later met with hostility as Kissinger and Nixon were determined to prevent a European political identity from coagulating 'against' the USA. The USA continued to conceive regional security in mainly military terms and therefore did not completely trust the EEC capacity to act as a political and security guarantee. Guia Migani's analysis of EPC discussions gives further insight into the difficulties met during the European search for a political role in the Mediterranean in the peak years of détente. During the second part of the 1960s, Western European countries were more sensitive to the general equilibrium in the Mediterranean for many reasons and prompted some EEC countries to replace the patchwork of agreements stipulated in the 1960s with a new strategy. In the preliminary stages, the Italian government launched a general discussion of the Mediterranean. Bonn supported the Italian proposal to further its relations with the Arab countries and to reassure its European partners after starting the *Ostpolitik*. The Benelux countries were more concerned about overlapping with NATO's policy in the area, whereas France rejected the idea of dealing with the Mediterranean as a whole. Moreover, Paris was unwilling to discuss military issues not covered by the EPC and promoted a bilateral approach (French–Italian) to the region. Studies conducted by the EPC Working Group stressed the key role of nationalism and Soviet activities. These discussions did not have a concrete outcome although they did offer a comprehensive acknowledgement of tensions and soft spots in the Mediterranean and proposals. The idea of EPC action towards the Mediterranean was definitively put aside after the Paris Summit which adopted instead the communitarian approach of the Global Mediterranean Policy. Nevertheless, the Mediterranean issues came to the forefront and encouraged European countries to conceive of the region as a single unit in need of a common policy. Acknowledgement of the existence of a link between Europe and the Mediterranean for Nicolas Badalassi was the limited, but unexpected result of the effort by some North African countries to have the Mediterranean included in the CSCE. In the main theatre of European détente, the overwhelming majority of the countries involved had no intention of melding European détente with the Mediterranean. The initiative, stimulating a kind of Franco-Italian rivalry at the Helsinki conference, was led by Tunisia and Algeria and aimed to link European security arrangements in the Mediterranean area with the Maltese attempt to reduce the military presence of the superpowers in the Mediterranean. The Arab countries, neutrals and non-aligned countries made an effort to shape their future, whereas Moscow and Washington shared a common view in marginalizing the Mediterranean dimension of security. Opposition parties in southern Europe also shared a vision of détente as an opportunity to downplay the blocs' control of the Mediterranean. Marco Galeazzi's reading of the Italian Communist Party (PCI) regional détente diplomacy narrates a diplomatic network in the perspective of a transformation based on the alliance between Western European working classes and southern countries' leaderships. From the mid 1950s, Togliatti agreed with Tito about the crucial role of countries struggling to be liberated from colonialism and the idea that the world was no longer strictly bipolar. At the beginning of the new decade, it appeared that the PCI was designated by the USSR as interlocutor for the liberation movements in Mediterranean Africa, thus replacing the French Communist Party. According to the PCI's strategy, the fight against neo-colonialism and true economic cooperation were the prerequisites for a coexistence aimed at overcoming the bipolar system and creating a common ground between democracy and socialism. This policy did not fit the Kremlin's approach and was also challenged by Italian communist leaders who were more cautious about the demise of the two blocs, or even favourable to their consolidation.

At the beginning of the 1970s, in Berlinguer's vision, a regional détente was a step towards the ambitious perspective of a new International Economic Order, although the PCI dialogue with Arab leaders was biased by a partial and rather dogmatic knowledge of Arab peoples and relations between Marxism and Islam. The rise of détente also promoted a wider strategy, Eurocommunism, set up by the three main Western communist parties in France, Spain and Italy. Valentine Lomellini demonstrates that Eurocommunism was intended to be an essentially dynamic policy that aimed to overcome the two blocs. Détente was a pre-condition for the Eurocommunist movement and was seen as essential to reforming socialism and shaping a new Mediterranean equilibrium, which limited the influence of the superpowers and the logic of blocs. As in the case of the PCI strategy towards developing countries, this ultimate goal clashed with the Kremlin's policy of freezing European borders and the political situation. Moreover, the three party leaderships held different views regarding the principal role of the Soviet Union. The PCI needed détente as a pre-requisite for obtaining the necessary credibility to become involved in government, but was not ready to openly challenge Soviet policy. The PCF embraced Eurocommunism essentially for domestic political reasons while the PCE firmly rejected any idea of maintaining the status quo in view of the final fight against Franco's dictatorship. Whatever the limits of these strategies, the deterioration of the situation condemned all these efforts to failure as long as détente remained essentially a European process.

Regarding the major Mediterranean crises in the détente period, Antonio Donno highlights the effects of the competition between the two superpowers in changing Mediterranean balances of power while the European continent was frozen by détente. After the 1967 war, the previous cautious policy towards Israeli requests for arms sales was abandoned by the Nixon administration. The Jewish state gradually became a strategic pillar for US containment in the Middle East. Israel was no longer only a regional ally but was considered on a more global scale as a Western stronghold in a vital area. Notwithstanding, the establishment of closer relations between Washington and Jerusalem proved difficult for many reasons. The US was willing to bring about an overall policy involving Arab countries on an anti-Soviet basis, whereas Israel was mainly interested in the purchase of American arms and remained suspicious of any proposal for an international conference. In this context, Kissinger's approach shaped a new stage in US Middle Eastern policy as a consequence of his clash with Rogers. Indeed, the Assistant to the President for National Security Affairs became more and more intolerant of US intelligence analyses stating that Soviet supplies of arms to Egypt had an essentially defensive purpose while Israel's intransigence was putting at risk Soviet–American confrontation in the region. In his essay, Daniele De Luca shows that this new trend was implemented by the Jordan crisis, which erupted in September 1970. According to the principal US decision-makers, the internal turmoil in Jordan marked a turning point: the credibility of American power was at stake and the Soviet Union's assessment of Washington's reaction should be carefully evaluated. At the beginning of the crisis, Nixon appeared more reluctant than Kissinger to deploy American ground forces, thus risking a serious confrontation with Moscow. Nixon also opposed any Israeli military moves unless he specifically approved them. However, when a small Syrian armoured force crossed the Jordanian border and King Hussein requested a British air strike, Nixon began to see the Soviets behind Damascus's initiative and prompted Jerusalem to deter the Syrians. This successful diplomatic move encouraged a decisive shift in US Middle Eastern policy, leading to a strategic partnership with the Jewish state.

The outcome of the Jordan crisis did not however prevent the Soviets from threatening the political and military equilibrium in the Mediterranean.

Backed by a repertoire of new evidence, Isabella Ginor and Gideon Remez argue that Moscow took an active part not only in training Egypt's armed forces for their offensive across the Suez Canal, but also in the war itself. The Kremlin's ambiguous policy did not pursue maintenance of the status quo in the name of détente. The Soviet leadership was informed of Egypt's war plan well in advance and did not deter its Arab clients from a large-scale military attack. In this case, détente was only partially disrupted by regional actors although the consequences of the October War spread on a regional level.

In this regard, John Sakkas shows how the cautious, if not ambiguous, Turkish policy during the conflict greatly concerned the Americans, already surprised by the initially successful Arab attack on Israel and the Soviet involvement in the region. In order to address this situation, the USA, and even Israel, did not oppose the partitioning of Cyprus. Indeed, a Turkish-controlled area on the island could increase Ankara's pro-Western posture and turn into a useful military asset to face the Soviet influence in the Middle East. Although aware of Turkey's concern about a Greek encirclement after installation of Nikos Sampson's government in Cyprus, the US administration was unwilling to act in the crisis with more than soft diplomatic instruments to prevent the invasion. Even Moscow seemed to accept a limited Turkish response provided that Cyprus's military and international status was preserved. Jan Asmussen argues for a link between the Nixon Doctrine and the cautious US policy adopted during the Cyprus crisis. The author stresses US responsibility in selling arms to Athens, thus prompting the colonels' regime to undertake the removal of Makarios under the auspices of an implicit green light from Washington. Although indirectly involved in the outbreak of the crisis, the USA appeared restrained by the Watergate scandal and failed to prevent partitioning of the island. The Cyprus crisis downplayed Kissinger's image and promoted replacement of a realistic approach with a moralistic one embodied by the Carter administration. Oliver Rathkolb's account of the attempt by major members of the Socialist International to contribute to the Middle East settlement underline the collective European endeavour towards North–South issues and the Middle East conflict, and the attempt to reduce the impact of superpower hegemony at a regional level. This detailed account aims to analyse the Brandt–Kreisky–Goldmann interaction as an example of a European network of international influence.

Besides playing a special role in global and European détente, the Mediterranean was home to national policies interacting with bipolar constraints. As argued by Houda Ben Hamouda, until the end of de

Gaulles's presidency, France opposed the development of EEC-Maghreb bonds owing to the persistence of conflicts and interests following the dismantlement of the colonial relationships: bilateral relations remained paramount until Pompidou accepted to support of EEC role in the area as a consequence also of the new Detente environment.

For Ankara, the clash with Athens came at a time when the country was involved in a harsh political and cultural debate about the prospect of further integration in the EEC. Mehmet Dosemeci argues that increased involvement in the European Common Market was not merely the continuation of a traditional policy but represented a historical opportunity to become part of modern European civilization. The EEC hinted at the possibility of political, economic and social union with Europe thus resurrecting the national debate about Turkish identity, modernity and 'Westernization', which lay at the core of Kemal's project. Within this framework, the Turkish anti-EEC front was internally divided into the left, the radical right and political Islam, though they shared a critical view of Ankara's integration into the European world. When the RPP–NSP coalition government led by Ecevit and Erbakan took power in 1974, a multidimensional foreign policy was adopted as a result of domestic pressure. The special attention given to Scandinavian countries, non-aligned and Arab countries marked disillusion with the EEC.

This new Turkish foreign policy signalled a partial detachment from the traditional pro-Western attitude and was a consequence of détente, as in the Libyan case analysed by Massimiliano Cricco. Indeed the purchase of a large quantity of Soviet weapons in 1974 and 1975 marked Libya's aspiration of playing a greater role in the Mediterranean. Since the beginning of the 1970s, Gaddafi supported the most radical Palestinian movements and many other terrorist groups around the world in order to gain more influence in the region. This Libyan reinforcement through the exploitation of East–West confrontation was achieved at the expense of a Mediterranean détente. It was the Reagan administration that decisively restrained Gaddafi's initiatives, even though this new trend took place after the failure of détente and the firm containment applied to international terrorism, Soviet aggressive design and challenges to the international order supported by Washington.

Although Gaddafi's policy was based on confrontation with the West, after their astonishing defeat in the Six-Day War, radical and populist Arab regimes faced a slowdown in their state-led economies. In order to reverse the decline in productivity, Massimiliano Trentin argues, these regimes promoted a limited degree of economic liberalization thus putting an end to the phase of Arab socialism. This new trend, coupled with the increase in constituencies including the private sector and conservative forces, was a global effort to reverse growing trade deficits by selling products to Western Europe and creating more business opportunities for their new constituencies. The inclusion of industrial cooperation, the introduction of financial assistance in the Cooperation Agreements of 1977 and the European effort to promote a free-trade zone in the Mediterranean meant that the EEC was supporting the political changes in the Arab region. This convergence took place when the Third World as a political and organized actor (1973 Charter of Algiers and 1974 New International Economic Order) was already declining. Unfortunately, the limits of the far-reaching goals of the Agreements soon became evident. The EEC Commission excluded some items, produced mainly by Arab countries, from reductions in custom tariffs (including textiles and most refined-oil products). Moreover, the Europeans tried to impose free-market dynamics and GATT rules on Arab oil producer investments, whereas Arab investors called for more guarantees and a special focus on industrial projects. Finally, many European corporations were sceptical about the regimes' economic policy and legislation that, in their opinion, did not involve any strategic shift toward privatization. The global pattern exchange between the two shores of the Mediterranean was asymmetric and, despite an increased volume of trade – excluding oil – the Arab countries still recorded a major deficit in the balance of trade with the EEC in 1979.

The contributions to the volume demonstrate that when dealing with the Mediterranean during the 1970s the usual conceptual framework based on détente is of scant value. The Mediterranean was a contested border between the peaceful relations that appeared to characterize most parts of the 'old continent' and the ongoing confrontation that shaped the 'Third World'. Although in different degrees the two superpowers were more and more committed to the aim of exerting a growing influence in those areas as the energy crises of 1973/1974 and 1979/1980 magnified the importance of this part of the world to both the Soviet Union and the United States. The Yom Kippur War was just the most evident example of the continuing conflict between Moscow and Washington, but other crises, such as Turkey's occupation of northern Cyprus, played some role in pointing out the permanence of long-term contrasts between the two superpowers. Moreover the conflicts and turmoil that characterized this part of the world demonstrated the importance of local factors and the difficulties the two superpowers had in controlling this area and to impose the rules of détente; in this connection it would be possible to point out long-term local conflicts, which had nothing to do with the Cold War, sudden crises, the emergence of revolutionary actors and forces which felt no allegiance to the traditional superpowers, the explosion of terrorist activities.

The conflicts in the Mediterranean, as well as in the neighbouring Middle East, appeared to influence southern Europe: from Portugal to Greece, from Spain to Italy, from Cyprus to Turkey. In such cases, however, the search for stability appeared to prevail. Nevertheless the United States and the Soviet Union did not play a leading role in finding a new acceptable balance. It was mainly up to local actors, to some western European nations, especially France and West Germany, and to the European Community to find out solutions that were based on new approaches that were largely based on political and economic instruments. In the late 1970s, in spite of serious difficulties, those policies had paved the way to valid forms of stabilization in most southern European nations. So it is not surprising that the new or 'second' Cold War had its origins, not only in Afghanistan, but mainly in central Europe as a consequence of the deployment of SS-20 Soviet missiles and of the Polish crisis. Moreover it is of some relevance that some sources of crisis and conflict on the southern and eastern shores of the Mediterranean are still there in spite of the end of the Cold War.

This volume originated in a conference held in Padua in July 2009 under the auspices of the Department of International Studies and of the Faculty of Political Sciences of the University of Padua and the LUSPIO University of Rome. The editors would like to thank all the persons and institutions which have contributed to the success of the conference, as well as to the publication of the proceedings, in particular Caroline Clarck and Massimiliano Trentin for their contribution to the editing process, and the staff of the Department of International Studies, which gave precious help to the organization aspects.

PART 1

The Mediterranean(s) in the Global Balance

CHAPTER I

Fault Lines in the Post-War Mediterranean and the 'Birth of Southern Europe', 1945–1979

An Overview

Effie G.H. Pedaliu

En Méditerranée, Georges Moustaki's elegiac and evocative lyrics epitomize the concept of a Mediterranean world, which is singular, unified and exists in a continuum. The Mediterranean world, however, has been historically a contradictory amalgam of difference and interdependence. This essay will look at how the Cold War and, in particular, the impact of super-power détente, compromised established bonds of interdependence and enabled the political, economic and societal fault-lines running through the Mediterranean to facilitate the 'emergence of Southern Europe'.

The 'High Cold War' and Decolonization in the Mediterranean

The American policy of containment was premised on a manichean view of the world where even the smallest shift in share of global power was perceived to be a major setback to the status and credibility of the USA and to its eventual ability to win the Cold War. The application of the policy was rigid and it was not amenable to a flexible implementation based on the special characteristics of each region.[1] One area in which the rigidity of the policy was experienced most profoundly was the northern Mediterranean littoral where, from France to Greece, the wartime experiences of

occupation, resistance and collaboration had resulted in profound political, social and economic tensions, which by the end of World War II had
coalesced into a maelstrom of insecurity and instability.[2] In such a precarious security environment, the prospect of communist victories at the ballot
box became a distinct possibility.[3] The chance of a communist electoral
victory in Italy came to be seen in Washington as signifying a substantial
victory for Soviet Communism and a near catastrophic loss of prestige for
liberal democracy and capitalism that could even tip the course of the Cold
War.[4] The situation in liberated France only helped to validate this conclusion. From Washington's vantage point, the volatility and politics of the
Fourth Republic appeared to be quite similar to the challenges facing Italy.
The French coalition government also included communists and socialists
as an integral component.[5] The civil war in Greece compounded American
concerns. They feared a communist-dominated Greek government would
clear the way for a similar government in Italy and probably increase
communist influence in the Middle East. Very quickly however, the US
State Department reached the conclusion that their British Allies were
mishandling the situation in Greece and even aggravating it through their
obstinate support for the Greek monarchy.[6] As the security situation on the
northern Mediterranean shore became increasingly vexatious to the USA,
the need to secure ready access to Middle Eastern oil was intensifying.
Europe needed to be weaned off its dependency on the heavily unionized
'King Coal' industry and oil was deemed the suitable replacement upon
which Western European economic reconstruction and stability should be
built. The value of the Mediterranean as an energy corridor came to be
cemented.[7]

Traditionally, Mediterranean security had been a British concern but,
in the post-war world Britain was displaying signs of being uncomfortable in withstanding the systematic probing by the USSR to its interests
in the northern Mediterranean and the Middle East which even during
the period of the 'Grand Alliance', the British Foreign Office had identified as a threat.[8] A recognition of this steered British foreign policy
towards cooperation with the USA in this part of the world until such
time Britain had overcome its economic weaknesses and was able to
become the 'middle of the planet' superpower that would promote its
interests unilaterally and even perhaps, to become the equal of the USA
and the USSR.[9] British weakness was exacerbated further by the troubles they encountered in their Palestine Mandate which were depriving
it of the friendship of Arabs and Jews alike.[10] By summer 1946, US State
Department's unwavering belief that a lone Britain was unable to defend

the Mediterranean route to the Middle East had become prevalent in other US government circles as well.[11]

By late summer 1946, developments in Germany, the negotiations for the Italian Peace Treaty, the Straits Controversy and the re-ignition of the Greek Civil War made it plain that the building of a post-war order in Europe based on a 'grand alliance' model was becoming increasingly problematic. America's reaction was to recast the countries of the northern Mediterranean littoral as impregnable anti-communist fortresses which turned the region into a Cold War frontline. The announcement of the Truman Doctrine earlier in March 1947, the 'exclusion crises' in May 1947 which excluded the communist parties of France and Italy permanently from government for the duration of the Cold War, the announcement of the Marshall Plan aid in June 1947 for countries which included France, Italy, Greece and Turkey now turned the US into a major Mediterranean power displacing Britain's dominance. The region was to become an invaluable weathervane for the Americans to gauge the effectiveness of containment and sharpen the capabilities and outreach of its newly acquired national security apparatus. The eventual outcome was the victory of the anti-communist parties in the Italian elections of April 1948 and by October 1949 the Greek communists had been defeated. However, Italy and Greece emerged as problematic democracies with limited sovereignty.[12]

The next step for the Americans in this process was to fortify the frontline. The most potent binding forces in this process were the Marshall Plan and the North Atlantic Treaty. The effects of the European Recovery Programme (ERP) were to be far-reaching and transformative for its Mediterranean recipients, which included the whole of the north Mediterranean littoral with the exception of Spain. During 1950–1973, *il boom* in Italy, *les Trente Glorieuses* in France and the Greek 'Economic Miracle' were to transform the economies and societies of these countries. From 1959–62, the Italian economy grew on average at a rate of 6.3 per cent per year.[13] From 1950 to 1973 the Greek economy achieved average growth rates of 7 per cent[14] and the French economy's performance was equally impressive.[15] This economic growth came in tandem with high wages which stimulated consumption, brought about affluence and transformed these countries into modern consumer societies. The ERP also forced these countries, despite a reluctance, to adopt a more American managerial and bureaucratic method in industrial production and relations.[16]

The Marshall Plan soon would be underpinned by security arrangements too. In fact, in the case of Greece and Italy, the Marshall Plan had a dual purpose as economic reconstruction aid was underpinned with secret protocols that provided military aid so that the two countries could stave off any communist threats. Italy became a founding member of NATO followed in 1952 by Greece and Turkey. This led seamlessly to the signing of the Madrid agreements in 1953 when the blindingly obvious value of Spain's real estate for American bases and the tighter application of containment could not be ignored. To allow General Franco to survive the economic impasse UN ostracism had condemned him to was deemed by the USA to be simply another necessary step towards protecting the 'free world', a Cold War mental construct which although not always compatible with the idea of 'the West' proved to be an essential tool to containment and building a robust anti-communist boundary.[17] By 1953, a coherent anti-communist security community was in place on the northern littoral comprising disparate countries from Portugal to Turkey. All differed in terms of tradition, institutions, religion, levels of development and punching power but all had been woven tightly together by a robust institutional framework.[18]

Over this formative period when the countries of the northern littoral were being drawn together, the experience of the southern shore was remarkably different. The incongruous fashion in which borders had been carved out to accommodate decolonization, the birth of Israel in a neighbourhood where it was not wanted and the intersection of decolonization with the Cold War had given birth to relatively unstable states. This had resulted in the rise of authoritarian leaders but also compromised economic development and commercial activities and bequeathed the region a tendency towards a relentless fragmentation. The tensions in the southern littoral proved difficult for Western powers to harness or even comprehend and their policies towards the region would be elaborated on outdated, even neo-colonialist assumptions. The aim of policy was to maintain influence and promote Western interests in the post-colonial era rather than to use and exploit a new understanding of the new world that was emerging in the Mediterranean South.[19] Despite American discomfort with the idea and practice of colonialism, until the Suez crisis in 1956, the assumption in Washington had been that the security of the Maghreb and the Mashreq coasts would be safeguarded in the main by the colonial arrangements of Britain and France.[20] President Truman's piecemeal approach to the region had been replaced by President Eisenhower's determination to build a coherent security system there. His efforts however, were to be compromised by the very force he had hoped would provide the USA with a tough shield against Communism – Arab nationalism. After 1948, this potent force would be directed not only against the colonial masters of the region but also, eventually, the USA itself, mainly because of President Truman's role in the birth of Israel. This bred anti-Western impulses that were abetted by the rise to power of Egyptian President, Gamal Abdel Nasser, in 1954.[21] Nasser used pan-Arabism as a clarion call to promote Egyptian leadership of the newly decolonized Arab world. As matters became more unsettled, Britain's failure to establish a Middle Eastern Command underscored the need for better defen/ ,rrangements for the Northern Tier to prevent Soviet encroachment ir ;he perceived gap between Turkey and Pakistan and this became even ,re urgent after the signing of SEATO in 1954.[22]

However, by 195/ ,e Eisenhower administration's adoption of the 'New Look' meant thar , USA was unwilling to take on more troop commitments. This had ,plications for Britain's plans for new defensive arrangements for the ,on but also for US policy both in the Maghreb and the Mashreq. E; ,ower tackled this in several ways. As the importance of the southern s ; for securing a more coherent Mediterranean strategy grew, his adm/ ;ration adopted NSC-5436/1 which repositioned US policy away f , shoring up Maghrebi security through French colonialism to one r / to accept the emancipation of the region and even, 'if the circumstar ultimately so require[d], to press the French to give full independen ,o Tunisia and Morocco', which he did indeed do.[23] He endorsed a c , against the Mossadeq Government in Iran, which secured easy access Iranian oil supplies, and he supported renewed British efforts to weave regional defence arrangement in the Middle East. The Baghdad Pact was signed in 1955. It comprised Britain, Iraq, Turkey, Iran and Pakistan but there was no Syria, no Jordan, no Egypt, no Israel and despite encouraging sounds behind the scenes from the Eisenhower administration, no USA. The pact was also overshadowed by the nascent moves by a group of countries towards non-alignment as manifested at the Bandung Conference in April 1955. This was a double blow to the West in the region as, by now, Nasser had decided that his plans were better served by manipulating the superpowers and engaging them in a game to outbid each other for his favour as his Czech arms deal revealed. It also highlighted with painful clarity the dilemma in which the USA was caught – an anti-colonial power whose closest allies against its mortal enemy were the very colonial powers striving to frustrate the efforts of the Third World to liberate itself. Thus, a window had opened for the Soviets in the region just when Nikita Khrushchev was about to embark on his 'Third World offensive'.[24]

Opportunities for the Soviets would multiply after the British, French and Israeli 'collusion' in reaction to Egypt's nationalization of the Suez Canal. Their actions at Suez in 1956 wiped out any residual European colonial influence in the southern littoral and also upset Eisenhower's delicately balanced policies there. As the Soviets were being invited to Egypt and Syria, Eisenhower was shelving his ambitions for constructing any encompassing institutional security arrangements for the South and he was left only with the option of announcing the more modest priorities of the Eisenhower Doctrine in 1957. The new doctrine was to be showcased in Lebanon in 1958 where it highlighted that the Middle East was not totally immune to Cold War tensions. In the meanwhile, as the countries of the southern littoral focused on constructing post-colonial identities there was a struggle in settling the shape of power relations in the region between the proponents of secular Islam as promoted by Nasser and those of political Islam as understood by the Wahabi Royal House in Saudi Arabia. Both would find that the Soviet Union cast a long shadow. Egypt's and Saudi Arabia's support of opposing sides in the Yemeni war clearly depicted this cleavage. In the years to come, authoritarian states in the Maghreb and Mashreq would attempt nation building on the foundation blocks of resentfulness towards the West, an inability to accept Israel and on non-alignment yet they failed to address issues of poverty, social justice, and civil rights which all promoted instability. The balance sheet for the Truman and Eisenhower years was that the USA had emerged as the dominant force in the Mediterranean but the Mediterranean South was devoid of institutional security arrangements and offered potentially rich pickings for the Soviets, especially as the region was turning inwards on itself. The generous amounts of Soviet aid to the states of the Mediterranean South increased substantially at this time so that between 1957 and 1970, economic assistance to Mediterranean and Middle Eastern states represented 40 per cent of total Soviet aid destined for non-communist states, with the largest beneficiaries being Egypt, Turkey and Syria.[25]

The seismic impact of decolonization promoted a dissociation between Europeans and non-Europeans in the Mediterranean region in a multitude of ways and concluded the process of separation that had started with the decline of the Levant. The inter-communal violence associated with the tensions of decolonization in Cyprus which were undermining Greco-Turkish relations, straining US and British relations with both countries and weakening NATO's southern flank, spilled over to Istanbul in September 1955. There were violent reprisals against the Greek community which led to the eventual exodus from their ancestral homes of nearly all the Greeks. The Evian Agreements of 1962 and Nasser's Egyptianization and Nationalization Laws of 1957 and 1961, led to the exodus and expulsion of British, French, Greek, Italian and Jewish minorities from the

Maghreb and Egypt. These developments signified the end of the era when heterogeneous Mediterranean populations of different religions and from both shores lived on the same soil, in large numbers. Their past interactions, in the main, may have been commercially based and far from perfect but from now on any co-mingling in the southern littoral became rare. Even the regional *lingua franca*, French, was replaced slowly by an extra-regional one, English. Cultural exchanges and familiarity that had existed for centuries were to be severed for years to come. The ethnic and cultural cleansing of European influences from the southern shore plus its huge democratic deficit, apart from Israel, reinforced the Cold War forces that were distancing the two shores from each other. By the late 1960s, the Cold War, the decrease in commercial opportunities for the nations of the northern shore and the fostering of ideas of the 'other' by many political forces in the South meant that the sea had lost most of its unifying qualities and by the late 1970s, any ideas of 'Mediterraneanism' appeared to be both questionable and superficial.[26]

By the early 1950s, the Marshall planners had succeeded in creating a hospitable environment in Western Europe for the seeds of European integration. The integrative process that gave birth to the Schuman Plan in 1950, had by 1957 culminated in the signing of the Treaty of Rome. The new European Economic Community (EEC) included among its founders two larger nations of the region – France and Italy both of which saw themselves as partly Mediterranean and partly Western. Soon afterwards, Greece in 1962 and Turkey in 1963, both gained EEC association status. The intermingling of security and a new prosperity intersected with a huge cultural transfer to these countries from the USA which drew out the European characteristics of the northern littoral countries and led eventually to their consolidation as Southern European nations via rapid modernization through Westernization/Americanization, exposure to Hollywood films, Coca Cola, rock 'n' roll and increasing conspicuous consumption.[27] The dictatorships in Portugal, Spain and later Greece, when curtailing political liberties, clashed directly with the messages of prosperity and pluralism reaching the inhabitants of these countries through advertising, film, music, literature and increased travel and tourism. These oppressive governments tried to minimize 'subversive ideas' penetrating their space but, in a world that was becoming ever more inter-connected, their attempts to isolate their citizens could be only partially successful. At the same time, by the 1960s, Western identity itself was undergoing major evolution. On the one hand there was Americanization and Atlanticism. One the other, with decolonization firmly behind it, a Western European identity was becoming ever more confident and coalescing around the universal values of civil liberties and human rights that soon came to be identified with the EEC. In contrast, at this time there was a realization by many Europeans that human rights could not be addressed in a satisfactory manner within NATO since many of the organization's members maintained that its status as a military organization obliged it only to preserve its strength and provide a credible deterrent to its enemies by maintaining its cohesion. However, by late 1960s the flagrant human rights abuses taking place in Greece coincided with the Portuguese colonial wars. Both were happening during a time of political radicalism which focused the attention of European public opinion on the actions of the southern European dictators. In order to appease their electorates and also conform to human rights policies Western European governments turned to the European institutions set up after the end of World War II to ensure that the ghosts of Hitler's Germany never revisited the continent. Thus, by the late 1960s and early 1970s, both the Council of Europe and the EEC were drawn into the fight for the restoration of democracy in Greece and stopping the abuse of human rights there. The Council of Europe eventually manoeuvred Greece into suspending itself from membership of the institution and the EEC suspended Greece's association agreement. Such actions strengthened and augmented European institutions and stimulated a distinctive Western European identity.[28]

'Bridge-Building' and the Mediterranean

From the early 1960s, the complexity of power relations in the Mediterranean as a whole had been increasing and in the South region in particular, which fuelled an intense proliferation of arms sales. This was fed not only by the superpowers but also by the European powers that wished to ensure that decolonization did not mean a total eclipse of influence and economic and commercial opportunity. President John F. Kennedy's attempt to cultivate closer relations with Nasser through personal diplomacy during 1961–1963 had foundered on the rocks of Yemen, Cuba and Albania. Nasser had needed weapons for his protégés in Yemen and when the USA prevaricated and declined to assist, the Soviets obliged as they needed to reverse any damage to their global credibility from the Cuban Missile Crisis and their expulsion from Vlore. Meanwhile Kennedy had decided to enable Israel to secure Hawk missiles.[29] By 1966, Ba'athism became an unassailable force in Syria. Soon the turmoil in the southern shore would also have security implications for the northern one. France, despite its seeming finely balanced poise between Arabs and Israel, was to emerge as one of the primary weapons providers for Israel and surreptitiously it helped it develop its own nuclear programme at Dimona. The reinsertion of France as a factor in Mediterranean affairs would increase greatly after the collapse of the Fourth Republic and the signing of the Evian Agreements 1962. For President Charles de Gaulle, an activist Mediterranean policy was not only a means for compensating France for the loss of its Maghrebi empire but also an integral part of his global challenge to American authority. The withdrawal of the French Mediterranean fleet from NATO Command in 1959 was a mere precursor to the French withdrawal from the military aspect of NATO in 1966.[30] The French were not alone in their Mediterranean ambitions however. Successive Italian governments had attempted to take advantage of French difficulties in the region after their retreat from the Maghreb. Italy sought to establish a firm Mediterranean presence in order to expand its commercial interests and become an energy player and Italian efforts would redouble in the years to come. The main difference between the two countries was in how they viewed their Mediterranean role. France was trying to minimize US influence and acquire a bigger sway, whereas Italy was satisfied with the role of the 'bridge-builder' between the southern Mediterranean world and NATO. Even the Spanish dictator General Franco decided to develop a Mediterranean policy to catch the attention of France, Italy and the USA as he sought to renegotiate better financial terms for the leasing of Spanish real estate for US bases.[31] Yugoslavia, emerging as one the pre-eminent powers in the Non-Aligned Movement (NAM) elaborated its own Mediterranean policy to increase the influence of the country beyond its borders and also later, to mitigate the menace of the Brezhnev Doctrine.[32]

Secretary of State Dean Rusk's reasoning that it was a 'false impression that Viet-Nam [sic] preoccupied [the USA] to the exclusion of everything else'[33] cannot be dismissed out of hand since President Lyndon B. Johnson and his administration had paid great attention to NATO's travails during the 1960s. However, when it came to international affairs America's lens became deeply distorted by Vietnam and for a while the Mediterranean dropped from its line of vision. America carried out some swift interventions in the area but, over the long run, it failed to promote security and stability there. Through the 1960s, the security environment of the region was further unsettled by a massive Soviet naval build-up, the increasing Arab–Israeli tensions, America's inattention due to Vietnam and its exploration of 'bridge-building' with Soviet Union. The region had now accumulated a dangerous level of tensions and threats to security. There had been no confidence-building initiatives to deal with the Arab–Israeli dispute and the deteriorating relations between Greece and Turkey were left to drift with just brief US interventions, which inflamed matters rather than offering long-term solutions. The year 1967 seemed to be the one that would define the future of the region for the coming years.[34]

The usurping of Greek democracy on 21 April 1967 and the increased tensions in Italian politics indicated that America's inattention combined with its attempts at 'proto-détente' were not exactly reconcilable and had exposed both Greece and Italy to intolerable domestic tensions. Elements from the political extreme right in both countries were losing their confidence in the USA and began to take matters into their own hands. As the surprise from the Greek coup was still sinking in, the outbreak of the Six-Day War in June focused, for a while at least, the attention of the Johnson administration on the area, especially since the Arab defeat could potentially give the USSR access to new naval facilities in Egypt and Syria.[35] However, Johnson was by now a captive of the Vietnam War and any concentration on Mediterranean matters was to prove too fleeting to be constructive. Where Greece was concerned, his administration just accepted the junta's anti-communist and pro-NATO credentials. The fact that the Israeli pre-emptive strike in June succeeded beyond even the wildest hopes of those who planned and executed it led the USA to upgrade the importance of Israel for containment and discouraged notions of promoting long-lasting solutions which may have meant coercing a reluctant Israel.[36] The efforts of the Four Power process and the Jarring Mission to seek out long-term solutions for the Middle East were deeply weakened if not compromised. This was not only because of Arab and Israeli mistrust but also on the calculation made that Vietnam would prevent the USA from being particularly active in the region, that the longevity of the Johnson administration was in doubt and also because the Four could not really agree on the best route forward among themselves. The Six-Day War also gave France the opportunity to re-orientate its policy in the Mediterranean away from alliance with Israel and accelerated its bid for a greater role in the area.[37]

From this moment on, some of the sinister offshoots of the Arab–Israeli conflict would spread and would not even be contained geographically within the Middle East. The Palestinian Liberation Front internationalized its campaign for a Palestinian homeland and attempted from 1968 onwards, to wage its war against Israel through increasing air piracy. This development compromised further the fragile security of many European countries especially those of the Mediterranean North. The expansion in scope of Palestinian operations in Europe came at a time when many European countries were facing internal challenges from domestic terrorist groups. The various terrorists formed links and set up networks that cut across national and even regional boundaries and the nature of security threats facing the region became more insidious and pervasive.[38]

The Mediterranean and Détente

By the time Nixon became president, he had to contend with a crescendo of calls demanding the neutralization and denuclearization of the Mediterranean. Such demands from many in the basin went back to 1964, but they were now getting very insistent and included even those the USA counted as allies such as Franco's Spain.[39] Others included countries that were members of the Non-Aligned Movement such as Algeria who called for the eviction of the superpowers. In fact, Houari Boumedienne, the Algerian President had relayed the very same message to Alexei Kosygin, the Soviet Premier.[40] Nixon had to cope with a region that was becoming more volatile, more complex and more polarized than ever. Three months from his inauguration, he faced the outbreak of the 'War of Attrition' in March 1969 and within nine months, the dethronement of King Idris of Libya by the volatile and unpredictable Muammar Gaddafi who lost no time in demanding that the USA vacate one of its most important real estate assets in the Mediterranean, the Wheelus air-base.[41] For Nixon the security environment facing the USA in the Mediterranean appeared almost apocalyptic. In an off-the-record discussion with journalists he painted the following picture:

> Over the past ten years the American position in the Mediterranean has been rapidly deteriorating and has deteriorated there more than any place in the world. Look at the Southern rim of the Mediterranean. Look at the eastern rim of the Mediterranean and the northern rim of the Mediterranean and see what has happened, and you will see why this is the case.[42]

The impact of the Cold War in such a semi-enclosed environment where stresses and frictions bounced off one another and created chain reactions of events with unintended consequences was encapsulated in Henry Kissinger's vivid description of superpower behaviour during the Cold War which still remains one of most spine-chilling depictions of the prevailing mindsets and paranoia behind policy formulation during the Cold War.

The superpowers often behave[d] like each side should know that frequently uncertainty, compromise, and incoherence are the essence of policymaking. Yet each tend[ed] to ascribe to the other a consistency, foresight, and coherence that its own experience belie[d]. Of course, over time, even two armed blind men can do enormous damage to each other, not to speak of the room.[43]

The adoption of a policy of détente did not mean that paranoia, mistrust, rivalry and jostling for position were to be jettisoned. These Cold War characteristics of superpower interaction remained deeply ingrained and were carried over into the period of superpower détente.[44] For its architects, President Nixon and his National Security Advisor, Henry Kissinger, on the one side, détente was merely just another permutation of containment which if implemented successfully would enable the USA to win the Cold War over the long run. For General Secretary Leonid Brezhnev, on the other side, it offered an opportunity to advance Soviet interests, and this included pushing back the boundaries of containment in the Third World. Kissinger, in one of his initial attempts to explain his ideas on détente to Nixon, set out the tortuous parameters within which détente would be pursued. He described the current state of the USA–USSR relations as a mix of 'containment and détente' and added that 'the most substantive East-West relations will remain in the realm of USA–USSR accommo-dation or cooperation within a framework of selective competition – a realm of political relationships that [is] inadequately expressed in the word "détente"'.[45] This selective competition would be at its most acute around the Mediterranean basin. The USA could not allow détente to create a vacuum in the Mediterranean because it would be filled by the massive Soviet naval build-up and just allowing the region 'to continue to dete-riorate as it ha[d] been deteriorating' would put US interests at stake.[46] At a time when American intelligence chiefs and policy-makers deeply distrusted each other the one thing on which they found common ground was the conclusion that 'the rivalry between the USA and the USSR in the Mediterranean [was] likely to persist at least as long as the contest between them continue[d] in the world at large'.[47]

The process of détente remained a profoundly theoretical exercise focused on arms reduction at the central front but in order to allow for maximum flexibility in their relations the superpowers were rather tardy in establishing agreed parameters of behaviour in other exposed areas. The USA saw the Mediterranean as an 'adjunct' of European security. This meant that as the détente process was still in its infancy, areas such as the Mediterranean could not be allowed to derail it or even worse, to allow détente to become an agent for a re-distribution of existing power in region. Soviet actions were to complicate US calculations in the Mediterranean further. During the years of détente the USA regarded Soviet attempts to improve their relations with the 'anti-communist' bastions of the northern littoral with real concern, especially as the Soviets proved to be quite undiscriminating over the democratic credentials of those who they sought to cultivate and even Franco's Spain and the Greek junta became targets for their overtures. The USA was not concerned that these regimes would advance relations with the USSR beyond the point of just trade but now, the whole of the North appeared less than stable.[48]

In order to ensure that no vacuums of power emerged in the Mediterranean region whilst it was pursuing détente, the USA excluded the area from the process and attempted to contain matters by increasing its control over political developments in its client states through an increasing use of covert operations and increased support for the dictators.[49] Thus, as tensions declined over the central front, in the Mediterranean they grew. The Nixon administration considered change to be a complication that needed to be resisted and even frustrated but stasis, however, created its own problems. The situation in Italy soon came to resemble that of a pressure cooker about to explode as the country was tested by social upheaval and growing political violence aggravated by its proximity to Greece. Nixon was dismissive of any suggestions that this situation could have arisen from any other contributory factors apart from 'the opening to the Left' and this precluded any proper consideration of making the Italian political system more inclusive.[50]

The exclusion of this coveted sea from the process of détente was experienced by the countries of the basin as a centrifugal force that compounded the disruptive effects decolonization and the Cold War had wrought on the region. The accumulation of tensions in the Middle East, which resulted in the Yom Kippur War in October 1973, caught the neglectful and complacent superpowers unaware. Détente was to be tested to its limits. No sooner had matters in the Middle East begun to be dealt with than a period of upheaval commenced in the northern Mediterranean shore. Portugal was to be the first southern European country to get rid of its dictators and a few months later, Greece followed. During the 1970s, the Greek junta's adventurist foreign policy had not been reined in effectively. The 'colonels' exported their anachronistic ideas to their neighbours. They struck up close relations with neo-fascist organisations in Italy and precipitated a series of crises in and over Cyprus.[51] Their recklessness culminated in the overthrow of President Makarios of Cyprus in July 1974. The subsequent invasions of the island by Turkey brought Greece and Turkey close to war, led to the junta's abrupt demise and nearly unravelled NATO's Southern Flank. In Spain, Franco's death allowed the country to take its place among the democratic nations of Europe. The sudden democratization of southern Europe and the short-lived uncertainty that followed was interpreted by the USA as being closer to a crisis than an opportunity.[52] Such concerns were misplaced. With the exception of Greece which left the NATO military command in the eventful summer of 1974 only to return in 1981, all the new southern European democracies entrusted their security to NATO in order to stabilize their political systems and safeguard territorial integrity. Even Greece admitted in private that it 'needed NATO as a shield although it was not sure how strong this shield was'.[53] For the USA, as far as Mediterranean politics were concerned, by 1974 the Nixon administration had come to view any changes towards democratic rule as a direct threat to détente.[54]

When the Portuguese dictatorship collapsed and the country had shifted to the left, Kissinger reacted impulsively and looked to a paramilitary solution. Cooler counsels, however, prevailed and under West German and British tutelage, Portugal was stabilized through elections and not through a coup d'état.[55] By the time the Greek dictatorship collapsed the whole of the Greek political spectrum, from left to right, had no desire to allow the USA any scope to mentor their newly found democracy.[56] In Turkey, a dislike for détente was to be compounded by the American Congress' decision to impose a weapons embargo and this undermined Turkish trust in the USA.[57] American actions and regional policy during this period of détente were to come under close scrutiny and the inability of the USA to protect and promote democracy within its sphere of influence was taken very seriously. President Carter could take credit for Camp David and the fact that the Italian elections of 1976 had returned the right result without overt American intervention but the reality was that the USA found its position in the region weakened.[58] The vacuum of power America feared did not occur, but a vacancy for a mentor did since both Ford and Carter were able to play only a limited role in this transitional period.[59]

The precariousness of the security of the southern flank had rattled not only the USA but also the Nine. The EEC focused on the democratic deficit of some southern European countries as being a source of instability rather than stability. This led them to re-think their toleration of authoritarian regimes within Western institutions. Furthermore, they realized that they would have to step in and take steps to safeguard democracy in southern Europe by containing the emerging tide of anti-Americanism and ensuring that political change in these countries was managed in a way that made them adhere closer to the West rather than merely becoming resentful states. At this point in its history the EEC was uniquely poised to undertake such stabilization. By the 1970s, it had grown in both size and wealth. Georges Pompidou's desire to make good the Gaullist aim of increasing French global influence through the EEC coincided with the emergence of European leaders such as Edward Heath in Britain and Willy Brandt in Germany. The three leaders wished to elaborate European solutions and resolve difficulties in European–US relations over issues such US policy towards Indochina, the Mediterranean and Greece, all of which had now become contentious issues in Western European domestic politics. The occurrence of such a degree of convergence in the national interests of its member states enabled the EEC to move towards acquiring a voice of its own in international affairs. This process was further accelerated by the intensification of the policy of superpower détente that was about to redefine the transatlantic relationship.[60] In 1967, the Harmel report had noted the European acceptance of détente in principle but it also identified the Mediterranean as an exposed area with 'special problems'. However, nearly all EEC member states held deep reservations that superpower détente, as practised by the Nixon administration, safeguarded their interests and security. At The Hague Conference of 1969, concerned by the possible effects of détente and prodded by the prospect of further enlargement, the EEC sought to explore avenues to move from just economic cooperation between members to political as well. The Davignon report gave birth to the European Political Cooperation process in 1970. Both the European Political Cooperation process and the Global Mediterranean Policy (GMP), adopted within two years of each other, were driven in the main by the internal impulses arising from impending enlargement abetted by the turbulence in transatlantic relations during this period.[61] Indeed, under Nixon the transatlantic relationship was to be tested very hard as America's European Allies faced the possible prospect of economic and physical annihilation whilst the USA sensed betrayal. The voiding of Bretton Woods by the Smithsonian Agreement in December 1971 severely tested European economies at a time of recession. Kissinger's 'Year of Europe' backfired when 1973 turned into an *annus horribilis* for the transatlantic relationship as allies became divided over how best to respond to the Yom Kippur War. The war exposed European countries to security threats ranging from increased terrorist activity on their soil to an oil embargo by OPEC which compounded the recession especially in the countries of the European

South. Détente had profoundly affected the EEC and the institution reacted by embarking on a search for a political identity to complement its Atlanticist one. The Helsinki process provided the EEC one such opportunity to acquire a new political role.[62] Another arose from the need for the EEC to mentor the stabilization of the new Mediterranean democracies.

This was not to be a 'top down' process. The years of dictatorship had strengthened respect for human rights and the greater proportion of political opinion in the democracies of the European South now aspired for a European identity rather than a Mediterranean one. In their search for models and know-how to underpin their new democracies, the southern European countries sought to take advantage of the adoption by the EEC in 1972 of its Global Mediterranean Policy.[63] This policy manifested both the growing economic clout of the EEC but also its desire to promote its economic interests directly by drawing both Arabs and Israelis into a closer relationship with the Community. The GMP had been, from the beginning, a disingenuous misnomer. It was supposed to treat all the littoral countries in a uniform fashion and yet the EEC applied different criteria in terms of engagement.[64] However, as the dust from the dramas of 1973 settled with the recovery in American and European relations, the increasing momentum of the Helsinki process which Nixon and Kissinger saw as a lever to improve transatlantic relations and with the northern Mediterranean countries seeking to join the EEC, the Mediterranean which the EEC had tried to construct in 1972 no longer existed. By 1974, under the pressure of events and with the determination of France to ensure that the northern intake of countries in the early 1970s did not permanently change the identity of the Community, the Mediterranean policies of the EEC had bifurcated into two distinct initiatives: the Euro-Arab dialogue and the stewardship of the fragile northern Mediterranean democracies. The Europe-Arab dialogue failed to prosper since the two parties had approached it with diametrically opposed objectives. The EEC had seen it as a means of dealing with economic issues and the challenges of energy security whereas the Arabs wished to utilize it as another international forum to bring pressure on Israel.[65] However, the other initiative which over time had developed into a potential Community enlargement proved to be much more successful. The EEC was able to take advantage of the geostrategic community the Cold War had created in the northern littoral. In this sense the so-called years of 'euro-sclerosis' after 1974 may have not been as flamboyant as those of the early 1970s but they were not exactly inert. They accomplished something very important in setting up the framework for the

Community's southern enlargement in the 1980s and helped stabilise southern Europe.[66] The troubles of the southern littoral were still important because of geographical proximity and the need to access its energy resources freely. After 1973, the actions of OPEC highlighted the potential of the South to undermine EEC cohesion. However, elaborating Community solutions proved difficult as different European governments adopted different stances to these problems.[67] The confluence of national interests that had been manifested over the stabilization of southern Europe did not occur over the southern littoral. Thus, EEC initiatives lost their clarity and purpose. Despite the inclusive rhetoric displayed by the EEC towards the South in practice, at Helsinki in 1975 and in Venice in 1980, an acceptance prevailed among the Nine that the priority with regards to the Mediterranean now was to strengthen southern Europe by integrating the new democracies into the EEC, thereby fulfilling a process that the Marshall Plan had set in motion in the 1940s. The EU would not turn its attention to the southern littoral again until the 1990s. In the South, the process of fragmentation that had begun with the collapse of the Ottoman Empire and that had been reinforced by decolonization would continue almost inexorably.[68]

Conclusion

In conclusion, the Cold War and superpower détente in particular stimulated the traditional fault lines running through the Mediterranean in economic, political, societal and security terms and hardened the 'North–South' divide in the region. This led to the emergence of 'Southern Europe'. The subsequent entry of Greece, Portugal and Spain into the EEC simply institutionalized the unambiguous disengagement between the two shores of the Mediterranean Sea which had been emphasized by the Cold War and completed by détente. This divergence has been difficult to reverse despite strenuous attempts by NATO and the EU in the post-Cold War era.

CHAPTER 2

The United States, the EEC and the Mediterranean

Rivalry or Complementarity?

Elena Calandri

By analysing the EEC–USA interaction in the Mediterranean, this chapter will review how the Mediterranean was included in the American vision of security and European policy. It will outline the United States' ambivalence to EEC relations with the Mediterranean countries, and analyse how a real EEC Mediterranean policy took shape during détente.

The United States and the Mediterranean in the First Decade of the Cold War

Since the early years of the post-war period, Southern Europe and the Mediterranean gained an important position in American foreign policy outlook. North Africa had been used in war to prepare and launch the liberation of Europe, while the USA became aware of the permanent strategic value of Morocco, Malta and the Eastern Mediterranean. Italy emerged as an important strategic platform. The Straits gatekeepers – Greece and Turkey – were acknowledged with the crucial role of keeping the '[Soviet] plug in the bottle', so much so that Washington replaced Britain as the economic and security provider, through the Truman Doctrine, even before initiating a comprehensive European post-war policy.

As the United States developed a containment strategy in Europe, the question of what place the Mediterranean should have in this strategy was dealt with in a piecemeal and pragmatic way. In the economic dimension of containment (i.e. the Marshall Plan and OECE), the USA adopted a comprehensive continental approach, which included all European countries west of the Iron Curtain who were willing and able to receive American aid and be part of a capitalist reconstruction. Strong bilateral links with the Southern European countries continued within the wider framework of European reconstruction. The African shore of the Mediterranean had no place in this design, as Washington was uneasy with the colonial ties still linking most of the North African countries with Europe. It was with regret that it had to accept France's use of Marshall aid funds to finance the consolidation of its shaky role in the Maghreb.

Regarding the military dimension of the containment strategy, the approach was even less comprehensive. On the launch of Atlantic Pact negotiations, Washington did not envisage including Southern Europe, or the Mediterranean. The military argued that US strategic rights and political influence would be better secured by the continuation of bilateral relations and saw no need to include in the alliance weak countries lying beyond the geographic purpose of the Atlantic initiative. The State Department was concerned with responding to the worries of the Brussels Pact countries. This opinion coincided with that of the majority of European governments involved in the negotiations. They considered the Southern European countries as more of a liability than an asset, and did not want the Atlantic Alliance to become involved in unrelated issues. The British wanted to build in the Mediterranean a second, autonomous, regional pact to enhance their position in the Near and Middle East. Only the French favoured a different solution: including French North Africa (i.e. Morocco, Tunisia and Algeria) and Italy in the pact. Italy would give more depth to France's defence, and by extending the purpose of the Atlantic Pact to the Maghreb, France would obtain legitimization of its 'Euro-African' geopolitical concept and its military and political presence in North Africa.

Neither of these situations appealed to Washington. Nevertheless, in the end, Italy and the northern departments of Algeria were admitted to the Pact in 1949. In 1950, Morocco and Tunisia were also included *de facto* in the area covered by the NATO military planning activities. Although France was the promoter, the USA was more forthcoming than expected, showing an increased strategic interest in the Western Mediterranean and using the alliance framework to facilitate negotiation of strategic rights in bases around the Mediterranean, in particular in Morocco. In 1952, Greece and Turkey also entered the Alliance thanks to the US doctrinal reassessment following the Korean War.

The Atlantic Alliance therefore became broader and more comprehensive than the OECE. The alliance allowed coordination and integration among different national forces, and strengthened the pro-Western leadership of the participating countries. More than anything else, however, it strengthened the United States' presence in the Mediterranean area. Spain and Yugoslavia became more closely linked to the United States than to European organizations by way of military and economic aid and/or military bases. Wheelus Field in Libya became a major American base. Everywhere bilateral agreements gave the US military very privileged status and rights. The United States built up a hegemonic position firmly established on military presence, political influence and economic means, and aid.[1] The extension to the alliance secured NATO's Southern Flank, and was designed to support military operations on the European continent; but it also projected US power through the Mediterranean into the Middle East, whose oil reserves and controlling positions on the Soviet Union were of great strategic value. The French and British, who had hoped to use the Atlantic Alliance to strengthen their own political and military roles in the region, were left with increasingly minor roles.[2] As the West European presence in North Africa declined, the USA had already built up a solid strategic presence in the area. American pre-eminence in Mediterranean security increased constantly during the 1950s.

Towards the end of the 1950s, European recovery also fuelled an increasing level of European economic re-integration. The Southern European countries, which had looked to the United States for help, became linked more closely to the continental economic locomotive. Furthermore, when US President Eisenhower, under pressure from the Congress concerning the size and limited effectiveness of foreign aid, asked the Europeans to 'share the burden', the poorer European countries were naturally at the top of the list of those expected to receive assistance from the richer European countries. Germany's contribution to Turkey and Greece's military build-up within NATO, Spain's admission into the OECE in 1957, the multilateral financial rescue of Turkey by a pool of European countries coordinated by the United States in 1958 and the establishment within the OECE of consortia designed to increase bilateral aid to Greece and Turkey, were examples of this shift of the burden of stabilization and development in Southern Europe back to Europe.

In other words, in the late 1950s, European economic dynamism and the US desire for 'burden sharing' prompted an increased role of the most developed European countries in Southern Europe, as a contribution to the economic Cold War. In the rest of the basin, European economic presence declined and had to be reinvented, as the North African countries became independent, amidst great conflict and mutual regret. For the United States, the end of European control of the Mediterranean and North Africa carried both advantages and risks. A solid network of bilateral relations, scepticism regarding plans for regional initiatives that were floated on various occasions, and a firm military and economic presence were the features of the US presence in the region.[3]

The Origins of the EEC Mediterranean Policy

The birth of the Common Market might be a turning point in a renewal of Europe's international economic role. At first, the Economic Community was considered in Washington to be a useful safety net for Southern European countries, and the EEC appeared to be ready to comply with US expectations. During the OECE negotiations for a European free-trade area, the State Department repeatedly signalled to the Six that the less developed European countries, i.e. Portugal, Iceland, Greece, Turkey and Ireland, should not be left 'out in the cold'. They requested that the other OECE members allow them important derogation to the free-trade area rules, as well as financial and technical assistance, and the Six hesitantly accepted in principle that they deserved to be helped.[4] Failure of the negotiations exempted them from implementing their promise, but during the initial period of the EEC grandiose projects were aired in many quarters and the EEC was seen as eventually becoming the pivot in a chain of regional arrangements, in which the Mediterranean had an obvious place.[5]

But new caution was now emerging in the United States regarding the economic role of the EEC. Eisenhower was elusive when approached by Italian Foreign Minister Fanfani about an EEC initiative in development assistance. A Belgian plan for a bold EEC initiative in external relations also won little appreciation. In fact, in his last year in office, Eisenhower tried to elaborate a Western initiative towards the Third World, encompassing the EEC. This resulted in the OECE being transformed into the OECD in 1960. The OECD Development Assistance Committee (DAC) would become the headquarters for coordinating increased bilateral aid from Western countries to developing countries.[6]

As President Kennedy arrived at the White House, both development aid and the relaunching of a renewed Euro-Atlantic partnership took centre stage in relations on both sides of the Atlantic. The United States welcomed the EEC Commission in the DAC[7] and the State Department and the Commission General Directorate VIII, in charge of development policy, established a somewhat clandestine information and consultation pact. In the DAC, however, and in other international forums, the Kennedy administration promoted a definition of aid (Official Development Aid, ODA) that virtually outlawed the combination of financial assistance and commercial preferences in the EEC association regime for African colonies of the member states – a model that Brussels seemed ready to replicate in its relations with other less developed countries. While in 1957 Washington had accepted, in 1962 it tried to prevent the perpetuation of this model in the Yaoundé Convention, which would replace the association regime. Washington was especially worried about the prospect of Britain's accession to the EEC, which could broaden the geographic scope of the association regime to include former British colonies. Although US nervousness diminished as the EEC–UK accession negotiations failed, Washington continued to oppose EEC preferential agreements with third countries.[8]

This principled position produced inconsistencies and friction in the Mediterranean. Many 'third countries' in the basin wanted access to the Common Market and hoped for financial aid, in some cases as a continuation of colonial-time arrangements; and the United States itself was trying to obtain a higher degree of European economic engagement for less developed countries. This was especially clear when, in 1959, Greece and Turkey applied for association with the EEC (that is, an agreement establishing preferential economic and political links, including common institutions), and exploratory conversations started in Brussels. The American silence avowed a lack of enthusiasm that contrasted with both their alleged support for the 'European pillar' and invitations to support the less developed European countries. Only after repeated Greek solicitations, and after more than a year of silence, did the State Department speak to the Six persuading them to be more forthcoming to Greek requests. However, it put clear limits: association should lead to full membership and not reflect negatively on Turkey. The State Department was very critical since the Athens Treaty, signed in September 1961, set full membership as a remote goal, while allowing Greece broad preferential access to the EEC that barely complied with GATT rules. As a consequence, it took a more rigid attitude towards the EEC–Turkey negotiations, which appeared to be geared toward an even more derogatory regime. The State Department made it clear, therefore, that the Greek formula was the 'bottom line' for acceptance. It stuck to this position until late 1962. A change in attitude was then prompted mainly by the Cuban crisis. As the Six (some of whom were perhaps looking for a pretext for not concluding the deal) disingenuously affirmed that the agreement with Turkey would be signed only if the

United States approved it, the State Department agreed. Association with the EEC would mend fences opened in Turkey by the 'Jupiter missiles deal' and consolidate shaky Turkish ties with the Atlantic Alliance.[9] Therefore, in one of the funding events of détente, the United States resorted to the EEC to strengthen a Mediterranean ally that it was sacrificing to the emerging détente logic. Nevertheless, the Ankara Treaty was an exception that Washington did not want to see replicated.

For its part, the Community welcomed applications from Athens and Ankara for political reasons, as proof of its international and 'Western' role. Quickly, however, the Six became aware of economic and institutional difficulties. Their initial ambitions for major international initiatives turned out to be unrealistic and clashed with the broader disagreements that opposed France to the other five. The Ankara Treaty was signed only at the end of tense negotiation and its ratification by France was included in the so-called 'synchronization' packet, in exchange for German ratification of the Yaoundé Convention. France openly disapproved of offering preferential trade, financial aid and special political ties to a country that it considered too closely bound to the United States. For different reasons, the Netherlands had also worked against the treaty and invented the 'preparatory phase' that led to the agreement being in a limbo for five years, except regarding financial aid. Both treaties set the goal of a custom union to be completed in more than 20 years and created joint institutions whose competence was restricted to association matters. In both the Athens and Ankara agreements, financial aid was *magna pars* of the deal. The Six allocated 125 million a.u. in loans to Greece and 175 million a.u. to Turkey in five years.[10] After the Ankara Treaty, no other Mediterranean countries reached a satisfying deal during the first decade, in spite of External Relations Commissioner Jean Rey's commitment.

Can it be argued that the EEC assumed the stabilization and development of Southern Europe as its responsibility? Or was it taking the first step in a regional policy in the Mediterranean? The answer is twofold. After initial enthusiasm, the EEC responses to requests from all the Mediterranean countries were spare and unenthusiastic. The Athens and Ankara treaties were the result of lengthy and bitter negotiations, and the goal of the custom union took so long that many considered it to be a cover for obtaining GATT approval rather than a realistic objective. Not until 1970 did Spain succeed in obtaining an agreement, and the Six refused it association. So while Germany ostensibly considered the associations to be a continuation and multilateralization of European solidarity and an allied obligation, for different reasons other member states were not ready to endow the EEC with this role.

On the other hand, while no proper Mediterranean policy emerged during the first decade, regionalism, in principle coupled with multilateralism, was an essential feature of the EEC. For historical/political and economic reasons, concessions made to Southern Europe rebounded in the rest of the basin. As the Athens Treaty was signed, and the Six hurried to argue that it could not be considered as a precedent, Israel and Spain proclaimed their right to similar treatment, and the Maghreb countries raised their requests as well. As GATT rules only allowed preferential trade within custom unions and free-trade areas, a regional approach including both north and south appeared to be a logical outcome, which could respond to both local requests and international rules, and foster the Community political and economic aims in the region. It was proposed by Italy as early as 1964, but met with scepticism. Indeed the Arab–Israeli conflict and the state of bilateral relations between the Six and the Mediterranean countries meant that the proposal seemed visionary, and certainly unrealistic.[11]

The Beginning of the Mediterranean's Long 1970s

Nonetheless, the EEC slowly increased its relations with the Mediterranean countries, which reached a critical threshold in the late 1960s. In the history of European integration, this late and overdue writing of agreements is usually considered to be due to the establishment of the common commercial policy in 1968 (which allowed the Commission to stipulate agreements with third countries) and the decreased Italian resistance after the adoption of Community rules for Mediterranean agricultural products, which protected Italian producers. The limited contents are attributed to the lack of interest of many members, to CAP protectionism and bilateral political quarrels, as well as to the limited interest of the Mediterranean countries themselves.

If one considers the broader picture however, and the changing Mediterranean balance after 1967, the agreements cannot be separated from the Six's attempt to assert Western presence in a period of increasing regional tensions, such as the USSR having obtained military bases and established close political and economic relations, and radical governments taking power in many Arab countries. The Six-Day War opened a period of increased regional polarization and danger, which impelled the Europeans to use economic leverage to promote peace.[12] The war deteriorated US and German relations with the Arab countries, while it opened a new era in France's relations with them, in coincidence with its withdrawal from NATO.[13] While at a structural level this configuration was a 'death kiss' for the EEC Mediterranean policy, in the short term the situation generated an impulse toward a renewed approach. The war also endangered the flow of oil supplies and this prompted the Commission to reflect on links between economic assistance and energy supplies. The Greek coup caused the Commission to reflect on the political risks of association and in connection with the second British application, it produced a type of doctrine. According to this, Southern European countries not yet ready for membership should have preferential agreements with the Community aimed at their economic development, but not association if they were not democratic.[14] This drew a clear political line, but at the same time confirmed that the EEC was not ready to accept American pressure to give up preferential agreements with developing countries, and that it intended to play a role in the Mediterranean whatever disagreements existed among member states, and with the major ally.

After the 1967 coup, the Greek association was partially frozen.[15] The current administration continued however, and during the 1967–74 'freeze', Greece benefited notably from economic integration with the Community. The EEC–Turkey relations also developed, as the Commission recommended, and the Council accepted, to overlook the scant economic results of the first lustre of association and to consolidate the EEC–Turkey political linkage: in 1970 a Supplementary Protocol to the Ankara Treaty opened the way for the gradual implementation of the custom union. The Turks considered the conditions too harsh, and feared that their economy would not be able to stand competition from the much more advanced European economies. However, the protocol committed 195 million a.u. in financial aid and confirmed that the goal of the association was Turkey's full membership. In 1970, Spain obtained a preferential agreement aimed at completely removing obstacles to trade in two stages. During the first, the EEC would lower tariffs on many industrial products by 70 per cent, while Spain accepted a cut of 40 per cent. EEC concessions were much more limited for agricultural products.[16] Malta, in 1970, and Cyprus, in 1972, also obtained preferential trade agreements, including financial and technical cooperation. Between 1968 and 1972 the Commission, under the presidencies of Jean Rey and Franco Maria Malfatti signed agreements with all Southern Mediterranean countries, except Libya and Syria. These agreements had commercial provisions similar to the Malta agreements, but no provisions for financial and technical aid, or for labour. A North–South divide followed.

For the United States, EEC agreements with Mediterranean countries, and more generally EEC association agreements remained a problem throughout the Johnson administration. Washington remained entangled in contrasting aims: not to encourage preferential trade, not to openly deny support to the 'European pillar' of the Atlantic Alliance, and to promote EEC economic engagement when it served Western interests. The EEC role in promoting stability could not be wholly dismissed since, in the second half of the 1960s, the Mediterranean ceased to be an 'American lake' and relations with local allies became tense. The 1964 Cyprus crisis complicated relations with Greece, Turkey and Cyprus itself. The notorious 'Johnson Telegram' blocked the Turkish invasion of the island, but strained US relations with Ankara and prompted Turkey's so-called policy of differentiation launched afterwards, which included closer relations with the Islamic countries and the Eastern bloc. Relations with Greece were never easy, either before or after the Colonels' coup in 1967. Military bonds remained strong, the Colonels carefully fulfilled Greece's obligations under the NATO alliance, the United States continued to be Greece's major source of military equipment and, in 1972, a homeport agreement allowed the precious stationing of US Navy carrier forces in the Athens-Piraeus area.[17] Meanwhile, US relations with Portugal suffered as a consequence of Portuguese colonial policy and relations with Spain also ran into difficulties, owing to the United States' inability to open the doors of NATO and to growing Spanish intolerance of US military rights. A 1970 agreement reduced the number of bases available to the United States and re-established full Spanish sovereignty.

The security dimension of the US presence in the region could be complemented by a reconstituted European influence. However, this was never the feeling in Washington. Washington could not dismiss the EEC's usefulness in specific cases, most of all because it was reducing its economic assistance to the region.[18] The State Department, however, maintained that association was bad in principle, and damaging to US interests.[19] In fact a degree of internal conflict existed within the Department, with the European Bureau more ready to accept validity of the EEC initiative. In the end, economic needs prevailed. In order to avoid doctrinal embarrassment, two categories of country were pragmatically considered appropriate for association: those with historical links with members, and potential member countries, i.e. European countries. The association of the Maghreb and Greece, Turkey, Spain and Austria therefore became acceptable, while for Israel, Nigeria, the Eastern Arab states, Malta and Cyprus, the USA was contrary. Washington was totally opposed to an EEC regional approach that would discriminate against American economic interests and legitimate regionalism at a global level, especially if it also led to preferential agreements between the EEC and Latin America.[20]

Initially, the Nixon administration did not pay much attention to the Mediterranean, except for the Arab–Israeli conflict. The implications of the Nixon Doctrine for the Mediterranean were unclear. While the Eastern Mediterranean and the Middle East remained a priority, the pragmatic attitude of the administration tended to reduce unnecessary commitment in the rest of the area, as in the Maghreb. Close association with Israel and questions about 'a future possibility of a greater influence and role for the Europeans'[21] in Mediterranean Europe remained unanswered and did not apparently concern the EEC. The EEC Mediterranean agreements were greeted with harsh criticism, owing to their preferential trade clauses. The serious deterioration in US–EEC relations, noted in Community circles at the beginning of 1970, due to mutual accusations of industrial and agricultural protectionism, gave the preferential agreements with Mediterranean and other European countries as the second bone of contention.[22] Once again, the prospect of Britain's membership made the EEC 'proliferating system of preferences' appear more dangerous, especially as commercial rivalries abounded.[23]

The EEC Mediterranean Policy

Given these economic, political and juridical obstacles, it was not obvious that the EEC would launch a Mediterranean policy. Indeed, the 'Global Mediterranean Policy' launched at the Paris summit of October 1972 was the result of a biased and complicated process. The first brick in the building was a Commission paper prepared in the late spring of 1970 at the Council's request. Aware of the strain caused by Mediterranean agreements in Atlantic relations, it asked the Commission to draw up a comprehensive proposal. The Commission recommended countering American criticism by moving from purely trade agreements to financial and technical assistance and manpower; by negotiating regional non-preferential agreements for special products, and launching a policy towards Latin America to counter the accusation of discrimination against that continent.[24] At the June 1970 Council meeting, the Six agreed to proceed. The strongest support came from the Italian Prime Minister, Aldo Moro. The EEC action was:

> A contribution to the political and social stabilisation in an extremely sensitive area, in which American presence is

insufficient not only quantitatively but also because the fronts in the Arab-Israeli conflict allow Europe to develop a role in the interest of peace and to strengthen the Southern Flank of the Atlantic alliance.[25]

For Moro, political and social arguments, rather than geographical-historical ones, should have been proposed in GATT and *vis-à-vis* the American government. Moro was aware of the economic importance of the Mediterranean region,[26] but he was especially concerned about political stability. In fact, he raised the Mediterranean question in every meeting with European, Atlantic and North African partners.[27] For him, the new Gaddafi regime in Libya had ruined the balance between moderate and progressive Arab countries, fragmented the Arab front and was causing increased instability. The PLO was an *incognita*, Yugoslavia was unstable and needed economic help, and Malta's future was unpredictable. The resources of the Six ought to be engaged in providing financial, technical and economic aid to consolidate the moderate governments.[28] In November 1970, Moro asked Commission president Franco Maria Malfatti to promote a Community initiative towards the Maghreb.[29] In spring 1971, he circulated a paper on the 'Mediterranean situation' to be discussed in the European Political Cooperation (EPC).

Moro's initiative was not welcomed in France:

> Ce document [argued the Quai d'Orsay] montre clairement que la préoccupation essentielle des Italiens est la menace soviétique, ce qui les conduit à concentrer leur étude soit sur les aspects propre-ment militaires, soit sur la pénétration politique et économique soviétique dans le monde arabe, et à identifier très largement les intérêts de l'Europe à ceux des États Unis.[30]

France wanted the Mediterranean to remain an area of national action and it proposed to Italy regular bilateral consultations and joint economic initiatives in the region.

> L'Europe aurait été présente en Méditerranée à travers la France et l'Italie sans que son action soit hypothéquée par les relations délicates de l'Allemagne occidentale avec les pays arabes, la quasi-absence de moyens du Bénélux dans cette partie du monde, ou tout simplement par l'appartenance atlantique de nos partenaires.[31]

The proposal for Franco-Italian cooperation was also an attempt to influence the Italian choice between the (German) Pal and (French) Secam television systems and to bind Italy into a Mediterranean television network by adopting Secam.[32] Behind the Italian proposal for a Community Mediterranean policy, Paris saw the hand of Brandt, who aimed to 'faire reconnaître la vocation naturelle des six [...] à agir solidairement en Méditerranée dans tous les domains', in order to foster German industrial interests.

However, since the Italians had raised the question, the French had to find a way to limit the damage. They certainly did not want to be involved in 'des vaines et fâcheuses entreprises communautaires qui paraissent forcément répondre à des considérations idéologiques ou stratégiques'.[33] From an ideological or strategic point of view only, for the Quai d'Orsay, the Mediterranean could be considered as a unity. However, this was an unsuitable basis for an initiative of the Six, either in the Community or in the EPC format. Furthermore, both visions were likely to involve NATO and the USA.[34] The French, therefore, worked on fragmenting Moro's 'Mediterranean question' into a multiplicity of separate 'Mediterranean problems'. In November 1971, a Working Group chaired by Andrea Cagiati, a close advisor to Giulio Andreotti, assigned each member country with a geographic portion of the basin to report on. Belgium had Greece and Turkey, Germany had the Iberian Peninsula, France had the Maghreb, Italy had Malta, Cyprus and Albania, and Britain had the Balkans.

By spring 1972, the Italians were changing their mind and Rome proposed that France take the lead: 'd'une approche en gros comparable à ce qui avait été en son temps le Plan de Colombo', aimed at: 'offrir aux pays non entierement développés de la Méditerranée l'accès à une sorte d'étage intermédiaire entre leur situation actuelle et celle de membres de la Communauté européenne, à laquelle ils ne peuvent raisonnablement prétendre'.[35] Italy, however, was also ready to accept France's proposal for national initiatives outside the Community framework. The model was probably Franco-Spanish-Italian military cooperation, and the UK–Malta agreement allowing British forces to use NATO structures.[36] Indeed Italy had been frustrated by the EEC reluctance to be more forthcoming with Malta, to reduce its flirting with Libya and the Eastern bloc.[37]

The breakthrough towards a regional EEC approach arrived in the summer of 1972, as the Six had to confront requests from the Mediterranean partners following the accession of Britain, Denmark and Ireland and after their adoption of the General System of Preferences for developing countries. A general reappraisal of existing agreements therefore could not wait. The EEC Commission, of which Sicco Mansholt had taken on the Presidency in March, did not play a particularly active role.[38] It was the French who proposed extending to Spain and Israel the formula currently discussed with Portugal, i.e. free trade for industrial products and selected concessions for agricultural products. The French formula appeared to have many advantages. It created a uniform 'Mediterranean regime' that was more acceptable to the GATT and escaped applying the GSP to countries that were not considered Third World.[39] During July and August, on the other hand, in view of the Paris October summit, the confrontation became heated on the future of the EEC development policy, as supporters of a 'global' approach tried to shelve the privileges of the former colonies.[40] In an effort to defend its African *protégés*, France was adamant that the *acquis* of relations with Africa *and* the Mediterranean could not be repudiated, and quickly launched the catchword of a 'global approach' to the Mediterranean.

At the Paris summit, the Nine launched the 'Global Mediterranean Policy', and the Mediterranean, as well as Africa, took priority over Latin America or Asia. 'Global' was meant to have both a geographical and a thematic meaning, but was above all a linguistic plot designed to assert the European political role in the area. The 'global approach' meant adopting a regional policy which encompassed a wide variety of provisions and instruments. The two catchwords of 'cooperation' and 'reciprocity' were also quite vague and nobody expected uniformity in dealing with all partner countries. In November 1972, it was agreed that Spain, Portugal, Israel and Yugoslavia would not receive financial aid, and that only agreements with the Maghreb, Malta and Israel would be signed within 1973, while the others would wait for development in the Middle East.

The American position regarding the GMP was outspokenly negative. Well before the Paris Summit, the State Department had tried to prevent its adoption by threatening

> un accroissement de l'incompréhension de l'opinion et du Congres
> à l'égard de l'Europe [...] [le danger qu'elle puisse avoir] des effets
> défavorables sur des importantes négotiations, telle celle relative à
> la reforme du système monetaire international et ne puisse même
> affecter les relations politiques et militaires entre les États Unis et
> l'Europe.[41]

Washington asked the Community to give up inverse preferences, to open its citrus fruit market and remove barriers to foreign industrial products.

Economic concerns became more important than any possible political dimension of the EEC initiative.

American irritation was expected and the Nine undertook to mollify it. They stressed that agreements were expected to be flexible and that the GMP was not intended to interfere with the Middle East peace process, and promised to consult regularly with the United States – as stated in the final communiqué of the Paris Summit.

As negotiations for implementing the Paris summit decision continued in the next months, it became clear that there was no agreement either on the geographical range or on the contents of the Mediterranean policy, and that US criticism had been heeded. The French became the standard-bearers of the new policy, which they wanted to develop independently of the United States.[42] The negotiations soon ran into problems, however. Many member countries refused to endorse the inverse preferences. For Britain, Denmark, the Netherlands and Ireland, only the Southern European countries, geared toward future adhesion, could be asked to open their markets.[43] Britain disagreed on the regional approach itself and argued that potential members should follow a different path from the others. Furthermore, owing to its major political meaning, Britain wanted Mediterranean issues to be a matter for the EPC. France took the lead in contrasting this: for France this would subordinate decisions to well-known American reserves and cause the Community to lose freedom. Others found that the intergovernmental and embryonic nature of the EPC would condemn the new policy to inconsistency, and supported the EEC role.

While French suspicions about Britain's 'Trojan Horse' role were to be expected, France seemed to be unaware of how promising the EPC appeared to Britain. The Foreign Office had pointed out the inconsistency between the EEC political aims in South-Eastern Europe and the limited economic means it deployed.[44] The political quality of the EEC Mediterranean policy appeared to be trapped in the EEC bureaucratic and technical approach while the economic resources were not enough to satisfy the partners' aspirations. The EPC could be the way out of this dilemma.

Conclusion

The resilient division between Cold War history and European integration history has usually considered analyses of European foreign policy separate from the general narrative of the Cold War.[45] In fact, in the high years of détente, the Italian initiative that, after many stops and starts, became the EEC Global Mediterranean Policy sprang from Moro's preoccupation with the growing instability in the Mediterranean. As he saw it, it was caused by increased Soviet presence and reduced American commitment in the area, rather than from a desire to further European integration and build up the international role of the EEC. A religiously inspired supporter of détente, Moro campaigned tirelessly for peace and promoted the idea of the Mediterranean as a 'peace lake', which was cultivated by many Italian Christian Democrat leaders. Confronted with instability and a changing balance in the Mediterranean, which he considered to be a consequence of Soviet policy, Moro cultivated relations with many regional leaders, but also appealed for an increased Western presence to counter a regional dynamic that could affect the Italian domestic situation. Moro was treading a fine line when dealing with the PCI, which the wave of détente had projected towards great electoral success and influence in Italian society. As a privileged area for the PCI's international initiatives, the balance in the Mediterranean and the spreading Soviet influence in the area had a global as well as domestic significance.

For Moro, as for many European leaders, multipolarism was a crucial dimension of détente, and the Mediterranean was the most natural area for the initiative of the European pole. Neither Moro, nor Prime Minister Andreotti were ardent Europeanists, nor did they pay particular attention to the institutional divide between communitarian and inter-governmentalism, that is between the EEC and EPC. They did not appear to be worried by competing initiatives, provided that the Mediterranean was not ignored on the outskirts of continental détente.

This was not the case for France. For Pompidou, the crisis in US relations with the Arabs was an extraordinary opportunity to relaunch France's Arab links, on the solid basis of armaments and oil and gas supplies. He saw in multilateral engagements in the area an obstacle to its policy based on bilateral relations[46] and a potential channel for US hegemony. The French therefore patronized the EEC 'global' role in the Mediterranean.[47]

The US idea of détente did not really permit the existence of a second pole within the West. This became clear in 1973 at the launch of the 'Year of Europe' initiative, and clearer still during the ensuing debate about the Atlantic declarations, the Yom Kippur War and the Atlantic crisis that followed.[48] The long established US adversity toward EEC policy in the Mediterranean was now topped with a determination to countenance European political ambitions and a European pro-Arab stance capable of interfering with US support for Israel and Kissinger's design for a US-brokered Middle East peace. The choice of the energy issue as a highly divisive test of European cohesion was a skilful move that led to profound divisions between the Nine and underlined the limits of the European Mediterranean design.

It is not surprising that only in July 1974, after an Atlantic Declaration had been finally agreed in June and European ambitions had been scaled down, were bilateral negotiations within the Global Mediterranean Policy authorized by the EEC Council. In the mandate the regional approach was virtually shelved. The ensuing political evolution in the Southern European countries, which led the way to their full integration into the EEC, opened a new phase in European commitment to stabilization and economic development in Southern Europe, but also strengthened the dividing line across the Mediterranean.

CHAPTER 3

Rediscovering the Mediterranean

First Tests of Coordination among the Nine

Guia Migani

Since the beginning of the Cold War, the Mediterranean was a theatre for the confrontation between the United States and the Soviet Union. After all, in 1947, the immediate cause of the Truman Doctrine was the need to preserve Greece and Turkey from Communism. During the 1950s, the Mediterranean became a sea under US control. The US Sixth Fleet guaranteed the security of the region (from a Western point of view, of course[1]), but the situation changed partially with the decolonization and birth of new Arab states. Moscow could penetrate the area, by providing economic and military aid to the new Arab governments. In 1967, the Six-Day War offered Moscow new possibilities to consolidate its positions in the Arab world.[2] The Soviet fleet could rely on important facilities in Egypt, and a series of political, economic and military agreements were signed with Algeria, Libya, Syria, Tunisia and Morocco.[3] Moreover, Moscow could count on the use of ship repair facilities in Yugoslavia.[4] The growing presence of the Soviet Union in the Mediterranean was of serious concern to Western European countries. Even if the Soviets did not represent a real danger, given the US predominance in the area, Moscow could now observe the US fleet, disturb their manoeuvres and add to the feeling of insecurity in Western European countries (and especially Italy). According to a French diplomatic note, written in March 1972, the Soviet fleet was sometimes larger than the US Sixth Fleet.[5] The sense of uncertainty in EEC countries was particularly strong because of US engagement in other parts of the world, such as Vietnam. This was at a time of growing instability in the Mediterranean area, due to the change of regime in Libya, where Gaddafi took power in 1969, and to the Arab–Israeli conflict – between Israel and Egypt there was a masked war throughout this period – while in Jordan a civil war broke out in 1970.

Another factor pressing Western European countries to give priority to the Mediterranean region was terrorism: 'Terrorism by Arab-Palestinian groups created a connection between the domestic arena of Western European countries, and the Middle East, the Mediterranean and the Arab world more generally.'[6] After the attack on Israeli quarters at the Munich Olympic Games in September 1972, all European governments knew that their territory could become the theatre of a terrorist operation. However, there were also economic reasons which made Western European countries (and the EEC member states) sensitive to the general equilibrium in the area. The strong activism of some Mediterranean states, such as Algeria within the G77 and the OAPEC (Organisation of Arab Petroleum Exporting Countries), for a New International Economic Order, and the need to secure oil imports (even before the Yom Kippur War and the oil shock) contributed to focusing the attention of European states on this region.

How the Mediterranean Started to Emerge in the Debate among European Countries

In spite of all these problems, Western European countries had not developed a common strategy towards the Mediterranean. For its part, the EEC had signed many agreements with Mediterranean countries during the 1960s, but they lacked a common framework.[7] They were a 'patchwork of agreements',[8] procuring for the EEC no visibility or influence in the region, as was pointed out by the European Parliament and the Commission.

However, some EEC member states were reconsidering the Mediterranean situation. This was especially true for Italy and France. Under the Pompidou presidency, France focused on the Maghreb in order to improve its relations with Tunisia and Morocco and to further its relationship with Algeria.[9] Nevertheless, although the Mediterranean was a crucial area for European interests at the beginning of the 1970s, the EEC member states did not share the same vision of the region and had different interests and priorities. The Mediterranean as a global area did not even exist for some EEC member states. If there were some bilateral consultations – between Italy, France and Spain for example[10] – nothing existed inside the EEC or the European Political Cooperation (EPC) frame, which was launched in 1970.

The situation started to change in 1971. Various initiatives adopted in different contexts (inside the EPC, by the Parliament or the Commission) led to the adoption, by the Nine, of a Global Mediterranean Policy (GMP) during the Summit of Paris in October 1972. In two years the Nine were able to agree on a common strategy for the area. Although this strategy was based on economic instruments (such as technical and economic aid, and commercial provisions) this did not mean there was not a common political reflection as the basis of the process which led to the GMP being adopted.

The Birth of the Mediterranean Working Group

The first discussions among the Six (soon Nine) regarding the Mediterranean started in May 1971. The proposal came from the Italian government after a bilateral meeting with Bonn. Italy, given its geographic position, was obviously interested in the general equilibrium in the Mediterranean.[11] Moreover, its dependence on Arab oil and the need to maintain good relations with all Mediterranean countries pushed Rome to take the initiative. The fact that this initiative was conceived in a European framework was a traditional feature of Italian foreign policy.[12] The Italian idea, as it was explained to the other EEC states, was to launch a general discussion on the Mediterranean, to define common priorities, harmonize national foreign policies, and then to agree on some common actions.[13]

The Italian proposal was strongly supported by the Germans. Bonn probably considered that coordination of the EEC member states' foreign policies was a good way to further its relations with the countries of the region. Moreover, at the beginning of the 1970s, Germany was the major client and supplier of Mediterranean countries as a whole.[14] From a wider political context, to manifest interest in the South of Europe permitted Bonn to equilibrate *Ostpolitik* and, to a certain extent, to reassure its partners.[15]

In May 1971, in preparation for the discussions, the Italian delegation circulated a paper analysing the Mediterranean situation.[16] Rome underlined the importance of the Soviet economic and military presence, barely contrasted by the Western states. The influence of Western Europe was lowered in the region because of decolonization, the Arab–Israeli conflict and Soviet penetration. In general terms, the policy of the two superpowers in the Mediterranean had reduced the autonomy of West European states.

The Italian paper concluded by pointing out the need for EEC action in the Mediterranean. In this regard, Rome observed that the EEC was present in the region thanks to some commercial treaties. However, these were not based on a coherent framework and the political gains for the EEC from these agreements were not significant.

The same position was expressed by some Italian officials of the *Farnesina* (the Italian Ministry of Foreign Affairs) to the French ambassador as he reported to Paris:

> Aussi estiment-ils [les Italiens] qu'en Méditerranée plus qu'ailleurs la politique est liée à l'économie. Pour renforcer la force des modérés, il faut faciliter la solution de leurs problèmes économiques et sociaux, leur fournir une aide financière, économique et technique qui sera d'autant plus substantielle qu'elle sera le fruit des efforts des six pays [de la CEE].[17]

The French Ambassador continued to explain that, thanks to economic agreements and the force of attraction of the EEC, Rome wanted to strengthen relations with the Maghreb countries, reduce the influence of Eastern European countries in Libya, assist Yugoslavia and help Sadat. 'Des Chefs d'Etat, comme Bourguiba, ne cessent d'ailleurs de pousser les Italiens dans cette voie.'[18]

The reaction of EEC foreign ministers to the Italian proposal was ambiguous. If the Germans approved it, the Benelux countries were concerned about duplicating NATO's work in the Mediterranean, and the French were extremely reticent. They did not agree with the idea of considering the Mediterranean as a whole. They were also concerned with the need to avoid duplicating NATO's work, and refused to consider the Mediterranean as the theatre of a confrontation between the two blocs, as this would have eliminated any possible autonomous (French) policy. In French opinion, there was not a Mediterranean area, but there were Mediterranean problems.[19] Last but not least, the French government did not want to discuss military aspects as they were not covered by the EPC. Paris would have preferred a bilateral (French–Italian) approach to the region, since this would have permitted better defence of its own interests. Nevertheless, Paris was ready to discuss some well-defined questions in order to exchange information and, in a second moment, to harmonize national positions. As Maurice Schumann, the French Minister of Foreign Affairs, explained to his ambassador in Rome (regretting the Italian decision), Paris was ready to take part in discussions between the Six without renouncing the idea of bilateral cooperation:

Dans la phase actuelle de la construction européenne, il y a la place pour le multilatéral et pour le bilatéral – l'exemple franco-allemand le montre – et les exercices de coopération politique des Six n'enlèvent rien aux responsabilités propres de leurs diplomaties.[20]

At the end of the meeting, which took place on 14 May 1971, the Council of Foreign Ministers agreed to have the Political Committee draw up a report on the Mediterranean situation which would be discussed in the context of the EPC. The Political Committee created a Working Group with the task of preparing the report in which it would present 'de manière motivée, dans le cadre d'une vision générale des problèmes de la Méditerranée, quels secteurs doivent être pris en considération en raison de leur intérêt prioritaire'.[21] This sentence was a compromise between Paris and Rome: the Working Group would have studied the Mediterranean problems (in the plural, as Paris wanted) but the idea of a general vision of the area, supported by Rome, was still on the table.

During its first meeting, in December 1971, the Working Group decided not to deal with the Arab–Israeli conflict (because it was already under study by another Working Group) and to divide the Mediterranean into four sub-regions. West Germany was responsible for the study of the Iberian Peninsula, France for the Maghreb, Italy for the Adriatic region, and Belgium and the Netherlands for the South-East. After the new EEC members were invited to take part in these discussions, London was in charge of the study of the Yugoslav case. The national reports had to take into consideration some common topics, such as relations between the EEC and Mediterranean states (non-members of the Community), the political and economic activity of the communist countries in the region, and energy supplies.

Italy, supported by the Netherlands, also wished to include an analysis of possible common actions or EEC initiatives. On the contrary, France wanted only to take into consideration the consultation or harmonization of national foreign policies.

The Mediterranean Working Group at Work: Studying Mediterranean Problems [...]

In February 1972, the Working Group approved an important document regarding the general principles on which the Six and the EEC should base their action in the Mediterranean. After mentioning the UN Charter, the document affirmed that any action undertaken by EEC member states

and the Community had to be based on the idea of economic cooperation in order to favour development of the Mediterranean states.[22] It also
recognized that agreements between the EEC and Mediterranean states
had been concluded without a common policy. In future, these agreements
should be harmonized, even if they included different clauses, as there were
many differences between the Mediterranean countries. This document,
conceived within the EPC framework, anticipated the reasons leading to
the launch of the EEC Global Mediterranean Policy.

This is even more evident if we take into consideration the report approved
in February 1971 by the European Parliament on the EEC commercial
policy in the Mediterranean.[23] The author of the report, André Rossi, criticized EEC policy because it lacked consistency, as the EPC document had
stated. However, the Working Group also seemed to share the Commission
proposals about a Global Mediterranean Policy (GMP).[24] The idea of a
Global Mediterranean Policy was emerging within the Commission at
the beginning of 1972.[25] 'Global' meant an approach towards all countries in the region and included commercial clauses, and technical and
financial assistance. The GMP was conceived as a common political framework within which bilateral agreements with the Mediterranean countries
should be stipulated.

At the meeting of the Political Directors Committee, on 15–16 February,
the Directors examined the first national reports on the Mediterranean
sub-regions. During the discussion, in which delegates of the new EEC
members states participated, the Italians and Germans emphasized the
need for greater concentration on the 'political' aspects of the problems
of the Mediterranean, for more oral exchange on the 'basic political problems' of the area, and (in the case of the Italians) for the development of an
overall policy towards the Mediterranean.[26]

The delegations of the Nine EEC member states agreed to prepare their
reports following the same scheme. Four aspects had to be taken into
consideration:

- Reasons for a European policy;
- Definition of the aims of a European policy (such as the need to rein-
  force links with Western Europe and to limit Soviet influence);
- Principal characteristics of the political and economic situation of
  the countries (to analyse relations with the United States, the Soviet
  Union, China [...]);
- Policies which EEC member states should adopt.

The vision of the Mediterranean emerging from these documents was very different from zone to zone, but all the papers stressed the role played by nationalism and Soviet activities. The Netherlands, in their document on the East Mediterranean countries, underlined the importance of Soviet penetration, prompted by the Arab–Israeli conflict.[27] Other regions, however, risked falling under Moscow's influence. Among them the most sensitive cases were Yugoslavia and Malta.

As Tito approached the end of his presidency, Western governments feared that the Soviet Union would try to exploit the new situation in order to reunify the communist bloc.[28] In the case of Malta, Western governments were concerned that after the end of the Anglo-Maltese military agreement, the Soviet Union would replace Great Britain and occupy the naval bases on the island.[29] In order to encourage Dom Mintoff, the Maltese President, not to stipulate such an agreement with Moscow, the Western European countries should build a new relationship with Malta, while the EEC should open negotiations for a new cooperation agreement.[30] The Nine should reinforce the non-alignment of Malta and Yugoslavia, and finance their economic and social development, encouraging their relations with the EEC. While the existing agreement between Malta and the EEC was a good basis for new negotiations, it was important to conclude some kind of agreement with Yugoslavia. As the British pointed out:

> In view of the present pattern of Yugoslav foreign trade, it is vital for Yugoslavia that there should be some form of continuing economic agreement with the Community. The political disadvantages of not making some accommodations for Yugoslavia's special position are great, as are the corresponding advantages if she could be offered a prospect of continuing and increasing a market for her products in Western Europe.[31]

The reports stressed the importance of the non-alignment and nationalism of the Mediterranean countries for the general equilibrium of the region. In the case of Libya it was affirmed that, in spite of the change of government with the arrival of Gaddafi to power, Soviet influence had not increased.[32] The German report on Spain and Portugal focused on the strategic importance of the Iberian Peninsula, which was still more relevant because of the growing Soviet presence in the Mediterranean. For this reason, it was important to support the efforts of Lisbon and Madrid in furthering their relations with the EEC. Without EEC help, the risk of political and economic regression of the two countries was very high:

Les pays européens doivent ainsi encourager le développement notamment pour contribuer à résoudre les problèmes de structure sociale et par là à créer une stabilité politique qui tienne compte toujours plus fortement des points de vue de démocratie et liberté.[33]

In the case of the Maghreb, the French document pointed out the internal economic and political problems of Tunisia, Morocco and Algeria, and called attention to attempts to coordinate between the three countries (in view of the creation of the Maghreb Union) and the importance of relations with European countries and the EEC (especially for Tunisia and Morocco). Finally, the report stressed the fact that, in spite of the recent agreement between Algiers and Moscow, the Soviet Union had not obtained all the facilities it had hoped for.[34]

... but Nothing Happens!

If these reports are interesting (in some cases, very interesting) the discussions among the Nine did not have any concrete outcomes. An Italian document proposing the elaboration of a Community strategy to oppose Soviet influence in the Mediterranean[35] was strongly criticized by the French representative, as the British delegate observed:

Signor Cagiati [the diplomatic assistant of the Italian Prime Minister] circulated (in the vain hope that we might even adopt it at this meeting) a somewhat ambitious paper suggesting that Soviet penetration should be contained through a Community Mediterranean programme of economic and technical cooperation of a non-political basis. [...] M. Jurgensen [the French representative] took the lead in getting section III and IV – the meat of the paper – set aside completely on the ground that even for French taste they impinged too much on economic matters that fell within the competence of the organs of the Community. I expect Signor Cagiati or the Belgian will return to the charge.[36]

In spite of the Italian efforts, the Political Directors agreed only that the Mediterranean Working Group should keep a careful watch on current events and report whenever necessary. The papers on the Mediterranean countries should remain national documents even if the group could use them as a basis for submitting agreed conclusions in the future.[37] For the British representative, it was clear that with the end of the Italian chairmanship, the Working Group was leaning away from the 'ambitious scheme of studies on the Mediterranean area as a whole.'[38]

In June 1972, after general debate, members of the Working Group agreed to concentrate their attention on Yugoslavia and Libya in order to arrive at a harmonization of the national foreign policies.[39] In particular it was agreed that 'The members' relations with Yugoslavia deserve special interest and that in due course the question of the Community's relations with her would deserve favourable treatment'.[40] In the case of Libya:

> The members should try so far as possible to improve their polit-
> ical and economic relations with her, and that the desirability
> of an eventual agreement between the Community and Libya
> should be borne in mind.[41]

In May 1972, the Political Directors, in their report to the Foreign Ministers, underlined the danger represented by the Soviet fleet (and, in general, the Soviet influence) in the Mediterranean. The tension created by this situation had led the governments of the Mediterranean countries to organize a conference of all 'neutral' countries in the area and to defend the idea of an arms limitation in the Mediterranean.[42] From now on, the debates between the Nine focused on the Mediterranean 'neutral' initiatives, in particular on a project for a conference of Mediterranean neutral states supported by Yugoslavia and Algeria – a project closely related to the convocation of the Conference on Security and Cooperation in Europe (CSCE).[43]

The Italian and Belgian efforts for a common approach to the region failed. In September 1972, the Belgian delegation presented a document on the common principles that should inspire the foreign policy of the Nine in the Mediterranean. After presenting the negotiations between the EEC and Mediterranean countries, and in particular the Commission's projects concerning Global Mediterranean Policy, Brussels indicated the need to elaborate a common vision of Mediterranean problems. In a second moment, this should lead to political cooperation among the Nine.[44]

The Belgian document was adopted as a 'useful' contribution to the consultations of the Nine that, in fact, did not take place. The EEC Council's adoption of the Global Mediterranean Policy prevented any serious discussions in the EPC. Work within the EEC progressed so fast that any proposal elaborated by the Mediterranean Working Group would not have had time to be taken into consideration. Moreover, within the Working Group, discussions did not go far because the Nine were unable to decide whether the Working Group was qualified to debate the political aspects of the Global Mediterranean Policy (as London argued) or not (as Paris claimed).

The situation was clarified only after the Paris Summit (held on 19–21 October 1972). The Nine decided that the political aspects of the Global Mediterranean Policy should be examined inside the EEC. For its part, the Working Group focused its discussions on the Non Aligned Mediterranean Conference project and on the request of the Southern Mediterranean countries to take part in the CSCE. Any idea of a common action towards the Mediterranean was put aside. In other words, the Working Group did not become a sort of Policy Planning Staff as some EEC member states had hoped when it was created, but it was transformed in a discussion forum on some specific questions related to Mediterranean equilibrium.

Conclusion

From the end of 1972, the debate within the Mediterranean Working Group lost much of its interest. However, it is important not to under-estimate its role in the elaboration of a coherent Mediterranean space. With the start of discussions at the beginning of 1971, the Working Group contributed not only to bringing the Mediterranean area to the attention of the Nine, but also to helping the EEC member states to conceive of the region as a single unity towards which it was necessary to elaborate a common policy. In doing this, it made a considerable contribution to the process leading to the approval of the Global Mediterranean Policy. The growing presence of the Soviet fleet, strong regional tensions, and the need to secure oil imports, made Europeans sensitive to the unstable equilibrium of the region. Détente, which existed in continental Europe, did not prevail in the Mediterranean. Here the situation was changing more than ever: Moscow was defying the US naval domination; the Arab states were counting on the competition between East and West in order to obtain more aid under the best conditions but, at the same time, they were also worried about the Cold War confrontation in the Mediterranean, as their request to link the region to the CSCE debates showed. In this context, some European states – Italy, among others – thought the EEC could play a role in the stabilization of the region. The Mediterranean Working Group was particularly useful, providing the Nine with an occasion to elaborate a common analysis of the problems of the region. From this point of view, it is very interesting that at the beginning of 1972, the Mediterranean Working Group and the Commission arrived at the same conclusions about EEC policy. Both focused on a lack of EEC influence in the area in spite of the agreements signed during the 1960s, and pointed out the need for a coherent and more ambitious development policy. After the termination of debate on national reports about the Mediterranean sub-regions, the work in the Mediterranean slowed down and focused on some specific questions. In any case, the Nine had already agreed that some kind of common action was desirable in the Mediterranean. In fact, they officially recognized the need for a common policy during the Paris Summit. In the declaration issued at the end of the Paris Summit (October 1972) it was affirmed that:

> The [Community] attaches essential importance [...] to the fulfil-ment of its commitments to the countries of the Mediterranean Basin with which agreements have been or will be concluded, agreements which should be the subject of an overall and balanced approach.[45]

The answer of the Nine to Mediterranean instability and the Soviet threat was the Global Mediterranean Policy, which was officially adopted during the Paris Summit. Moreover, thanks to the GMP and the agree-ments to be signed by almost all the Mediterranean countries, the Nine hoped to strengthen their influence, and to contribute to the (capitalist) development of these countries.

It is beyond the scope of the present article to evaluate the success or failure of the GMP. What is important here is that even if it is not certain that the Nine shared the same vision of the Mediterranean area, they shared at least a common vision of the Mediterranean problems. The work of the Mediterranean Working Group showed that the Nine agreed on both the importance and danger of the growing presence of the Soviet Union in the Mediterranean. They also agreed on the fact that many countries in the region were going through a crucial phase of economic development and transformation, Arab leaderships were facing important political challenges and the EEC could contribute to stabilization in the region.[46] The fact that these considerations did not lead to the adoption of a common foreign policy[47] (as the Italians or Belgians had proposed) but to an economy-based initiative was not a sign of limited interest of EEC member states. An economic approach was the customary EEC strategy towards developing countries. Moreover, the South Mediterranean coun-tries were very interested in the EEC economic cooperation proposals and were awaiting them.

CHAPTER 4

Sea and Détente in Helsinki

The Mediterranean Stake of the CSCE, 1972–1975

Nicolas Badalassi

In July 1973, 33 European countries, the United States and Canada met in Helsinki for the Conference on Security and Cooperation in Europe. The Soviets considered it an achievement of East–West negotiations, which were designed to confirm the political and territorial status quo in Europe. The Western intention was to make the Russians and their allies agree on some fundamental principles such as the possibility of changing borders by peaceful means, respect for human rights, improvement in cultural exchange, and a better circulation of people, ideas and information between the East and West. In brief, they wanted to overcome the negative effects produced by the Iron Curtain.

Nevertheless, according to some European countries and North African states, security as defined by CSCE was imperfect. Détente may have been established in Europe, but it was not the case in the Mediterranean region where tensions, particularly in the Near East, were growing. As a consequence, Algeria and Tunisia tried to take advantage of the most important European meeting organized since the Congress of Vienna in 1815 to make European states and both Soviet and American superpowers become aware of the unbreakable link between security in Europe and security in the Mediterranean. This raises the question of the geographical aspect of détente: should the CSCE negotiators have considered only regional issues or should it have been enlarged to a global level?

This chapter tries to show how the CSCE contributed to the promotion of European–Mediterranean ties and made it a central parameter of the East–West relationship during the 1970s, when the first oil shock, the Turkish military intervention in Cyprus and the growing Soviet influence in the world became involved in the debate about disarmament and Near East conflicts.

The question of security in the Mediterranean was progressively included in CSCE negotiations. The North African states first introduced the issue in Helsinki but it was the strong support for the Maghreb initiative from the neutrals and non-aligned states, particularly Malta, which placed great emphasis on this question during the CSCE. The invasion of Cyprus and European Political Cooperation (EPC), as well as the Yom Kippur War, pushed each conference member to take a stand on the situation in the Mediterranean.

The North African Initiative in Helsinki

In 1971, Algeria and Tunisia informed the main Western Mediterranean countries – France, Italy and Spain as well as Yugoslavia – that they wanted CSCE conclusions to be applied in the Mediterranean zone. Indeed, there were various reasons for this request: first, tensions were growing in the region because of the Near East war which had started up again with renewed vigour since 1967; second, the North African countries complained about the increased activity of the Soviet naval fleet in the region because of the Arab–Israeli conflict. There were more Soviet troops in Egypt and Syria, and later, the USSR signed a friendship and cooperation treaty with Iraq on 9 April 1972. In addition, the Algerians and Tunisians denounced the American attempts to increase the Sixth Fleet in Greece by establishing a base near Athens. The Algerian and Tunisian governments considered the Mediterranean to be slowly becoming the main area of power competition. They feared a partition between two zones or, at the very worst, an East–West military conflict near their territories.[1] As a consequence, they called for the departure of Soviet and American fleets.

The CSCE project crystallized these fears. While the Mediterranean was becoming an area of power politics and competition, and détente in Europe seemed to transport tensions towards southern regions, the North African states tried to become involved in the security organization and ensure the involvement of the Mediterranean in the détente process. Further, Algeria did not see the CSCE as a real regional meeting since it brought together almost all the industrialized world, four permanent members of the UN Security Council, and all the great military powers, which spent 85 per cent of the world defence budget and owned almost all of the world's nuclear armament.[2] Consequently, Presidents Boumedienne and Bourguiba asked for their countries to take part in the Conference, directly calling French President Georges Pompidou.[3] The Yugoslavians, and the leaders of the non-aligned countries including Algeria, strongly supported the Arabian initiative but wanted the Maghreb states to be only associated with the CSCE. On the Western side, positions were less categorical.

When the 32 European countries, the United States and Canada – Monaco joined the group in September 1973 – met in Dipoli, near Helsinki, from November 1972 to June 1973, to establish the agenda and organization of the Conference, Algiers and Tunis immediately gave the Finnish government and other state delegations a letter in which they officially expressed their desire to be associated with the CSCE and the need to link security in Europe with security in the Mediterranean.[4] Delegations of both countries were also sent to Helsinki to put direct pressure on Western and Eastern diplomats. Of the Western states, France and Italy were of particular interest because of their propensity to intervene in the Mediterranean area. Algeria managed to create real competition between Rome and Paris to determine who would be the best representative and defender of the Mediterranean countries' interests.

As an official neutral state, Franco's Spain was the closest from an Algerian point of view, and called for a Mediterranean pact which would unite all coastal countries so that they might be directly concerned with their own security. Italy, however, did not wish to promote a project that would replace the protection of the US Sixth Fleet. Rome would have preferred to organize a Conference on Security and Cooperation in the Mediterranean which included the United States and USSR, thus blocking the North African initiative.[5] First, France, which was the only Western state invited to the Conference on the Mediterranean organized by Algeria in the summer 1972,[6] was reluctant because of Soviet hostility towards the presence of observers or representatives from non-European countries apart from Canada and the United States. Paris, which sought to recover its status as the USSR's special partner as during the de Gaulle years, tried not to offend Moscow.[7] However, for France, this status had to be compatible with the need to maintain French political pre-eminence in North Africa. The French foreign Ministry had to individuate a position which would accommodate all partners.

From March 1973, Algeria and Tunisia were not alone; Morocco, Egypt, Lebanon, Libya and Syria also wished to participate in the Conference, which led to greater European concern. In turn, Israel, via its Paris embassy, asked to be considered on the same level as all governments of the southern side of the Mediterranean. The main Israeli goal was to avoid the CSCE speaking about the Near East conflict.[8] On the contrary, the Maghreb states welcomed the Conference as an opportunity for appeasement in the region. The Algerian foreign ministry believed that bringing up this issue in Helsinki was inevitable since security in the Mediterranean depended largely on Israel, heavily armed and flaunting its weapons.[9] The initiative that forced the European states to establish a tie between security in Europe and security in the Mediterranean came from Malta.

The Maltese Rebellion

Neutral and non-aligned countries, especially Yugoslavia, played a central role in discussion about Mediterranean issues during the CSCE, particularly by supporting the North African initiative. While this proposition had only a limited impact on the Conference, the question of security in the Mediterranean became a hot topic since spring of 1973. The Maltese delegation caused a *coup de théâtre* which dampened the atmosphere during the last days of the preparatory multilateral talks in Helsinki.

Valletta toughened its attitude towards full participation of Arab Mediterranean states, arguing that Maltese security was closely dependent on the security of these countries. Malta attempted to demonstrate that its vision of détente was global, based on negation of a bloc-to-bloc relationship and self-assertion of the small countries. Moreover, Valletta stressed the solidarity existing between former Western colonies. Ambassador Saliba threatened to block consensus on all the Helsinki recommendations if his expectations were not satisfied.[10] This meant that consensus at the CSCE, one of its basic principles, might never come to be since Malta could hinder the détente process. The Maltese ultimatum took all delegations by surprise and provoked a collective protest as nobody, particularly in Eastern countries, thought the final clash would be about the Mediterranean. This event showed heightened sensibility in East–West relations created by the Near East war. All delegates knew that getting into this issue during the CSCE meant the end of détente, given the divergent positions on the Arab–Israeli conflict.

On the one hand, Malta finally agreed to the Helsinki recommendations but, on the other, Valletta vigorously resumed its demands during the negotiating stage of the CSCE in Geneva, from September 1973 to July 1975. On 11 September 1973, the Maltese delegation submitted a document directly expressing Prime Minister Dom Mintoff's view that Malta might withdraw from the military structures of NATO. Indeed, Mintoff, in contrast with his Nationalist Party predecessor, who favoured NATO ties and the visits of the Sixth Fleet, followed a neutralist and opportunist foreign policy, which allowed him to accept assistance from any source. According to the US Department of State, 'Mintoff, from his first day in office, has set about systematically to reduce Western influence in Malta in favour of closer ties with the non-aligned world, particularly Libya, the Arabs, and China'.[11] Malta remained, however, heavily dependent on revenue derived from the British military presence.

Malta's purpose in Helsinki was to denounce superpower hegemony in the Mediterranean. The most controversial point of Malta's document was the call to transform the Euro–Arab dialogue into an autonomous federation, enlarged to include Iran and the Gulf countries, areas in which East–West confrontation was heating up. Malta thus proposed to the CSCE 'to create a control committee in charge of stimulating evolution of this dialogue in order for political understanding to be led to a concerted political action for peace in the Mediterranean and South Europe'.[12] In others words, the CSCE's decisions concerning security and cooperation would be unsuccessful if the geographical borders of European security were not extended. Malta complained that the CSCE participating states were only interested in issues arising from the Iron Curtain and ignored the more distant European states. The security of these countries depended not only on the political situation of the continent, but also on the Near East.

The Turkish intervention in Cyprus during the summer of 1974, following the Greek coup d'état against Cypriot President Makarios, was central to the Maltese line of argument and a key moment in the process which led European leaders to realize the close connection between European and Mediterranean situations. Indeed, the intervention occurred when the delegations of the first committee in Geneva were negotiating principles such as the inviolability of frontiers and the non-use of force. This constituted the main goals of the Soviets during the Conference since, according to the Kremlin, it allowed confirmation of the status quo. European countries, to which mention of border issues suggested the Iron Curtain, suddenly had to confront a new process of territorial division. Turkey and Greece, both involved in the Cyprus crisis, were not only members of NATO but also active contributors to the CSCE, as was the Republic of Cyprus itself. The CSCE's credibility in the face of public opinion was severely threatened.

As expected, the Cypriot issue was included in the Geneva negotiations, and almost all European delegations wanted to speak about

Cyprus. Security in the Mediterranean intruded dramatically into the talks about security in Europe, and led to a reappraisal of the principles negotiated by the 35 countries in the previous two years. It also created serious second thoughts about the success and achievement of the CSCE, whose goal was to consolidate détente and avoid a return to the Cold War. The head of the Cypriot delegation in Geneva, Mavrommatis, listed principles and provisions discussed during the Conference which had been infringed by Turkey. He consequently described the CSCE as 'the non conference of the century'. Like his Greek colleague, Mavrommatis said his government would not sign any final text as long as his country was occupied.[13] In addition, the Turks vehemently opposed the presence of the Cypriot leader Makarios at the CSCE stage III, and made approaches in favour of some form of Greek–Turkish–Cypriot representation.[14]

Malta reappraised a large part of the first basket devoted to the principles drawn up to regulate relations between states and confidence-building measures (CBM). The CBM included pre-notification of military exercises – a country planning military exercises had to previously inform its neighbours – and exchange of foreign observers during troop movements. The main goal was originally to prevent misunderstanding and accident, particularly in border areas, but for Malta, the Cyprus invasion proved that these measures were inefficient and inadequate:

> Notwithstanding all guarantees of security provided by some great countries and involvement of a considerable contingent from the United Nations, use of force led to a tangible violation of sovereignty and integrity of a territory. For the little independent nations, previous notification is an empty measure and we have to search for other measures designed to reinforce confidence.[15]

According to Valletta, which became the champion of the neutral and non-aligned states, the only ways to reinforce confidence were dissolution of the military bloc, disarmament, and independence of Europe from both superpowers – measures complemented by a Euro–Arab organization. This meant the departure of Soviet and American troops from Europe and the Mediterranean, and extending the mutual and balanced reduction of forces to the whole of both areas.[16] In view of these demands, reactions were lukewarm. The USA and USSR, embarrassed, tried to get around the debate by giving the Nine of the European Community an opportunity to demonstrate their ability to ease tensions.

Stasis of the Superpowers, Dynamism of the Nine

As we have seen, the Maghreb states' request to take part in the CSCE was first made towards the most powerful countries on the northern side of the Mediterranean. The North Africa states were in fact thankful that the French, Spanish and Italian governments understood the need to create a binding tie between Europe and the Mediterranean area.

Regarding France, its Mediterranean policy was similar to the Gaullist European conception. It favoured bilateralism, condemned bloc-to-bloc relationships and rejected mutual force reduction. The French refused the full participation of some Arab countries in the CSCE because they argued that the Conference had to preserve its European character. Georges Pompidou tried to make Bourguiba understand this in July 1972, but he was glad to allow Eastern countries to express a more categorical opposition in order to avoid disagreement coming from France.[17]

A Paris–Rome–Madrid triangular relation was therefore established and was coupled to the consultations of the Nine to reach a common position. Pompidou contributed to the adjustment of EC Mediterranean policy during the European summit of Paris in October 1972, and thus made it possible to define a global approach to this issue. Furthermore, since November 1970, the Foreign Ministers of the Nine had identified the CSCE and the Near East as the main consultation issues which should be included in European Political Cooperation (EPC) formulated in The Hague in December 1969. The first goal of EPC was to allow Western Europe to speak with one voice against Soviet–American pre-eminence in East–West relationship and the Arab–Israeli conflict. For France and the United Kingdom, EPC also provided a means for claiming to be medium powers in the Near East where their influence had become restricted since the Suez crisis in 1956.[18] Tackling the question of security in the Mediterranean at the CSCE amounted to bringing together both main issues of EPC.

During 1972, the states participating in the CSCE were confronted with an alternative: either North African countries sent observers to the Conference – at the risk of introducing the Near East war into the Geneva negotiations, which everyone wanted to avoid – or one of the thirty-five participating delegations expressed these countries' point of view. This latter idea, which came from Madrid and Belgrade, was favourably considered by the Nine. In addition, the Italians suggested that their Western European partners plan a parallel information system about the CSCE discussions towards south-side Mediterranean countries.

Moreover, Italy took part in several multilateral meetings concerning security in the Mediterranean and made a pledge to Malta, Libya and

Tunisia to raise the problem during the Conference.[19] Rome's dynamism on this issue led the French to become aware of their own passivity. During the autumn of 1972 and the following winter, they made sure that other Western countries did not become interlocutors who North Africa would prefer to deal with.[20]

At the beginning of the Multilateral Preparatory Talks (MPT), the head of the Algerian diplomatic mission in Helsinki tried to convince the French delegation that his country's participation in the CSCE was the only way to decline the Soviet proposal concerning a friendship treaty similar to the Soviet–Egyptian one.[21] At the same time, Paris said France was ready to regularly inform the Algerian, Tunisian, and Moroccan diplomatic missions about the discussions of the MPT.[22] For Pompidou, who wanted to improve French–North African relations, which were marked by several strained periods,[23] France had to take on this role because of the 'Mediterranean and African extension' which history and geography had given France.[24] By linking the Mediterranean to Europe, Charles de Gaulle's successor showed he was anxious to balance the continent towards the south, using the traditional opposition between Latinity and Germanity. In addition, on the eve of the October 1973 oil crisis, Paris sought to diversify its supply of hydrocarbons, and initiated negotiations with several Arab states. As a consequence, it was not the moment to put France in the wrong from political and international points of view.

In Helsinki, France, Italy, and some neutral and non-aligned countries such as Yugoslavia, Spain, Switzerland, and Malta stood up for the Algerian and Tunisian initiative in front of the Soviet–American reluctance to tackle the issue during the CSCE – the Mediterranean was in the middle of the US and Soviet military systems. It was a French document which, among the Nine in Helsinki, served as the basis for the agenda paragraph about the Mediterranean, despite the continuing reluctance of the USSR. According to this text, 'the conference and its committees will be able to acquaint themselves, in conditions they will work out, with points of view that some non-European and Mediterranean states may wish to express concerning issues on the agenda'.[25] Paris did not hesitate to tell all Arab countries that the text which authorized them to present their ideas to the CSCE was French.[26] The rivalry created by Boumedienne and Bourguiba thus worked perfectly, even if numerous participants considered the Italians as the leaders in Mediterranean issues during the whole Helsinki process.[27]

However, there was still a fear of the Arab–Israeli conflict being introduced into the Helsinki and Geneva talks. Such a situation would jeopardize European détente. To avoid this, the Quai d'Orsay suggested that the countries concerned promise not to tackle the issue – otherwise they would not continue to be supported by France. Paris also suggested not speaking about security in the Mediterranean itself, but rather, to insert instructions about the connection between the issues dealt with in these committees and the Mediterranean problems in the mandates of several committees or under-committees of the CSCE. The first basket on security and the second on economic cooperation were specially targeted. The French, with ulterior motives, thought it was possible to apply the principles of cooperation among states, confidence-building measures, environmental measures, and, of course, cooperation over raw materials and energy resource exploitation to the whole Mediterranean area.[28] However, the North African delegations were resolute, and as the MPT came to an end, numerous discussions were organized with the French. They stressed that each Mediterranean country had to subscribe to the principles of the first basket in order to settle the Near East conflict.[29] Finally, the speeches of the North African states representatives at the CSCE took place in October 1973, a few days after the outbreak of the Yom Kippur War, which slightly affected negotiations since all delegations had decided not to speak about the conflict.[30]

The Soviets only really intervened in the debate once Malta stopped the MPT. Malta had hoped for the full participation of the Arab countries and the withdrawal of the Soviet and American fleets from the Mediterranean. The Russians, who did not agree with the Mediterranean states' point of view, were furious. On 6 June 1973, the Soviet representative Mendelevitch, in a memorable speech citing the 20 million Soviets who died during World War II, protested against the fact that only one government could jeopardize an enterprise aimed at securing peace in Europe.[31] Moscow did not want to allow Malta to eradicate its military system in the Mediterranean and to deadlock a conference which sanctioned the Soviet authority over Eastern Europe.

The Soviets repeated their refusal to connect European security with Mediterranean security when the Cyprus crisis broke out. In order to avoid the Turkish intervention which would have caused the failure of a conference which they had taken seriously since the 1950s, they suggested a United Nations conference to settle the Cyprus issue. The Kremlin wanted, at all costs, to avoid the topic of Cyprus, but Malta and Greece thought it was the most important point in the CSCE agenda. Inviolability of frontiers and refraining from the threat or use of force were the two crucial principles designed to prevent any reappraisal of the European status quo, which had been damaged by Turkey.

From the outset, the United States was quite unconcerned about the Helsinki process since they preferred to favour direct dialogue with Moscow.[32] Moreover, Washington gave priority to military rather than political détente. The human and financial cost of the Vietnam War and the numerous requests from senators to reduce the American military presence in Europe led the Nixon administration to privilege the MBFR and SALT negotiations. It was, however, out of the question for the White House to reduce the number of troops in the Mediterranean while the Arab–Israeli war was at its height and USSR was making endless attempts to establish itself in the Near East and Africa. The USA was concerned that too much attention was being given to the Mediterranean in the CSCE, especially from the political and security angle. This would have not only disrupted the Conference but would have complicated rather than facilitated relations with the Mediterranean states. In particular, they could not accept the neutrals' suggestion for an extension of confidence-building measures in the Mediterranean or 'the completely unrealistic Maltese proposal for a permanent committee on Mediterranean security'.[33] They considered this request to be beyond the Helsinki mandate.

The Nine of the EEC, like USSR, did not want the CSCE to end in failure. On the one hand, they were about to succeed in introducing respect for human rights into the East–West relationship and in making the Soviet bloc agree to improve exchanges in the fields of culture and education, human contacts and the freer and wider dissemination of information. On the other hand, the CSCE was the only field in which the Nine consistently managed their policies in the EPC framework. As a consequence, they opted for a strategy in which the main goal was to persuade the Maltese to be less intransigent, and in compensation for their understanding, they would be implicated in Euro–Arab dialogue developments. The new relations between Malta and the Nine were immediately fruitful, and Valletta appreciated the ECP's part in overcoming the bloc-to-bloc situation. The EEC delegations thus managed to have the Maltese agree to some texts which corresponded to their common project and to abandon some important and sensitive points such as an extension of the confidence-building measures, relations with non-participant states and suppression of tensions in the Mediterranean. The United States and the USSR, who were reluctant to intercede with Malta because they did not want to increase its hostility towards the division of Europe in two blocs, avoided conferring disproportionate political dimensions to the Mediterranean issue.[34]

Finally, in order to have the protagonists of the Cyprus crisis agree to the final provisions of the CSCE, the Nine suggested adding, in an independent paragraph, a declaration about the Mediterranean. This would encourage mutually favourable cooperation, especially in the economic field, between both sides of the Mediterranean. It would be submitted in Geneva by Italy and the participant states would reaffirm the tie between European and Mediterranean security. The United States and the USSR, however, refused a separate text for fear that it would give the Arab countries the right to take part in the third stage of the CSCE, in which the heads of states and governments would meet. They also feared the superpower presence would be further challenged in the Mediterranean. Nevertheless, the Soviet delegation in Geneva allowed the Americans to express their disapproval. The USSR interceded only to oppose the idea of 'economic interdependence' between both sides. The document was consequently changed at Moscow's request and was then registered.[35] The declaration was combined with the political part of the Final Act, which gave it a certain importance. Finally, when Makarios decided to go to Helsinki (he was given the opportunity by the CSCE to present Cypriot interests), Athens and Nicosia were no longer reluctant to sign the Final Act.[36] Concerning the Turkish attitude towards the presence of the Cypriot leader, Washington firmly discouraged the Turks from pursuing their line, on the grounds that it would have been counter-productive and would have forced all CSCE participating states to reiterate their recognition of the Makarios regime as the only legitimate government of Cyprus.[37] By early July 1975, all CSCE issues seemed to have been settled.

During the final period of negotiations in Geneva, Malta tried again and undermined its own work. An ambassador of Dom Mintoff's came to Switzerland and expressed two demands. The first was for Valletta to be mentioned in the Declaration of the Mediterranean desire for the participant states to improve the dialogue with the coastal countries, i.e. with the Arab states. It also called for a clause on the progressive departure of American and Soviet troops from the area. This event paralysed the Conference for an entire week. Malta refused to agree to several proposals as long as its own proposals were not agreed to. In order to overcome this situation, the Soviets tried to enlist Western support for some strong-arm tactics to isolate Malta and move on to the CSCE final summit in Helsinki without it, if necessary. Indeed, the Maltese initiative was out of place for the USSR, which was reinforcing its Mediterranean fleet in June 1975.[38] However, for the USA, signing the Final Act without Malta would have been a violation of the consensus rule prevailing in the Conference, and would have been rejected by many Western allies, as well as neutrals.[39]

Finally, thanks to joint pressure from the USA and the USSR, who were keen to finish the CSCE,[40] agreement was reached on a toned-down text, planning 'reduction of the armed forces in the area', while 'amplification of the contacts and dialogue' was agreed. The Maltese annoyed all delegations during this week: the Soviets were ready to ignore the Maltese and to conclude an agreement without them; the smaller states were worried about abuse of the idea of consensus; the United States was angry because they had no intention of reducing their forces in the Mediterranean; France did not appreciate Malta's initiative because of its strong opposition to mutual forces reductions. During a NATO caucus meeting on 11 July 1975, the Turks emphasized their dislike for Mintoff's call for a reduction in armed forces in the Mediterranean. The Maltese amendment was in fact read by the Turks as being partly directed against them, in particular in regards to the Cyprus context.[41] To show its general disapproval, the Conference reduced the importance of the document about the Mediterranean, which lost its status as a declaration and was separated from the political documents.[42] In spite of this, Malta, Algeria and their neutral and non-aligned partners all managed to introduce a lasting relation between European and Mediterranean security, even if, as the Algerian Foreign Minister Abdelaziz Bouteflika noted, 'the principles laboriously perfected by the CSCE are not applicable as it is to the area and have to be completed by the Third World's principles, more particularly the principle of non-alignment.' He regretted that, 'considering international responsibilities of some powers, the issue of decolonization in Africa, and the question of Palestine and Middle-East did not receive attention of the conference'.[43]

In 1975, the 'Mediterranean dimension' of the CSCE was aimed more at demonstrating to the Soviet bloc that détente was indivisible geographically, than about taking North African hopes into account. Therefore, the extension of confidence and security measures in the Mediterranean was postponed until 1983. Two reasons explain this European refusal. First, they did not want to mix European issues with the Near East question. Second, they wanted to keep the naval forces that were not subject to any manoeuvre notification measures in an area outside of the NATO zone and where the provisions of the CSCE could not be applied.[44]

The Mediterranean's intrusion into the Helsinki process finally leads to a double observation. On the one hand, both the United States and the USSR measured up to competition with new actors: the Arab states, neutrals and non-aligned states, which tried to take their future into their own hands. On the other hand, Western Europe tried to regain influence in an area which it dominated over several centuries, now by using the new Community instruments. Nevertheless, bipolar logic still prevailed until the end of the Cold War because of EPC's failure to harmonize the Nine's positions about the Near East, and the increased number of conflicts in the Mediterranean area.

CHAPTER 5

Regional Détente or a New International Order?

The Italian Communist Party, Non-Aligned Leaders and the Mediterranean, 1964–1980

Marco Galeazzi

After World War II the Italian Communist Party (PCI) pursued a new strategy aimed at the European context. This decision was based on both the new party's desire to take root in Italy and the beginning of the Cold War in 1947. To this end, Togliatti declared: 'the colonial powers do not have a decisive role in determining our policies'.[1] This policy was to change only at the beginning of the 1950s as a result of Stalin's death, the end of the Korean War and the development of neutralism. Less than a year after the African–Asian Bandung Conference the PCI Secretary laid down the Five Points that had emerged from the Indonesian summit as:

> The most modern and state-of-the-art foreign policy programme that was presented, in that it contained a detailed and precise formulation of the most civil and human way in which the relations between the great organised communities can be regulated today, thereby avoiding the risk of conflict and providing a solid basis for permanent peace.[2]

During this period Togliatti devised the thesis of polycentrism, which, together with an end to the guiding state, constituted one of the pillars of Italian socialism.[3] While this strategy was undoubtedly shaped by Khrushchev's foreign policy,[4] it was also influenced by Togliatti's dialogue with Tito, which culminated in their spring 1956 meeting in Belgrade. Although the two leaders expressed different views on Stalinism and the role of the USSR, they agreed on the new role of countries struggling to be liberated from colonialism and the idea that the world was no longer strictly bipolar.[5] However, after the Suez Canal Crisis[6] and Soviet intervention in the Hungarian revolution the PCI had to backtrack from the aspirations of the previous months and go along with the line of bipolar stabilization in international relations. As a result of the Middle East crisis in the summer of 1958 much of the PCI leadership began to accentuate the link between the anti-colonial struggle and the USSR's anti-imperialist movement. For this reason Giancarlo Pajetta was critical of both Nasser[7] – who had been forced to seek Soviet aid – and Tito's policy of wooing Asian and African nations, which was judged harshly during the PCI and the CCP bilateral meeting held in Beijing in April 1959.[8] The Italian Communist Party was inspired by an eschatological notion that the 'uncommitted' countries of the two blocs would end up adopting the socialist model of development. This conviction was expressed by Togliatti at the end of 1956[9] and recounted in the PCI press following the African and Asian Peoples' Conference in Cairo (December 1957–January 1958):

> The main champion of the movement embodied in the conference is socialism, toward which the peoples inhabiting the immense areas of Asia and Africa inevitably lean, while at the same time addressing the issue of total liberation from the influence of imperialism.[10]

Tito's fierce opposition to power blocs was further criticized by the Italian Communist Party, which saw it as a taking away from the USSR's peace policy.[11] Moreover, the PCI was worried about the relations between the Communist Party of Yugoslavia (LCJ) and the Italian Socialist Party, especially because many Arab countries were showing signs of discontent with bipolarism, and they were distancing themselves from Moscow.[12] Further evidence of such concern can be seen in the PCI's effort to internationalize the Algerian conflict between 1957 and 1962. Available documents appear to confirm that the PCI had been designated by the USSR as interlocutor for the liberation movements in Mediterranean Africa, replacing the French Communist Party (PCF),[13] which had become isolated in de Gaulle's France and entertained colonialist leanings. As early as 1937

Algeria was defined as a 'nation en formation' by Thorez,[14] an issue that Togliatti was highly critical of, though only behind the closed doors of the Party leadership.[15]

The Impact of Decolonization

At the beginning of the 1960s, after the Twelfth Session of the UN General Assembly's condemnation of colonialism and the emergence of the under-development issue, the PCI renewed its dialogue with Yugoslavia. The First Conference of Non-Aligned Countries held in Belgrade on 4–9 September 1961 was given special mention in the Party press[16] and by Togliatti himself who took advantage of the occasion to highlight the West's hostility towards self-determination of peoples:

> This situation was clearly and vigorously denounced by most of the participants at the conference in Belgrade, the initiatives and decisions of which we approved and still approve, but the true contents have to be unequivocally determined with no hypocrisy or allusion if we wish to perform a positive deed so that we can avoid catastrophe.[17]

Togliatti needed to expand his horizons beyond the communist move-ment, even if the non-aligned countries themselves were beleaguered by regional crises, such as those between Beijing and New Delhi over Tibet, India and Pakistan, and Algeria and Morocco. While, on the one hand, the 'double loyalty' and its privileged relation with Khrushchev's USSR, even more in the wake of the Cuban missile crisis of October 1962, were not brought into question, on the other, the party's ideological ortho-doxy of the past[18] had changed, prompting Togliatti to adopt a policy of neutrality.

> We propose a policy of neutrality, Italian disengagement from conflicts and from aggressive alliances between the great powers, which corresponds entirely to the traditions of the Italian workers' movement, to which we want to and will remain faithful.[19]

It was becoming clearer within the PCI that it could play a role on the front lines of international politics, even though this role was not supported by any theoretical premises that addressed the incongruences between Third World nationalism and the now obsolete categories of the Third International.

In 1963–64 PCI diplomacy was visibly shaped by Togliatti, whose final years were characterized by intense theoretical and strategic activity. Such diplomacy was dictated by the need to move beyond the 'camp' lines and the limits of Khrushchev's policies without, however, reneging on its support of the now isolated Soviet leader within the CPSU.[20] The Party's foreign office was reactivated under Galluzzi's leadership, and Longo's mission in Algiers,[21] Ingrao's in Cuba[22] and Togliatti's in Belgrade in January 1964[23] testified to their desire to develop a plan of regional détente, that would later evolve into a premise for formulating the New International Economic Order to come.

During their meetings in Algiers, Longo and Ben Bella set out a series of common aims, ranging from the struggle for socialism in Europe to aiding African countries in their liberation from colonialism.[24] Even though the PCI's involvement in the Algerian struggle for independence was more emotional than intellectual and their knowledge of Arab peoples and the complex relation between Marxism and Islam were partial and dogmatic, there still prevailed a desire to transform the Mediterranean basin into a denuclearized area and, more importantly, into 'a sea linking all the coastal peoples around economic, technical and cultural exchanges'.[25] Liaising between the Italian ruling elites and the Southern countries fuelled PCI commitment: even though it was an opposition party, it was seen as an almost independent sovereign entity by some European and non-European diplomacies. Evidence of this attitude emerges from the Italo-Yugoslav summit held in Belgrade in January 1964, when Togliatti and Tito laid down a common strategy based on the relation between the workers' movement of European capitalistic and non-aligned countries effectively isolating the French Communist Party, which remained loyal to the Kremlin line.

At the summit, Togliatti and Tito outlined the most important themes of international relations, which included the tensions in Latin America, the transition of the USA after Kennedy's assassination, East–West relations, under-development and the role of Third World countries.[26] They were particularly worried about the situation in the Arab world, and Tito highlighted the positive relations between Yugoslavia and Egypt. While he was critical of Nasser's anti-communist repression, he portrayed positively the direction Egypt was taking, which, although certainly not socialist, was well on the way to adopting advanced economic and political solutions.[27] The Yugoslav president was concerned about both the contrasts taking shape among newly independent countries and China's expansionist designs in Africa.[28] The latter concern was shared by Togliatti, who stated that the most effective reply to Beijing's dogmatism was:

To establish the most organic relations possible with the liberation and progressive movements of these countries. A stronger unity between Western communist parties and the liberation movements of Africa, Asia and Latin America should be created. This is the true response to the Chinese and, if done effectively, this would be much more valuable than contention.[29]

Tito wholeheartedly supported[30] Togliatti's proposal to organize a conference between communist parties, representatives of the liberation movements and European progressive forces. The struggle against neo-colonialism and true economic cooperation were the prerequisites for a coexistence aimed at overcoming the bipolar system and creating a synthesis between democracy and socialism.[31] This requirement was reaffirmed by the PCI Secretary in his report to the Central Committee in April 1964[32] and, a few months later, in his treatise, considered his political last will and testament, *The Yalta Memorial*.[33] The divisions within the communist movement, that he saw to be waning, and the difficulties of the non-aligned countries preyed on Togliatti's mind, and his opening to the progressive governments of newly independent countries stemmed from a view of a now interdependent world. Nonetheless, with his political background the Italian leader was unable to formulate a strategy fit for the challenges of the future. There still remained, however, a valuable, albeit unfinished, legacy that he would leave to his successors. But although these leaders reaffirmed their support for Togliatti's (and Gramsci's) doctrine, they still had to come to terms with their considerable isolation from the other communist parties, insofar as the PCI's great prestige among the liberation movements and non-aligned countries, especially in the Mediterranean basin, was not sufficient to endow it with a true sense of hegemony in international politics. Khrushchev's removal in October 1964 provoked contrasting reactions and deep uncertainty in both the communist movement and the Third World leadership.

The bilateral meetings between the PCI and the Algerian National Liberation Front (NLF) were inconclusive: the loss of such a valuable interlocutor as Khrushchev weakened Ben Bella's government, and his prospects in the difficult reconstruction of the country were becoming more and more uncertain.[34] The PCI delegation at the ceremonies for the Tenth Anniversary of the Algerian revolt could not fail to notice, on the one hand, Mozambican FRELIMO's caution ('the liberation movements do not want to compromise themselves', commented Dina Forti),[35] and, on the other, the PCF's and the Polish PUWP's palpable hostility in the wake of Berlinguer and Bufalini's stormy meeting with the new Soviet leadership.[36]

No less important was the internal debate among the new PCI leadership. Their ties with the USSR seemed even more important than they had to Togliatti, thereby hindering the PCI's development of an original culture and full autonomy. Pajetta's condemnation of China's anti-Soviet exploits in the Third World was countered by Berlinguer's view that stigmatized the USSR's refusal to recognize China's role as a great power and, in his own words, its 'more reasonable' foreign policy.[37] At the end of 1964 the dispute between the Chinese and the Soviets and the issue of the International Conference sought by the CPSU provoked a defensive attitude and overwhelmed the PCI's attention to Third World issues. These countries, however, were still of great interest to the Italian Communist Party, which decided to focus on the positive aspects of their liberation from colonialism, and to underplay their economic and social contradictions, and their inability to avoid the bipolar rationale and to elaborate their aspirations for a New International Economic Order.

Romano Ledda, who was sent as an observer to the Second Conference of Non-Aligned Countries in Cairo, viewed the movement in positive terms. It had matured beyond the limits of Bandung's 'noble moral testimony' and the 'vague equidistance and considerable passivity' vis-à-vis the power blocs expressed in Belgrade in 1961.[38] In Ledda's view, influenced by Togliatti's line of reasoning, the European workers' movement, the Socialist countries and the Third World liberation movements shared the responsibility to seek 'solutions to help the current affliction of the world'.[39] Such a view fostered a form of all-round diplomacy with key non-aligned countries, especially those in the Mediterranean basin. Pajetta and Galluzzi's visit to Cairo in February 1965 was particularly important in this regard.[40] The dispatches sent by Ambassador Magistrati to Moro, the Minister of Foreign Affairs,[41] confirm the interest of the Italian diplomacy in the PCI, which was no longer confined to its role of opposition and testimony: in the wake of La Pira and Fanfani's 'Mediterranean calling' the Christian Democracy Party's foreign policy, while still ostensibly anti-communist, shared some important positions with the PCI, the privileged interlocutor with the new participants in international politics. Pajetta was quite positive in his evaluation of Egypt's domestic situation and its foreign policy, and he portrayed it as a country which was pursuing a non-committed and overtly anti-imperialist type of politics, cooperating with socialist countries:

> A special type of country that is against imperialism but that sends troops to Jemen [sic] and Iraq and sends arms to the rebels

in the Congo, etc. [...] Just the type of leanings that we should be interested in.[42]

Such optimism, however, stemmed from an inadequate understanding of the culture and outlook of Arab societies. Years later Galluzzi would write: 'Even though we openly questioned the Egyptians' beliefs and proposals, we did not completely gauge their meanings and the perils of the radical turn that Nasser had forced upon the Egyptian politics and which would prove to be fatal'. In contrast to a line of argument favoured by Pajetta and widespread in the PCI in the 1970s, he went on to say that 'the idea that Arab socialism could be realized was so complex and far-fetched that it appeared at the time more of an ideological abstraction than actual fact'.[43]

Berlinguer's position differed from Pajetta's. At the beginning of 1965 he was interested in the East–West dialogue because he thought it was important to link 'the strategy of coexistence with the struggle for liberation'.[44] He voiced this idea officially at the Moscow summit of March 1965, where he argued matter-of-factly for the need to overcome the ideological schematizations of the communist movement, recalling the PCI's recent meetings with the NLF and the Arab Socialist Union.[45]

The dialogue between the European workers' movement and the non-aligned countries however did not advance. The Algerian coup in June 1965 was unexpected among the ranks of the PCI, even though the *Unità* correspondent had pointed out the weaknesses in Boumedienne's leadership.[46] The 'second Bandung' that was supposed to take place in the Algerian capital was postponed indefinitely, confirming the crisis among the non-aligned countries.[47] Furthermore, the Vietnam War, the KPI massacre in Indonesia, and the dispute between Cuba and Yugoslavia on anti-imperialist strategy (i.e. armed struggle or diplomacy) made the ambiguities in the PCI position all the more evident. Thus, while Longo clearly acknowledged that 'the Soviets and French are inclined to start something that could compromise our autonomy',[48] it was almost impossible for the Italian communists not to take into account the influence the CPSU and the PCF had on the results of their dialogue with the Mediterranean countries. In the meetings between Longo and Rochet, which had been called to bring together Togliatti's and Thorez's rich legacies, a number of important differences emerged on the enlargement of the anti-imperialist front beyond the communist parties.[49] At both meetings between the two secretaries and the bilateral talks held in Sanremo in May 1966 the PCF explicitly requested that the issue of relations between the working class of European capitalistic countries and the liberation movements be shelved.[50] Nonetheless, the PCI still stressed differences with both the French and the Soviets, demonstrating important similarities with the LCJ's line: they were both particularly concerned with the non-aligned countries, notwithstanding questions about the pressures of imperialism, the contrasts between the leading countries of the movement and the irreparable rift between China and the USSR. What they had to do, in other words, was to determine 'if the movements in underdeveloped countries should be considered as allies or reserves' of the most advanced communist forces in Europe in hopes of overcoming the bipolar balance of the world.[51] This phase was characterized by the important debate initiated at the Eleventh PCI Congress in 1966, that highlighted the role of the internal left and its susceptibility to the deep-rooted transformations in the world balance, support of the role of the colonial revolutions and Maoist China, and opposition to maintain close ties with the USSR, the dominant view among the party ruling group.[52] Thus, for example, despite his rather fierce criticism of the CPSU in his meeting with Tito in January 1967, Longo urged the Yugoslavs to take part in the Kremlin's Worldwide Conference seeing it as a valuable form of support for his own party's autonomy. Tito's refusal was categorical, however, citing the original inspiration of the non-aligned movement. Belgrade's role was in jeopardy, as it would have been damaged by a rapprochement with Moscow's foreign policy.[53] Even with such dissent, however, the Italian communists still considered entente with Yugoslavia to be an essential part of their international policy, within which there was a growing sense of mistrust towards the Soviet-led communist movement and an ever growing awareness of the interdependence of world processes. Berlinguer expounded upon this view during the Communist Parties Summit in Budapest in February 1968 affirming the need to create a dialogue with the new forces at work in the world so that anti-imperialist action could be reinforced and the crucial point of development confronted.[54]

Within the PCI, however, there was also a great deal of dissent of Yugoslav policy. During a meeting with the Mediterranean communist parties, Ledda voiced criticism of Belgrade's renewed refusal to allow American and Soviet ships in the region: Tito's inflexible non-alignment risked weakening the anti-imperialist struggle that the PCI, like many Arab parties, based upon their relationship with the USSR.[55] The PCI was finding it difficult for its new internationalism to take hold due to its disagreement with Yugoslavia and the worsening situation in the Middle East after the Six-Day War.

New elements and defensive positions coexisted in the PCI perspective. Ledda himself expressed deep-rooted criticism of the line taken in the previous years towards the Third World. In his opinion, decolonization had made no noteworthy advances, while non-alignment had been transformed into a veritable equidistance between the two blocs, and the PCI itself had misunderstood these 'processes underway', by re-proposing Comintern categories that were inadequate for the particular conditions of the societies and economic development of the South.[56] Third-Worldism appeared to be an unfruitful and unproductive category, while at the same time new political and social forces were becoming involved in the anti-imperialist struggle.

In mid-1969 the PCI reiterated its opposition to NATO in the Mediterranean,[57] yet it continued to stress the need for unity among the liberation movements, socialist countries and the workers' and progressive parties as its main sphere of internationalist activity. Although this policy had been veiled by Togliatti, at the beginning of the 1970s it gained new momentum from a growing awareness of the limits of the Soviet model and the USSR's actions in the Third World. The international policy of the Italian communists was now built on two strategic pillars: the development of closer relations with European social democrats and active support of non-European peoples, whose complex characteristics were noted by Berlinguer in his speech at a June 1969 Moscow conference. Not only did the PCI underline its courageous differentiation from the communist movement closely tied to Soviet positions, it reiterated its ambition to become a hegemonic force that could join the North and the South at the nexus between nation and internationalism and respond to the challenges of interdependence.[58] Deep-seated uncertainties within the PCI point to a number of unresolved problems: anti-Americanism, a normalization of relations with the CPSU after its condemnation of the Czechoslovakia invasion,[59] fear of international isolation, and the Stalinist legacy standing in the way of reimagining their own identity. Despite these problems, PCI policy remained focused on the Mediterranean and a growing and more systematic commitment to overcoming bipolarism.

In February 1973, while the worsening conflict in Vietnam induced Berlinguer to claim that 'the world was veering to the Left',[60] he again entertained talks with Algeria, Egypt and Yugoslavia in order to stiffen the hypothesis of a regional détente as part of his ambitious perspective of a New International Economic Order. There were a number of differences between the PCI and the NLF regarding the Arab–Israeli question, the types of struggle being pursued by Fatah and the PLO,[61] and the relations between PCF and NLF, which preoccupied the Italian leaders. Yet, this aspect did not deter the Party foreign office and *l'Unità*'s correspondents from devoting more and more space to economic issues and raw materials (such as natural gas and oil), making Boumedienne's regime an invaluable partner of both the Western powers and the Eastern bloc.[62] This importance was made clear at the PCI–NLF bilateral summit in October 1971:[63] the Algerian representatives' emphasis on the strategic meaning of non-alignment could not go unnoticed by Berlinguer, and the seeds of his global outlook of the first half of the 1980s can begin to be seen. Communist leaders painted a complex and problematic picture of the situation in Egypt after Nasser's death, and demonstrated once again how much their positions were influenced by wishful thinking, giving too much importance to the role of the communist minority and the continuity of Egyptian foreign policy despite the pro-Western turn initiatied by Sadat with the expulsion of Soviet technicians.[64]

It was still the relationship with the LCJ as a true strategic alliance that make it possible for them to imagine the possibility of overcoming bloc politics and a central role for non-aligned countries. Certainly they were concerned with the internal situation in Yugoslavia, where Croatian nationalism was spreading and there was the problem of Tito's succession; but the meetings between Berlinguer and Tito in May 1970 reaffirmed their common vision of the global crisis and the need for a more active role for the non-aligned countries before the Lusaka summit.[65] However the meeting made the polarization within the PCI leadership more evident: on the one hand, there was Berlinguer himself, who considered the policy of non-alignment as a means of moving beyond the bloc system, while, on the other, there were those who were more cautious about the end of the bipolar system, or even favourable to its consolidation.[66] In the Central Committee report of November 1971, the future PCI secretary drew attention to the national question, so fundamental for the development of internationalism, founded on a unitary action of the European workers' movement and southern countries.[67] The PCI leadership, however, lacked a full understanding of the limits of Allende's experience and Cuba's role in creating a deadlock in the Non-Aligned Movement. The Chilean coup dampened hopes of fortifying the anti-imperialist movement and Berlinguer's former optimism of a possible détente and multi-polar world. Overcoming bloc politics was no longer considered a *prius*, but a gradual process to which a 'neither anti-Soviet nor anti-American' Europe should actively contribute.[68]

Berlinguer was convinced that 'history is on the road to becoming global insofar as peoples from every continent are joining it as its subjects and protagonists'.[69] Although he envisioned a supranational government that could take on the challenges of modernity, serious doubts loomed on the horizon. In fact, how could a scenario be imagined in which capitalism, considered to be in trouble but not yet ready to fall, might cooperate with the very forces that were striving to bring it down? Moreover, how might there be a convergence of the superpowers to resolve the problems of humanity, and, at the same time, a desire for a strategic alliance among socialist countries, the European workers' movement and Third World countries in anti-imperialistic terms and whose victory was written in history? PCI strategy continued to be influenced by an antagonistic view of international relations. Egypt's attitude in the Yom Kippur War and OPEC's decision to raise oil prices were praised as responses to the challenges of imperialism and neo-colonialism. But the Party clearly underestimated the complexity of the Arab countries, which were considered to be part of the global revolutionary front, while some of it had long taken a pro-Western line. The opulence of United States' finances was much more attractive to African and Middle Eastern leaderships than the economy and ideology of the Soviet Union.[70]

In the mid-1970s Berlinguer and other Italian communists still had an ambivalent understanding of détente, based on an oversimplified view of capitalist means of production that ignored the structural weaknesses of the Soviet model, far superior, in their view, from a moral point of view. In addition to such dogmatism, however, an original line of thought was also developing, which was focused on resolving the problems of humanity. In this view, opulent society was urged to reconsider its privileged position and to understand the contradictions of the Third World. Such a world was 'neither homogenous nor autonomous', but rather crossed by deep-rooted divisions between and within states. Berlinguer noted:

> We know well that among the countries in these areas of the world and within each one of them, as in, for example, the Arab world, there is a contrast between the privileged and reactionary forces and social forces and progressive policies.[71]

Due to the structural differences created by colonialism and yet to be resolved he spoke of a 'Fourth World', condemning the growth of countries he defined as sub-imperialist,[72] whose expansionistic courses of action and possession of nuclear weapons would raise 'the risk of a show of force between capitalist and Third-world countries'.[73] From such reasoning resulted the need to recognize the supremacy of Western Europe and its hegemony over the countries of the Mediterranean, a view being advocated more and more frequently by the PCI secretary.

At the Non-Aligned Countries Summit in Algiers in September 1973, the PCI seems to have been hoping that the contrast between Gaddafi's position, opposed to both superpowers, and Castro's pro-Soviet line would be thwarted through Tito and Egyptian mediation.[74] Still, not only should the Third World be weaned from its dependence on financial capital and neo-colonialist rationale, but also it was necessary to elaborate a common position and autonomy of the West European countries.[75] Despite the radicalism of the Algerian regime, during the XIV Congress Berlinguer insisted on the positive role played by Boumedienne at the OPEC summit at the beginning of 1975.[76] The North–South question prompted talks with the most important representatives of social democracy in Europe, ranging from Brandt to Palme. Relations with the SPD had, in fact, been constant, and not sporadic as has been claimed.[77] Nevertheless, at the Puerto Rico Summit of June 1976 the political development of the Southern NATO countries after the fall of the Portuguese and Greek regimes and just before Spain's turn distressed Western representatives, making Italy, much more than in the past, a frontier country where the possible victory of a communist-led government was firmly opposed by both the United States and European governments, especially by Bonn and Paris.[78]

During a meeting in Belgrade in March 1975, before the Helsinki Conference, Berlinguer reinforced the strategic alliance with Tito.[79] Both leaders expressed a negative view about the situation in Portugal and the communist movement's inadequacy to embody the hopes of a socialist-inspired evolution in contemporary society. They were more optimistic, however, about the Non-Aligned Movement. The decline of the movement would become clear to them only at the end of the decade with the disagreement between Tito and Castro at the Havana Conference in 1979 and the war in Afghanistan, while its downfall would come with the Sino-Vietnamese and Iran–Iraq wars.

Although the PCI's project was definitively derailed in Italy after Moro's death and the party's return to opposition, from an international perspective, despite the second Cold War and the weak and contradictory position taken in relation to the EMS and the installation of Euromissiles in Italy, Berlinguer's stance at the beginning of the 1980s reveals at the end a capacity for analysis worthy of the global challenges of the time. In the autumn of 1978 tensions with the USSR nearly led to the breaking-off of relations, while the last meeting between Tito and Berlinguer reinforced the two parties' common strategy.[80] Berlinguer adopted an original line of reasoning in the 1979 Charter for Peace and Development,[81] in his speech in Cancùn to the Mexican Communist Party in October 1981 and in the heated debate with Castro at the same time about the Third World's independence from both superpowers.[82] He promoted economic and financial aid for Southern countries, which were to become active participants in their own progress, as the way for 'equal cooperation between the West and the Third World towards common goals of civility'.[83] It might be asked if such statements can be interpreted as the unbearable tension between moving beyond bipolarism and an abstract view of Communism's mission to reform.[84] While the contradictions in the Party's history are indisputable, 'Europeanism and its concern with Non-Alignment had brought the PCI to acquire, for the most part, a point of view unrelated to Soviet communism'.[85] If this meant that Italy was to enjoy a privileged role in the Mediterranean, the global vision expressed in Berlinguer's last considerations anticipated the yet unresolved conflicts in a world where international relations imposed cooperation among all states in a new social, political and economic order removed from the hegemonic ambitions of the great powers.

Chapter 6

A Window of Opportunity?

Eurocommunism(s) and Détente

Valentine Lomellini

In the mid-1970s, the fall of continental authoritarian regimes led a significant sector of the West European left to believe that the time had come to create a democratic and free Europe. In 1974, the regime of the Greek colonels was overthrown and in the same months, Portugal experienced the Carnation revolution. A few months passed and even Spain took the path of democratic transition after the death of the *Generalísimo*.[1]

According to the three main communist parties in Western Europe, Partito Comunista Italiano (PCI), Parti Communiste Français (PCF), Partido Comunista Español (PCE), events in the Mediterranean area – by which was meant south Europe rather than a more complex geopolitical concept – were the direct outcome of détente. Briefly, Eurocommunist parties considered that dialogue between superpowers meant overcoming blocs and leaving people free to choose their own fate.[2] The belief in a peaceful coexistence became the pillar of agreement between the three most powerful Western communist parties. It was a common ground on which to build a new kind of democratic socialism, that is, Eurocommunism. Détente was considered to be both a pre-condition for Eurocommunism and the main aim of the movement itself.[3]

This chapter argues that all three parties shared the same idea of détente, considered essential to shaping a new Mediterranean equilibrium, free from the influence of superpowers and the logic of blocs. However, we can also use détente as a paradigm for understanding why Eurocommunism failed.

Despite following a common goal of establishing a new Mediterranean, the PCI, PCF and PCE were unable to construct a shared strategy to pursue this aim. There were two reasons for this inconsistency. First, the need to take into account the champion of détente – the Kremlin – and its understanding of peaceful coexistence. Supporting the Soviet idea of détente caused divisions in the three Western communist parties. Second, domestic needs prevailed over attempts to construct a shared international strategy which could lead to a consistent common ground which the Eurocommunist movement could rely on. These two limits in the three Parties' reassessment of détente led Eurocommunism to implode at the dawn of the second Cold War.

This chapter, based on primary sources, is an attempt to reconstruct the European communist strategy for each country, as related to the phenomenon of détente. The study relies on sources from the Central Archive of the Istituto Fondazione Gramsci (Rome), the Archives départementales de la Seine Saint-Denis (Paris), and the Fundación de Investigaciones Marxistas (Madrid), concerning the investigation of Eurocommunist parties' press, an analysis of the literature and some interviews with protagonists of the period.

Détente in Joint Eurocommunists' Statements

Before defining each Eurocommunist party's policies regarding détente, it is necessary to focus on the phenomenon of Eurocommunism. Was it a complex strategy – as the promoters themselves presented it – or was it just a tactic?[4]

One of the main shared ideas in the literature about Eurocommunism – especially among studies of the 1970s–1980s – was that it was a potential destabilizing factor,[5] since it appealed to Eastern Europe.[6] Eurocommunism has its roots in the events of Czechoslovakia in 1968 – the Prague Spring was considered to be a forerunner of Eurocommunism. The three Parties welcomed as positive the new path chosen by the General Secretary of the Czechoslovakian Communist Party, Alexander Dubcek.[7] Then, when the Warsaw Pact invaded Czechoslovakia, the communist parties of Italy, France and Spain unanimously condemned the foreign policy of the Soviet Union for the first time.[8]

Western communist parties shared some common goals: the quest for autonomy from the USSR was probably the most important.[9] The search for new political interlocutors (Yugoslavia, Romania, and Czechoslovakia under Dubcek), accepting to live behind the Iron Curtain in the opposing bloc, and opening to the European Common Market and to Europe, soon became common ground between Parties.[10]

A long-range effort to exploit détente was undoubtedly another common point. Although the Soviets used their ideological interpretation of détente in Europe to strengthen cohesion within the international communist movement, the PCI and PCF began to work towards autonomous initiatives in the international arena.[11] The organization of a pan-European conference of communist parties was the outcome of private talks between Rome and Paris. The conference had two main aims: to affirm the different attitudes of Western communist parties concerning internationalism and to establish an informal platform of aims among communist parties in Western Europe.[12] These goals obviously irritated the Soviets, who were annoyed by Western communist attempts to create a different pole of attraction of communism in the world.

These events allow us to see the first archetypal dynamics between the PCF and the PCI. Rome, unwilling to break relations with the Soviets, decided to maintain its position. Although its attitude towards Eastern failures regarding democracy in socialism was softened, common ground in foreign policy, essentially détente, was stressed.[13] On the other hand, the PCF took a more pro-Soviet attitude. The feeling which developed during preparatory talks for the pan-European CP Conference, suddenly dissolved when the Portuguese crisis emerged.[14] The PCF, aligning itself with Soviet policy, supported the communist Álvaro Cunhal, betraying the PCI, whose support lay with the Socialist Mario Soares.[15]

The principal axis of Eurocommunism – the relationship between the PCI and the PCF – continued unsteadily during the brief term of the movement. After several months, French communists were again prepared to sign a joint declaration, and the Secretary of the PCE, Santiago Carrillo, probably played a key role in this renewed dialogue. He relaunched cooperation between Western communist parties in a joint declaration between the PCE and PCI, after an exchange of delegations in July 1975. According to the two Secretaries, the end of dictatorships in the Mediterranean and the process of détente opened up new possibilities for a leftist development in the southern part of Europe, and launched new challenges to Western communist parties. Berlinguer and Carrillo solemnly declared that their belief in a democratic socialism was not a tactic but 'strategic persuasion' and supported the idea that détente must be shared with the USSR, Eastern countries and Western communist parties. Their task was to promote détente in the Mediterranean area.[16] The Spanish–Italian encounter was followed by a French–Italian meeting a few months later. An entire paragraph in the final declaration was devoted to peaceful coexistence as the only way to avoid global war. Both Parties stressed the crucial contribution of the Soviets to the promotion of détente, while underlining that it should be interpreted as consolidation of the status quo. Détente was the key factor in the struggle against imperialism, democracy and socialism.[17]

The same faith in détente was one of the main pillars of the joint declaration after the Conference of European Communist Parties, in Berlin, June 1976. On that occasion, Berlinguer reaffirmed the PCI's role in the wider context of international relations and its aim to gradually overcome the blocs.[18] The Italian communists' strategy in the Eurocommunist movement appeared to prevail in a reassessment of détente which would not jeopardize relations with the Soviets. In a joint declaration, the tone often used by Spanish communist leaders was thus mitigated. While underlining the independence of the European CPs, the signatory parties stressed the important role of socialist countries in preventing a new world war, strengthening international security and pursuing the development of détente. The main point was, again, a dynamic vision of peaceful coexistence, which 'could not mean in any case maintaining a political and social status quo'. Détente provided better conditions for the working class and for a free and conscious choice of regime.[19] After the Berlin Conference, the Eurocommunist movement seemed to be a reality.

The meeting between the three Parties in Madrid, in March 1977, was celebrated by the international press as a new and decisive step towards the creation of a true movement. Even the literature seemed to predict this development. Nonetheless, as Sergio Segre (former Head of the International Department of the PCI) pointed out in our interview, the Madrid meeting marked the effective end of Eurocommunism. The Soviets were irritated and warned (as will be highlighted in the Italian part of this article) that building a platform of Eurocommunist parties meant creating a schism in the international communist movement.

The Soviet threat led the Eurocommunist parties to stress their internationalist legacy. Détente was clearly part of it, as the main pillar of Soviet foreign policy. Thus, the Eurocommunist idea of détente – overcoming military blocs for a democratic, free and independent Europe and a peaceful Mediterranean[20] – turned out to be a distinctive feature. The communist internationalism prevailed: the Eurocommunist idea of détente began to overlap with the Soviet demand for dialogue between superpowers.

The Italian Communist Party: Détente as a Sweetener?

From the end of the 1960s, the PCI began to believe that it could not avoid distancing itself from the image of the Soviet Union. News from the Soviet bloc of human rights violations and cases of well-known dissidents who denounced the repressive USSR system (e.g. Solzhenitsyn, Sakharov, Bukovsky) underlined the questionable behaviour of the Soviets in domestic policy. The Warsaw Pact invasion of Czechoslovakia also meant that it was necessary to promote a new image of communism in the world.[21] The idea of strengthening relations with the Western communist parties and new interlocutors was mentioned first by Berlinguer during talks regarding PCI participation in a world Conference of Communist Parties in Moscow, in June 1969.[22] There was increased concern among Italian leaders since seeking new interlocutors meant weakening ties with the USSR, which was central, not only for financial reasons, but also for its role as defender of revolutions and promoter of détente in the anti-imperialist struggle.

From the early stages of the CSCE preparations, the PCI expressed strong support for Soviet action in promoting détente.[23] Détente was essential to Italian communist action in domestic politics. Right-wing terrorism caused great concern in Italy and it was clear that the danger of fascism was not over, as hoped.[24] Moreover, détente was essential to attain the democratic legitimacy needed by the PCI to accomplish its strategy of 'historical compromise'.[25]

If hopes for peaceful coexistence were shared by both the PCI and the CPSU, the idea of détente was very different. The Italian communists' concept of a peaceful coexistence was a dynamic one: its main aim was to overcome superpower blocs. For its part, the USSR promoted a static vision of détente, which was intended to consolidate blocs and maintain European boundaries and political situations. Nonetheless, the PCI was clearly committed to supporting the USSR in the process of détente and, moreover, in handling Eurocommunism, in order to prevent a head-on collision with the Kremlin.

The more Eurocommunism became a well-defined political movement, the more the PCI avoided noting publicly any elements of contrast with the USSR, apart from criticism of the connection between socialism and democracy.[26] Criticism of the conceptualization of détente was confidential. In Italian private talks, détente was the necessary pre-condition for establishing new relations between brother parties, thus pushing the Soviets towards democratic socialism.[27] Italian communists were using détente to predict a new internationalism and a new path towards socialism. This goal was evident during the above-mentioned conference in Berlin. Western CP and Eastern communist leaderships had to be involved in a common reassessment of the idea of peaceful coexistence.[28] The Kremlin could not agree on this attempt – reformulating détente would have meant a clear effort to create a new magnet for the communist left in Western, and probably even Eastern Europe.

This concern became central to relations between the Italians and Soviets in the following year. On the occasion of the meeting between the three communist parties in Madrid, in March 1977, Moscow clearly warned Berlinguer:

> Our concern [...] is that during this meeting, the platform of the so-called Eurocommunism could be elaborated and approved. As far as we know, the main thesis of such a platform, the elaboration of which, it seems, has been carried out by fellow Carrillo, would be characterized by a non-objective criticism of the CPSU and the structure of the Soviet society. [...] In our opinion, the elaboration and approval of such a platform would mean the beginning of a new and very serious division in the communist movement. [...] We hope you can reassure us regarding these concerns, at least about the intents of the PCI.[29]

These fears were strengthened by the PCI's criticism of the Soviet attitude toward the Final Act of Helsinki. After August 1975, on several official occasions, the Italian communists pointed out the need for complete respect of the Helsinki Agreement, in particular according to the principles indicated in the Third Basket[30] concerning human rights.

Détente was still central to the PCI, drawing up domestic and international strategies. On the domestic level, its development permitted obtaining the necessary credibility to get into government, promoting Eurocommunism in the international arena, and, indirectly, reform of existing socialism. If détente were necessary, the PCI could not challenge the champion of détente – the USSR – on these grounds. The Italian communists' choice was then to stress détente as a shared point while arguing with the Soviets about the reliability of democratic socialism. With the second round of the CSCE conference in Belgrade approaching, the Soviets became anxious about judgements concerning implementation of the Third Basket. The *Direzione* of the PCI discussed its attitude towards the important meeting in Yugoslavia. Positions seemed to converge on some central points: first, the PCI had to avoid contrast with the Kremlin;[31] second, although fighting for autonomy, the PCI had to avoid breaking relations within the international communist movement. This meant that the Italian communists would continue to support détente and not consider the Conference of Belgrade as a chance to break away from the communist movement. In contrast, the Italian communists avoided speaking to the Soviets in the tone of Carrillo and Marchais. The link between the defence of human rights and détente was not considered a priority.[32] The Soviet idea that the Eastern dissidents jeopardized détente was then shared by the Italian communists. In an Italian–Soviet meeting in January 1977, Zagladin stressed that talking about dissent would damage the process of détente, and have negative effects on Western communist parties.[33]

The first aim of the PCI was Eurocommunism, and in order to realize it Italian communists needed détente. This made indispensable the link with the main promoter of peaceful coexistence, the USSR, and support for its international politics dealing with détente. The Soviets showed their appreciation of the PCI stance, which differed from the PCF and the PCE, by positively commenting on its foreign policy position and international unity politics.[34]

Détente became the main pillar of cohesion between the PCI and CPSU even when, in the late 1970s and early 1980s, the PCI harshly criticized the Kremlin for its realization of 'developed socialism'. A letter from the CPSU to the PCI in 1979 clearly outlined that the two parties 'really share common positions which constituted a safe ground for developing solidarity and cooperation' in the international arena.[35] The Soviet invasion of Afghanistan was clearly a turning point with regards to relations between the PCI and CPSU. In an editorial published by the communist newspaper *L'Unità*, the PCI condemned Soviet intervention in Afghanistan, defining it a 'non-admissible violation' of the sovereignty of Kabul.[36] The Second Cold War was already underway. The Eurocommunist belief would soon be jeopardized by this new international trend and the consequent stance by their French counterparts.

The French Communist Party: A Eurocommunist Crush?

The image that history projects of the PCF is that of a loyal and orthodox party.[37] The present research cannot deny this *topos* found in the international literature. Nonetheless, we can try to provide some food for thought in reassessing the history of the Eurocommunist period of the French Communist Party.

Eurocommunism emerged unexpectedly in the history of the loyal and pro-Soviet Marchais leadership. If it is true that the PCF condemned the Soviet invasion of Prague in 1968, the French communist attitude towards Czechoslovakian normalization confirmed their strong tie with the Soviet Union.[38] In the early 1970s, support for détente was a key common point with the Kremlin: Moscow was considered the principal architect of détente. Nonetheless, in the book *Le défi démocratique*, Marchais stressed the hope of French communists for the 'dissolution' of the two military blocs, to be replaced with a system of collective security which would allow France, and other European countries, to pursue their own independence from any military-political bloc.[39] During the following months, détente became central to French communists' discourse – a point which could be used as a weapon in their favour in domestic policy, especially regarding two issues. First, the PCF used it to stress the instrumental nature of the anticommunist and anti-Soviet campaign of its adversaries. Second, Jean Kanapa – the Head of the Department of International Relations – denounced the French government's foreign policy which was deeply involved in 'cette voie de l'abdication nationale' and 'd'hostilité à la détente internationale'.[40] In this phase, the PCF avoided using its particular idea of détente in international policy, either as a tool to distinguish PCF foreign policy from that of the CPSU, or as a means to lay the foundations for building a new kind of unity with other Western communist parties. The events of 1974 seemed to jeopardize the possibility of a close tie with potential Eurocommunist interlocutors. Confrontation with the Italians arose regarding the French communists' normalization and, as mentioned, dealing with the PCF's alignment to CPSU policy in supporting the Portuguese communist leader, Álvaro Cunhal.[41] This latter event was crucial to the deterioration of relations between the two parties to the point that, in April 1975, a member of the PCI Direzione, Giancarlo Pajetta, noted a profound change in the PCF position: 'It seems that our relations with the PCF have fallen behind by several years'.[42] A couple of months later, Pajetta referred to the sudden turning point of the PCF. The negative outcome of the PCF at the presidential elections of 1974 – when François Mitterrand, leader of the French socialists, became the most credible candidate of the left – strongly conditioned the French communists' foreign policy. As Pajetta said, the PCF started considering with suspicion the politics of détente and began to discuss it openly with the Soviets and Poles.[43] Pajetta did not go further, also because, as he admitted, the event was not clear to the PCI itself because of difficulties in maintaining contact with the PCF. The PCF began to be dubious of other fraternal parties: Marchais was probably afraid of losing votes and isolation in domestic policy, also in the international arena. His ally Mitterrand seemed to be his most feared enemy. He managed to get votes and become an important actor within the French left as it opened a new channel of communication with the PCI, with whom the PCF had long been having difficulty with dialogue.[44]

In the difficult situation of being an ally to its worst potential enemy, the French Communist Party began to lend more weight to domestic aspects than international ones. The positive and fruitful relations between the French government of Giscard d'Estaing and the USSR irritated the PCF, which felt the Kremlin considered government relations more important than internationalist ones.[45] This is probably one of the reasons why the PCF welcomed the Eurocommunist route. In June 1975, during a meeting with Marchais and Kanapa, Italian leaders noted the French communists' wish to break the tension. It emerged during the reunion that the reason for the French communists' attempt to establish a new kind of relations between the two parties had to be found in domestic politics and relations with the PSF, as well as in recent international events. In this regard, the anonymous author of the document commented that 'a strong critical charge' emerged against Eastern countries because of their opening to the French government.[46]

From that moment on, the PCF began to emphasize strong disapproval towards the USSR. Its position in favour of Eastern dissidents, its criticism of the outcomes of Soviet bloc socialism and its astonishing decision not to attend the XXV Congress of the CPSU were examples of its shouted disapproval of the USSR.[47] French leaders also tried to persuade the PCI to take common initiatives on human rights.[48] The Soviets threatened their French counterparts with public denunciation of the anti-détente initiatives of the dissidents.[49]

Rifts in the shared strategy of peaceful coexistence started to appear. During negotiation of the final document of the Conference of the European Parties in Berlin, the French seemed very concerned about Soviet attempts to influence orthodox parties' idea of détente.[50] As Elleinstein pointed out, hopes for a democratic socialism were mainly based on the fact that détente was there to stay.[51] The first signs of the second Cold War quickly destroyed any hope for a different model of socialism. French elections in 1978 did not compensate the PCF in terms of consensus. Thus, the failure of détente and the need to change domestic strategy led the PCF to suddenly abandon the Eurocommunist perspective.

The Spanish Communist Party: The Champion of the True Détente

The PCE was undoubtedly the brother Party which went further in its criticism of the Soviet Union. Since the Czechoslovakian crisis of August 1968, and through the following decade, attacks of the USSR concerned and focused on the Soviet conception of peaceful coexistence.

The Spanish communists' particular situation called for taking a well-defined position regarding the need for peaceful coexistence which would have led to overcoming the blocs. The relaxation of diplomatic tensions between superpowers allowed Western communist parties to stop supporting some aspects of Soviet foreign policy. In the Spanish case, this opening was reinforced by the need to take further the possibility of defeating authoritarian regimes in the Mediterranean, in particular, that of Franco.

From the early 1970s, the PCE harshly criticized the Soviet Union, regarding two aspects in particular: first, the violation of human rights and the realization of a democratic socialism; second, the Soviet policy concerning peaceful coexistence. Regarding the latter, the resolution of the Eighth Congress of the Spanish Communist Party in August 1972 was clear: peaceful coexistence could not mean an end to class struggle.[52]

The Spanish Communist Party clearly opposed the idea that peaceful coexistence meant renouncing the fight against dictatorship as well as imperialism. The idea that détente could not mean freezing the political and social status quo ('La coexistencia pacífica no es la congelación del statu quo político-social') was clearly stated in the final resolution. However, it seemed to be linked more to the situation in Indochina than aimed at the Spanish situation.[53] Nonetheless, the PCE recognized the key role of the Soviet Union in the fight against imperialism, as well as the great industrial and economic successes and equality of rights and high cultural standards.[54]

The idea of a different conception of détente was defined more precisely by Manuel Azcárate, head of the PCE Department of International Relations, from 1968 to 1981. Azcárate clearly wished to determine the type of coexistence the Party was seeking: could Spanish communists accept a policy aimed at maintaining the status quo and stopping the forces opposing imperialism? The rhetorical question was not an easy one since it involved the PCE's attitude towards the Soviet conception of détente. Azcárate admitted that the coexistence policies of socialist countries were generally advantageous to the revolutionary process, by decreasing the danger of war and atomic destruction and helping, for example, Vietnam and anti-imperialist movements. At the same time, however, Spanish communists had to acknowledge that there were 'contradictory moments', 'at which the foreign policies of certain socialist states also aimed at "freezing the status quo"'.[55]

The participation of Franco's Spain in the approaching European Conference on Security and Cooperation added a further point of disagreement. Azcárate accused socialist countries of confusing their support for coexistence and a favourable attitude towards the participation of Francoist Spain in the European security conference. In 1973, the Spanish Communist Party went further. In the declaration of the Executive Committee published in *Nuestra bandera*, critical of the re-establishment of diplomatic relations between the Popular Republic of China and Spain, the PCE stated that the politics of coexistence, 'in its Leninist sense', did not mean supporting status quo in the world.[56] Again, Azcárate provided more precise information. While not underestimating the USSR's contribution to the development of détente, the PCE had to follow its own particular responsibilities, which included fighting against all attempts, 'wherever they may come from, even on the part of our friends', to equate détente and world status quo. The specific task of Western communist parties was to fight for the advance of détente and 'the elimination of the systems of blocs'.[57] This goal could only be pursued within a wider framework of close cooperation with other Western bloc communist parties which shared the idea of a dynamic détente.

In the months which followed, as mentioned above, cooperation was strongly conditioned by the upcoming events in Portugal, and the forthcoming Conference of Brussels. Moreover, the Spanish Communist Party was very much absorbed by domestic episodes. The events that took place in the Spanish domestic arena made transition to democracy possible. The death of Franco, on 20 November 1975, marked a turning point which made it impossible to postpone the democratization process.[58]

The process of transition made the PCE even more willing to affirm its autonomy from Moscow, as made clear by the official Party programme in 1975. The PCE moved away from the Soviet Union, its concept of socialism and its idea of détente. While criticizing the concept of 'modelo unico' of socialism, the PCE argued for a new idea of internationalism. According to the PCE, peaceful coexistence had created favourable objective conditions for the struggle for socialism, giving more strength to national identity in the class fight. The role of détente provoked a re-definition of traditional relations between brother parties. Peaceful coexistence not only allowed, but compelled communist parties to permit national characteristics to emerge. In this regard, the PCE proudly declared its total independence from any other state, 'including Socialist States'. The Spanish communists' politics could not be determined by the need for defence of Eastern countries.[59] This autonomy was also underlined in the declaration of the Executing Committee of the PCE.[60] Attention to autonomy was central in a series of interviews released by PCE leaders in 1975. Carrillo wanted to stress the authenticity of democratic beliefs and complete autonomy of the PCE from the USSR. The iron link could negatively influence the image of the PCE in domestic politics.[61]

As Valenta pointed out, none of the Eurocommunist parties had any desire to cut relations with ruling parties of 'developed socialism', nor did the Spanish Communist Party have this intention.[62] However, the PCE was the Western Communist Party that went further in this action, and it did it in a rather devious way. If the CPSU could face criticism of human rights violations in the Soviet Union by arguing that reports were merely imperialist propaganda, how could the Kremlin face the charge of promoting partial détente, destroying its own allies' hope for a change in the country they fought for?

In 1977, Carrillo's disagreement became intolerable for the Soviets. His last book – *Eurocomunismo y estado* – supported the idea that Eurocommunism would have been different from models of socialism which prevailed in the Eastern bloc. This approach was criticized harshly by the press in Eastern countries, who charged Carrillo with discrediting socialist ideas and supporting bourgeois propaganda.[63] Regarding the Eurocommunist reassessment of the Mediterranean area, Carrillo asked for disarmament only as a guarantee of peace, and wanted to relaunch the role of Spain in the wider picture of multipolar equilibrium. The PCE sought a Europe independent of both the USA and the USSR – a Europe of people, oriented towards socialism, where Spain could maintain its own personality.[64] In Carrillo's speech at the Madrid meeting in March 1977, the same demand for full independence of countries was linked to the claim of complete autonomy for Parties within the international communist movement.[65] This tendency was also strengthened at the dawn of the second Cold War, in the last stages of Eurocommunism. Calling again for the 'elimination of the existing military blocs' in the resolutions of the Ninth Congress of the PCE,[66] the Spanish communists defined their commitment to overcome the blocs. In Azcárate's statement to Radio Free Europe, the close tie between a dynamic détente and Eurocommunism also emerged clearly. Azcárate said that Eurocommunism was the only European option which lay outside the two blocs.[67] The Spanish communists' criticism of the Soviet idea of détente was not welcomed at all by their Eurocommunist partners. In the late 1970s, the different positions taken by the three CPs regarding the Afghan and Polish crises clearly indicated the failure of Eurocommunism. Even if these events had not taken place, the PCI and PCF, for different reasons and to differing degrees, were not ready to say officially that Moscow was no longer the Rome of communism.[68]

Conclusion: A Movement that Never Existed

Very briefly, the different attitudes shown by the three Eurocommunist parties towards détente reveal the inner meaning of Eurocommunism to each of them. For the PCI, Eurocommunism was an attempt to accomplish its universal mission of reforming communism. For this reason the Italians preferred to stress détente as a point in common with the Kremlin. Breaking relations with the Soviets meant failing in a global reform of communism. If it was necessary to question the Soviet model, they preferred to choose a more sensitive and less common point (the link between socialism and democracy). To Marchais, Eurocommunism had an instrumental role. When the French communists felt betrayed by Moscow's pro-French behaviour, they used Eurocommunism as a warning. Moreover, distinguishing their idea of détente from that of the Soviets implied shaping their new image on domestic ground. When they believed this tactic did not work, they suddenly returned to a pro-Soviet attitude. Carrillo, for his part, believed that a new pole of attraction of European communism was possible. His remarks about détente clearly demonstrated not only criticism of the USSR, but also his strong conviction about the need to overcome blocs in Europe. This hope was shared by the PCI, but Rome was persuaded that détente was not possible without Moscow.

Finally, different attitudes toward détente, which three Eurocommunist parties sought, mirrored the reasons why the Eurocommunist project failed on its eve, or why it never really existed.

PART 2

War and Diplomacy in the Middle East

CHAPTER 7

The American–Israeli 'Special Relationship' in the Nixon–Kissinger Years

Antonio Donno

When we mention the American–Israeli special relationship during the Nixon years, we should keep in mind that Nixon was the first US President to make Israel a strategic asset for the United States, raising the question explicitly compared with his predecessors. Israel matched US interests in the Middle East within a global Cold War context and contrast with the Soviet Union in the region.

Why did Nixon and Kissinger decide to back Israel's cause? Although during the Eisenhower, Kennedy and even Truman administrations the two countries had a very close relationship, this rarely produced satisfying dividends in terms of common strategies able to safeguard Israel's existence and at the same time US interests in the area.[1] On the contrary, it was easy to note 'the unwillingness of the United States, under either Kennedy or Johnson, to countenance a bilateral security treaty with Israel'.[2] Nor is it possible to affirm that this was due to events leading to different, and sometimes opposing, policies. Instead, this all took place thanks to very precise choices of the American administrations, as Dean Rusk writes in his memoirs: 'the United States shares important interests with Israel, but Israeli and American interests are not identical'.[3]

Israel's policies implemented by Nixon's predecessors can be summarized in the following way: after recognition of the State of Israel and under pressure from the Department of State (always against the foundation of a Jewish state in Palestine), Truman issued a total arms embargo towards

Middle Eastern states – then ratified through the Tripartite Declaration (United States, Great Britain, France) of 25 May 1950 – which objectively harmed the newborn State of Israel in the face of massive Arab superiority in terms of armaments. Eisenhower and Dulles launched a new international policy, mainly focused on relations between the USA and Arab states, above all Nasser's Egypt, a country considered as the keystone for an effective contrast to Moscow's aims in the Middle East. Israel was put to the side compared with Eisenhower's pro-Arab policy, and its arms requests were ignored.[4] Kennedy highlighted the question of Israeli nuclear power, and was persuaded to withhold arms sales, in particular Hawk missiles, unless Israel permitted inspections of the Dimona site, in the Negev Desert.[5] The confrontation continued on through the Johnson years,[6] until the astonishing Israeli victory in the 1967 war turned the tables. This was the breakthrough which produced the ensuing Israeli policy revision by Nixon and Kissinger.

In fact, Johnson had inherited from Eisenhower and Kennedy only an informal type of alliance with Israel. Conventional weapons issues, combined with the much more serious nuclear ones, had prevented Johnson from reaching an agreement which could turn the Jewish state into a real strategic asset for Washington's Middle East policy. Moreover, victory in the 1967 war meant that Israel could be much less concerned about the need for a special relationship with the United States, also taking into consideration that in view of Moscow's bitter political defeat, Washington had come out politically triumphant from the war.[7] After the war elation, Jerusalem realized that it was the right moment, after its military victory against the Arab states and Washington's political success against Moscow to form a closer tie, both political and military, between Israel and the United States. In conclusion, we can say that the 1967 war showed Washington that Israel played a key role during the Cold War by containing Soviet penetration of the Middle East. It also showed that the Americans had underestimated this role, considering Israel's potentialities only on a regional basis.

Hence, in the Nixon years, due to the very positive outcome of the 1967 war for both America and Israel, military and economic aid given to the Jewish state by the United States in the previous decades immediately acquired an unexpected political and strategic value. Washington basically changed its perception of Israel's role in the Middle East, regarding both exclusively regional questions (Israel as a safeguard against Moscow-backed Arab states wishing to destroy the Jewish state) and on a more global level (as a pro-West stronghold in a strategically and economically very large area – i.e. oil – pivotal to the bipolar context of the times). At the same time, although the United States had steadily helped Israel from its foundation onwards, it also true that, unlike America's Arab 'allies', Israel never attacked US interests. These remarks, together with the events of the times, persuaded Nixon and Kissinger to establish the special relationship that had been *in nuce* in the previous decades.

It was not such an easy process, but Nixon's pragmatism was able to overcome the difficulties. As Raymond Aron has wittily underlined, 'Nixon accepts also the dissociation between ideology, which has internal uses, and relations between states; he even accepts that it is entirely normal for the superpowers to have rival interests'.[8] This was Nixon's basic idea for the Middle East, too, but Israel also allowed him to inherit a very good position due to the 1967 war. Kissinger then acted cleverly so that such an advantage would not be missed, but rather augmented. In fact, in a memorandum to Nixon, written a few days after his inauguration, Kissinger recommended doing nothing which would 'jeopardise Israel's basic interests';[9] or even worse 'force an unconditional Israeli withdrawal which would not aid the interests of the United States within the Arab world'.[10] In short, although Nixon considered the region to be vitally important to US interests, he had the tendency – at least at the beginning – to regard Israel as a hindrance to an effective American policy in an area where the Arab world was largely predominant. On 14 March 1969, Nixon met the Israeli Foreign Minister, Abba Eban, in Washington DC, debating with him possible four power talks which could resolve the Arab–Israeli problem. Jerusalem opposed these talks, fearing they would produce an outcome contrary to their interests, and expressed preference for bilateral meetings with Arab countries. Nixon responded firmly: 'we need your help. Don't make our role impossible',[11] meaning that American renunciation of the Four Power Talks could damage Washington's position on an international level, and towards Arab countries.

What Israel feared most was increased involvement of the great powers in the Middle Eastern conflict. As Bernard Lewis wrote, 'more immediately relevant [was] the Israeli conviction that any compromise likely to be reached among the four powers would be at Israel's expense'.[12] Finally the State Department's position, and that of the Secretary himself, left no uncertainty as regards the American will to start the Four Power Talks. Since Nixon had delegated Middle Eastern issues to Rogers, Kissinger did not have a big voice in the matter. Although he advised the Israelis to avoid dealing with the Secretary, whose positions he did not share, he could not openly expose himself as hostile in front of the President.[13] Hence, if

Rogers warned Nixon about Israel's toughness towards the great powers, considering it as an objectionable obstacle to the effectiveness of American diplomacy in the region,[14] Kissinger, on the contrary, recommended the President take Israeli concerns into account: 'we hope Israel will be willing to specify boundaries to which it will withdraw, but we know Israel cannot withdraw without an Arab assurance of peace'.[15] The breakthrough took place when Rogers, on 9 December 1969, released his Middle East Plan, which Nixon met with great scepticism: 'I knew that the Rogers Plan could never be implemented',[16] for it was unacceptable to Israel.

In short, the negative opinion of the Rogers Plan, as shown by both Nixon and Kissinger, indirectly brought the President's position closer to that of his National Security Adviser. The safeguarding of the Middle Eastern status quo, as it stood after the 1967 war, gave the United States a strategic edge over the Soviet Union, which could be undermined through unsuitable initiatives potentially able to favour a resumption of Soviet political adventures in the region. This was the aftermath of the failure of the Four Power Talks, similar to the Washington–Moscow ones. There was no agreement between the two superpowers, something Israel welcomed greatly, having always believed that 'the idea of an imposed peace [was] odious'.[17] Kissinger explained to Rabin that, according to him, 'the Soviet Union would not be able to stand by and accept another Arab defeat'.[18] Therefore Moscow, too, was not interested in stirring the current situation in the area. In fact, as Kissinger pointed out to Rabin, the consultation between Americans and Soviets 'was merely an exercise in multilateral mediation, or stylized group therapy, with the added benefit of an insurance policy on the side'.[19]

However, this did not represent at all a rapprochement between Washington and Jerusalem which could pave the way towards a special relationship. On the contrary, two questions remained open: weapons and the different interests of the two countries in the area. Israel continued to request weapons from the United States, stating that it had to restore the arms balance with the Arabs, who were in fact receiving large amounts of weapons from the Soviet Union. The Department of State hesitated, however, in order not to appear too imbalanced towards the Jewish state. In this regard, a long memorandum to Kissinger from Melvin R. Laird, Secretary of Defence, clearly illustrated the American administration's perplexities on any further arms supply to Israel. The United States, Laird concluded, wanted to supply Jerusalem with a quantity of weapons 'sufficient' for its defence needs, but it was not possible to exceed this amount without provoking an arms race in the Middle East.[20]

The divergence of the countries' political interests in the area is a much more complex question. The outcome of Golda Meir's visit to Washington on 24 September 1969 shows clearly the difficulties that the link with Israel produced in the implementation of the American Middle Eastern policy. Nixon told Meir that, as the United States was aiming for a solution to the conflict and an overall settlement of issues in the region, Washington could not take a partisan stance, although it was ready to work with the Israelis to pursue their common goals.[21] Meir did not request weapons only. She also sought assurance that talks with the other powers would not go ahead, above all those with the Kremlin. In this regard, Nixon could not deny Rogers's initiatives, at least for the moment. He could do nothing but accept Meir's request for 25 Phantom jets and 80 Skyhawk fighters, after National Security Council analysis and approval.[22] However, on 31 January, a letter from Kosygin to the American President stopped the shipment. Kosygin threatened to supply the Arab countries with a large quantity of arms, should Washington provide arms to Israel. In order to avoid an arms race in the Middle East – as Nixon wrote in his memoirs – it was decided to stop the shipment of weapons to Israel. It is interesting to note what the US President wrote thereafter: 'I also believed that American influence in the Middle East increasingly depended on our renewing diplomatic relationships with Egypt and Syria, and this decision would help promote that goal'.[23]

The Soviet threat had an effect. Nixon was worried that Arab rearmament could improve the Soviet position in the Middle East. In short, Israel pursued national security within a deeply hostile area, trying to reach a real alliance with the United States. The Americans, however, wanted to develop an overall policy not only aimed at the defence of Israel, but rather involving Arab countries on an anti-Soviet basis. Nixon thought that the 'Israeli occupation of Arab land only strengthened anti-Western radical forces in the region'.[24] He also thought that obliging Israel to relinquish the conquered territories would appear as a sign of weakness towards Arab requests and an advantage for Soviet, but not for American interests.

Several factors affected Nixon's hesitation. The War of Attrition between Egypt and Israel, triggered by Nasser, caused a massive and sometimes tough Israeli response, considered as exaggerated by the American administration itself. The Israeli government's strictness in condemning Four Power Talks, such as the Soviet–American ones, was regarded by many in the State Department as offensive interference in American political decisions and unacceptable pressure. The Israeli demand that American Middle

Eastern policy be limited only to the needs of the Jewish state seemed inappropriate compared with wider American interests in the region, especially in relation to the Soviet presence. The massive Soviet rearmament of the Arab countries implied, according to Nixon, the organization of talks in order to avoid a new arms race in the Middle East. Nixon wrote in his memoirs that it was misleading to think that support to Israel automatically meant opposing the Soviet Union in the Middle East.[25]

Israel was very unhappy about American policy regarding the Arab–Israeli conflict. The aired restitution of the Occupied Territories, according to leaks from the talks with the Soviet Union, rocked the boat of Israeli diplomacy, since 'the newly occupied territories gave Israel enhanced strategic position with more defensible borders and early-warning time as a result of greater strategic depth'.[26] To give back the territories for nothing in exchange, that is, definitive peace with the Arab countries, would have been a sign of weakness which Israel could not afford. The rumours circulating, said Rabin to Kissinger, '[had] undermined Israel's position in future negotiations with her neighbours whenever they come about'[27] and made the Israeli–American bond appear weak, if not unreal. Hence, despite Kissinger's formal reassurance of the relationship between the two countries and the important American interest towards the integrity of the Jewish state,[28] the Israeli government feared that the bilateral talks and those among the Four Powers could give rise to something negative for Jerusalem and that such decisions could be imposed as a diktat. Israel pursued a privileged relationship with Washington, but at the moment it was impossible for Nixon to accommodate it with the strategic American stakes in the Middle East.

Kissinger had obtained from Nixon the opportunity to bypass federal bureaucracy. Therefore, he set up an ad hoc group within the National Security Council in charge of canvassing Israel's military requests. The consequent report allowed Kissinger to directly confront Nixon on the issue and thus obtain a green light from the President. In the memorandum sent to Nixon, which included the report, he wrote with satisfaction: 'for the first time, a President will be able to make his political decisions on Israeli aid requests with a clear view of their military and economic consequences'.[29] Kissinger was replacing Rogers in the Middle Eastern dossier, thus establishing a hotline with Nixon on the Arab–Israeli question. This was important within the administration, and later led the President to cast a new light upon American–Israeli relations, following an outlook which, according to Kissinger, was profitable for Washington and Jerusalem at the same time:

Nobody could make peace without us. Only we, not the Soviet Union, could exert influence on Israel. [...] If we remained steady and refused to be stampeded, the pivotal nature of our position would become more and more evident.[30]

Kissinger was persuaded of American superiority in the Middle East, even more so because Arab radicals would never reach an agreement with Israel. There was no reason for setting the wheels in motion, as this could allow the Russians to recover some room for action. As far as the Israelis were concerned, Kissinger wrote, they had realized that the question for the Arabs had nothing to do with boundaries or similar, but rather with the very existence of the Jewish state. In a long memorandum dated 2 January 1970, and in the following the one on 5 January in response to new Israeli arms requests, the ad hoc group, chaired by Kissinger, underlined some extremely important political data concerning Israeli–American relations, which set the question within the wider frame of the Soviet–American confrontation in a strategically pivotal region where Israel played a crucial role.[31] Therefore, when Nixon (despite Kissinger's opposition) decided to postpone the delivery of the Phantoms and Skyhawks to Israel, on the grounds of the prediction that it would increase the Soviet commitment towards their Arab clients, a groundswell of opposition was raised in a large sector of the American political world, in the face of which the President was 'obliged' to dictate Kissinger another memorandum which said: 'we are for Israel because Israel in our view is the only state in the Mideast which is pro-freedom and an effective opponent to Soviet expansion'.[32]

Nixon's statement was not double-faced, but down-to-earth. Kissinger, however, had good reasons too. He thought the deployment of Soviet missiles in Egypt implied a clear and unequivocal American response through the delivery of aircrafts and missiles to Israel; all within the frame of a firm stance against Moscow in the region, in order to regain the American superiority acquired through Jerusalem's overwhelming victory in the 1967 war.[33] Nixon realized Israel's centrality in American anti-Soviet policy in the Middle East, but with the same realism he thought it was not convenient to 'tease' Moscow on the arms race issue, for there was the risk of wasting the edge gained until then. Instead, he and Rogers believed that Israel maintained certain superiority over Arab enemies, in spite of Soviet missiles for Egypt.

The problem of arms for Israel underlined the simmering conflict between Kissinger and Rogers. On the same day, 3 March 1970, two memoranda, completely different from each other, arrived in Nixon's office – one from Rogers and the other from Kissinger. Rogers started from the observation that after the 1967 events, the Arab–Israeli conflict needed a diplomatic speed-up, with the purpose of involving the Soviet Union and its Arab clients in a negotiation process which could lay the foundations for a settlement to the Arab–Israeli dispute. As a consequence of this, Rogers said, the arms delivery to Israel would irretrievably harm the process and exacerbate the conflict. Hence, it was necessary to postpone delivery, being careful that 'this decision [was not] being made under pressure from the USSR', and trying 'to exploit it to the maximum in the Arab world, and to take advantage of the breathing space it offers to put pressure on Cairo and Moscow to take some positive steps towards getting negotiations started between the parties', and finally highlighting that such a decision would not affect American support to Israel.[34]

Kissinger, on the other hand, stated that Rogers's three recommendations were incompatible with each other. In the case of postponement of delivery, it was impossible for Moscow not to realize that the American administration had rather distanced itself from Israel, due to its attempt to resume dialogue with the Arab world. Moreover, 'the appearance of bowing to Soviet pressure cannot be disposed of by simple denial'. Kissinger's suggestion, therefore, was that 'the announcement should be made by the State Department, not the White House',[35] in order for Nixon not to be affected by the resulting inevitable criticism. On 8 March, Golda Meir wrote a concerned but resolute letter to Nixon, the crux of which was that 'our enemies, including the Russians, would, for the first time, really believe that we are at their mercy'.[36] This concept was resumed by Rabin during a meeting with Kissinger and Saunders: 'from the political point of view the Arabs and Soviets will inevitably interpret a negative decision as a public abandonment of Israel'.[37] Kissinger certainly shared these statements, as he contemplated approaching the President at the right moment, even if in his memoirs he reveals that it was a mistake not to oppose such a decision: 'in retrospect I believe that I erred in not being more emphatic'.[38]

In late March 1970, the Middle Eastern situation had evolved into what Kissinger had planned. The ongoing Soviet supply of arms to Egypt, the presence of Russian pilots in the country,[39] and certain political unrest in the Arab world aimed at immediate revenge finally persuaded Nixon to act and ship the Phantom jets to Israel, though as a replacement for the Israeli aircraft which were lost in the War of Attrition. In his memoirs, Rabin recalls a remarkable conversation with Nixon, during which, at a certain point, the President said:

You can be sure that I will continue to supply arms to Israel, but I shall do so in other, different ways. The moment Israel needs arms, approach me, by way of Kissinger, and I'll find a way of overcoming bureaucracy.[40]

Moreover, Kissinger was tired of reading US intelligence documents stating that Soviet supplies to Egypt had an essentially defensive purpose, that Moscow's policy was simply oriented to defending its own position in the Middle East, and that Israel's intransigence was in fact the true element of danger to a Soviet–American confrontation in the region.[41] The contrast between Kissinger and the Department of State was by then open. 'Once the Soviets established themselves with a combat role in the Middle East – Kissinger wrote in his memoirs – and we accepted that role, the political balance would be drastically changed'.[42] Kissinger's point of view, at that moment, paved the way for a new stage of US Middle Eastern policy as a consequence of the open conflict with Rogers. Nixon was unsure about it, and this irritated both Kissinger and Rogers, though for different reasons. In July, Meir herself sent a letter to Nixon, warning the President that the Soviet rearmament of Egypt imposed arms supplies to Israel in order to reach a true balance, and that the peace process, which Rogers resolutely pursued, did not exclude any arms delivery to the Jewish state. Indeed, this balance was supposed to produce an effective path for negotiations.[43] In fact:

[Israel] argued that the installation of the missiles was an aggressive, not a defensive act; that they were there in support of Nasser's offensive attrition strategy and hence must be seen as fulfilling an offensive function.[44]

In March 1970, the American government proposed a cease-fire between Egypt and Israel, stating that if Jerusalem accepted the proposal, then Nixon would deliver the armaments Israel requested. For the Israelis the offer was blackmail, and Kissinger did not like it either.[45] Nasser soon accepted the proposal, thus making things difficult for Israel, which in turn was obliged to comply, so that it would not be again in contrast with the American administration. It was clear, however, that the two countries were experiencing a moment of crisis. Symptomatic of this was the final exchange of statements between Laird and Rabin. In a meeting in late July, Laird rather provocatively asked Rabin why the situation of the Arab–Israeli conflict was still blocked in the 1950s. At that point, Rabin replied that everything had got worse because in the Middle East 'the Soviets had injected their own forces',[46] thus alluding to the ineffectiveness of American policy in the area. However, in spite of the cease-fire, the Soviets continued to supply Egypt with weapons and SA-3 missiles. Rabin readily forwarded this information to Kissinger, who, in turn, related it to Nixon with this warning: 'the Soviet/Egyptian build-up has created a new situation for Israel',[47] with the purpose of prodding the President into action, and shipping the armaments Israel had requested.

The difficult relations between the United States and Israel represented a plus point for the Soviet Union. However, on 23 October 1970, Kissinger explained to Dobrynin that the possible start of negotiations should not undermine Israeli–American relations and that, in any case, Washington and Jerusalem would hold identical positions within the United Nations.[48] It was the Jordan Crisis in September 1970 that led to a clarification between the two countries. The internecine war between King Hussein's Army and the Palestinian organizations located in Jordan – the latter aimed at overthrowing the King and turning the country into a PLO base against Israel – led Syrian troops to hint at an intervention in Jordanian territory. At that point, Nixon and Kissinger, believing that the Soviet Union was backing Syria, asked Israel for help. Jerusalem threatened Syria by saying it would intervene in defence of Jordan, while Washington, in turn, warned Moscow that it would not tolerate any Soviet intervention against Israel. The outcome of this was that Syria immediately withdrew and Hussein came to a showdown with the PLO applying tough repression. Nixon greatly appreciated the effective Israeli collaboration in the Jordan Crisis, thus paving the way for a true understanding between the two countries.[49] As Douglas Little observed, 'for top U.S. policymakers the outcome of the Jordanian crisis confirmed what Ben-Gurion, Eshkol, and Meir had been saying for more than a decade: Israel could serve the United States as a strategic asset'.[50]

There were a further three steps which led Nixon to make up his mind and opt for an Israeli–American special relationship: the signing of the first agreement between the two countries, in November 1971, on the grounds of which Washington committed itself to steadily supplying the Jewish state with arms;[51] Jerusalem's assured support of Nixon's re-election in November 1972, implemented through strong pressure on the American Jewish community; and finally, a few months earlier, on 18 July 1972, Sadat's decision to distance Egypt from the Soviet Union and to start a process of rapprochement of his own country to the American position. This was, therefore, the end of a long, and often contradictory, path which led the United States of Nixon and Kissinger to establish a firm and lasting tie, recognizing in the Jewish state a pivotal partner for the safeguarding of US stakes in the Middle East and, at the same time, ensuring its support for Jerusalem's survival.[52] It is appropriate to underline that Nixon's choice in favour of Israel was also due to 'Israel's military superiority in the region'.[53]

The Yom Kippur War (1973) consolidated Israeli–American overconfidence. The outcome led Nixon and Kissinger to no longer consider the Middle East through the Cold War lens, but to regard the domestic factors of the area and the more general ones of bipolar confrontation as inextricably intertwined.

CHAPTER 8

'The Gods of War were Inspecting their Armaments'

The United States and the 1970 Jordan Crisis

Daniele De Luca

Henry Kissinger wrote in his memoirs:

> As 1970 began, the gods of war were inspecting their armaments, for it was clear they would soon be needed. There was daily combat along the Suez Canal. Then in January Israel began 'deep penetration' air raids with bombing attacks around Cairo and the Nile Delta, designed to demonstrate Nasser's impotence and force an end to the so-called War of Attrition. [...] On the Jordan front the vicious cycle of fedayeen raid and Israeli reprisal accelerated. Israel and Syria clashed in the Golan. Finally, at the end of January, Nasser suddenly paid a secret visit to Moscow. Thereafter, the problems of the Middle East began increasingly to merge with the relations of the superpowers.[1]

There was a serious problem of comprehension within the American government regarding this question. From the Department of State's point of view, the root of the difficulties for the United States was the territorial dispute between Israel and the Arab states. Once the problem was resolved – according to the experts – the influence of the radical

Arabs would decline and with it the Soviet role in the area.[2] Kissinger had serious doubts about this analysis; as he wrote in a memorandum for President Nixon:

> Arab radicalism had five sources: Israel's conquests of territories; Israel's very existence; social and economic dissatisfactions; opposition to Western interests; and opposition to the Arab moderates. Only the first of these components would be affected by a settlement. The others would remain. Western capitalism would remain anathema to the radicals. Arab moderate regimes would continue to be unacceptable. The causes of social and economic unrest would persist. Israel would still be there for the Arab radicals to seek to erase. And Israelis understood this. It was precisely because the issue for them was the existence of Israel, and not its particular frontiers, that they were so reluctant to give up their conquest.[3]

In any case, on 7 August 1970, a cease-fire between 'radical' Egypt and Israel came into effect, putting an end – for just a few days – to the War of Attrition (one of the points of the so-called Rogers Plan). According to William Quandt:

> It seemed as if both the State Department and the White House could feel satisfied that their preferred policies had produced a successful outcome. Within days, however, the provisions of the cease-fire were being violated and a new crisis was in making. The [...] delicate balance between the State Department and the White House concerning the Middle East was also shattered.[4]

The new crisis in making was the Jordan Crisis. Some considered this crisis as unusual because 'it was seen as quintessentially lesson-bearing from the very beginning'.[5] This was the consequence of three factors. First, the Jordan Crisis was the climactic, largely unexpected, conclusion of the Nixon administration's first major foreign policy crisis known as the War of Attrition, which witnessed the introduction of Soviet combat pilots into Egypt. It was, therefore, the object of intense scrutiny as defining a precedent for a US approach to subsequent crises in this and other areas. Second, the crisis was seen by the principal US decision-makers at the time to be, above all, part of a 'superpower psychodrama' in which success in the careful orchestration of words and deeds would cast a long light – or shadow – over the credibility of US power and the success of its diplomacy. Third, some of these decision-makers actively interpreted the crisis in terms of the effect it would have on both the Soviet Union's assessment of US resolve and diplomatic skill, and in settling a divisive debate within the government over US Middle East policy.

Since the first Arab–Israeli war of 1948–49, Jordan had to face the complicated problem of Palestinian refugees. In Jordan itself – and on the West Bank – the question was the increasing power of Palestinian radical groups such as the Palestine Liberation Organization (PLO). In particular after the 1967 Six-Day War, for every Palestinian attack on Israeli territory, there was reprisal action by the Israel Defence Force deep into Jordanian land. As a further consequence of the 1967 war, the Third Armoured Division of the Iraqi Army was in Jordan with the false excuse of protecting the weak Hashemite reign. For this reason, since the beginning of 1970, King Hussein felt that he was under heavy pressure and started to react.

Within their camps, the fedayeen groups enjoyed considerable administrative autonomy, had their own finance departments and ran their own welfare services. Outside the camps, they enjoyed freedom of movement and special rights, while exercising increasing influence over the Jordanian part of the population. By the beginning of 1970, the Palestinian resistance movement had, to all intents and purposes, established a state within a state in Jordan.

> They drove noisily around Amman in jeeps with loaded weapons, like an army of occupation; they extorted financial contributions from individuals, […] in their homes and in public places; they disregarded routine traffic regulations, failed to register and license their vehicles, and refused to stop at Army checkpoints; they boasted about their role of destiny against Israel and belittled the worth of the Army. Their very presence in Amman, far from the battlefield, seemed like a challenge to the regime.[6]

The arrogance and the indiscipline of the fedayeen placed King Hussein in an acute dilemma. If he used force to crush them, he would alienate his Palestinian subjects and the Arab world. Yet if he failed to act against them, he would lose the respect of his Jordanian subjects and, even more seriously, that of the Army, the mainstay of the regime. In February 1970, Hussein went to Cairo to see President Nasser and won his support, or at least his acquiescence, in a tougher policy dealing with the fedayeen.

Nasser was prepared to use all his influence with the fedayeen to have them reduce their pressure on the regime, provided Hussein restrained his Army from openly clashing with them. Upon his return, King Hussein published a ten-point edict, restricting the activities of Palestinian organizations. In particular, the new regulations prohibited carrying arms in public, storing ammunition in towns, and holding unlawful meetings and demonstrations. The fedayeen reacted sharply and violently to this, and forced the King to back down and freeze the new regulations. He also yielded to fedayeen pressure by dismissing the hard-line Minister of Interior, Major-General Muhammad Rasul al-Kilani.[7]

It was now quite clear that Hussein was preparing for the next round: his concessions to the fedayeen were a tactical move designed to buy time. Moreover, he began to mobilize external support to help in his battle against his internal opposition. The two countries he turned to were the United States and Israel. Both had their drawbacks as allies but for King Hussein there were no other options. On 17 February the U.S. deputy chief of mission in Tel Aviv, Owen Zurhellen, delivered an urgent message from Hussein to Foreign Minister Abba Eban. In this message, the King put three questions:

> 1. Does Israel agree to avoid taking advantage of the opportunity of Hussein having to thin down his forces on the border to deal with subversive elements at home? 2. Can Israel agree to avoid responding to provocations by the terrorists, who will try to carry out attacks while Jordanian forces are being thinned down, with the purpose of drawing Israel into retaliatory actions? 3. Can Hussein count on Israeli forces to assist him should the forces of neighbouring countries come to the aid of the Palestinian terrorists while he tries to knock them out?

With the message sent via Washington, Eban realized that Jordan was also looking for an American guarantee. Notwithstanding the opposition of the Defence Minister Moshe Dayan, the Israeli cabinet responded positively. [8] In the following months, there were more new Palestinian attacks on Israel and heavy *Tzahal* retaliations in Jordanian territory. Once again, King Hussein wrote to the Israeli government (again using the American channel) calling for a period without reprisals, and only would he take strong measures against the fedayeen. Jerusalem decided to give the King what he wanted; the strength of his language on this occasion impressed them: 'Jordan Army under orders to shoot to kill any fedayeen attempting to fire rockets and fedayeen leaders had been told again evening of 3 June that violators would be shot on sight'.[9] In July, Jordan and Egypt decided to accept the Rogers Plan. The Plan stated that the West Bank was to be under King Hussein's authority, which was unacceptable to the more radical organizations. The Popular Front for the Liberation of Palestine (PFLP) of George Habash, and the Democratic Front for the Liberation of Palestine (DFLP) of Naif Hawatmeh opposed the plan, attacking Nasser and Hussein directly in very strong language. The central committee of the PLO condemned the proposals as a plot to liquidate Palestinian resistance. In August, the PFLP and the DFLP began to challenge the Jordanian regime. Their leaders started to demand more openly for the reactionary Hashemite monarchy to be overthrown as a prelude to launching a popular war for the liberation of Palestine. Further fighting broke out between the Army and the fedayeen towards the end of August. It was time for civil war.

It was the radical fedayeen that precipitated the crisis. On 1 September, King Hussein came under heavy fire on his way to the airport in the second attempt on his life in three months. The regime responded immediately by bombing Palestinian positions in Amman. With 17,000 Iraqi troops stationed in eastern Jordan and ready to intervene in support of the fedayeen, Hussein was wondering about Israel's possible moves. While waiting for Israeli or Iraqi moves, Hussein's authority at home came under serious challenge. On 6 September, the PFLP hijacked four Western-owned airliners with several hundred passengers and forced them to land in Dawson's Field, near Zarka, in Jordan[10] (another attempt to hijack an El Al airliner failed because of the reaction of armed guards on board).[11] It was a strange event, the one that took place that day: when the Jordanian Army arrived at Dawson's Field, they found that Iraqi troops had taken position on the ground. According to King Hussein there was clear collusion between Iraq and the terrorists on how to carry out the hijack operation.[12] On 12 September, the hijackers blew up the airliners in front of the world media and released all but fifty-four passengers (most of them Israelis). On 15 September, the fedayeen took over Irbid and declared it a liberated area under a people's government. It was now time to act. As Avi Shlaim wrote:

> Hussein was extremely patient by nature and knew the importance of timing. He wanted to leave his people in no doubt that he had done everything in his power to avoid bloodshed. The hijacking of planes and the holding of hostages finally tipped public opinion at home and abroad against the fedayeen. The time for action had come.[13]

On September 15 King Hussein declared martial law. The news of martial law led Kissinger to prepare a memorandum for the President in which the National Security Adviser was of the opinion that the most effective role for the United States was to rapidly and threateningly increase the US military forces in the Mediterranean to deter intervention by radical Arab regimes in Jordan; to provide psychological support for the King; and to match and overwhelm a Soviet response (including military intervention if necessary). The massing of US military power in the Mediterranean and the ambiguity of Washington pronouncements would be used to strengthen Hussein's position, discourage his opponents, and deter the Soviets.[14] Reading Kissinger's memoirs we discover that 'unexpectedly, his [President Nixon's] reaction was vehement'. Nixon who strangely does not recount the episode in his memoirs:

> questioned whether there had been any need for an emergency WSAG [Washington Special Action Group] meeting and covered my report of the WSAG's views with angry scribbled comments. He wrote that he preferred no confrontation at all; if it was unavoidable he wanted American forces used; he opposed any Israeli military moves unless he specifically approved them in advance, which he strongly implied he would never do.[15]

Kissinger hoped that the President would have second thoughts, and asked the White House Chief of Staff Bob Haldeman to put pressure on Nixon.[16] On 17 September, King Hussein ordered his Army to enter Amman, thus, civil war broke out. Heavy fighting was reported in the British and American Embassy area of the town, and in the north of Jordan around Palestinian populated areas in the towns of Irbid, Salt, Sweileh, Baq'aa and Zarqa. Washington decided to inform King Hussein that they were sympathetic to his efforts and his request for material assistance.[17] Meanwhile, the aircraft carrier USS *Saratoga* was ordered to join the USS *Independence* off the Lebanese coast. A third carrier, the USS *John F. Kennedy*, was dispatched to the Sixth Fleet from Puerto Rico. The helicopter carrier USS *Guam* – with a group of marines – was on its way to the Mediterranean. There could have been a problem with Soviet intelligence but Nixon and Kissinger agreed that 'we should be enigmatic and say nothing. They will pick this up [US military movements]'.[18]

Meanwhile, on the ground, Jordanian fears of external intervention in the conflict were soon realized. On September 18, a small Syrian armoured force crossed the border near Rathma and headed for Irbid,[19] the fedayeen 'liberated area'. Later in the day there was a second incursion across the border but not on a large scale. The Syrian tanks had Palestine Liberation Army (PLA) markings, but since the PLA had no tanks it was obvious that the invaders were regular Army units. Considering the situation on the battlefield, Hussein had the authorization of his government to ask for external help. Sunday, 20 September, was a long and stressful day. Events on the ground influenced the manner in which King Hussein used the mandate he had received. The request was for an airstrike against invading Syrian forces by the British Royal Air Force.[20] Because of communications difficulties between the King and the American Embassy in Amman, it was not clear if Hussein was also asking for a US and Israeli attack,[21] nevertheless Washington was considering action.[22] The following day, a very worried King Hussein sent an urgent message to Nixon:

> Situation deteriorating dangerously following Syrian massive invasion. Northern forces disjointed. Irbid occupied. This having disastrous effect on tired troops in the capital and surroundings. [...] I request immediate physical intervention both air and land as per the authorization of government to safeguard sovereignty, territorial integrity and independence of Jordan. Immediate air strikes on invading forces from any quarter plus air cover are imperative. Wish earliest word on length of time it may require your forces to land when requested which might be very soon.[23]

Nixon, in particular, saw the Soviets behind the Syrian invasion and a challenge that had to be met. He shared the conviction that Moscow orchestrated the Jordan Crisis in order to challenge US credibility in the Third World. In his memoirs Nixon wrote:

> We could not allow Hussein to be overthrown by a Soviet-inspired insurrection. If it succeeded, the entire Middle East might erupt in war [...]. The possibility of a direct U.S.-Soviet confrontation was uncomfortably high. It was like a ghastly game of dominoes, with a nuclear war waiting at the end.[24]

Kissinger, on the other hand, told Soviet Ambassador Anatoly Dobrynin two months later: 'During the Middle East crisis in September the Soviet role was ambiguous. No one in Washington thought that the Soviets started it, but at the same time no pressure was put on Syria until it was nearly too late'.[25]

In any case, the first thing to do was to give the 'green light' to the Israelis for an attack against Syrian forces within Jordanian territory,[26] and prepare contingency plans for a possible Soviet response.[27] Moreover, Nixon placed the 82nd Airborne Division on full alert; ordered the Sixth Fleet to move demonstratively towards the area of tension in the eastern Mediterranean; a reconnaissance plane to fly from an aircraft carrier to Tel Aviv to pick up target information and signal that American military action might be approaching; and a warning to be delivered to the Soviets to restrain their Syrian clients.[28]

The real turning point was 22 September. Encouraged by American and Israeli backing (and by the fact that the Syrian Air Force – under General Hafez al-Assad – stayed out of the combat), Hussein ordered his small Air Force to move against the Syrian forces in the north of the country. Both the Air Force and the Army went into action and inflicted heavy losses on the Syrians who started to withdraw from Irbid and the area around it. It was clear that Assad had no intention of intervening as the entire invasion was already condemned. Assad had held back the Air Force for reasons linked to his internal power struggle with Salah al Jadid, the deputy secretary-general of the Ba'ath Party, who had ordered the invasion. Shortly after the Syrian defeat in Jordan, in November, Assad seized power in Damascus.

The Syrian withdrawal – with the Iraqis always neutral – enabled the Jordanian Army to shift the offensive against the fedayeen and drive them out of the cities and their major strongholds. The Palestinians sustained further heavy losses and some leaders were captured. Political pressure from the Arab world forced Hussein to call a halt to the fighting. Nasser convened an emergency summit in Cairo. Hussein flew to Cairo on September 26 to a hostile reception from Arab leaders and a chilly meeting with Yasser Arafat. The next day, an agreement was signed by King Hussein and Arafat in the presence of President Nasser. This was to be the Egyptian leader's last act in the cause of 'Arab unity': he died of a heart attack the following day. The crisis was over and the two leaders shook hands over a sea of blood.

One further point should be added: the Jordan Crisis led to a definitive bureaucratic shift within the Nixon administration away from the State Department and Secretary Rogers to the White House and Secretary-to-be Kissinger.[29] The 'real' Secretary of State was Kissinger, while the President in the hottest hours of the crisis was in Chicago. The Washington Special Actions Group was the core of the decisions, Henry Kissinger the star and William Rogers just a dummy on a stage which was too complex for him.

CHAPTER 9

The Middle Eastern Test of Détente

The Direct Role of the USSR in the Yom Kippur War, 1973

Isabella Ginor and Gideon Remez

I remember how L. I. Brezhnev spoke at the Central Committee plenum in September 1974 – the speech was read out at Party assemblies. [...] He criticized Sadat and explained that the USSR did not know about Sadat's planned operation. – 'Mir Vam' (peace upon you)

As the grandson of a Soviet admiral, I declare: No less than 5,000 Soviet military advisers took part in the operation itself. Of these, 1,500 took part in combat, especially pilots and anti-aircraft defence experts. – 'Lishenets' (disenfranchised) [exchange in Novaya Gazeta readers' forum, 27 October 2004][1]

The Soviet role in the Yom Kippur War of October–November 1973 has posed vexing questions for historians, as it did for the national actors at the time. On the one hand, the mass evacuation of Soviet civilians, including the dependants of military advisers, from Egypt and Syria that began on 4 October – two days before these countries launched their attack on Israel – was taken to indicate that Moscow was, until then, unaware at least of the date for this offensive, and that it was so reluctant to get involved that it was willing even to compromise the advantage of surprise for its allies. The USSR's subsequent support of the Arab side, both politically and by means of a massive military resupply effort, would then have to be considered as practically imposed on the Soviets by their clients as the price for maintaining any regional influence.

At a critical juncture, when Israel threatened to reverse the initial Arab gains, the Soviets were believed to have entered into the equation even their own nuclear capability, thus triggering a commensurate US response. Still, Moscow was rarely held to have *deliberately* jeopardized global détente by putting it to such a severe test. On the contrary, the Soviet leadership had exhibited, in two summit conferences and countless other contacts, its commitment to the relaxation of superpower tensions, which extended to the Middle East and to other arenas of the Cold War. It was the Soviets' fulfilment of this pledge that supposedly convinced its clients (notably Egypt's President Anwar Sadat) that they could not expect any backing for their war aims, thus leading them to act alone, disregarding Soviet interests and entreaties.

On the other hand, even the limited evidence available at the time hardly appeared to support this interpretation. The very fact that there was a large apparatus of Soviet military advisers present in Egypt – and that only their dependants were evacuated, while the advisers themselves remained for the duration of the war – contradicted the already established concept that Sadat had banished the advisers in July 1972 because of the Soviets' supposed refusal, in the détente context, to provide offensive weapons. In another paper at this conference, 'The Secret Price of Détente: The Moscow Summit and the So-Called Expulsion of Soviet Advisers From Egypt', we expanded on our previous publications to demonstrate that this conventional concept is in fact incorrect.

The mass exodus of Soviet personnel that did take place was not a unilateral eviction but a consensual withdrawal, agreed upon not only between Moscow and Cairo, but also with the United States. The Soviet servicemen who left Egypt were not advisers, but the personnel of a Soviet expeditionary force of up to 20,000 troops (at a time) that was posted there from 1969–70. These integral Soviet formations (mainly an anti-aircraft division and several squadrons of MiG-21 fighters) took an active part in the War of Attrition. The aerial defence array, in particular, achieved its main mission by shooting down Israel's newly acquired F 4 Phantom jets at an unsustainable rate. This compelled Israel to accept a cease-fire in August 1970, which the Soviets and Egyptians could violate with impunity by moving the SAM batteries up to the Suez Canal. The resulting no-fly zone for Israel created the precondition for an Egyptian offensive across the canal, for which the Soviet advisers had been training and equipping the Egyptian Army. The 'expulsion' permitted repatriation of the Soviet units without ever confirming their presence. There is also strong evidence that the 'expulsion' was intentionally designed as an elaborate deception to mislead the Israeli side – which, in any case, was the outcome.[2]

Recently declassified papers have underlined the importance of the détente context, and especially of the Moscow summit in May 1972, in motivating both the American and Soviet sides first to negotiate this arrangement and then to misrepresent it. This contributed signally to both contemporary consequences and the historical record. In particular, US National Security Adviser Henry Kissinger felt constrained by the needs of his global policy to portray the 'expulsion' as the opposite of what he had demanded and ultimately achieved, and to conceal the actual agreement from Israel, with disastrous results for the latter. For our initial study, we had mainly the transcripts of formal US–Soviet talks, which have been released over the past decade, to compare with Kissinger's voluminous and ubiquitously quoted memoirs. But more recently, the joint Russian–American publication of Kissinger's and Dobrynin's reports to their respective bosses about their otherwise unrecorded back-channel meetings has strongly confirmed our conclusions – in addition to providing some entertaining and revealing observations about each other.[3]

Motivations and intentions are tricky to ascertain and almost always debatable, but factual evidence, when available, can suffice at least to rule out claims that cannot be reconciled with deeds. As we found with respect to previous stages of the Soviet intervention, it was precisely because of the discrepancy between Moscow's declared policy in the heyday of détente and its simultaneous actions in this regional arena that we now have a considerable body of such evidence to juxtapose with official documents. Like the huge deployment of Soviet regulars and their withdrawal, their partial return to take an active part in the 1973 war was never confirmed by the USSR. In the October War, unlike the War of Attrition, the same was also true of the individual Soviet advisers attached to Egyptian units, most of whom had supposedly been sent home over a year earlier. Nothing was entered in their papers to indicate they were war veterans, and they were required to sign lifelong pledges of secrecy about their Middle Eastern combat record. It was only toward the disintegration of the Soviet Union, and for a while afterwards, that they began to demand their rights and recognition as *internatsionalisty*. One way to do this was by publicizing their stories.

This process has declined markedly in the last few years. This is due, at least in part, to an official campaign, which included the creation in May 2009 of a presidential commission 'to investigate and counter falsified versions of history that damage Russia's international prestige'. As a result, many have had to exercise renewed caution.[4] However, while it lasted, the relatively free rein that the veterans enjoyed produced a sufficiently large and variegated volume of accounts to permit cross-checking and verification. Vladislav Zubok's recent, authoritative Cold War history acknowledges that 'the Soviet role in this war has long been the subject of great controversy. Today, this story can be analyzed with much more clarity, thanks to the recollections of ex-Soviet veterans'. He too maintains rather ambivalently that Sadat 'kept the Politburo and Soviet representatives in Egypt in the dark, although the KGB and military must have known about the preparations […] the Kremlin leaders could not control or restrain their foreign clients'.[5]

However, our study of veterans' testimonies largely removes any remaining doubt that – notwithstanding détente – the USSR was not only aware of, but was actively involved in, planning, timing, and conducting the war. The following sampler will refer mainly to the opening stages of the war, as the subsequent phases of Soviet intervention may be attributed to response rather than initiative. Likewise, we should mention only briefly that the Soviet veterans of the War of Attrition, as well as official Russian publications about their role in 1969–1972, claim proudly that they 'prepared' the Yom Kippur War.[6] Even if we allow for retrospective self-glorification, these preparations may have made their input before the Soviets' purported expulsion in July 1972. The following examples therefore include mainly Soviet contributions that clearly reflect subsequent knowledge and endorsement of the ultimate Arab battle plan and its timing.

The weapons that Sadat sought *were* provided, with the advisers to oversee their induction. Two examples are particularly relevant to the preparations for the 1973 war. One illustrates the continuity of this process – contrary to suggestions that Soviet–Egyptian collaboration did stop, but was renewed after reconciliation in October 1972. Andrei Yena, the deputy commander of a fighter 'battalion', was sent to Egypt in June 1972, to oversee the assembly of Su-20 planes (the stripped-down export version of the swing-winged Sukhoi-17). His mission should ostensibly have been cut short by the expulsion declared by Sadat on 18 July. His project not only went on, uninterrupted, to its planned conclusion, but his posting was even extended for another two months, to help introduce the fully equipped Su-17s, which began arriving in November.[7]

The supply of another clearly offensive system, the Scud surface-to-surface missile, was *initiated* well after the supposed rift with Moscow: 'In the middle of July [1973], together with the hardware for deployment of an Egyptian operative-tactical brigade, a group of Soviet missile specialists arrived in Cairo under the command of Colonel Sal'nikov', as recorded by the outfit's interpreter. Any suggestion that the missiles' ultimate use in the Yom Kippur War – which will be discussed below – violated the terms of their supply is negated by the fact that at the outbreak of war, 'the Egyptian "Scud" brigade was urgently supported by a group of specialists and regulars-instructors and brought up to battle read   s.'[8]

This occurred after at least one postponement of   zero hour for Egypt's cross-canal offensive which exemplified Sovie   luence on its determination. A former Soviet diplomat has claimed th   was delayed from May to October at the Soviets' behest, in order no   disrupt the summit talks in June 1973: '[General Secretary Leonid] B   nev visited the United States and Sadat was told to wait a bit after the   was over, not to weaken our position.'[9] Sadat himself (among several ra   ales that he gave for the postponement) claimed that *he* had preferred   wait the outcome of the summit.[10] However, the transcripts of Kissinge   reparatory talks with Brezhnev in Moscow on 7 May show that the Un   States was aware of an Egyptian and Syrian military build-up, and co   onted the Soviets about it:

> *Kissinger*: [...] There is a possibility that there is a plan to do som thing before the summer, to force us into action [...].
>
> *Brezhnev*: That's not bad intelligence. Israel also is calling up reservists [...] certain preparations are under way. [...] We can tell the Arabs not to fight [...] But [...] we might not be able to contain the status quo [...] All good things done by us in the direction at the Summit of achieving détente and avoiding a confrontation will be scrapped.[11]

Brezhnev, then, warned that the Soviets' power to restrain the Arabs indefinitely was limited, but he also let slip that the Americans had found out something. This suggests that the Soviets relayed Kissinger's disclosure to Sadat, and the offensive was actually delayed not only to save the summit, but until the element of surprise could be restored.

Another obvious indication of Soviet involvement in the Arab war plan came when the offensive was launched. The air and sealift of munitions from the USSR began too quickly and effectively for an unforeseen contingency. Faced by these inconsistencies in the USSR's declared détente policy, most Western scholarship tended to skirt the question with such formulations as 'Soviet policy was dualistic [...] providing the wherewithal for hostilities while nonetheless urging the Arabs to forego their war plans.'[12] Soviet (and then Russian) spokesmen continued well into this century to deny any complicity in the Egyptian–Syrian attack. A recent official history attributes to a figure as high up as Foreign Minister Andrei Gromyko not only utter surprise at learning about it only two days in advance, but also the response 'they didn't listen to us!'[13]

Setting the Date and Gearing Up

An Egyptian–Syrian protocol, quoted by Arab officers for research at a Soviet military academy that was published as a book in Russian, is one of the sources that pinpoint the final setting of zero hour:

> From July 3 to July 5, 1973, Cairo hosted meetings with the participation of Syrian and Egyptian officers [...]. Between August 11 and 26, 1973, the Supreme Council of the Egyptian and Syrian armed forces conducted meetings at Navy headquarters in Alexandria. [...]. After prolonged discussions the day of October 6 was chosen.[14]

The place and precise dates (20–23 August) were confirmed by General Baheiddin Noufal, Egypt's Chief of Operations for the Federal Command, who related that this meeting posed a logistical nightmare: how to camouflage the arrival of the top six Syrian military officers – including Defence Minister Mustafa Tlas. Tlas himself confirmed the Soviet involvement in an interview in the 1990's: 'We travelled on board a Russian ship, wearing civilian clothes. The Soviet Ambassador accompanied us and told the captain: "This [...] is the Syrian Minister of Defence. Protect him during the journey and don't tell anyone who he is"'.[15]

At this point, it is worth quoting a little-noted statement that the former US Ambassador in Egypt, Hermann Eilts, made in 1998:

> As far as I know, nobody has mentioned that in the weeks before the 1973 war, Marshal [Andrei] Grechko, the then minister of defence of the Soviet Union, came to Egypt and was taken around

the military installations. It was apparently suggested to him that the Egyptians might attack, not with any indication of date.[16]

Eilts arrived in Egypt only after the war, to take charge of the US interests section in Cairo and reconstitute it as an embassy. He did not clarify whether the section had learned of Grechko's visit and supposed remarks in real time or only in retrospect. At any rate, Eilts's comment that 'nobody has mentioned' the visit still holds true to the best of *our* knowledge. At the conference where he referred to it, none of the Egyptian or Soviet participants is recorded as challenging his statement. If true – especially given the disclosure of the Alexandria meeting within the same time frame and at Grechko's level of defence ministers – it would strongly corroborate Soviet complicity in setting the date for the Egyptian–Syrian offensive.

Lest it be argued that the Soviets were not privy to the decisions in Alexandria, we can track their part in the operational preparations that began in short order. The Soviet Navy's Fifth *Eskadra* in the Mediterranean had been reinforced unobtrusively by a technique that was also used before the Six-Day War. Units were sent into the Mediterranean as though for normal rotation, but the ships they were ostensibly replacing stayed put.[17] The order of battle was thus raised to an unprecedented 120 units.[18]

As a former Soviet naval officer relates, 'at the end of August 1973, the *Eskadra* – according to the plan to assist Syria at preparing a war with Israel, in an atmosphere of the strictest secrecy […] carried out an operation to transport a brigade of Moroccan troops from Algeria to Syria […] under cover of supposedly conducting landing maneuvers.'[19] On 13 September, an Israeli air patrol west of the Syrian ports of Latakia and Tartus (which also housed Soviet naval facilities) spotted Soviet ships unloading tanks, artillery and missiles. A Syrian attempt to intercept the patrol triggered a massive dogfight, in which the Syrians lost 13 planes to Israel's one.[20]

On 28 September, the Soviet Baltic Fleet's marine force was put on alert. Part of its complement, under Lt. Col. V.I. Gorokhov, was flown in transport planes to Sevastopol with personal arms only. There, it was loaded, with full battle gear and weapons borrowed from the Black Sea Fleet's counterpart regiment, onto a BDK (large landing ship). Additional units followed from Baltiisk the same day by train, and embarked on two medium landing ships (SDKs). All of them then set sail for the Mediterranean. Also on 28 September, another reinforced marine battalion steamed to the Mediterranean directly from Baltiisk, on the Baltic Fleet's own BDK *Krasnaya Presnya*. The Baltic Fleet marines had maintained a rotating presence at Port Said from before the Six-Day War till the end of 1971, but it was then discontinued and was never at this level. The urgency and mode of the marines' dispatch indicates preparation for a highly extraordinary development. The then-lieutenant who recorded it, notes that his men's 'combat service' (until they landed at Tartus on 7 December) was 'very difficult'.[21]

Likewise, an entire 'brigade' of 10 submarines, with their tender ship, were dispatched from the Arctic Fleet early enough to pass Gibraltar on 3 October, the earliest date given for Sadat's alert to Moscow – without the previous 'garrison' being withdrawn. According to a Russian naval historian, Aleksandr Rozin, the submarine skippers were puzzled by some of the orders that the fleet commander gave them in person. Two of the subs were to take up positions off the Israeli coast and 'upon the outbreak of hostilities' were to search and destroy enemy vessels 'approaching or leaving Israeli ports'. One of these subs was positioned 'south of Cyprus and west of Haifa' to 'protect transports'. The brigade commander received an angry response when he asked for clarification.[22]

Going Public: 4 October

All the above tends to obviate the ongoing confusion – or intentional obfuscation – whether Sadat specified the exact date and hour of the attack to the Soviets on 3 or 4 October, and how this information was transmitted. Many low- and mid-level Soviet officials and officers may be entirely truthful in attesting that *they* were first warned of the impending war less than two days in advance, that is, on 4 October, after Sadat served notice on the Soviet Ambassador Vladimir Vinogradov the day before. Sadat related retrospectively that he did give Vinogradov a *general* warning on the 3rd, without stating the precise time.[23] Vinogradov describes this in even vaguer terms: 'Sadat raised the possibility that Egypt might take retaliatory action against a big Israeli provocation, and promised to inform the USSR when this came about'.[24] Vinogradov's deputy, Pavel Akopov, did not clarify the issue much when he stated in a retrospective interview that Sadat disclosed the exact date 'two or three days before the war started,' saying 'it is my duty to warn you because you have too many people and specialists here'.[25]

According to Sadat, the precise zero hour was divulged to the Soviets by Syrian President Hafez al-Assad on the 4th, as the two Arab leaders had prearranged.[26] In the best-known 'insider' account, Victor Israelyan confirms that the Soviet ambassador in Damascus, Nuritdin Mukhitdinov, did meet Assad on the 4th – but received the same general declaration as his colleague in Cairo. Likewise, Mukhitdinov was finally given a few hours' notice only on the morning of the 6th.[27] Given Mukhitdinov's role in the August council at Alexandria, and the evacuation of Soviet citizens from Syria already underway, either these meetings, or the accounts about them, seem to be a choreographed charade. Israelyan writes that he failed to find the crucial information in *any* dispatches from Cairo or Damascus. He concluded that the Soviet leadership must have received it through 'special channels', and 'its "special connection" in Cairo or Damascus remains undisclosed.' He stresses that this does *not* allude to KGB representatives in either Arab capital reporting to Moscow without informing the ambassadors.[28] On the other hand, an official Russian history even claims that on 4 October, Moscow was not notified by the Egyptians at all, but rather learned about the impending war from its own intelligence. The KGB *rezident* in Cairo at the time, Vadim Kirpichenko, stated at a conference on the war in 1998 'we learned the date of the military action about five or six days in advance'.[29]

At any rate, Soviet actions make it unnecessary to sort out this tangle, and these actions now shifted from military preparations that could at least be partly concealed to high-profile moves that could not avoid being detected – indeed, were intended to be. By 7 pm on 4 October, when Gromyko convened senior Foreign Ministry officials to tell them that 'the Egyptian and Syrian leaders had made their final decision to attack Israel', he stated that 'the matter had already been discussed at the "highest level" in the Kremlin', and 'steps were being taken to evacuate Soviet civilian personnel and their families'.[30] It is not necessary for the purposes of this paper to inquire whether this move was initiated by Moscow or, as Akopov stated, was prompted by Sadat. The former possibility seems more plausible. Upon receiving the order from Prime Minister Alexei Kosygin, Vinogradov tried to object out of anxiety that such a massive, overt measure would give away the Arab plan. However, he was not able to attain his usual direct access to Brezhnev. Gromyko evaded a similar question when one of his aides dared to pose it, and would not instruct them how to explain the evacuation if asked. He laid down the official Soviet line by repeating several times that the war would start on Saturday, 6 October, at 2 pm and that 'neither [he] nor Brezhnev supported the Arab decision [...] the Soviet leadership had done everything it could to talk Sadat and Assad' out of it.[31]

It is just barely possible that there was time to convene the Politburo following a surprise message from Cairo, and to take practical measures within a few hours. The evacuation, however, clearly could not have been implemented on 4 October if it had been ordered on the same day. For example, Akopov – who was charged with organizing it – let slip that there were fewer Soviet tourists than usual to look after, as 'we had already sensed [the war]' and 'limited the number of tourists to Egypt.' Akopov related that within a day and a half 1,700 people were sent home by planes alone. The rest – Israelyan quotes a total of 3,700 – were driven to Alexandria, and there boarded naval vessels for Odessa, including submarines.[32]

An *airlift* might conceivably be mounted within a few hours, but the presence of adequate *ships* on such short notice is more remarkable. Indeed, the *Eskadra*'s commander, Vice-Admiral E.I. Volobuyev, is reported to have received his instructions before 01:00 hours on 4 October – that is, several hours before his superiors in the Kremlin supposedly ordered the evacuation. He then commanded all available craft to head for Egyptian and Syrian ports. This indicates that the requisite ships were already within a few hours' sailing distance, if not in harbour.[33]

Prior preparation for the evacuation is also attested by a professor of medicine from Kiev. He remembers that on 3 October he was unable to reserve a room in any hotel in town for a subordinate, who was about to arrive for a weekly tutorial. When he tried to use his connections, a friend told him in strict confidence that 'there was an order to clear all hotels from 4 October, for imminently arriving evacuees from the Middle East'.[34]

The target date for evacuation was thus set in advance, and disclosed to both Egyptians and Soviets at various levels on a need-to-know basis. Its timing is explained by the frequently cited Egyptian assessments of the period that Israel would need to call up and deploy its reserves. In early planning, Minister Ahmad Ismail estimated that if the Israelis learned the date of attack only four or five days in advance – preferably, three – this would suffice to preclude a full IDF mobilization. On 2 October, Chief of Staff Saad Shazli opined that it was already too late for Israel to mobilize ahead of an attack on the 6th.[35] Sadat echoed this on 3 October, as:

> A careful study of the Israeli mobilization system [...] led him to believe that it would be impossible for Israel to mobilize armoured formations and deploy along the Canal in less than 72 hours, [nor] for the entire mobilized strength of Israel to be deployed [...] in under five to six days.[36]

The prominence of this consideration indicates the purpose of feigning a secret, last-minute warning to Moscow. It would effectively be revealed by the easily detectable mass evacuation, which could (and did) provide the Soviets with deniability vis-à-vis the United States and others, without endangering the Egyptian operation on the ground. For the same purpose, it was also on 4 October that a massive Soviet propaganda campaign was launched accusing Israel of the provocation that Sadat had invoked. Regarding this – as with the Kiev hotels – Soviet media had been instructed:

> To keep space available for stories on the Middle East. Consequently, in the last two or three days before the war, Soviet broadcasts and the press had been disseminating an increasing number of reports of an alleged Israeli military build-up.[37]

At the same time as the frenetic exodus of Soviet civilians *from* Egypt, there was a much less ostentatious movement of military personnel in the opposite direction. A respected Soviet Major General, the late Viktor Kutsenko, then a colonel in the Corps of Engineers and ultimately its commander, wrote a detailed account how '60 officers of the Moscow military district [...] were rousted out at 6 a.m., by 8 were at Chkalovsky Military airport and by 8 pm had already reached a briefing room in Cairo.' Kutsenko published his reminiscences in the third person, as purported fiction. He explained that – as already noted for the veterans in general – 'in 1973 [...] I signed [a paper] for the state security authorities that I would never reveal my participation in those events. Who knows, perhaps that signature may still be binding, but what counterintelligence can complain about a story?' Still, though he names his own character in the narrative 'Col. Vasily Bodrov', it is undoubtedly a factual memoir of his own experiences.

Kutsenko's timeline clarifies that his dispatch to Egypt was on 4 October at the latest, possibly the day before. Either way, especially given the time difference between Cairo and Moscow, the order to send these officers had to be prepared and was even implemented before Sadat's supposed announcement. The officers' transport plane, the late General Kutsenko recounted, was escorted by fighter jets.

The mission entrusted to Kutsenko's *alter ego* in the story is of special significance. He was to replace the chief engineering adviser to one of the Egyptian army corps, who had suddenly fallen ill. What follows is a detailed account of the Soviet advisers' role in the Canal crossing. They not only constructed pontoon bridges for the Egyptian tanks within 35 minutes, but before this, towed fire engines across the canal on makeshift ferries to blast breaches in the Israeli sand rampart. The narrative features such minute detail as the model of the Soviet-made outboard motors on the rubber dinghies used by Egyptian infantrymen for the initial crossing – and it checks out neatly against accounts from the Israeli side.[38] So does the use of Soviet-made high-pressure water cannon, which were supplied as late as January 1973.[39]

Advisers who were already in Egypt might perhaps have been caught up willy-nilly in these operations. If that had been the case, a replacement would hardly have been posted so urgently for a key adviser who fell ill so conveniently. The Soviet defence attaché in Cairo at the time, Nikolai Ivliev, adds that a dozen senior Soviet officers arrived in Egypt on the morrow of the war's outbreak, and he led five of them across the canal on the same day in order to tour the battlefield as the Egyptian forces advanced into Sinai – not exactly a gesture of displeasure.

One of these senior officers was apparently Robert Bykov, a GRU (military intelligence) operative and missile expert with special-operations experience worldwide, who is also described – remarkably – as 'a veteran of the 1967–1976 Egyptian campaign.' Bykov, who retired as a colonel of the General Staff, told a Russian television interviewer in 2003 how, in the Yom Kippur War, he was given the task of overseeing the Egyptian forces in the use of the new Malyutka (Sagger) anti-tank missile, in its first major combat test:

> We took a poorly trained peasant, put him behind a small stone in the desert, a sandstone, gave him 10 of these Malyutkas and left. The Israeli tanks could be heard from far away. Later, all of a sudden we could not hear any movement, any noise normally produced by tanks. We arrived there and saw the peasant literally clapping his hands and pointing a Malyutka at our armored vehicle. We said 'Point it away, what are you doing!' He pointed it away and showed us six destroyed Israeli tanks in the distance.

The Soviets may have somewhat exaggerated the Malyutka's success when they credited it with 800 Israeli tanks, but it did take a lethal toll and went down in Israeli military lore as a deadly surprise. Still, the Soviets were not entirely pleased, and used this battlefield test to improve the system. Another such example follows.[40]

Ivliev stated in an interview that for the same purpose, he was charged with collecting samples of Israeli or US-made armaments. He is credited with sending exemplars of several dozen weapons systems to Moscow during the war. The Soviets took some of the Egyptians' booty, but also made sure of getting the most sought-after items themselves. Among their best prizes, Ivliev reports, were a downed UAV and a brand-new M-60 Patton tank with only 100 kilometres on the odometer, which these advisers themselves captured immediately after crossing.[41]

Another testimony reveals that Soviet *Spetznaz* (special forces) units were not only present in Egypt but also went into combat. Within the first few hours of the war, it was noticed – evidently by Soviet advisers – that Egypt's newly-supplied T-62 tanks were unexpectedly vulnerable to the cannon of presumably outdated Israeli Centurions. Soviet commandos twice went behind Israeli lines to obtain these British-made tanks to inspect their Israeli-upgraded gun. In raids on October 8 and 9, they succeeded in killing two Centurion crews while disabling the vehicles only in such a way that they could still be driven back over the pontoon bridges to Cairo and flown urgently to Moscow.

The *Komsomolskaya Pravda* report of this exploit backs it up with a facsimile of the transport plane's flight log. As with Bykov's story about the Malyutka operator, for anyone with a military background, this account is further authenticated by an anecdote that rings unmistakeably true. The first tank's turret was immobilized with the cannon pointing sideways, and it would not go through the cargo plane's back door. After hours of vain attempts, an Egyptian begged: 'Mr. Officer, just cut it off!' To which *Spetznaz* Major 'Ivanov' replied: 'I'd sooner cut off my you-know-what.' Finally both Centurions were loaded and flown to the USSR. One was used for testing weapons, and the other is still exhibited at the Kubinka testing ground near Moscow.[42]

Air and Sealift

The timing of the Soviet operation to resupply Egypt and Syria also casts serious doubt on the conventional assumption that it was undertaken only in response to the heavy losses that the Arab side sustained in the first days of fighting. Recent Russian sources put the departure of the first cargo ships from the Black Sea ports of Illichivsk and Oktyabrsky as early as 7 October – barely 24 hours after the first shots were fired. Each of these ships was by then loaded with up to 92 armoured vehicles. It stretches the imagination to suppose that such a mass of armour was marshalled from scratch, moved and loaded in that space of time, or for that matter, even after the formal announcement of Egypt's plan to Moscow on the 3rd or 4th – which would in itself indicate Soviet support for the imminent attack.[43] This differs significantly from both previous Western perceptions and official Soviet/ Russian statements, which dated the first shipments on 9 October.[44]

If we factor in the Politburo approval that under Soviet procedures was required for transfers of such magnitude, this necessarily puts the resupply commitment even earlier. It is remotely possible, but highly unlikely, that this complex operation was authorized only when, according to Gromyko (as quoted by Israelyan), 'the matter was already discussed at the "highest level" in the Kremlin'. It was in the afternoon of 4 October that the Politburo decision was taken within a few hours and carried out within two days. Considered together with the evidence already cited, it seems a safe assumption that the transports were standing by well in advance, ready to go as soon as this easily detected measure could be presented as a response to a *fait accompli*.

The same applies to several subsequent instances of direct Soviet intervention in the war, of which only the most prominent are listed here. While the first flights of the Soviet airlift were devoted to replacement weapons and 'experts' to supervise them, beginning on 13 October, 12 An-22 and 72 An-12 sorties were needed to fly 'Special Air Detachment 154' to Cairo-West airbase. This formation consisted of four MiG-25RB aircraft, with seven pilots, ground crew and support staff totalling over 220 men. It had been alerted on 11 October for deployment to Egypt. The personnel were stripped not only of documents and insignia, but of any item identifiable as Soviet, from wristwatches to matches. The planes' Soviet military markings were painted over, but unlike the MiG-25s' previous stint in Egypt in 1971–72, the red stars were not replaced with Egyptian marks 'as no one would believe it anyway.' Once reassembled, they carried out four 'uniquely important' reconnaissance sorties by the war's end. The photos and audio material were flown to Moscow within hours.

When the 154th arrived in Egypt, the headquarters of a Soviet 'air group' was already there to receive it. This group had been set up under the command of Major-General M.S. Dvornikov 'on the war's sixth day, when luck turned against the Egyptians', and posted at the Soviet embassy in Cairo to prepare an air intervention on the Arabs' behalf. However, 'its full deployment' never materialized and the MiG-25s remained the only Soviet aircraft in Egypt.

The aviation writer Viktor Markovsky, who based the above description on participants' accounts, also makes an unsourced claim that GRU units began practical training for 'another insane plan'. This plan was to 'land' in Israel's Negev desert (presumably by helicopter or parachute; there were a series of attempted helicopter-borne raids by Egyptian commandos in Sinai). The Soviet operatives were to set up radio beacons to guide aircraft for an attack on the Israeli nuclear complex at Dimona with burrowing missiles that would destroy the site's underground facilities. Markovsky does not specify whether this was to be implemented by the MiG-25RBs (the reconnaissance-bomber version), but states that when dispatched from Moscow, the pilots were instructed to prepare for both kinds of mission. He does note that the planes were designed, and the pilots thoroughly trained, to launch standoff nuclear weapons from a range of 40km. Whereas at the start of the war, Israeli anti-aircraft defences successfully intercepted 'winged missiles' (apparently Kelts) fired by Egyptian Tu-16s, the Israelis had nothing that could cope either with the MiG-25's altitude and speed or intercept their nuclear weapons once launched. Markovsky claims that 'as the military situation changed daily against the Arabs, an attack on Tel Aviv [...] was seriously considered,' but he does not state that the requisite nuclear weapons were actually delivered to Egypt, nor whether their use was contemplated as a nuclear first strike – contrary to the USSR's long-standing doctrine – or only in response to an Israeli nuclear blow.[45]

However, Professor Aleksandr Minayev of Moscow State University clarified this point in an article in 2008. Minayev's late elder brother Alexei, an aircraft designer who in 1973 was deputy minister for the aircraft industry, convened a consultation whether the MiG-25s could safely overfly Tel Aviv. The context was:

> The eventuality of an Israeli air strike on the Aswan Dam [...] which might cause a nuclear war [...] it was rumoured in the highest corridors of power in Moscow that in response to such a development, our air force would have to land a nuclear blow on Israel.[46]

It hardly seems likely that the contingency of such an Israeli move, and the appropriate response, were discussed in Moscow only a week into the war. How seriously the nuclear option was considered is illustrated in the memoirs of Zinaida Freydin, the widow of physicist Ilya Livshits. In a volume commemorating the thirtieth anniversary of his death in 1976, she related that in October 1973 his colleague and close friend, the nuclear weapons developer Yakov Zeldovich, left a note with Livshits (both Jews), to be opened if the USSR launched a nuclear attack on Israel – in which case Zeldovich intended to commit suicide.[47]

The global significance of the MiG-25 deployment to Egypt, regardless of détente commitments, is illustrated by the simultaneous dispatch of a Foxbat squadron to Poland.[48] In the event, the MiG-25 detachment only carried out a reconnaissance sortie over Tel Aviv. Minayev and other ex-Soviet writers have asserted that the Israelis' awareness of this threat, and their inability to counter the Foxbats, is what *prevented* the use of Israeli nuclear weapons, which had reportedly been readied in the early stages of the war when the Egyptian and Syrian onslaught appeared to jeopardize the Israeli heartland.[49] This claim seems dubious, as by 13 October the

Syrian advance had been reversed, the Egyptian incursion had stalled, and a renewed thrust into Sinai was repulsed, so that any Israeli doomsday scenario was by then obviated. Precisely this turning in the war's tide lends credibility to the offensive plans attributed to the Soviet MiG-25s.

The nuclear option associated with them adds a new twist – but not much more credibility – to the much-debated reports that US intelligence identified emissions from Soviet nuclear weapons on board a ship heading for Egypt. This was retrospectively cited as the climactic motivation for the decision by Kissinger (who in September 1973 had been appointed Secretary of State) to declare a worldwide Defcon-3 alert during the night of 24 October, that is on the 25th, Middle East time. So far, these alleged nuclear munitions were held to have been warheads for the Egyptian Scud missiles.[50]

The ship was first spotted on 22 October entering the Mediterranean from the Black Sea. It docked on the 25th at Port Said – an unlikely port, unnecessarily close to the combat zone to risk such a cargo if the supposed warheads were destined for the Scuds *or* Foxbats, both of which were stationed near Cairo. If nuclear weapons for the MiG-25s ever reached Egypt, they were probably among the 'armaments' that, as Markovsky writes, were airlifted with the disassembled planes themselves. Regarding the Scuds, well before the suspect ship arrived – on the 22nd, as the first ceasefire was about to go into effect – two conventionally tipped missiles had already been fired at the Israelis' canal counter-crossing point. Though versions differ as to who pressed the button – Soviet or Egyptian operators – authorization was required and given by Marshal Grechko from Moscow. Israelyan describes his order as an offhand response to Vinogradov's request from Cairo, but Grechko could not have made such a momentous move without Politburo approval (which had till then been denied) – or at least, he could not have done so without being called to account later.[51]

Taken separately, each of these cases might be construed as a *post factum* attempt by the Soviets to make the best of an undesired predicament. Cumulatively, they reinforce our conclusion drawn from the earlier examples. The USSR's conduct in the 1973 war allows for a range of interpretations as to its intent, from a genuine commitment to global moderation that was disrupted by regional clients wagging the superpower dog, to a deliberate deception that used this pretence to hide aggressive moves. The facts as they have now been fleshed out definitely narrow down the spectrum of tenable hypotheses by ruling out the possibility that an unwitting and unwilling Kremlin merely tried to cope with a war it had tried to avoid in the name of détente.

CHAPTER 10

Conflict and Détente in the Eastern Mediterranean

From the Yom Kippur War to the Cyprus Crisis, October 1973–August 1974

John Sakkas

On 15 July 1974, the Greek military junta carried out a coup against the elected President of the Republic of Cyprus, Archbishop Makarios, deposed him and installed the puppet government of Nikos Sampson. Using as a pretext the restoration of constitutional order on the island and the protection of the Turkish-Cypriot minority (around 18 per cent of the total population) from Greek nationalists, Turkey, in a two-stage operation (20–22 July and 14–16 August 1974), invaded and occupied an area of about 36 per cent of Cyprus.

The Cyprus conflict cannot be analysed and understood in any depth without seriously and systematically taking into account the determining political influence and degree of involvement of external agents in Cyprus. This chapter focuses on the attitude of the superpowers during the Cyprus crisis in the summer of 1974 and examines their strategic objectives in the eastern Mediterranean and the Middle East in relation to major regional actors such as Turkey and Israel. The author's central hypothesis is that the 1974 invasions took place for reasons other than those claimed publicly by Turkey – to protect its minority and to prevent *enosis* (union) of the island with Greece – and that the USA and the USSR were primarily concerned with the island's effect on the balance of power in the Near/Middle East rather than with the geostrategic significance of Cyprus itself. For the Americans, Turkey and Israel were of enormous value in terms of both global and regional strategy; for the Soviets, Turkey was a key country in their policy of peaceful coexistence with the West.

The first section deals with US interests in the eastern Mediterranean and the Middle East. The second section addresses the impact of the Yom Kippur War on American policy in Cyprus. Very few scholars have linked the Arab–Israeli conflicts to the problem of Cyprus. One of them, Vassilis Fouskas, has argued that the Cyprus crisis of 1974 was a conflict with global dimensions seen in the context of a generalized Middle Eastern situation in which the security and defence of Israel was of paramount importance for the USA. Israel itself was greatly interested in Cypriot affairs, even before the establishment of Cypriot independence in 1960.[1] The third section concentrates on the strategy of Henry Kissinger, then US Secretary of State, in the eastern Mediterranean and the reasoning behind his acquiescence to the Turkish policy of partitioning Cyprus, while the last section analyses the way the Soviet leadership perceived the Cyprus crisis and its eventual settlement.

Apart from published sources, which include the last two volumes of memoirs by Kissinger covering the period from the second administration of Richard Nixon (January 1973) to the electoral defeat of President Gerald Ford in 1976, this chapter uses evidence drawn from US diplomatic papers published in the Foreign Relations of the United States (henceforth FRUS). Some additional material on the Yom Kippur War is drawn from files at the British National Archives.

American Interests in the Eastern Mediterranean and the Middle East

Though many areas were strategically important in the emerging Cold War era, the Eastern Mediterranean was particularly so because of its location astride three continents, its crucially situated waterways and ports, and its proximity to both the Soviet Union and the Middle East. Closely linked to American interests in maintaining the eastern Mediterranean under firm Western control was Washington's protective attitude towards the vast petroleum resources of the Middle East. In the 1970s, European and Japanese dependency upon Middle East oil was well over two-thirds of total consumption, while the Americans imported half their oil – half of which came from the Middle East.[2]

As the old colonial powers were beginning a process of evacuation from this major strategic zone and the Soviets were trying to extend their influence to the south, a new version was recreated of the power vacuum situation that had been the focus of rivalries in the eastern Mediterranean in the nineteenth century. In 1958, John Campbell, a former State Department official, with the help of a study group from the Council on Foreign Relations, published *Defense of the Middle East* – a revealing account of the concern with which the foreign policy establishment viewed trends in the region. The fundamental problem was the Soviet threat to the security, even the survival, of the USA in the face of the global Soviet challenge. As for the Middle East:

> The entrenchment of Soviet power in that strategic region would bring a decisive shift in the world balance, outflanking NATO. Soviet control of Middle Eastern oil could disrupt the economy of the free world. And the triumph of Communism in the heart of the Islamic world could be the prelude to its triumph through Asia, Africa and Europe.[3]

In 1946–1947, the USA established close relations with two key countries in the Eastern Mediterranean, Greece and Turkey, which were already under heavy Soviet military and political pressure. In Greece, a civil war had broken out with the Eastern bloc encouraging and assisting communist guerrillas in the northern part of the country. With regard to Turkey, the Soviets were demanding bases in the Straits in addition to territorial adjustments on the Soviet–Turkish border. The communist uprising in Greece and the Soviet territorial demands on Turkey led the two countries to seek an alignment with the USA through the Truman Doctrine (1947) and their membership of NATO (1952), which marked their military commitment to the West as well as economic dependence.

Greece and Turkey were seen in Washington as a united strategic bloc, an essential part in the US foreign policy notion of a 'Northern Tier'.[4] But Turkey was of far greater geo-strategic importance than Greece. Turkey shared borders with the Soviet Union, was near the Persian Gulf, had strong armed forces and played a crucial role in the Middle East defence system as a member of the Central Treaty Organization (CENTO). For Kissinger:

> Bordering the Middle East, Central Asia, the Soviet Union, and Europe, Turkey was indispensable to American policy in each of these areas. Turkey had been a staunch and loyal ally in the entire Cold War period. Turkish troops had fought with distinction at

our side in Korea. Twenty-six electronic stations were monitoring Soviet missile and space activities from Turkey territory.[5]

When, on the eve of the second Turkish invasion of Cyprus, President Ford asked Kissinger what the USA would do if the Turks proceeded with their military plan, the latter simply replied that 'we certainly do not want a war between the two, but if it came to that, Turkey is more important to us.'[6]

Another important country for the US Middle Eastern policy was Israel. The 'special relationship' between the USA and Israel began to evolve in the second Eisenhower administration and strengthened further after the Six-Day War of 1967, when Washington realized Israel's military prowess and strategic value. Consequently, Israel became the recipient of unprecedented quantities of US arms intended to maintain a favourable balance in the region.[7] In the early 1970s, a more formal US–Israeli link was forged – largely due to the efforts of Henry Kissinger. Kissinger regarded Israel as a strategic asset for the USA in the global struggle against Communism. He presented Israel's interest in holding on to Arab territory and in retaining ascendancy over the Arabs as an American interest to exclude Soviet influence from the Middle East. He therefore managed to marry the USA's global concerns with Israel's local ambitions. This was the fundamental premise of his Middle East thinking when he took control of US foreign policy as National Security Adviser (then also as Secretary of State). As Nixon sank into the Watergate scandal, Kissinger's influence increased, as he became the architect of Washington's new diplomacy, with almost presidential powers.

The October War, Israel, and Cyprus

On 6 October 1973, Egyptian and Syrian troops launched a surprise attack on Israel in an attempt to regain territories occupied by the Jewish state since 1967. Despite its overwhelming military superiority and American military assistance, Israel failed to achieve a rapid victory and suffered heavy losses, which shocked the country and destroyed the myth of its invincibility. Furthermore, Kissinger emerged as the key peace broker in the Middle East, since he was heavily involved in working out the ceasefire of 22 October 1973 and, thereafter, in a series of intense negotiations with the Egyptian and Israeli governments that came to be known as 'step-by-step' or 'shuttle' diplomacy.

The October crisis brought to the surface the divergence between US and European interests and their perspectives on the Arab–Israeli conflict. The

Europeans regarded the war primarily as a regional conflict with potential global implications. As they were almost totally dependent on Middle Eastern oil, the key threat to them was the energy crisis. They conducted a policy of neutrality during the war, and were primarily interested in a rapid end to the fighting, a lasting settlement of the conflict, and an end to the Arab 'oil weapon'. By contrast, Nixon and Kissinger perceived the October War essentially through the prism of the Cold War. Preoccupied with Moscow's expansionist conduct and with the global balance of power, the USA focused on the active protection of Israel and on containment of the Soviet Union.[8]

The Europeans (with the exception of Portugal) refused to facilitate the American airlift and banned American planes from flying over their territories to re-supply Israel. London made it known that it did not want its bases at home or on Cyprus to be used for either the airlift or intelligence collection. It was keen to see a solution to the Arab–Israeli conflict on the basis of the UN Security Council Resolution 242, which challenged both US regional plans and Israel's hegemonic policy in Palestine.[9] Bonn had initially tolerated the airlift, but following the ceasefire, it publicly asked Washington to stop shipments of American equipment to Israel from West German ports using the argument that the Middle East crisis was not a case of common responsibility for the Alliance, and that military supplies to Israel were for purposes which were not NATO's responsibility.[10] The most severe criticism against American policy in the Middle East came from Paris. Michel Jobert, the French Foreign Minister, denounced the USA for not consulting its allies during the Yom Kippur War and for its attempt to monopolize the Middle East settlement, while Europe was left 'a forgotten victim of the conflict [...] more a pawn than an instrument or an asset in the arbitration of the great powers'.[11] What followed was a period of drama in transatlantic relations, marked by a war of words and active US efforts at bringing the Europeans in line with Kissinger's Middle Eastern policy and Washington's leading role within the West. While it was the French who were to blame most for the transatlantic strains, it was the British who became involved in the sharpest exchanges with Washington. James Schlesinger, US Secretary of Defense, accused the Heath government of pursuing a policy of 'decayed Gaullism' and insisted that London could no longer count on the continuation of the special relationship. Heath retorted that Kissinger could not expect the Europeans to fall into step behind him if they disagreed with the substance of his policies. He added that the Americans had long urged the EEC to speak with one voice, but now did not seem ready for it.[12]

Turkey and Greece also denied the USA the use of military bases in their territories. Turkey, in the process of its newly found understanding with the Arab countries and the Soviet Union, allowed Soviet planes to fly over its territory to supply Syria, while denying the USA the right to use its territory to supply Israel. Leaders in Ankara advised the Americans that Incirlik Air Base and other American facilities in the country were available for NATO purposes only; and could not be used for anything to do with the Middle East war. On 11 October, they went public with this position.[13] The Greek military regime, declared itself neutral in the conflict, but this was due to historical, geographical, and commercial links with the Arab states rather than hostility toward Israel. Prime Minister Markezinis stated that 'many ties connect us with Arab countries, but nothing divides us from the state of Israel, which has also the right to have a place under the sun'. A public announcement to this effect was made by Foreign Minister Xanthopoulos-Palamas on 13 October. He stated that 'Greek sea and air space is not being used for any activity whatever related to the state of war in the Middle East and especially against the Arab countries with which Greece maintains good relations'. However, the Greek government secretly cooperated by allowing the USA to use communications facilities in Greece and airports in Athens and Souda Bay in Crete, while no restrictions were placed on the movements or supply of the Sixth Fleet.[14]

The Arab ability to plan, coordinate and execute a successful military attack on Israel and to profoundly disturb the Middle East status quo, Soviet assistance to the Arabs, and Britain's and Turkey's refusal to allow the USA to use Cyprus and the eastern Mediterranean area in an integrated military manner to support Israel, led the Americans to realize the urgency of filling the existing power vacuum in the eastern Mediterranean. As the British were preparing to reduce their forces stationed in Cyprus,[15] and the Soviets were increasing their naval presence in the eastern Mediterranean,[16] in Washington's view Turkey should be allowed, or even encouraged, to reverse the negative balance of power in the region by 'solving' the Cyprus problem in its favour. The American strategic assumption seems to have been that the division of the island would not only satisfy Turkey, which might then attempt to restore its relations with the USA, but, more importantly, would transform the island into a Western carrier serving the security and defence needs of Israel as well as Kissinger's diplomacy in the Middle East. A few days after the second Turkish invasion of Cyprus, Kissinger remarked to State Department senior officials that 'the Turks can give us trouble in the next Middle East war. We have to be careful not to get too far separated from the Turks'.[17]

Like the USA, Israel viewed favourably the emergence of a friendly regime in a Cypriot state that was both geographically proximate (220 miles to the west) and non-Arab. At the same time, it considered ties with the Turks of Cyprus as a means of further enhancing its relationship with Ankara. In February 1961, it managed to establish an embassy in Nicosia by exploiting the Turkish-Cypriot factor against Makarios's pro-Arab stance.[18] However, Turco-Israeli relations began to cool in the mid-1960s, when Ankara decided to break out of the international isolation so clearly manifested in the December 1965 UN vote on Cypriot sovereignty and against 'outside' intervention on the island. As expected, Turkey attempted to improve and expand its relations with the non-aligned countries, especially those in the Middle East. Illustrative of Turkey's new policy in the region was its support for the Palestinians after the 1967 Arab–Israeli war and its pro-Arab stance in the Yom Kippur War.[19] In the summer of 1974 Turco-Israeli relations continued to be tense. But Turkey, like many other countries, had learned to appreciate the technical expertise of the Israelis and wished to continue to benefit from it. According to an Israeli source, Tel Aviv collaborated with Ankara in the invasion of Cyprus by providing arms and technical know-how.[20]

Turkish Territorial Aims and the 'Balance of Forces' in Cyprus

In his last volume of memoirs, Kissinger claims that 'the United States, preoccupied with Watergate, did not believe the situation was approaching a critical point' and that 'no one expected, not even Makarios, the explosion of 15 July'.[21] Kissinger could not predict and therefore could not forestall it. In fact, the State Department had been inundated by reports of an imminent coup against Makarios since March 1974. These reports came from various sources: the Department's Cyprus Country Director Thomas Boyatt,[22] the American Embassies in Greece,[23] Cyprus,[24] and Turkey,[25] even from the Undersecretary of State Joseph Sisco.[26] In early June 1974, Senator William Fulbright, chairman of the Senate Foreign Relations Committee, visited Kissinger and warned him of the junta's intentions. Kissinger rejected Fulbright's suggestion that he should avert the coup by arguing that the USA should not interfere with Greek internal affairs.[27] On 20 June, the head of the military regime Ioannides informed a CIA operative in Athens that Greece had decided to remove Makarios from power.[28] In view of these warnings, the argument that the State Department and Kissinger himself had not been informed about the impending Greek move against Makarios must be dismissed outright. However, the crucial question here is why, in 1974, was there no decisive American initiative to prevent Ioannides's proceeding with a coup on Cyprus, in contrast with 1972 when Henry Tasca, US ambassador to Athens, effectively dissuaded dictator Papadopoulos from a similar course of action? In later years, Kissinger claimed that he did not condemn the coup because of his desire 'to keep Greece in the Alliance and provide Turkey no pretext for invasion'.[29] In fact, Kissinger had no reason to be dissatisfied with the developments in Cyprus. The pro-American Greek military regime had brought Cyprus under its firm control and Makarios, who relied on the local communist party internally and on the Non-Aligned Movement internationally, had been removed. Moreover, the coup provided an ideal opportunity for the Turks to expand their influence in Cyprus and the eastern Mediterranean.[30] In the evening of 15 July, the Turkish Finance Minister, Deniz Baykal, told the National Security Council (NSC) that as a result of détente, the superpowers' reaction to regional crises had changed. Instead of interfering, the superpowers had begun to appease the parties in regional conflicts, and states which took the initiative and created *faits accomplis* were now in more favourable positions. He added: 'the most important aspect of today's coup is not the installation [to power] of Sampson, the murderer of Turks and British, but the inevitability that Greece would soon be our southern neighbour. Greece is about to take this last step. This should be prevented'.

Ecevit supported Baykal's remarks and argued that as a result of the coup, central and southern Anatolia were within range of the Greek air force.[31] These words prove beyond any doubt that the prime motivation of Turkish policy in Cyprus was strategic. If Cyprus was united with Greece, Turkey would be 'encircled'. But if Cyprus was divided, Turkey would block Greece's aspirations in the island while bringing the eastern Mediterranean under Ankara's control.

Officially, the American objectives after the coup were to prevent a war between two NATO allies that would destroy the Alliance's eastern flank and open the way for Soviet penetration in the Mediterranean, and to preserve the existing constitutional structure in Cyprus.[32] According to Kissinger, the USA was opposed to Turkish intervention, but Ecevit 'proved impervious both to American warnings and to the Greek concessions'.[33] However, evidence from US documents seems to imply that although the US administration was aware of Turkey's military plans – the first invasion was widely predicted in newspapers two or three days before and there were reports of Turkish ships moving towards Cyprus – and territorial goals, it was unwilling to intervene with more than diplomacy to influence the course of events as long as peace in the region was not endangered. Thus, Secretary Kissinger refused to comply with suggestions from State Department officials that the US Sixth Fleet be deployed near Cyprus (Tasca) or that UN forces be deployed on the northern shores of Cyprus (Sisco) to indicate American dissatisfaction with Turkey's expected invasion. On the evening of 19 July, Kissinger told Schlesinger that 'if the Turks want a piece of the island then in my view we have to work for *double enosis*[34] and give the Greeks the other part of the island'.[35] An hour later Kissinger discussed Turkey's territorial goals with William Colby, the Director of the CIA:

> *Kissinger*: But what do you think they're after? They're not after the whole island, are they?
> *Colby*: No, no. What they would be after would be Famagusta and Kyrenia and kind of a line between the two [that is the northern third of Cyprus].
> *Kissinger*: That kind of a quadrangle in the north east.
> *Colby*: Yeah. Well, call it almost (inaudible) from roughly Baranaka [Larnaca?] on up and then just assert themselves and give themselves a position to bargain with [...]
> *Kissinger*: Do you have any good ideas what we should do?
> *Colby*: Well, I think the biggest thing is to get the Greeks not to fight. To say all right, let's negotiate and discuss what ought to be done.
> *Kissinger*: OK.[36]

On 10 August, Kissinger told Ford that the Turks might proceed with their plan: 'the Turks want a quick result leading to partition of the island into Greek and Turkish parts with sort of a general federal government [...] They have about 15 per cent and want 30 per cent. They might try to grab it'.[37]

That American officials had prior knowledge of the 'final' line of the Turkish advance is further confirmed by the findings of two Greek-Cypriot journalists, Costas Venizelos and Michalis Ignatiou. In their well-researched study, they claim that a key intelligence map was handed to Kissinger on 13 August detailing the areas the Turkish army intended to occupy in the second phase of the invasion, and that the following day Kissinger's advisor, Helmut Sonnenfeldt, argued that the partition of Cyprus was inevitable: 'assuming the Turks quickly take Famagusta, privately assure Turks we will get them a solution involving one-third of the island with some kind of federal arrangement'.[38] The occupation of a third of the territory of Cyprus, a Turkish aim since the late 1950s,[39] was regarded by the Americans as a means for changing the 'balance of forces' in Cyprus at the expense of Greece. The following discussion in Washington on 21 July is indicative of Kissinger's approach:

> *Kissinger*:   I'm trying to understand what the *balance of forces* [italics added] would be when negotiations start so that we can chart a course.
> *Colby*:   If there is a ceasefire, it would seem to me that the Turkish effort failed. They wanted to seize a substantial area – more than they have now – and they have failed.

And a little later in the same discussion:

> *Kissinger*:   Seems to me that Ecevit is not doing well militarily. They are doing lousy militarily [...] What is going to be *the balance of forces* if we get a ceasefire?
> *Colby*:   The National Guard is doing quite well, they have some 40,000 troops.
> *Schlesinger*:   I don't think we can get an accurate picture of the *balance of forces* because the only thing we have is a ceasefire. They can bring in more troops under a ceasefire, reinforce here and there. That would change the whole picture.
> *Kissinger*:   It is against our interests to have the Greeks in there. *A strong Turkish presence would be highly desirable.*[40]

At the beginning of August 1974, Kissinger described the course he adopted on Cyprus to top officials of the State Department: 'in the early stages of a crisis, it is our responsibility to determine *the balance of forces*, assess the likely evolution and, above all, to shape these factors into a policy that serves the national and public good'.[41] Since the balance of forces had not yet been altered in favour of the Turks, he was not prepared to take any drastic initiative or to sanction or accept military moves by either Greece or Britain to thwart renewed military operations by Turkey, despite the fact that the legitimate leadership of Cyprus had been restored in the person of the then parliamentary speaker Glavkos Clerides. With regard to the Soviet Union, Kissinger and Nixon made every effort to keep it on the sidelines, warning Moscow that the United States 'opposed external interference in the affairs of Cyprus whatever the source'.[42] Thus, faced with no military reaction from West or East and having reinforced its troops on the island since the ceasefire of 22 July, Turkey was allowed to expand its area of control totally unhindered.[43]

Turkey, the Soviet Union, and Détente

President Lyndon Johnson's tough diplomatic intervention in June 1964 against Turkey's planned invasion of Cyprus was the catalyst that prompted Ankara to re-evaluate its foreign policy. Turkey's leaders were forced to recognize that their strict adherence to a pro-Western alignment in a period of a changing international system had left the country virtually isolated in the world community. The process of détente, which slowed down inter-superpower rivalry, also made it possible for small members of alliance systems to have broader relations with the other states disregarding military blocs. In such a fragmented world, Turkey had to improve and expand its relations to the countries of Eastern Europe and the Third World in order to take full advantage of its economic and political potential.

One of the major changes in Turkish foreign policy in the late 1960s was rapprochement with the Soviet Union. Although there had been a movement toward rapprochement with the Soviets as early as 1959 because of economic need, the real thaw in Turkish–Soviet relations started after the 1964 Cyprus crisis and Khrushchev's fall from power in October. In the following years, talks and official visits between Turkey and the Soviet Union increased and the dialogue covered Cyprus and other matters of mutual interest. Turkish exports to and imports from the Eastern bloc expanded rapidly and their share in Turkey's total trade increased from 7 per cent in 1964 to 13 per cent in 1967.[44] In 1967, Premier Süleyman Demirel visited Moscow and the Soviets agreed to build a number of industrial plants in Turkey, including a steel mill, an aluminium smelter, and an oil refinery. By the end of the 1960s, Turkey became the recipient of more Soviet economic assistance than any other Third World country.[45]

For its part, Moscow exhibited a persistent concern with the fate of Cyprus. In addition to being the focal point for Greek–Turkish confrontation, Cyprus was the site of two important British bases, which were of strategic value to NATO. Moscow's key objective was to see these bases closed down. Therefore, it consistently expressed its support for the continuing existence of an independent and non-aligned government in a unified and demilitarized Cyprus. After 1964, it recognized 'the legal rights of the two national communities', which might choose federation as a form of government, but continued to consider Makarios as a legitimate political leader. [46]

The coup against Makarios in July 1974 convinced the Soviet leaders that the military regime in Athens aimed at *enosis*, which would bring Cyprus under the firm control of Greece and thus NATO. The Turkish Ambassador in Moscow met Foreign Minister Andrei Gromyko on 19 and 20 July and informed him of Turkish intentions in Cyprus.[47] The Soviets indicated that they were ready to accept a limited Turkish action provided that Cyprus's military and international status was preserved. When the Turkish invasion took place, they chose to remain silent. For the communist superpower, Turkey was a much larger prize than Cyprus. According to an undated paper prepared in the US State Department on the eve of the second Turkish operation, 'they [the Soviets] were skilful in managing their relations with Ankara during the initial period of the Turkish intervention by maintaining a posture of benevolent neutrality. Strains developed only when Moscow began to suspect that Ankara was seeking partition rather than federation'. During the first Turkish invasion Kissinger sought to coordinate his actions with the Soviets, who asked for American help in the evacuation of their personnel from the island.[48] On 14 August, Kissinger met the Soviet Ambassador to the United States Anatoly Dobrynin and 'told the Soviets to lay off, and they agreed to do nothing'.[49] At the same time, Moscow proposed a joint initiative with the USA which involved a joint guarantee of the outcome of negotiations and joint intervention in the case of war according to the agreement.[50] Throughout the crisis, the Americans were certain that the Soviets would not take any military initiative 'given the NATO alignment and the likely repercussions of Soviet saber-rattling in the absence of a threat to USSR territory'.[51]

Although the most important factor for the Soviet inactivity in the Cyprus crisis was the maintenance of good relations with Turkey, Moscow's stance can also be attributed to its desire to preserve the climate of détente with the USA that had been established in the early 1970s. In 1964, the Soviets had publicly announced that they would defend Cyprus's freedom and independence from a foreign invasion, and warned Turkey that they could not remain indifferent to the threat of an armed conflict near the Soviet Union's southern frontier. However, in 1974, possible gains in the eastern Mediterranean and the Middle East had to be weighed up carefully against the risks of endangering détente. Besides limitations on the arms race and acceptance of existing borders and arrangements in Europe, 'peaceful coexistence' also meant trade and credit from the West.[52]

Conclusion

The author of this chapter does not subscribe to the conspiracy theory that there was a 'back-stage' secret diplomatic activity between Greek, Turkish and US officials under the aegis of the CIA which aimed at the downfall of Makarios and the division of Cyprus between two NATO allies.[53] Kissinger's first concern in the area was to maintain the Western defence-deterrence capability, which required NATO cohesion, the maintenance of US/NATO facilities in the eastern Mediterranean, and Greek–Turkish harmony. The existing evidence leads to the conclusion that Kissinger remained inactive because the coup, and the inevitable invasion which followed, served America's wider interests in the eastern Mediterranean and the Middle East as they were evolved and formulated *after* the Yom Kippur War. The expansion of mainland Turkish control over the island would solve once and for all the Cyprus problem and, more importantly, would maintain the balance of power in the region in favour of NATO and the USA.

Kissinger was reluctant to antagonize Turkey, an ally with a major strategic importance for the USA, and he, therefore, acquiesced to Turkish occupation of a third of Cyprus. As he told President Ford, there was 'no American reason why the Turks should not have one-third of Cyprus'.[54] In order to help Turkey reach its territorial objectives he adopted a 'wait and see' approach and throughout the crisis he remained strongly opposed to a military option to avert the invasion.

Israel was another important regional actor in American foreign policy. The Yom Kippur War showed that Israel could not be defended effectively without the support of friendly and cooperative regimes at its periphery. The strategic importance of Cyprus in that particular conflict brought the rift between Britain and Kissinger to the surface when Makarios and Britain denied the use of bases and their facilities for gathering intelligence. If Cyprus remained strong, independent and non-aligned under the leadership of Makarios, it might put at risk Israel's security and Kissinger's policy planning in the Middle East. By contrast, a divided and weakened Cyprus would be the best way of serving the regional interests of the Western alliance. It would stop local communists from gaining control over key areas of the island's government and keep crucial military facilities available for Western use.

In order to avoid the internationalization of the Cyprus crisis, the USA sought to coordinate its actions with the Soviet Union. Thus, despite declarations of its willingness to protect the Republic of Cyprus from foreign interference, Moscow remained remarkably self-restrained in the period under consideration. Having achieved an understanding with the Turks, it undertook no initiative to stop them and did not condemn the invasions. Other strategic factors that influenced its stance were a fear of Cyprus becoming a NATO stronghold in the eastern Mediterranean after the coup against Makarios, and its emphasis on the continuation of Soviet–US cooperation, not only for bilateral relations, but for world peace and international security.

CHAPTER 11

The Post-Cold War Legacies of US Realism

The 1974 Cyprus Crisis in Perspective

Jan Asmussen

Cyprus: Conspiracy, Realism or Fiasco?

The independent Republic collapsed after the 1963–1964 civil war between Greek and Turkish Cypriots. While the Greek Cypriots retained control of state institutions in the now solely Greek Republic of Cyprus, Turkish Cypriots retired into enclaves, surrounded by Greek-Cypriot troops and observed by the United Nations Peacekeeping Force in Cyprus set up on the island in 1964.

On 15 July 1974, Greek-Cypriot nationalists in cooperation with the Greek National Guard deposed the Greek-Cypriot President Archbishop Makarios III. After the failure of international diplomacy to avert war between the two NATO allies, Turkish troops landed in Cyprus on 20 July. The subsequent confrontation resulted in the partition of the island. The story also involved the United States and Great Britain. The existence of Europe's biggest communist party outside the Soviet Block, the Greek-Cypriot AKEL, a lingering ethnic conflict between Greek and Turkish Cypriots and the presence of a United Nations peace force stationed in Cyprus since 1964, all provided the perfect backdrop for the development of many conspiracy theories.

O'Malley and Craig, for example, argued 'that the Cyprus crisis was no failure of American diplomacy, but a deliberate Cold War plot to divide the island and save the top-secret spying and defence facilities from the twin threats of a communist takeover or British withdrawal.'[1]

But what was really behind the Cyprus crisis of 1974 and what were the principles guiding British, and especially American, policy? In April 1976, the House of Commons Select Committee on Cyprus published its report and asked: 'Why in fact did not Britain intervene?' It concluded, that 'the full truth will never be known unless and until all official papers of the period can be seen.'[2] The 30-years restriction on opening British government files of 1974 has now passed and the papers are available for review. Similarly US files have been released. Newly published research indicates that US and British policy on Cyprus had little to do with organized and carefully planned strategic policy.

The US Government had conflicting evidence about the coup and the CIA was probably misled by the Greek colonels. Britain had no idea when exactly a coup d'etat would take place – but knew that it might come. Neither the USA nor Britain considered intervening on behalf of Makarios. For some hours or days the ambassadors on the ground even thought about acknowledging the coupist Sampson Government. The US Government favoured the replacement of Sampson by Clerides instead of a return of Makarios. British and American intelligence reports revealed knowledge of the objectives of the Turkish military operations in advance. US contingency planning was opposed to 'partitioning' Cyprus since it would continue to form a bone of contention between Greece and Turkey. In the light of the danger of a Greco-Turkish war and its negative repercussions on NATO's southern flank, the Wilson Government was prepared to halt the Turkish advance. As the danger of such a war waned Britain abandoned the idea of intervention altogether. At no point was the US Government prepared to intervene and confront vital NATO allies. Henry Kissinger did not believe in the real danger of a Greco-Turkish war. In addition, he trusted his diplomatic skills to contain the Turks through personal conversations with his 'student' Bülent Ecevit. The US Government convinced the Turks to abandon their aim of partitioning in favour of a cantonal solution. However, the affair – like the entire crisis – was so badly handled that the outcome of the initiative led to rejection by all other parties. All US contingency planning was based on the assumption that the US could contain any conflict in Cyprus *before* it evolved.[3] There was no contingency planning for a failure to do so. In the event, US policy was quickly running out of options and resulted in a terrible failure.[4]

US Foreign Policy in Transition

American foreign policy during the 1974 Cyprus crisis has to be considered against the background of three elements which guided or influenced American conduct – that is, the Nixon Doctrine, the policy of détente and the Watergate affair. Under the Nixon Doctrine, more responsibility for regional security was attributed to local partners of the United States. For the Eastern Mediterranean, this meant that Turkey was regarded as the most vital ally in the region. Its continued allegiance to US international strategic goals was the main aim of US foreign policy-making in the region. Secondly, Greece was seen as an important element in the security puzzle in the Levant. In order to remain in line with US interests, the Nixon administration turned a blind eye to human rights violations there. However, if there were to be a conflict between Greece and Turkey the US would back the more important partner, Turkey. Cyprus did not play an important part in this American strategy. It was basically seen as a bone of contention between Greece and Turkey. As long as both were satisfied with the situation on the island – the United States would be fine with whatever happened there as well.

The aim of this chapter is to bring the Cyprus crisis of 1974 into the assessment of US international relations during the Nixon administration and to attempt to analyse the long-term effects the crisis had on US foreign policy-making. The guiding question here is whether the Cyprus crisis can be seen in the framework of the Nixon Doctrine and the policy of détente. Was the Cyprus crisis special because it coincided with the final phase of Watergate? Are there any parallels with other conflicts of that time? Moreover, did the experience of Kissinger's handling of the crisis affect the general outlook of American politicians on international relations? Another issue to be tackled is the question of whether the roots for contemporary neoconservatism can be found in the disputes that surrounded Kissinger's foreign policy-making.

The Nixon Doctrine and Détente

To many observers it came as a surprise when Richard Nixon chose Henry Kissinger as his National Security Advisor. Kissinger had at first considered Nixon as 'the most dangerous, of all men running, to have as President,'[5] and Nixon was on record for his unwillingness to share foreign policy decisions with anyone. He said that he had 'always thought this country could run itself domestically without a President. All you need is a competent Cabinet to run the country at home. You need a President for foreign policy; no Secretary of State is really important; the President makes foreign policy'.[6] However, the Nixon–Kissinger relationship turned out to be a fruitful one. Subsequently, Kissinger served in both the Nixon and Ford administrations as National Security Advisor from January 1969, and as Secretary of State from September 1973 to January 1977.

Kissinger was a brilliant academic and expert in international relations, but he lacked an understanding of the fragile relationship between the White House and Congress. The squabbles of domestic policy and the importance of reassurance for foreign policy measures remained largely out of his sight. Personalization, concealment and concentration of power in the White House replaced cooperation with Congress and other government agencies. Nearly all parts of the foreign political machinery of the United States government were excluded from the decision-making process.[7] As seen in the case of Cyprus, foreign policy-making was mainly confined to the White House and Kissinger's inner circle of advisers. Coral Bell described the Department of State's long decline as the primary policy-maker, a decline that 'began with the McCarthyite attack of the early 1950s and Mr Dulles's failure to resist it.'[8]

Kissinger, upon his promotion in September 1973, did not use his abilities to reform the State Department or to strengthen it. Instead, he continued to bypass foreign policy experts and relied on his own wisdom and that of his few advisers. The new China policy mentioned below was the first, but not the only, example of how American foreign policy was carried out without consulting the main professional agency designed for this purpose.

On 25 July 1969, President Nixon, during a news conference on Guam, redefined the new foreign political foundations of the USA as a Pacific power. In what was later to be known as the Nixon Doctrine, he declared a shift from an era of confrontation to one of negotiation that would lead to a new order of peace. The Nixon Doctrine narrowed the term 'American interest' and suggested that more engagement on behalf of its allies should soften the responsibilities of the United States.[9] It constituted a fundamental shift in US foreign policy. The new line redefined America's role in world politics and departed from the principle of global moral commitment as defined by Truman and Kennedy. Instead, it declared that America could not vouch for the defence of the entire free world. It could only help if this help was indispensable and in the interests of the United States. This new strategy meant that United States world policy would, in future, concentrate on areas that were vital to America's role as a world power. Nixon listed Europe, in particular, and those countries which depended on the protection of America's nuclear shield. The countries which Nixon regarded as of marginal importance would have to rely on their own means of protection of security and independence, and could only expect limited American aid. Thus, the Nixon Doctrine was designed for emergencies that were not covered by alliance agreements and were not at the heart of world politics.[10] Kissinger described this by saying that the principal challenge of a new administration and the American people was that of 'relating our commitments to our interests and our obligations to our purposes.'[11]

The first country subject to this policy shift was Vietnam.[12] Nixon and Kissinger were determined to reduce the American commitment especially as they were realistic enough to understand that America would not be able to win.[13] Following the conclusion of the Vietnam agreement, Nixon had indeed reached the climax of his popularity. His foreign policy had strengthened the United States' role towards former enemies, and after years of domestic polarization and strife the agreement promised to bring about external and internal stability. In fact, the agreement contained the nucleus for the South Vietnamese defeat in 1975. It legalized the presence of North Vietnamese troops in the South, leaving a 'Trojan horse' that would inevitably lead to further military confrontation. Thus the agreement was nothing but a fig leaf for American withdrawal.[14]

However important the policy shift on Vietnam was, the main rationale for the Nixon Doctrine was the conviction that the USSR had reached equality in the atomic arms race. Thus, the policy of deterrence had become ineffective.[15]

The idea of détente between the superpowers had originated during the Kennedy and Johnson administrations. However, the implementation of its main principles came in the Nixon era. Nixon and Kissinger's new policy, which became known as 'realist', departed from the global-democratic approach founded by Wilson and developed by Roosevelt. Worldwide democratization, as defined by Wilson, ceased to be the method to secure world peace. Instead, the old European concept of preservation of the balance of power between leading nations was reintroduced. Kissinger's preferred tool for this new policy was the linking of several issues into a package that would enable compromises.[16] 'The challenge of our time,' he said, 'is to reconcile the reality of competition with the imperative of coexistence.'[17]

Opponents of Kissinger accused him of trying to appease the Soviet Union and of accepting the situation in Eastern Europe. Kissinger developed what Litwak termed an 'enlightened policy of the possible.'[18] He countered criticism that his policy was immoral by asserting that peace was probably the most important moral goal.[19] Litwak has questioned whether the Nixon–Kissinger foreign policy was actually a fundamental re-evaluation of American foreign policy or just a readjustment in the face of new realities i.e. the emergence of the Soviet Union as a fully-fledged global military power.[20] Litwak's evaluation has its merits, but fails to see that the nuclear dimension had resulted in a policy of realism differing sharply from Truman's containment policy. Instead of containing communist advance wherever it emerged, Nixon and Kissinger defined areas of interest in which the United States would actively challenge the Soviet Union and others in which they would abstain. In terms of internal policy, Cyprus certainly belonged to the second category.

The strategic significance of Cyprus to the United States must be seen in the broader context of United States' strategy for the Eastern Mediterranean. US military installations on the island were far less important than those in Turkey and Greece. In addition, the conflict on Cyprus included two NATO 'partners', but the Soviet Union was not involved. The communist AKEL was under the firm grip of the conservative Makarios. Subsequently, the USA would have accepted any solution that did not endanger NATO's southern flank and kept out the Soviet Union. The aim of keeping out the Soviets is the main parallel to the Yom Kippur War. The principal difference is that the Soviets did not make any attempt to be part of it in the first place. Thus, as far as the Nixon Doctrine was concerned, the responsibility for Cyprus remaining in the Western sphere rested in the hands of Greece and Turkey. This turned out to be a dangerous gamble and might have led to a serious weakening of NATO in the region. Kissinger might have taken a more determined stance if the Soviet Union had shown more interest.

Watergate, Cyprus and Growing Opposition to Kissinger's 'Realism'

One major element hindering effective policy-making during the Cyprus crisis was the negative effect Watergate had on the efficiency of decision-making in Washington.[21] Not only did Watergate absorb much of the Nixon administration's time which could have been spent on policy-making, but it also seriously damaged trust in the administration's abilities on the part of Congress and the press. One of the tragicomic features of Watergate was that Nixon had abandoned uncritical anti-Communism in American foreign policy, but at the same time was obsessed with the existence of domestic communist conspiracies. He believed himself to be entangled between two fronts: external against North Vietnam and internal against communist conspirators, who would try to overthrow the United States and its traditional values. In his eyes, the USA was surrounded by external enemies and infiltrated by internal ones. Press and TV were cooperating with 'enemies of the state'.[22] The tax reports of government critics were double-checked by White House inspectors to discover irregularities. A whole chain of criminal acts was set in motion, which culminated in the burglary of the Democratic headquarters at the Watergate Hotel. It was the result of Nixon's paranoia, which originated in his fear for the survival of American morals, freedom and pride.[23] The Nixon administration tried to distract public opinion from Watergate by taking a determined stance on foreign political issues. Nixon's rhetoric during the energy crisis that followed Yom Kippur in 1973 was already influenced by Watergate. He pictured himself as a determined leader as he announced a national emergency. While Kissinger and Nixon had moderated the American people's fears regarding the Soviet Union and China, they now exaggerated the threat of a communist take-over in Italy and Portugal.[24] Watergate almost totally absorbed Nixon's attention during the greater part of his last year in office. Kissinger had more responsibility than ever, but often less leeway. As détente came under fire from a large, and strong, group of opponents, Kissinger could not enjoy his newly acquired freedom.[25] In fact, he came under suspicion himself. During his confirmation hearings Kissinger was queried on his role in an earlier White House order for the FBI to wiretap some of his own staff.[26] The repercussions of this wiretap controversy hit Kissinger at a sensitive time. Shortly before the Moscow summit meeting in June 1974, and just after his return in triumph from the successful negotiations on disengagement in the Middle East, Kissinger was dismayed to be assailed at his first news conference in Salzburg, Austria, on June 11 and threatened to resign unless 'innuendos' regarding the wiretapping were cleared up.[27] On July 12, Nixon finally wrote to Senator William J. Fulbright that the responsibility for wiretapping the White House officials was entirely his, and the committee cleared Kissinger.[28] This clearance did not change the fact that Kissinger's relations with congress were severely damaged by Watergate.[29]

Another blow to Kissinger's foreign policy-making was struck by the 1973 Cooper–Church amendments. The Congress made amendments to the Department of Defense Procurement and Development Act that prohibited the use of American ground troops in Laos, Thailand and Cambodia without congressional approval. It was the first time in American history that Congress restricted the deployment of troops during a war and voted against the wishes of a president.[30] Before the end of that year, Congress passed a law preventing American troops from returning to Vietnam, and signalled its intent to hold trade relations with the Soviet Union subject to Soviet performance in human rights issues, specifically the freedom of Soviet Jews to emigrate.[31]

Kissinger reacted to the atmosphere of paranoia that emerged during Watergate by casting himself as a heroic loner.[32] As Bell put it, Kissinger's 'rather abrasive relationships with the foreign-office bureaucracy in the State Department and the intelligence community probably owed something to this self-image.'[33] Kissinger's paranoia regarding leaks to the press and the workings of State Department officials against him cannot only be attributed to the repercussions of Watergate. Kissinger's uneasy relationship with the intellectual foreign policy elite in America did not help either.[34]

The American liberal establishment had enthusiastically supported the war in Vietnam and was now utterly disillusioned with the outcome. Kissinger, who had been rather sceptical about the entire affair from the outset, was now to arrange the withdrawal of American forces. The 'guilty disillusionment' among American intellectuals after 1968 severely damaged Kissinger's own standing with the establishment.[35]

Another blow to Kissinger's ability to conduct US foreign policy came from Senator Henry M. 'Scoop' Jackson, who was aspiring to the presidency and had consistently combined a liberal stand on many domestic issues with a hard-line anti-Soviet position, and now stepped up his campaign against SALT.[36] Moscow finally renounced the 1972 bilateral trade agreement in January 1975 amidst angry charges that the Jackson–Vanik Amendment constituted an unprecedented attempt by the United States to interfere in the internal affairs of the Soviet Union.[37] Congress had thereby virtually destroyed a vital element of Kissinger's linkage policy: the ethics of ideology had triumphed over that of reason.[38]

Whatever the repercussions of Watergate on foreign policy may have been, Kissinger could still have pictured himself as a successful Secretary of State. The Cyprus crisis altered even that image, marking a major defeat for Kissinger.[39] Together with Watergate, Cyprus had a devastating effect on Kissinger's ability to conduct foreign policy. His failure to prevent division of the island was now seen as the result of an entirely false and immoral approach to foreign policy regarding Greece and Turkey. The Nixon and Kissinger posture towards Greece followed the rationale of 'containment' by supporting authoritarian regimes to maintain regional stability. The Johnson administration had bridged the dilemma of wanting to support the Greek junta despite fierce domestic opposition, by withholding shipments of important arms such as planes and tanks while allowing other military aid to continue. Nixon changed this policy by aiming to remove even the appearance of disapproval of the Greek military regime.[40] Kissinger met with Greek Foreign Minister Panayotis Pipinelis on 11 April 1969 and informed him that the Nixon administration would change American policy by removing all restrictions and bringing an end to any political pressure on the junta. Kissinger said that 'he could report categorically that the policy of the President is for the United States not to involve itself in the political affairs of other countries, but to concern itself only with the foreign policy of another country.'[41] The Nixon administration continued to invoke 'overriding requirements of national security of the United States' to legally bypass congressional prohibitions on the sale of arms to Athens.[42] For Kissinger, Greece's strategic position, American military installations in that country, and Soviet presence in the Eastern Mediterranean were 'ample justifications for this waiver'.[43] In the light of the Nixon administration's indifference towards human rights in Greece, there can be no doubt that the Greek colonels expected little objection as they went ahead with their Cyprus adventure. Their mistake was the failure to appreciate that there was a power regarded by Washington as even more important to regional stability – Turkey. There is not much to suggest that Washington would have bothered to interfere if Greece had tried to strike a deal with the Turks about Cyprus before turning against Makarios. Stoessinger has rightly argued that 'Kissinger, beset with the problem of the Middle East and besieged by Watergate, dealt with Cyprus cavalierly and haphazardly, alienating both Greece and Turkey.'[44] In addition, he had 'thought that his telephonic persuasion [of Ecevit] and a bit of luck had saved the situation.'[45]

Détente had not only reduced the dangers of a global war, but it also diminished the amount of pressure a superpower could exert on one of its allies. It is questionable whether a stronger stance by Kissinger, first against the Greek colonels and later, against Ecevit, might have resulted in any other behaviour.

Following the crisis, Kissinger saw himself as confronted with a hostile Congress which insisted on cutting off military aid to Turkey. The Greek lobby often aligned itself with the pro-Israeli lobby, which was anxious about the possibility that Kissinger would sell out Israeli interests in order to secure peace in the Middle East. Finally, there were those among the Democrats who hoped to run successfully for presidential nomination, and saw a chance to gain credit in attacking the 'immoral' politics of the Secretary. Kissinger chose to fight Congress on the issue of the arms embargo and lost. The arms embargo resulted in the temporary loss of twenty-six American monitoring bases in Turkey, the vital function of which was related to monitoring the growth and alert status of Soviet missile forces. As such, they were an important element in the vast invisible net of mutual surveillance on which the maintenance of the SALT agreements depended. Congress's action in imposing the ban, which moved the Turks to reduce their military effectiveness and threatened NATO's southeastern flank future, was obviously some strategic bonus or 'windfall gain' for the Soviet Union.[46]

As the United States entered the 1976 presidential election year, détente and Kissinger's diplomacy came under increasingly severe attack from both ends of the American political spectrum. To right-wing opponents of Administration policy, détente had long been viewed as a 'one-way street' tantamount to 'appeasement'.[47] Ronald Reagan managed to insert a deliberate snub to Kissinger's détente policy into the party programme at the Republican convention of 1976. The goal of Republican foreign policy was defined as one that would recognize the tyranny of the Soviet Union and called for unilateral favours not to be granted in the pursuit of détente.[48] On the orthodox left of American politics, liberals (primarily in the Democratic Party) claimed Kissinger's diplomacy was inconsistent with the core values that US foreign policy had traditionally sought to protect.[49] They advocated the eschewal of *Realpolitik* in favour of adopting a new foreign policy agenda embracing such concerns as human rights and the North–South dialogue.[50]

Criticism from both quarters was often cast into the form of moral reproach. The accusation of 'having no values' normally meant 'not adhering to my values', whether those values are of the left or right.[51] Kissinger defended himself by emphasising fundamental cultural differences between the United States and others. 'A legitimate order', he said, 'is merely an order accepted by all its major members; it does not imply adhering to a common constitutionality or ideology and it should not be confused with justice'.[52] Moreover, Kissinger stressed that the realities of the Cold War necessitated a quest for stability that would ensure peace.[53]

While he accepted the importance of freedom, Kissinger insisted that moral callousness would not achieve the proclaimed goals. Instead, American foreign policy should aim for more realistic achievements such as the preservation of human life and society.[54]

He saw himself in the tradition of great statesmen like Metternich who did not achieve final greatness 'through resignation', but by having 'the strength to contemplate chaos, there to find material for fresh creation.'[55] He claimed that the 'test of a statesman is his ability to recognise the real relationship of forces and to make this knowledge serve his ends.'[56]

Moral attacks on US foreign political conduct were not confined to the Nixon Doctrine and détente, but called into question the entire philosophy of 'containment' since Truman. One of the most criticized elements of the Nixon Doctrine was the resulting support for right-wing dictators and enforced order to achieve containment and stability. The United States had increased its arms sales and overall support for a number of nations, such as Indonesia, Greece, Iran, and the Congo, despite domestic criticism of these regimes. Moreover, containment and the establishment of order in Latin America were considered especially vital to the Nixon Doctrine and American national security.[57]

The Senate Select Committee on Intelligence, or Church Committee, proved that the United States had been involved in the overthrow of governments in Iran, Guatemala, Congo, Chile, and other countries, and had attempted to assassinate foreign rulers.[58] The Committee's report concluded that US policy was still based on the same assumptions that had led America into the Vietnam War.[59] It recommended better statutory guidelines for the intelligence community and control over 'excessive and at times self-defeating use of covert action' and called for a ban on assassinations and the subversion of democratically elected governments.[60]

The first immediate impact of the Church Committee on American foreign policy-making came in December 1975 as the Senate voted to block military expenditure in the former Portuguese colony of Angola.[61] Despite failure in Angola the Ford administration continued its support for right-wing dictatorships if their perseverance was regarded as vital to American interests. Ford openly consented to Indonesia's capture of East Timor in December 1975 in order to stabilize the Suharto regime.[62]

The long-term effect of Watergate was a deep distrust of any White House or State Department activities on behalf of Congress. Henry Kissinger's policy of 'realism' – long regarded as having eternal wisdom – was now seen as immoral and un-American. Critiques from the left and right of the American political spectrum called for a new moral foundation on which the United States should build its dealings with other countries. This shaped the rhetoric of Carter's presidency – albeit not its real conduct when vital US interest were concerned. The Carter administration, contrary to its proclaimed emphasis on human rights, did not totally depart from the idea of relying on local powers instead of direct American involvement. The Iranian Revolution in 1979 marked the end of the Nixon Doctrine era with its emphasis upon the role of preponderant local powers.[63] This event constituted the greatest American foreign policy setback since the collapse of South Vietnam. Under the Nixon Doctrine, increased reliance on regional middle powers in the performance of vital functions (in Iran's case, maintaining access through the Strait of Hormuz) had the net effect of placing Washington, in its role as principal weapons supplier, in the precarious position of being dependent on the survival of particular regimes.[64] Moreover, the long-term operation of such a client system was contingent upon the existence of a close correspondence (if not actual congruence) of interests between the regional actor and the United States.[65] The Iranian Revolution marked the end of the Nixon Doctrine era of American reliance on regional surrogates.[66]

On the conservative side, Ronald Reagan engaged in a moral crusade against the Soviet Union, claiming to set new moral standards for international conduct. In this he was supported by the neoconservatives, a group originating in and around the Democratic Party, whose members were disillusioned with the outcomes of détente and realism. The neoconservatives formed alliances with more traditional, but anti-realist conservatives, like Dick Cheney and Donald Rumsfeld. This new alliance would later build the backbone of George W. Bush's support for the Iraq War in 2003.

Realism and Neoconservatism

The downfall of the realist approach had an immediate effect on US foreign policy. It brought back an outward moralist approach that was coupled with human rights rhetoric during both the Carter and Reagan administrations. Moreover, it had a long-term effect on the development of international relations theory.

Different international relations theories emerged in reaction to Kissinger's traditionalist conservative realism. Kissinger was neither a liberal nor did he follow the path that American conservatism took in the late twentieth century. Bell has emphasized that in the contemporary foreign-policy debate in America, the name 'conservative' has been pre-empted by the right-wing sector of opinion he qualifies as 'simplistic nationalism'. While this form of conservatism was represented by Ronald Reagan and his followers, and transformed later into neoconservatism, Kissinger's conservatism can be termed 'traditionalist conservatism'.[67] Given the origins of the movement in left-wing anticommunism, it is not surprising that neoconservatives would, for the most part, end up opposing the realist foreign policy of Henry Kissinger during the 1970s. Realism, as defined in international relations theory, begins with the premise that all nations, regardless of regime, struggle for power. Realism can at times become relativistic and cynical about regimes; realists by and large do not believe that liberal democracy is a potentially universal form of government or that the human values underlying it are necessarily superior to those underlying non-democratic societies. Indeed, they tend to warn against crusading democratic idealism, which in their view can become dangerously destabilizing

Fukuyama emphasized the personal legacy that opposition to Kissinger's realism had on supporters of the Reagan administration. Walter Wohlstetter, Paul Wolfowitz, Richard Perle, Henry M. Jackson, and Paul Nitze would fall into this category.[68]

One of the most vigorous supporters of a merging of neoconservative and more traditional conservative policies in the George W. Bush administration was Donald Rumsfeld, who had already served in the Nixon and Ford administrations. While originally not totally opposed to détente, he increasingly turned against it as Defense Secretary under President Ford (1975–77). He had only played a minor role during the Cyprus crisis as he was the US ambassador to the NATO council. In 1976, he helped to set up the so-called Team B that claimed that the United States had lost out against the Soviet Union during détente. In 1997, he signed, alongside Dick Cheney, Francis Fukuyama, and 22 mainly neoconservative intellectuals, the 'Statement of Principles' of the 'Project of the New American Century' which called for a return to 'the essential elements of the Reagan Administration's success: a military that is strong and ready to meet both present and future challenges; a foreign policy that boldly and purposefully promotes American principles abroad; and national leadership that accepts the United States' global responsibilities'. Therefore, the United States should have increased defence spending significantly and modernized its armed forces; strengthened its ties with democratic allies and challenged regimes hostile to American interests and values; promoted the cause of political and economic freedom abroad; and accepted responsibility for America's unique role in preserving and extending an international order friendly to its security, prosperity, and principles.[69]

Fukuyama has since departed from his original support of neoconservatism that, as he claims, 'was based on a set of coherent principles that during the Cold War yielded by and large sensible policies both at home and abroad'.[70] The realist and neoconservative positions were defined partly in opposition to each other during the Cold War, and both were inadequate to the world that was emerging in the twenty-first century.[71] He calls for a 'a more realistic Wilsonianism' that differs from classical realism 'by taking seriously as an object of US foreign policy what goes on inside states'.[72]

Richard Falk has tried to revise the Westphalian world order according to the needs of the twenty-first century. He sensed that, against the background of Machiavelli, Hobbes, and Clausewitz, the prevailing view of international society has been one in which the role of law and morality has been marginal in relation to statecraft.[73] To the extent that stability and order produce 'peace', it arises from the capable and prudent management of relative power, and not from norms of law and morality. He argued that the Cold War managed to stifle thinking about alternative world orders based on the centralization of authority over nuclear arms.[74] However, there are several types of actor, or transformative agent, pushing consciousness and perceptions beyond Westphalian categories: there are global corporations and banks that conceive the world as a marketplace for production, consumption, and investment; there are the transnational actors of civil society who conceive the world as a human community in which the needs and basic rights of all persons are upheld; there are transnational networks of extremists animated by post-Westphalian visions of community (for instance, the Islamic *umma*); and there is a global state that projects power, and claims to exercise authority with limited deference of sovereign boundaries. These transformative agents seek alignment with governments and popular movements, and each exerts a measure of influence.[75] Falk defined four post-Westphalian dead ends as being the global marketplace, world government, the global village, and global empire.[76] Successful management of these fields could lead, as he concluded, to a:

> Future [that] can evolve positively either as a new stage of a fundamentally Westphalian world of sovereign states or as 'the moment' when regionalism and globalism provide political communities with their security and identity to such an extent that it would be appropriate to label as post-Westphalian the new reality.[77]

Kissinger himself contributed to the discussion of American diplomacy for the twenty-first century, which can well be regarded as his political testament. Kissinger evidently continued to feel at ease with his realist convictions and translated them into a form suitable to the new century. He described American self-perception as being 'both the source and guarantor of democratic institutions around the globe'.[78] He quoted the example of the Balkans where the United States was 'performing essentially the same functions as did the Austrian and Ottoman Empires at the turn of the century, of keeping peace by establishing protectorates interposed between warring ethnic groups'.[79] Kissinger sensed that this foreign policy-making was confined to a tiny group of professionals while the American interest in foreign policy was at an all-time low.[80] For him, American actions were based on the assumption that 'the United States needed no long-range foreign policy at all and could confine itself to a case-by-case response to challenges as they arise'.[81]

Realism in the Twenty-first Century

It remains unclear where American foreign policy will ultimately turn. The American-led humanitarian intervention in Bosnia-Herzegovina in 1995 cannot be explained by the end of the Cold War alone. It would have been unthinkable without the official shift from realism to morality that set in after the Cyprus crisis. The principle of non-intervention was set aside, citing the overriding value of human rights. However, as many contemporary cases of non- or belated intervention show, the principle of American self-interest remained in place after the end of the Kissinger era. The rhetoric and actions of the Obama administration appear to lie somewhere between Fukuyama's 'Realistic Wilsonianism' and Falk's 'post-Westphalian new reality.' Whatever the outcome, realism appears to persist as the driving force of US policy and goes far beyond its Cold War origins.

CHAPTER 12

The Fact-finding Missions of the Socialist International in the Middle East, 1974–1976

Political Networking in Europe's Policy Towards the Middle East in the 1970s[1]

Oliver Rathkolb

This chapter explores the functionality of a specific political network in the context of the Middle East conflict resolution efforts between 1973 and 1983. At its core the nucleus of this network consisted of two social democratic politicians: Willy Brandt, chancellor of the Federal Republic of Germany between 1969 and 1974 and Socialist International (SI) president between 1976 and 1992,[2] Bruno Kreisky, Austria's federal Chancellor between 1970 and 1983. Nahum Goldmann, founder and president of the World Jewish Congress 1948–1977 joined the professional politicians temporarily. Previous studies have underlined the importance of the 'triumvirate' of the Socialist International Brandt–Kreisky–Palme[3] but even biographical accounts[4] have left the dense mesh of relations that developed between these protagonists largely untouched. This is not to say that these three did not also form close personal relationships outside the triumvirate with other high-ranking SI members and – as will be shown – with outside networkers like Nahum Goldmann. Brandt for instance made it repeatedly clear that François Mitterrand was as close to him as either Kreisky or Palme.[5] The fact that especially Brandt and Kreisky included other personalities temporarily into their network has so far been completely neglected both by political science and contemporary history. They both included outside political actors in their networking strategies.

What was unique about those two politicians, however, was the high reciprocity of their mutual esteem and political affinity. They themselves tried in an early publication to draw attention to the symbolic significance of their collaboration.[6] For them the SI functioned as an institutionalized transnational network of networks of social democratic and socialist parties and movements, whose tradition dates back to the Second International created in Paris in 1889. It is the functions of this personal network that this chapter will explore in greater detail. In order to be effective both Brandt and Kreisky opened the political network to outside personalities as non-state political actors such as Goldmann.

Policy Entrepreneurs in Track II Diplomacy
Especially Brandt and Kreisky made use of the SI network as a basis to enhance their activities as policy entrepreneurs both in a European and a global context. The concept of the policy entrepreneur, which was originally conceived within the framework of operations research, is also applicable to political processes of decision-making: 'Policy entrepreneurs advocate new ideas and develop proposals, define and reframe problems; specify policy alternatives; broker the ideas among the many political actors; mobilize public opinion; help set the decision making agenda'.[7] In what follows below this approach will be linked to a model of conflict resolution that was proposed in 1981 by the US diplomat Joseph V. Montville and that has undergone further theoretical refinement since then.[8] This approach, which is embedded in debates on applied political psychology, explores what potential informal contacts outside the channels of inter-state diplomacy and negotiations at governmental level ('track II') may bring to conflict resolution as inter-state diplomacy ('track I'). Track II diplomacy played a key role in debates centring on the Middle East conflict. This had to do with the fact that US Secretary of State Henry Kissinger had declared contacts with the Palestinian Liberation Front (PLO) inadmissible by 1975 and that most west European member states of the European Communities (EC) toed the line regarding this marginalization strategy, at least initially.

Track II diplomatic contacts, which may involve government representatives in addition to civil society opinion leaders, aim to develop a shared appreciation of the problems at hand through intensive talks and to get to know the perspective of the other side in greater detail. A basic distinction is made between 'soft track II' talks[9] and 'hard track II' talks. The primary objective of the former is to provide opportunities for getting to know the representatives of the other side and for establishing an atmosphere of trust; the latter set the scene in more concrete terms for track I negotiations. The overall aim of track II diplomacy is to recast the shared traumatized perceptions of the conflict as a problem that affects both sides and that in principle is capable of resolution.

For the moment it still remains to be seen whether it will be possible to establish a more direct link between the three political protagonists mentioned above and the development and wording of EC policy decisions regarding the Middle East. It has to be borne in mind in this context that Brandt was involved in EC decision making only for part of the period under discussion, namely until the end of his chancellorship in 1974, and that he must be considered a non-state actor after that date. In the case of Kreisky, who was in power throughout the period in question, it is important to remember that he represented a neutral state that was not a member of the EC at the time – as opposed to West Germany. At the same time he was also active in the framework of the SI, which enabled him to cooperate closely with social democrats in EC countries. In addition to this, there were connections to a category of networks, which, as international commissions, were both only temporary in character on the one hand and on the other, distinguished by a high profile owing to their highly publicized agendas.[10] In a broader sense Bernd Faulenbach has even characterized the 1970s as a social democratic decade.[11] Brandt and Kreisky made intensive use of these informal networks: Brandt as the head of the Independent Commission on International Development Issues founded in 1977, which presented its report, 'A Programme for Survival', to the Secretary General of the United Nations (UN) in 1980; and Kreisky – at Brandt's instigation – as co-chairman of the first North-South Summit in Cancún in 1981.[12] In this article I will focus on the Middle East policy arena despite the fact that the three policy entrepreneurs were also active in such fields as North–South issues and détente policies.

In addition to the good chemistry between these two politicians, the SI network in a broader sense also required clear assignments of tasks and responsibilities.[13] Mitterrand was to address himself to human rights issues, which he did until he was elected President of France in 1981; Palme, the committed critic of the Vietnam War, was to be in charge of the anti-apartheid strategy in regard to South Africa from 1977, and Kreisky was to focus on the Middle East conflict from 1974. Brandt's assignment included above all Latin America and North–South issues. The Spanish socialist Felipe González, who became prime minister in 1982, was never more than a potential candidate to be coopted to the group of SI policy entrepreneurs should the need arise but he did take part in the ineffectual mission to free the American hostages in Iran in May 1980.[14] Gro Harlem Brundtland, Norway's first female prime minister, was another member of that kind of B team from 1981; this team was never as closely knit as the Brandt–Kreisky–Palme triumvirate, however. Despite the fact that the SI was primarily an informal forum for ideological debate, the three social democrats succeeded through the use of media and other communication channels in having an impact on the setting of political agendas. Public perception of the triumvirate's effectiveness was such that the Christian democratic and conservative parties felt compelled to reorganize at the European level, one of the direct consequences of the 'close dialogue between the three socialist statesmen as well as the then Socialist dominance in the European parliament'.[15]

Brandt and Kreisky belonged to the same generation and had been driven from their home countries by National–Socialism – Brandt for political reasons, Kreisky above all because of his Jewish descent. Both had been active in the International Group of Democratic Socialists in Stockholm between 1942 and 1945 alongside sixty other socialists from twelve different countries.[16] In 1958 and 1959 Kreisky tried repeatedly to initiate talks between the mayor of Berlin, Willy Brandt, his close friend from the days of their Swedish exile, and the Soviet leadership but was held back by US interventions and Brandt's personal reserve. Kreisky was more successful as a political communicator in his passing on of confidential assessments from sources in the Soviet Union and in communist satellite states, to which he appended his interpretations and analyses, to the USA and other Western countries.

In the 1960s the two pooled their resources to found the Wiener Institut für Entwicklungsfragen,[17] which was designed to raise public awareness of North–South issues. Consistent with Bruno Kreisky's social democratic beliefs (as was clearly apparent during his tenure as Foreign Minister in the early 1960s) he actively involved himself in the process of decolonization, the struggle of the former colonies in the Southern hemisphere for independence and the considerable economic and social problems faced by those newly independent states. In the first years of his time as Foreign Minister he met prominent leaders of those new states for talks. Among them were politicians like Pandit Nehru, Kwame N'krumah, and Ahmed Ben Salah, among others. Long before the general public in Austria had become aware of the scale of the problems of development policy, and also of their potential global political impact, Bruno Kreisky recognized the need to give long-term support to the newly independent states' socio-economic development. In the end Austria actually benefited in various ways from its political support for these states, for instance, from the decision of the UN General Assembly to make Vienna the third UN seat, and from the appointment of the Austrian Kurt Waldheim as UN Secretary-General. In the early 1960s, first in a speech to diplomats in Salzburg in 1963 and in the following year at the first world trade conference (UNCTAD) in Geneva, Kreisky proposed a 'New Marshall Plan' for the Third World. By this and a whole range of other political activities and initiatives he won Austria a good reputation among the young states of the Third World. In the end, however, because major questions about financing and political aims were not resolved, the Western states did not even begin to implement the 'New Marshall Plan' – not even at the time of the global economic crisis between 1973–1974 and the early 1980s, when Kreisky strongly urged the view that a programme of that kind would have the added effect of compensating for the low demand for the products of the industrialized countries, thus leading to a new worldwide economic upturn. Finally, it has to be said that even in the economically and politically euphoric first phase of his period as chancellor (1970–1974) Kreisky did not succeed in providing sufficient Austrian state budgetary resources for development cooperation to have a significant impact. There was too little public support, and above all such ideas did not meet with a positive response from the 'social partners' in the neo-corporatist domestic political system who at that time wielded great political influence.

After Palme became the leader of Sweden's Social Democratic Party in 1969,[18] he joined Brandt and Kreisky; the triumvirate was now in place for the intensive debate of burning global issues and for the joint search for solutions. An excellent example of the extended network that the three protagonists were able to rely on is Austrian industrialist Karl Kahane. Kahane and Kreisky had been on friendly terms since the 1960s. Kahane had been driven into exile in Palestine during World War II. After the war he and his father devoted all their energy to reversing the 1938 'Aryanization' of the family's Montana Corporation. Despite his close ties to Israel, Kahane was increasingly supportive of Kreisky's policy, which aimed to make the PLO a partner in efforts to bring about peace in the Middle East, and also got involved in the Peace Movement in Israel. He also became Kreisky's informal emissary to Arab countries, above all to Egypt, and maintained close contacts to Issam Sartawi and US Ambassador Milton Wolf, a successful real estate developer and investment banker in Cleveland, Ohio as well as a noted Jewish community leader. One of the consequences was a meeting between Wolf and Sartawi in 1979, despite contacts with the PLO having officially been ruled out by the State Department.[19] Especially Kreisky but also Palme did not limit their SI network to social democratic politicians but opened it to independent personalities such as Karl Kahane, a rich businessman.

European Community Policy Towards the Middle East

Despite the negative economic consequences of the oil crises of 1973–1974 and 1978, which were to a significant extent a by-product of the unresolved Israeli–Arab-Palestinian conflict, there was no stringent common EC policy towards the Middle East until 1980. The field continued to be dominated by different national interests. In the EC traditional approach, bilateral trade and economic agreements replaced a more dedicated Middle East policy. The EC negotiated the first such agreements as early as 1964 with Lebanon and Israel. In the 1970s these agreements took on a more systematic form in the shape of cooperation agreements but remained without traction on the political level. Such cooperation agreements were concluded in 1976 with Morocco, Algeria and Tunisia and in 1977 and 1978 with Egypt, Jordan, Syria and the Lebanon.[20] Similar in its ineffectiveness was the European–Arab Dialogue, which was initiated by the EEC after the Yom Kippur War with the declared aim of 'putting above all economic cooperation on a secure long-term basis and of shoring it up with mutual understanding and trust'.[21] The Arab states sought to broaden this forum to include a political dialogue, as the USA and Israel had feared they would, but EC representatives refused to follow suit and restricted talks to economic issues.

The joint declaration by the nine EC countries of 6 November 1973[22] produced apprehension and criticism on the part of the Israeli government. Israel's foreign minister, Yigal Allon, considered the declaration to have an 'anti-Israel' thrust and to constitute an 'encouragement for Arab intransigence', and Prime Minister Yitzchak Rabin stated on 8 May 1975: 'What we are expecting from Germany is a more balanced political position. A position that is different from the one that the nine members of the European Community committed themselves to in November 1973.'[23] Despite the cautious diplomatic formulations that were used, Israeli politicians of all colours agreed that the subsequent declaration on the Palestinians' right to self-determination, which the European Council agreed on 29 June 1976,[24] was biased in favour of the Palestinians.

The positions held by different member states within the EC in regard to the European–Arab dialogue and the political consequences indirectly linked to it may be subdivided into three groups: the cautiously pro-Arab group (France, Italy, Belgium and Ireland); the centrist group (Britain, Germany, and Luxembourg); and the ostentatiously pro-Israeli group (Netherlands, Denmark).[25] It was not until the Venice Declaration was issued in 1980, in spite of the warnings by the USA to the EC not to depart from the American geopolitical line, that the EC signalled a readiness at least at a symbolic level to take up an independent stance in regard to the Middle East:

> A just solution must finally be found to the Palestinian problem, which is not simply one of refugees. The Palestinian people, which is conscious of existing as such, must be placed in a position, by an appropriate process defined within the framework of the comprehensive peace settlement, to exercise fully its right to self-determination.[26]

This EC declaration met with a great deal of international criticism, from which only a few countries such as Japan abstained. True to its traditional pro-Palestinian line, the Soviet Union criticized it for not explicitly putting the blame squarely on Israel. Even though an official recognition of Yassir Arafat's PLO was not mentioned, demanding its involvement in peace negotiations amounted to breaking the taboo established by the Israeli government under Menachem Begin and supported by the Carter administration. The role of the three policy entrepreneurs Brandt, Kreisky and Palme in this context was in fact significant.

Brandt, Kreisky, Goldmann and the Middle East Conflict

It is remarkable that Kreisky was perceived as not being loyal in Israel after his fact-finding missions to the Middle East and above all after his official meeting with Arafat in 1979, particularly in view of his Jewish descent, whereas Brandt was regarded as loyal to Israel even more than his successor, Helmut Schmidt. These divergent perceptions, which the two politicians made use of wittingly or unwittingly in their Middle East activities, can be explained against the background of their different socialization in their national and ideological contexts.

The worldviews of Brandt and Kreisky were both shaped by the experience of World War II. Brandt went into exile to Norway, returned under cover to Germany and then went back to Norway and then Sweden. Kreisky was imprisoned for 15 months by the Dollfuss regime in 1935 and by the National Socialists for another five months in 1938. He was eventually forced into exile in Sweden, from where he returned only in 1951. As secretary of the Stockholm International, Brandt succeeded in getting the representatives of the workers' movement to jointly formulate their peace aims in 1942–1943. In the 1970s he sought to overcome the fragmentation of socialist parties by deepening their international cooperation. Kreisky's main concern was for political actors to take the initiative in preventing a conceivable third world war. Together Brandt and Kreisky developed ideas and strategies for international conflict resolution of the kind known as 'global management' today, with which they hoped to address Cold War issues. They engaged intensively in détente policies but at the same time intervened in favour of political opponents of, and refugees from, the communist bloc.

In 1975 Kreisky was one of the few politicians present at the signing of the Helsinki Final Act of the Conference for Security and Co-operation in Europe who focused on the following basic issue:

> We are therefore ready for this confrontation and one reason why we subscribe to the Conference for Security and Co-operation in Europe is because the principles that have been hammered out here have the potential to make this confrontation possible on a worldwide scale and by peaceful means. This is in any case how we interpret the passage in the declaration of principles where it is stated that every participant state is entitled freely to choose and develop their own political, social, economic and cultural system.[27]

The Soviet Union displayed all the symptoms of temporary irritation and substantially downgraded Kreisky's imminent visit to Moscow in terms of diplomatic protocol. Brandt even directly engaged in meetings with Soviet opposition – such as with Lew Kopelew in 1975.

This stated readiness to continue ideological confrontation with Communism and the Soviet Union was followed up by practical political measures, for instance the reception and integration of members of the Czechoslovak opposition movement Charter 77 in Austria or interventions for imprisoned human rights activists such as Václav Havel or Andrei Sakharov. Both the Czechoslovak and Soviet leaderships criticized this policy. Bilateral relations with neighbouring Czechoslovakia were strained as a result. Kreisky and Brandt, who actively sought direct contact with communist leaders to assist the opposition within the Eastern bloc, were assisted by Mitterrand, who symbolically staged meetings with Havel and the Polish trade union leader Lech Walesa.[28]

The Middle East conflict demonstrates the extent to which the two politicians reflected the socially and politically dominant mainstream in their respective countries in the 1970s. As early as 1938 Brandt had addressed the persecution of the Jews by the national socialists and advocated the foundation of a Jewish state. Later, he was able to draw on the anti-fascist tradition of the Social Democratic Party of Germany (SPD) of Kurt Schumacher, its first leader after World War II; the German social democrats not only made sure that their former party members were recalled from exile but that they were also integrated politically on their return. Kreisky on the other hand had to deal with the prejudices within the Socialist Party of Austria (SPÖ) against Jewish members in general and those coming back from exile in particular. In regard to the issue of the restitution of, and compensation for, material losses of the Jewish victims of National Socialist terror the SPÖ continued to drag its feet, whereas the German SPD supported the initiative of the Christian Democratic Chancellor Konrad Adenauer to ensure far-reaching compensation for individuals and substantial payments to the state of Israel in the 1950s.

Kreisky was confronted with his Jewish identity again and again and got to know anti-Semitism not only outside of his own party but also within it – both before 1938 and after 1945. Despite this the SPÖ was an environment in which he felt at home. Already as under-secretary of state from 1953 and then as foreign minister from 1959 onwards he tried to steer clear of 'Jewish' issues like restitution, particularly as he was already burdened with the negative associations invariably connected in those days with someone who had returned from exile. In the context of the Middle East question Kreisky sought early contacts with Arab states without ever calling the right of existence of Israel into question, where in fact his brother Paul lived. Following the pattern of German policy under Chancellor Brandt, also in regard to the supply of weapons, Kreisky initially aimed to establish good contacts with Egypt as well as Israel. It was only after the SI's fact-finding mission of 1974 that Kreisky shifted more and more towards emphasis on the involvement of the PLO and its leader, Yassir Arafat, as the key dialogue partner for Israel in the search for a peaceful solution of the Middle East problem.

Neither Brandt nor Schmidt were prepared to criticize Israel's policies in public as they felt that, in light of the Holocaust, they lacked the moral legitimacy to do so. Brandt pursued his Middle East initiatives and his basically pro-Israel policies despite increasing economic relations with the Arab world. He never lost sight of the hope that a deliberate confrontation with its National Socialist past would make Germany in the eyes of the USA, Western Europe, the Soviet Union and Eastern Europe appear more trustworthy so that one day a peaceful German reunification or at least humanitarian aid for people in East Germany would become possible. It was therefore imperative to downplay the idea of yet another German 'Sonderweg', or special path. Kreisky in contrast drew upon a completely different domestic discourse in regard to the country's past role in National Socialism, which was still prevalent in Austrian society at the time, that is, that Austrians had been victims only, not (also) perpetrators. With his recognition of the PLO on 11 March 1980 he severed the already badly damaged relationship with Israel's Labour Party for good.[29]

Goldmann was older than Brandt and Kreisky – born in 1895 in Vishnevo, than in the Russian Empire (now Visneva, Belarus). He moved to the German Empire with his father, who was a convinced Zionist, when he was six years old.[30] In 1913 he visited Palestine for the first time and published the book *Eretz Israel, Reisebriefe aus Palästina*. He became very active in publishing a Zionist journal and with Joakob Klatzkin he initiated the *Encyclopedia Judaica*. Goldmann was able to escape the Nazi Gestapo after 1933, was outlawed and went to the USA, representing the Jewish Agency. In 1936 he co-founded the World Jewish Congress. Already during World War II he pleaded for a compromise with the Arab states and supported the foundation of two states in Palestine – pressing for an increase of immigration from Nazi-occupied Europe. Goldmann clearly addressed the danger of genocide in Europe already in 1942. After the end of World War II he was involved in the establishment of the State of Israel but preferred a diplomatic arrangement with the Arab neighbours. As chairman of the Executive Agency of the Jewish Agency he coordinated and negotiated a reparations and restitution agreement between the Claims Conference and West Germany.[31] He always was a critical observer of Israeli politics including the negotiations after the Six-Day War in 1967. Several times he used indirect contacts with President Nasser to arrange a personal trip to Egypt to talk to Nasser in 1970 or even arrange meetings with the Israeli Prime Minister and Foreign Minister with their Egyptian counterparts, but failed to succeed.[32]

Track II Diplomatic Contacts

Immediately after the Yom Kippur War or October War between Israel and its Arab neighbours the SI convened a conference on the situation in the Middle East on November 11, 1973. On this occasion Kreisky tabled again his six-year-old proposal of a fact-finding mission. After an intensive debate – Israel's Prime Minister Golda Meir being present at the conference – a decision was delayed until January 1974, when Kreisky was finally nominated as head of delegation. The primary objective was to gather information as a precondition for a peaceful solution. In 1976 Kreisky published the results. These eventually were to play a role in the peace treaty between Israel and Egypt in the form of a conditional recognition of Israel if the occupied territories were returned.[33]

One of the key results of the Middle East fact-finding mission was Kreisky's realization, following a meeting with Arafat on 11 March 1974, that in him the Palestinians had a leader who might be capable of abjuring violence and of playing a part in a peaceful resolution of the conflict. This first meeting did not lead to any concrete results. In fact, Kreisky remained guarded throughout, stressed his loyalty to the Israeli Labour Party and signalled his readiness to make a contribution to a 'humanitarian solution of the Palestinian problem'.[34] In the beginning Kreisky was not sure whether Arafat would be crucial to a resolution of the conflict and focused much more on bringing the Egyptian leader Anwar al Sadat in touch with the West and the USA as a conversation with President Richard Nixon in 1974 shows:

> All the Arabs are in favour of a Palestinian state, because then things will go in a different direction. The first question is its relationship to Jordan. Then there are so many Palestinian groups who don't feel represented by the PLO that maybe there should be a Palestinian Congress to decide what the Palestinians want. Arafat is weak [...] I talked to Ghanim [Head of the Arab Socialist Union in Egypt] and he said we are building up Arafat. This is an illusion. Kosygin said the Soviet Union had a good impression of him. But I doubt he will be the leader of the Palestinians.[35]

Relatively soon after his meeting with Nixon, however, Kreisky changed his position and began to back Arafat. Even more important than the official communiqués after the various Middle East fact-finding missions was the permanent media interest in what were – for Kreisky – the main preconditions for the conflict to be resolved. A case in point was his trip to Berlin in early December 1977, where he delivered a speech on the occasion of the annual dinner of the Berlin Press Conference in the presence of a large number of opinion leaders from Berlin, which culminated in an appeal to Israel 'to take the leap' and create the nucleus of a Palestinian state by returning the Gaza Strip and the West Bank.[36] Kreisky made use of this type of political communication strategy in several EC states – for instance in a talk he gave at the Royal Institute of International Affairs (Chatham House) in London on 4 July 1978 and after the subsequent meeting with the British Prime Minister James Callaghan and Foreign Secretary David Owen. Kreisky's topic was the policy of détente of which the Middle East issue was a central part:

> Détente will be jeopardised whenever tensions arise in other areas of the world, because the great powers will invariably be involved in them. One such area of particular importance to Europe is the Middle East. Unfortunately, the democratic countries of Europe have not yet shown the active interest that would be impera-tive when dealing with the problems of this area – although I do understand that many European countries still have certain inhibitions in this regard because of the fate of European Jews.[37]

At the press conference that followed, he devoted most of his time to the forthcoming meeting in Salzburg between Sadat, Brandt and Shimon Peres, the leader of Israel's Labour Party from 1977 onwards, and the posi-tion of the PLO.[38]

Brandt and Kreisky realized that it was necessary for the diametrically opposed notions concerning the options in the Middle East conflict to be discussed by high-ranking representatives from the elites of the conflicting parties in Israel and in the Arab world in the form of a closed workshop. Their first joint effort to persuade intellectuals and scholars from the Arab world, Israel and the USA to adopt their approach to a possible solution of the Middle East issue failed in 1978, despite the fact that both Brandt in his capacity of former German chancellor and Kreisky as Austrian chan-cellor had extensive contacts they could draw upon.[39] Both were also in touch with others whose views on this question differed from those of the mainstream, such as the president of the World Jewish Congress, Nahum Goldmann, who helped to plan a confidential meeting in 1978 with the goal to explore the basis for a negotiated settlement of the kind that was eventually reached in Oslo in 1993. The leading force in this project was Goldmann, who first approached Willy Brandt, who would function as the host. Jewish and Arab intellectuals and opinion-makers from the USA, Europe and the Middle East were to be contacted to participate in this 'Jewish-Arab Conference'.[40] In early June 1977 Goldmann contacted Kreisky too and asked him to approach the Syrian President Assad to back this conference.[41] Dr Nahum Goldmann was convinced that participants from Egypt, Tunisia and Morocco would come, but the Syrian attitude would influence both Palestinians and the Lebanon. On June 23, 1977 Kreisky convinced Goldmann that this conference should take place in Vienna. Brandt's invitation letter emphasized 'the theme of this gathering would be Arab-Jewish relations in their historical perspective and cultural context'.[42] The conference which was designed by Brandt and Kreisky as an informal forum and should not discuss the recent political agenda but should concentrate on three topics: 'Jews and Arabs in the Past', 'Jews and Arabs in the Present' and 'Jews and Arabs in the Future'.

Nothing came of the project, however, mainly because of a lack of trust on the part of potential Arab and Palestinian partners. Intellectuals and opinion leaders as well as scientists and a few former politicians such as Noam Chomsky, Saul Friedländer, Henry Kissinger, Pierre Mendès France or Amos Oz were to form the core of the conference participants. Brandt hoped in his invitation letter that:

> By giving the possibility of a frank and open exchange on the mutual perception and experience between Arab and Jewish intellectuals, Vienna might contribute in small and indirect ways to the process of a peaceful and just resolution of the Middle East conflict. I am convinced that the very fact of such a gathering will constitute a moral achievement.[43]

Goldmann was convinced that Arafat himself discouraged the invited Arab participants to join this meeting of 1978 in Vienna,[44] in general the new situation in the Middle East after the unilateral move by the Egyptian President Sadat to conclude a peace treaty with Israel had irritated the Arab world.

Sadat, who strongly backed this Goldmann–Brandt–Kreisky initiative, was completely isolated in the Arab world. In December 1977 only seven Arab participants had agreed to participate compared with thirty on the Jewish side – one month after the invitation letter had been sent out. So far the following personalities were expected to speak: Mohammed Arkoun, Professor of the history of Islamic thought at the Sorbonne, and Professor George F. Hourani, one of the preeminent scholars of Islamic Philosophy and Near Eastern History, State University of New York at Buffalo. Both agreed to come. The other three key personalities on the list of most wanted speakers had not answered yet: Abdallah Laroui, novelist and prominent Moroccan historian at the University Mohammed V in Rabat, one of Morocco's leading intellectuals, Mohamed Sid-Ahmed, a life-long activist in the communist and progressive movements, one of Egypt's leading political writers and intellectuals, and Ihsan Abbas, open-minded professor at the American University of Beirut, who was considered a leading figure in the field of Arabic and Islamic literary studies both in the East and in the West. Goldmann's list of Arab participants was strongly influenced by Professor Abraham L. Udovitch, the Chairman of the Department of Near Eastern Studies of Princeton University.

Goldmann, who had almost singlehandedly negotiated the treaties between the Federal Republic of Germany and Israel and with the Jewish Claims Conference in the 1950s, was a highly articulate critic of the policies of Israel towards the Palestinians and its Arab neighbours.[45] In 1975 he said in an interview with the German weekly magazine *Der Spiegel*: 'What Golda Meir has done was completely unrealistic: not to acknowledge that there is such an entity as a Palestinian people. The fact that there has never been a Palestinian state is beside the point.'[46] In November 1977 Goldmann has been quite active with the Israeli peace movement and joined a meeting in Tel Aviv with international personalities like Mendès France, Lord Caradon and George Ball as well as representatives from the Arab community in the West Bank.

In 1979 the triangle Brandt–Kreisky–Goldmann seemed to be successful as far as the integration of the PLO under Chairman Arafat was concerned. In September 1979 Judith Wyer, an experienced analyst of the Executive Intelligence review even thought that these efforts might end up in a 'Camp David with a Balkan face'.[47] Here another actor was mentioned, the Romanian president Nicolai Ceauşescu, since Romania was the only communist country still keeping up diplomatic relations with Israel. Especially the Palestinians tried to get Ceauşescu involved in public dialogues with well-known international personalities such as Mendès France or Kreisky.[48] With regard to this 1978 initiative communist diplomatic channels seemed not to have been used or contacted by Kreisky. Brandt, however, wanted the Soviets directly involved whereas Kreisky tried to keep them out.

Since 1977 a new player appeared on the scene, who very much impressed Brandt, Kreisky and Goldmann: Issam Sartawi, a former US-trained physician, born in Acre, Palestine, in 1935, who soon interacted between these three men as representative of Arafat in Europe. Sartawi met Brandt and Kreisky regularly since 1977, and soon Nahum Goldmann became one of his regular contacts in Paris.[49] Two years later – in 1979 – Kreisky and Brandt met Arafat in Vienna (July 7th and 8th) – pressing hard to convince Arafat to acknowledge the right of existence of the State of Israel and at the same time convince the Israeli government to start negotiations with the

PLO. In the meantime the opposition against direct talks with the PLO had considerably decreased within the SI – only the Israeli Labour Party and the British Labour representatives still opposed this new course.[50]

Sartawi, too, tried in early 1979 to continue along the lines of the Goldmann model, that great men can overcome the political barriers of the present, and proposed in March 1979 to Brandt a meeting of Arafat with Kreisky, Brandt, Senghor, Mendès France, Ribicoff and Caradon.[51] During such a meeting Arafat should guarantee the right of existence of the State of Israel on the basis of the UN resolution 242, and that the PLO will be accepted as a negotiation partner. Sartawi furthermore reported that the USA allegedly would back a meeting between Arafat and Goldmann, but asked for more concessions from the United States (e.g. an end of the ban to enter the USA after Sabri Jiryis and Isam Sartawi had been ousted from the USA after the opening of an office to represent the Palestinian people in 1975). Goldmann indeed considered such a meeting but then accepted the advice by Moshe Dayan to decline an option for such a meeting as proposed by the King of Morocco Hassan II already earlier in 1970.[52]

Goldmann, who continued to maintain his good contacts with the German government under Chancellor Helmut Schmidt, however, was more radical than Brandt in condemning the Israeli intervention in Lebanon in 1981. Kreisky started a bitter dispute with Brandt which even seemed to destroy their friendship when the SI refused to harshly condemn the Israeli intervention. Due to the divergent memory politics concerning the Holocaust the Austrian chancellor – because of his Jewish background – showed no obligation towards Israel, whereas Brandt continued the established West German *Vergangenheitspolitik*: taking responsibility for National Socialism and the Holocaust and showing strong loyalty towards Israel. Both Kreisky and Palme begged to differ, but all three agreed to back the continuity of the state of Israel, which was non-negotiable for them.

Kreisky tried first of all to involve Sadat in a negotiated settlement and organized the meeting between Sadat, Brandt and Peres in 1978, which caused quite a stir in the international media, even though concrete results were confined to statements of principles, personal assessments and a general four point plan. Even the Carter administration commented favourably on the meeting, which also involved talks between the Israeli and Egyptian defence ministers.[53] Even though this and other meetings with SI representatives, who included several prime ministers from EC countries, did not win Peres over to endorsing more moderate ideas regarding a solution of the Palestinian question, he did at least acquiesce to what was increasingly the majority opinion within the SI in public communiqués. Recognizing the PLO under Arafat's leadership was still out of the question. Yossi Beilin, Peres' long-time assistant and one of the architects of the Oslo Plan, has suggested that Peres, who was made a vice-president of the SI in 1978, wanted above all to improve his standing with influential people in the SI but had no intention for the time being to change his political positions on the Middle East conflict.[54]

While Kreisky, Brandt and Palme were undertaking efforts to prepare a resolution of the Middle East conflict, the EC also started various initiatives. Gaston Thorn, a liberal politician from Luxembourg, who was later to become president of the European Commission (1981–85), regularly sought Kreisky's advice, as did many other leading European statesmen. Thorn attended the Opera Ball in Vienna in 1977, when he and the French Gaullist leader Jacques Chirac were Kreisky's personal guests. The extent to which Thorn's fact-finding missions as foreign minister of Luxembourg and president of the EC Council of Ministers, which he undertook to the Middle East after the Venice Declaration 1980,[55] were modelled on those by Kreisky on behalf of the SI in 1974–75 is difficult to say without further research. There were obvious parallels as regards the objectives of the two sets of fact-finding missions, even though the Israeli position under Begin was even more intransigent than in the first half of the 1970s. Thorn's mission took place in a vacuum in terms of Middle East politics because of the transition of power from Carter to Reagan and the forthcoming elections in Israel. Thorn had to threaten his departure to be allowed to meet with Sadat, who found words of praise for the Venice Declaration and for the 'contribution of the Western Europeans to the resolution on Jerusalem passed by the Security Council' but lost no time to warn against European initiatives lest these were to interfere with the interests of the US and the ongoing Camp David process.[56] In addition, Sadat dismissed the role of the PLO and of Arafat for a peaceful solution as 'insignificant'.

It is clear that the slow evolution of the EC's policy on the Middle East issue was in part fostered by its increasing strategic economic dependence on oil imports from the Arab countries. 40 per cent of the exports of the member states of the Arab League went to the EC (90 per cent of which was crude oil), 16 per cent to Japan and 9 per cent to the USA.[57] It was not until 1979 and after the second oil crisis that the EC made first tentative moves towards developing a political strategy for the Middle East conflict characterized by somewhat greater independence from the USA. In 1979 the Irish Foreign Minister Brian Lenihan Sr, speaking at the UN General

Assembly as the representative of the Irish EC presidency stated 'that [...] the representatives of the Palestinians must play their full part in the negotiation of a comprehensive settlement'.[58] He named the PLO among the parties who would have to be involved in this process. Thus, 1979 was designated by the London-based Middle East International 'as the year in which the EEC countries would decisively move away from support of Israel and toward the Arab cause'.[59]

The Socialist International Network and EC Decision-Makers

How did the SI network influence political actors in the EC, if at all? It became obvious in 1979 that France in particular sought once more to play a more prominent role in international politics including the Middle East conflict. Five years earlier, the newly elected President Valéry Giscard d'Estaing had categorized the meeting between Jean Victor Sauvagnargues, French Foreign Minister in the government led by the Gaullist Chirac, and Arafat in Damascus on 21 October 1974 as a 'mistake'.[60] At the same time, however, Giscard himself had already used the formula of the Palestinians' right to a 'homeland of their own',[61] which the EC only adopted in its London Declaration of 29 June 1979. In 1979 the French President embarked on a high-profile tour of Kuwait, the Gulf States and Jordan. From Giscard's point of view, West Germany was unsuitable as a mediator in the Middle East for historical reasons. Britain in turn was too close to US positions on foreign policy matters.[62] Thus, the French President and government also put their stamp on the Venice Declaration. The British government reacted to the French initiative with some misgiving, which was at least partly owed to the fact that, even though Giscard had contacted Schmidt and leading politicians in Italy, Belgium, Ireland and the Netherlands to inform them of his trip and to discuss it with them, Britain had received no such advance notice.[63] Following British interventions, the original draft of the EC declaration was watered down considerably. Care was taken not to call into question the US position on the Middle East question.

Media coverage of Giscard's trip, which culminated in a joint press communiqué expressing support for the Palestinians' right to self-determination, was upstaged by the diplomatic recognition of the PLO by Austria at Kreisky's initiative. Kreisky's attempts to draw Schmidt (despite personal and political differences between the two men) into the 'pro-Palestinian' camp by supplying him with direct information failed. Rather like Kreisky in his first years in foreign policy-making, Schmidt originally supported a policy of equidistance in Middle East politics. In talks with the Syrian

Foreign Minister Abdul Halim Khaddam in Bonn on 12 May 1975 Schmidt argued: 'We do not believe that we have the greatest expert knowledge in the world in Middle East matters but we are resolved not to favour one side over the other; we will pursue a balanced concept instead.'[64] In any case, Schmidt lost a vote of no confidence in the German Bundestag in 1982 and the subsequent elections to Helmut Kohl in 1983. The Christian Democrat Kohl was more inclined to follow Margaret Thatcher's line, however, which supported a resolution of the Middle East conflict brokered by the USA.[65] Kreisky continued to advocate the strategy of involving the PLO directly in the negotiation process. For instance, he passed the summary of a conversation between the Austrian ambassador to the UN and the mayor of Bethlehem, Elias Freiij, on the situation of the Palestinians in the West Bank on to the newly elected French President Mitterrand.[66] Rather like Thatcher and Kohl, however, Mitterrand was not really interested in a joint active Middle East policy by the EC and Western Europe.[67]

Arguably, Kreisky and Brandt's initiatives concerning the Middle East conflict had the greatest long-term influence on decision-making processes within the EC through their endorsement of contacts with the PLO. It all started with a PLO platform in Europe, initially centred on Said Hammami, a representative of Arafat, who was based in London and sought to establish contacts with Israel from November 1973. After the publication of two articles in the London *Times* on 16 November and 17 December 1973, in which he underlined the PLO's readiness to participate in peace conferences and sketched a two-state solution involving mutual recognition, contacts with Israeli and Western European politicians ensued. In 1975 Hammami met the Knesset member and peace activist Uri Avnery in London for the first time. Hammami subsequently gave a public address on the 'two-state solution' at the National Liberal Club. He also established contacts with the Egyptian-Jewish activist Henri Curiel, who lived in Paris at the time. In September 1976 Hammami was replaced by Issam Sartawi, a medical doctor recently returned from exile in the United States.[68] Brandt first met him during a meeting with Arafat in Vienna on 8 July 1979.[69] Sartawi was Arafat's European spokesman. He was based in Paris, where he was involved in a series of secret talks with Israeli peace activists around Reserve Major General Matti Peled.[70] These contacts had been authorized by Arafat, who was subsequently forced to defend them in the plenary sessions of the Palestinian National Council.[71]

Shortly before Christmas 1978 Sartawi worked with Kreisky and a number of other well-known social democrats, most of whom had formerly held leading positions. This group was to develop a peace plan that would form the basis for the recognition of the PLO and its integration in peace negotiations. The precondition was, however, to get Arafat both to sanction the group's claims on behalf of the Palestinians for the 'legitimate rights of the Palestinians' and – crucially – to indirectly recognize Israel's right to exist; this recognition would be couched in a 'formula which [...] conforms with the internationally accepted criteria for a just solution'.[72] Alongside Kreisky, the group included Leopold Sédar Senghor, Brandt, Palme, Pierre Mendès France and Ted Heath. The spokesman of the German government, Klaus Bölling, was also involved. Even though this plan was ultimately not realized, Sartawi benefited from the Brandt/Kreisky network. Among other contacts it enabled him as has been mentioned to get in touch with Nahum Goldmann. Kreisky for his part kept Sartawi up-to-date about his interventions in favour of the PLO. In a letter to Sartawi written by Kreisky's advisor on foreign policy, Georg Lennkh, Lennkh listed everyone Kreisky had contacted on the subject including Schmidt, the British Foreign Minister Peter Carrington, the French Foreign Minister Jean François-Poncet and the US Secretary of State Edmund S. Muskie.[73] In conversations with Schmidt on 6 September 1980, Thatcher and Carrington on 16 September 1980 and the French Prime Minister Raymond Barre on 25–26 September 1980, Kreisky plied his pro-Palestinian agenda. These activities peaked when a number of high-ranking Jews – among them Nahum Goldmann, Philip Klutznick (former US Secretary of Commerce and President of both the World Jewish Congress and B'nai B'rith International), and Pierre Mendès France (former President of France) – in a public declaration came out in support of involving Arafat in peace talks on 2 July 1982 on the occasion of Israel's military intervention in Lebanon. The journalist Mark A. Bruzonsky reported on the first page of the French daily newspaper *Le Monde*:

> In their responses to this historic statement Yasser Arafat and the PLO Representative in Europe, Dr. Issam Sartawi, considered this 'Paris Declaration' to be a Balfour Declaration for the Palestinian people that would hasten the creation of an independent Palestinian State and lead to a general Middle East peace between Israel and the Arab States.[74]

Sartawi and other pioneers of the dialogue between Europe and the PLO such as Hammami and Curiel were assassinated.[75] On the day before he was killed Sartawi wrote to Brandt to underline the historic significance of the Lisbon SI Conference, in which he took part as the PLO's official representative. By means of different declarations, such as the acceptance of the Brezhnev and the Fez Plans, he had attempted to construe the formula of a 'just, honourable and lasting peace' to imply an indirect recognition of Israel's right to exist. Sartawi's close contacts with Jewish leaders had cut him off from the Palestinian mainstream, however, even though he had always been at pains to keep those contacts secret. He took a first symbolical step towards making these contacts public when he accepted the Kreisky Human Rights Award together with Lova Eliav in 1979,[76] even though he had not been authorized by Arafat to do so. Kreisky made use of the award ceremony to strengthen the acceptance of Arafat and the PLO as interlocutors in the peace process, after the Palestinian leader had also been received in Madrid and Ankara.

Conclusion

Policy entrepreneurs develop political visions, which they subsequently try to realize in the medium term by creating a substantial public and bringing key political actors on board. What was so remarkable about the Brandt–Kreisky–Goldmann connection within the loose overarching network of the SI was the impression that they created of continuously and closely working together even if only one or two of them who were working in a particular political arena at a given time. As regards Middle East policy, it was Kreisky and Brandt who prepared the ground for the PLO to be accepted as a partner in the peace talks by making skilful use of the media, by supplying relevant actors with an endless stream of information and by exploiting personal contacts. Here especially Nahum Goldmann became an important dialogue partner since 1977 and joined various activities but tried to use the network for his own purposes. Arafat's 'ambassador to Europe' Sartawi was also given access to this network and introduced to important interlocutors including even the US ambassador to Vienna, Milton Wolf. All three – Brandt, Kreisky and Goldmann still believed that respected international personalities could influence considerably the political agenda and especially include the PLO into future peace negotiations. In the end the political environment neither in Israel nor in the USA was prepared to accept this major change of perspectives at the time. In this sense they overestimated their agenda-setting power and the power of rational arguments and negotiating skills. Despite the fact that the network was relatively open and included discreet personalities from the business world (e.g. Karl Kahane) and lobbyists like Issam Sartawi it functioned well as if driven by game theory. The participation of the Soviet Union and Romania, however, was partly a disputed issue in this network.

Palme was very active initially regarding the PLO issue. He met Arafat in 1974 and only a year later, the PLO opened an office in Stockholm.[77] Later on, especially after Kreisky retired from politics in 1983, Palme and other Swedish social democrats, who (with the exception of the SI Secretary General Bernt Carlson) had initially been on the margins of Middle East politics, carried the basic idea of Palestinian–Israeli negotiations to achieve a long-term settlement forward. In 1988 the 'Swedish connection'[78] around Foreign Minister Sten Anderson revived the old Goldmann–Brandt–Kreisky idea of establishing contacts between the PLO and representatives of the US American Jewish Community in order to overcome the PLO's ostracism by the USA.

In his correspondence with Arafat Anderson fleshed out the model he had in mind. On 21 November 1988 he initiated the first meeting in Stockholm. Harold Saunders, a US diplomat and expert on the Middle East, who had last been assistant secretary of state for Near Eastern and South Asian affairs under President Carter, summarized the significance of this ultimately ineffectual initiative, the last one before the Oslo Agreement, as follows:

> Insiders working from outside government [...] produced a precise formulation to help the US government and the PLO begin a formal dialogue. Most unofficial meetings concentrate on helping citizens on both sides of a conflict to understand each other more fully. In this case, however, Rabie Mohamed and former senior National Security Council staff member William Quandt worked closely with political authorities.[79]

In the meantime, evidence has come to light which demonstrates the intensive use that was made of the SI network by Norway's Labour Party, which initially maintained close ties exclusively with Israel. The party leader Gro Harlem Brundtland met Arafat in the wake of Sartawi's assassination and discussed the option of a secret forum for direct Palestinian–Israeli talks.[80] After the Labour Party had come back to power in 1986, Foreign Minister Thorvald Stoltenberg indicated that Norway would henceforth adopt a somewhat more 'pro-Palestinian' attitude. However, it took until 20–22 January 1993 for this new contact to become operational and for secret talks in Oslo to start.

Had it not been for the intensive and very open communication work by Kreisky, Brandt and Palme, the SI would arguably not have developed into a forum that made the PLO acceptable as a dialogue partner and that turned one of the most pro-Israeli social democratic parties, the Labour Party of Norway, into an ideal host of the Oslo negotiations. Without the unceasing work of the three policy entrepreneurs Brandt, Kreisky and Goldmann (a Zionist and not a social democrat) as well as Palme, the EC would arguably not have considered the PLO as an important factor in the equation of the Middle East, at least not so soon, even if the recognition of the PLO remained out of bounds for most EC countries for a long time. Even the government of Germany – Israel's second largest trade partner and particularly close to it on account of the Holocaust – held secret talks with different PLO representatives in Lebanon as early as 1974. But it was not until after the first official talks in 1979 between Kreisky and Brandt on the one hand and Arafat on the other that the PLO representative in Bonn, Abdallah Frangi, was perceived in a more positive light in public.[81] The first de facto acts of diplomatic recognition, the opening of official PLO offices, were initiated by Spain (1977) and Portugal (1978),[82] followed by Austria in March 1980, and France, Italy and Greece. Arafat was not officially received in Spain until he had met with Kreisky and Brandt in Vienna, however. Here too the pioneering role of the SI network is clearly in evidence.

That the Venice Declaration ended up not being more pronouncedly pro-PLO was due to the fact that for Thatcher a pro-Palestinian policy was tantamount to an SI policy, which she refused to endorse. At the same time she sought to follow the line endorsed by the Reagan administration in its early days and to act as the extended arm of the USA in the EC. On a bilateral level she strove for improved relations with Israel and wanted to get rid of the historical burden dating from the times of the British Mandate for Palestine. Kohl also favoured restraint in Middle East politics. These developments point to a weakness of the social democratic network, which became evident in the 1980s. Its Middle East activities largely depended on socialists implementing the new approach in government. When more and more Christian democratic and conservative governments were formed again in the 1980s, the SI network was no longer able to translate its track II activities into track I-type inter-state negotiations.

PART 3

Regional Actors and Dynamics
from Détente to the Second Cold War

CHAPTER 13

France, the European Community and the Maghreb, 1963–1976

From Inertia to Key Player

Houda Ben Hamouda

Since the end of World War II, two phenomena have significantly modified the relationship between European states and their overseas territories: decolonization and the 'unification' of Europe. These two major developments have forced the leaders of European states and those of newly independent states into an ongoing effort to adapt the terms of their relationship to a changing situation.

At the time of preparations for the Treaty of Rome, several countries that would become independent a few years later still had the status of dependent territories. Political dependence led to a phenomenon of economic domination on the part of the 'métropole'. Therefore, the progressive unification of customs and excise between the Six included special measures toward these territories. Regarding the situation in 1957 in the countries of North Africa, Morocco and Tunisia had already achieved independence before the signing of the Treaty of Rome. As their trade relations with France were particularly close, special arrangements were made: the 'Protocole relatif aux marchandises originaires et en provenance de certains pays et bénéficiant d'un régime particulier à l'importation dans un des États membres' and the 'Declaration of intent to association with the EEC independent countries of the Franc zone',[1] allowed preferential trade between

France, Morocco and Tunisia to continue. Between Algeria and the Six, the problem was different. Since it was considered part of the territory of the French Republic, Algeria was treated according to the provisions of the Treaty of Rome. After the Evian agreements of 1962, however, the question arose about how to settle relations between independent Algeria and the EEC.

During the 1960s, many difficulties became evident in the development of a European policy towards North Africa. This was mainly due to a lack of interest by member states and the passive role of France. Why did France not encourage other partners to pursue a policy of cooperation towards the Maghreb? Only in the early 1970s did France become a key player. The economic crisis, the rise in terrorism, tensions in the Middle East, but also Pompidou's awareness of the strategic importance of the Mediterranean area, led France to use its influence to build true European cooperation towards the Mediterranean.

The aim of this chapter is to analyse French action in the European Community regarding the relations between the EEC and the Maghreb. The first part deals with French inertia in the Euro-Maghreb issue from 1962 to 1969, while the second part analyses the peculiarity of the Algerian case. Finally, the active role of France in boosting cooperation policy toward North African Mediterranean countries in the 1970s will be considered.

The First Negotiations between the EEC, Morocco and Tunisia, 1963–1969

In 1959, North Africa started to open up towards the EEC, and EEC relations with certain countries of the Maghreb began,[2] but with difficulty. Concerning Tunisia, as a newly independent state, it had to take the initiative to engage in relations with the Community. Discussion followed, although the Tunisian delegation did not indicate clearly the nature of the preferred agreement, nor did they explicitly clarify their intentions. While President Bourguiba favoured cooperation with the EEC in order to reduce dependence on France, much of the Tunisian political elite saw it as 'the birth of neocolonialism'. Because of the difficulties in Tunisian–French relations, Bourguiba withdrew into a 'policy of precaution' by observing the association negotiations with Greece and, in particular, awaiting the end of the Algerian war before starting negotiations on Tunisian association with the Community.

King Mohammed V of Morocco did not demand dialogue. On the one hand, given his distrust of Europe, he preferred to turn towards the United States and his Arab neighbours. On the other, his priorities were for unification of the kingdom and consolidation of its independence and territorial integrity. Further, the King was not in favour of the idea of an association with the EEC: also for the Moroccan political elite the association project had negative political connotations. Only from December 1963 did Mohammed V's successor, Hassan II, ask for negotiations to draw up an agreement – although he avoided using the term 'association' until 1967.

The Community, for its part, was in its initial stages. It adopted an equally cautious position, thinking that any association risked being premature.[3] Furthermore, it was considered appropriate to leave the initiative to North African countries. Within the Community, contrasting positions can be observed. The Commission supported the immediate opening of a political dialogue to establish agreements for drawing up an aid policy for developing countries. On the other hand, the Council considered that negotiations concerning the association of the Maghreb and other countries were premature. This position of the Council emerged strongly in the reports:

> Lors de la Réunion du Conseil des ministres de la CEE, le 25 juillet 1961, M. Spaak a fait part de son souci d'éviter d'allonger la liste des négociations avec des pays tiers avant que ne soit ratifié l'accord avec la Grèce et que ne soient connues les initiatives britanniques; ce souci est partagé par la plupart des membres.[4]

Moreover, France did not support these negotiations at all. Since their independence in March 1956, the Maghreb countries had been involved in many crises and tensions with France: land occupied by the *colons*, the presence of French troops, and Tunisian and Moroccan support for the Algerians[5] in the war of independence. The difficult relations between France and Tunisia and Morocco meant that relations between the Community and these countries were not part of the European agenda for France, whose priorities were, instead, the installation of the Common Market and resolution of the Algerian war.

The watershed year was 1963 when the Maghreb states officially asked for a definition of their relations with the Community.[6] The context was more favourable because the Evian agreements had ended the Algerian war. Besides, the signing of the treaties of association with Greece and Turkey, and the British candidature, consolidated the success of the common market. The EEC's positive perception of the Maghreb countries helped to set in motion their demands to open negotiations in 1963.

The first session of negotiations took place in July 1965 on the basis of a partial Council mandate. This mandate was so restrictive that it did not allow the negotiations to advance.[7] It concerned trade only and even in this restricted domain, there were many gaps. In particular, two funda-mental products of the Moroccan and Tunisian economies – olive oil and citrus fruits[8] – were excluded from the list of products whose tariff could be negotiated. In October 1967, the EEC Council of Ministers gave the Commission a new mandate for negotiations. This second mandate intro-duced into the discussion certain new points (olive oil and citrus fruits), but removed others (wine[9]), nor were financial and technical assistance, or the question of workforce, considered. Tunisia and Morocco, however, agreed to resume negotiations, which may be explained by the difficult economic situation, particularly for Tunisia. Since Bourguiba had decided to nationalize lands in 1964, the French grant was interrupted. For these two Maghreb countries, although the mandate was partial, it was essential to become less dependent on France.

The negotiations with Tunisia took place on 14–16 November 1967, and with Morocco on 22–24 November 1967 and it was only in March 1969 that the agreements of association were signed. Algeria was again excluded. It was only after a long, twenty-eight month period since approval of the first mandate that Tunisia and Morocco attained the agreements they were seeking. These concerned only limited commercial matters and it had to be accepted that Algeria was again omitted.

Since the start of talks in 1963, numerous difficulties slowed down the elaboration of the agreements. The implementation of the Common Agricultural Policy delayed negotiations on agricultural products, such as wine, which was included in the first mandate (1965) but missing from the second in 1967. On the other hand, for other goods, in particular olive oil and citrus fruits, the institution of single markets allowed the Community to formulate offers in Tunisia and Morocco.

Certain member states also hesitated, partly for political and partly for economic reasons. The political considerations were raised by the Belgian and German delegations. The Belgian government questioned the sense of granting advantages to these countries, particularly in the case of Algeria, which was hostile towards Belgium because of the Congo question. The German delegation also wished to settle by treaty the relations between all the Maghreb states and the EEC, although the Algerian position towards Egypt was of concern. In addition, there were the general objections of other member states: the Dutch considered the EEC involved too far south and regretted the lack of balance in relations with neighbours in the north and west. The Italian delegation wanted these agreements to be considered in a wider perspective, within the elaboration of a regional approach to the Mediterranean. The French delegation participated very discreetly in the negotiations because of the numerous tensions with former protectorates. They also wished Algeria to be included in the mandate granted by the Council.[10]

Finally, since it was clear that an even longer time would be necessary to discuss financial aid and workforce politics, the Commission advised the Maghreb countries to accept this partial agreement as a first step. The agreements would last five years from their coming into force, and then new negotiations would lead to new agreements with broader contents.[11] These agreements were based on article 238 of the Treaty of Rome.[12] It was the first time that the Community used the term 'association' for agreements, the contents of which were purely commercial.

A political analysis of negotiations from 1963 to 1969 reveals, first of all, the reasons for this specificity in EEC external relations, and that the initiative came exclusively from the Maghreb. Certainly, the Treaty of Rome clearly expressed the faculty to stipulate association agreements in this region of the world, in conformity with article 238 and the introduction. Indeed, the Commission thought that by leaving the initiative to the African states, this would free the Community of any suspicion of neo-colonialism.

The reasons for the slow pace of these negotiations can be explained, on the one hand, by the passivity and indifference of France. Indeed, the stormy political context involving the Maghreb countries clearly disturbed relations with the EEC. The main reasons for tensions between France and its former protectorates were the crisis of Bizerte for Tunisia,[13] Ben Barka's arrest for Morocco,[14] these countries' support for Algerian independence, and the nationalization of lands belonging to former *colons* and the subsequent suspension of French grants to Morocco and Tunisia. On the other hand, de Gaulle wished to maintain superiority in bilateral relations with the former protectorates.

The Commission adopted a line of neutrality and waited for a more serene climate to conclude any agreement, not wanting to instigate the hostility of other members towards France during negotiations. Indeed, the difficulties met during the negotiations can also be explained by the internal crisis within the EEC. De Gaulle refused to strengthen the powers of the Commission and the European Parliament, leading to the 'empty chair' crisis in 1965, and also opposed Britain's request for membership twice in 1963 and 1967.

There was also opposition from some member countries, in particular the Netherlands and Italy, regarding financial concessions made within the framework of association agreements. For this reason, the Commission, not benefiting from the financial competence that was indispensable to implementing more comprehensive agreements, was forced to deal exclusively with commercial aspects.

Indeed, without being concerned about reactions from certain member states – France in particular – regarding its ambitions and new influence, the Commission used the means provided by the treaty to encourage a policy of cooperation with the African countries and assumed an autonomous position in these meetings and in political initiatives toward these countries:

> La Commission me paraît abuser de ces droits pour tout ce qui touche à ses rapports avec les États de la Communauté [française]. Des experts sont envoyés sans qu'il nous soit demandé au préalable la moindre autorisation [...]. En bref, une habitude se crée qui consiste à oublier non seulement que c'est la France qui, en fin de compte, et elle seule, a la responsabilité politique de la Communauté à l'égard de la coopération européenne.[15]

The Algerian Case: Preservation of the Commercial Status Quo

With the signature of the Treaty of Rome, Algeria was an integral part of the French territories and the main provisions of the Treaty were applicable to Algeria in accordance with the provisions of article 227, paragraph 2, of the Treaty. After independence, on 24 November 1962, the Algerian government asked to retain its privileged status as granted by the Treaty of Rome.[16] Member states agreed to grant this, in view of Algeria's recent independence and the French pressure on the Council not to penalize the Algerian economy. Thus Algeria continued to benefit from a situation very close to that established by article 227. It set up a contingent system and a customs tariff on three levels (France, other EEC member states, and other countries). It was also during 1963 that the Algerian government made the political decision to open exploratory talks with the Commission. These were aimed to establish, first of all, a complete balance sheet and, second, to propose working hypotheses and solutions to be sought.[17]

The delegations met three times in 1964, without achieving concrete results, since the Algerian government was not able to clarify its intentions.

In fact, the Algerians wanted consultations with France before defining their intentions toward the EEC. The purpose of these consultations was to protect their economy by maintaining the aid and commercial preferences granted on independence. The French delegation, however, pointed out that the Algerian authorities showed no intention in this sense, which is explained by the Algerian government's desire to maintain the status quo as long as possible. In response to the Algerian waiting game, the Commission warned that member states and the Community would modify the conditions of trade with Algeria, by considering the provisions of article 227 as no longer valid.[18] During the session of 14 June 1965, the Council asked the Coreper to open negotiations with Morocco and Tunisia. Under French pressure, it was decided that negotiations with these countries should take place so that the envisaged solutions could be widened to include Algeria. In other words, the Council made no decision regarding Algeria, but it made sure that, when the time came, negotiations with Morocco and Tunisia would not hinder a future agreement with Algeria. Indeed, since the opening of the negotiations with Tunisia and Morocco in 1965, France had persuaded its European partners that agreements with these countries should not damage Algeria. The Commission supported France because it wanted to undertake a regional policy in the Mediterranean, harmonize its trade policy and not penalize other Mediterranean countries. During meetings of the Council, France had also repeatedly asked its European partners to preserve the status quo so that Algeria would not be penalized because of its fragile economy.

On 10 November 1965, the Coreper, in the absence of the French representative, again examined the case of Algeria in the perspective of community tariff reductions. By then, the EEC authorities had continued to treat Algeria as a third country similar to a member country, in spite of the opposition of member states. In this particular case, the question was to decide whether Algeria would be considered as a third country or if the Community would apply a 10 per cent reduction in customs duties by delaying regulations on the contents.[19] This latter solution was adopted.

According to the Commission report,[20] numerous internal difficulties hindered the talks – among which the 'empty chair' crisis, implementation of the common agricultural policy (CAP), and differences of opinion within the Council were perhaps the most disruptive elements.

On 1 January 1966, the attitude of five member states (excluding France) was no longer consistent on the question of extending 'intracommunity' tariff reductions to Algeria.[21] Thanks to Italian pressure, some decisions were taken in 1968 regarding wine regulations. This was the beginning of a clarification of situation of exchange agreements between Algeria and members of the Community; but negotiations were opened only in 1970. Indeed, on 7 May, the Commission proposed that the Council define the regime regulating the import of Algerian products into the EEC. It suggested granting 70 per cent of rights of the Common Tariff for industrial products and 50 per cent for agricultural products, while reserving a decision on wine because organization of the wine market in the community was not yet regulated. While postponing examination of the question to a later date, the Council decided nevertheless to proceed towards standardizing the economic contents of the norms applicable to Algerian imports in the Community, by way of a one-sided decision (without excluding the possibility of contact with Algeria) to provide a legal basis for the regulation of these products.

In 1968, the situation of Algerian products in the EEC was thus rather vague. Each member country applied a different regime to Algerian imports. Italy pointed out that the absence of community intervention had led to a rapid increase in sales of Algerian agricultural products, in particular in Germany and the Netherlands, to the detriment of Italian products.[22]

From 1 January 1968, Italy dealt with Algerian products in the same way as for third countries. All member states followed Italy's example and in this particular context, Algeria asked the Commission to receive a delegation of senior officials. The aim was to discuss the Algerian government's intentions of setting up a new tariff in Algeria and, especially, to follow up the exploratory talks begun in 1964.[23]

Nevertheless, on 30 July, the Council again refused to open negotiations with Algeria. Several members of the Council (particularly France) considered that these should take place within the framework of the Maghreb. However, an ad hoc regime was allowed, which applied to Algerian wine imports to Germany and the Benelux countries. The possibility of importing wines from Algeria under privileged conditions was limited in these countries to certain quantities and certain qualities of wine.[24] Finally, the 3 February 1970 Council resolution concerning the regulation of the wine market marked a step in relations between Algeria and the Common market. It assimilated Algeria to an associated country and it was therefore exempted from the general regime of imports from third countries.[25]

The implementation of a common wine policy made member states aware of the problem underlying relations with Algeria. The urgent need for normalization of relations between the EEC and Algeria was often emphatically underlined, as well as the need to conclude an agreement.

On the other hand, the Commission officially stated its desire to engage in negotiations with Algeria and on 15 April the Commission expressly asked for authorization to open negotiations. The French position, too, was more assertive at the beginning of 1970. On 7 April, the Minister for Agriculture, Mr Duhamel, declared to the Senate that 'il appartient à l'Algérie de rechercher avec la Communauté les associations qu'elle souhaite'. Jean Basdevant, French Ambassador in Algiers, declared to the Algerian Economic General Confederacy: 'la France a insisté auprès de ses partenaires de Bruxelles pour que soient pris en particulière considération les préoccupations et les intérêts de l'Algérie dans la perspective d'un accord entre la CEE et l'Algérie'.[26]

To conclude, 'l'Algérie demeura dans une situation aléatoire et para-doxale'[27] unlike its Maghreb neighbours. This was explained in particular by the peculiarity of French–Algerian bilateral relations. Algeria was less keen to negotiate an agreement at the beginning of its independence, since, until 1968, it had benefited from an advantageous status quo. This special treatment was in line with the numerous concessions granted to Algeria by de Gaulle, in the name of preserving a bilateral privileged relation between Algeria and France. It is in this frame that France maintained the free entry and freedom of import applied to Algeria, except for certain products subject to duties at the time of independence. In fact, France made every effort to defend and maintain the status quo for Algeria within the Community throughout the 1960s. Finally, the Algerian position towards the political situation in the Middle East and the reserve of the Netherlands[28] did not permit the negotiations to start.

The Turning Point of the 1970s

At the end of the 1960s, the association policy of the EEC towards the Mediterranean countries was under scrutiny for various reasons. First of all, the international context was extending into the Mediterranean basin. Détente was well installed in Europe but in the Mediterranean, the Cold War was very present. The strong Soviet presence, the tensions of the Israeli–Palestinian conflict, and terrorism worried the Community.[29] Besides, the extension of the EEC to include three new European countries had consequences on agreements with the Mediterranean countries. Indeed, Great Britain's membership, which had important economic relations with the Mediterranean countries, and Israel in particular, made it necessary to adapt the agreements so that Great Britain's regime of exchanges with the Mediterranean countries was not penalized by its membership of the EEC.[30] Finally, Georges Pompidou's coming to power in 1969 brought some changes in the European policy of France. Pompidou continued along the lines of his predecessor in the policy towards Arab countries, which had been inaugurated in 1967 by General de Gaulle.[31] In contrast, unlike de Gaulle, Pompidou wanted the Community to adopt a similar policy for the three Maghreb countries. At the beginning of his presidency, he made it clear to Algeria that there would no longer be special treatment.

President Pompidou was convinced that although France needed to develop a 'European hinterland', history and geography had assigned it a Mediterranean and African locality. This Mediterranean policy, which consisted in maintaining the 'best possible relations' which were 'closer' to all the coastal states of this almost enclosed sea, had to be organized around three main axes: a southern balancing of the European Community, by openly supporting the application of Spain; maintaining and strengthening privileged relations with three countries of the Maghreb: Tunisia, Algeria and Morocco; defending Europe's interests in the Middle East and developing a French influence there.[32]

It was also at the instigation of the European Parliament that President Pompidou began to lead a general policy towards the Mediterranean countries. Indeed, on 23 January 1969, the Committee on Foreign Economic Relations, represented by Socialist members of parliament (Metzger, Valleys, Wohlfart, Vredeling and Dehousse), proposed a resolution which recommended an overall policy towards the Mediterranean countries.[33] It was the Rossi Report in particular that made the Commission and France aware of the importance of the Mediterranean basin. In this report, André Rossi insisted on the fact that relations between the Community and the Mediterranean countries had been formed in a disorganized manner. Indeed, during the 1960s the European Community had not defined a coherent policy towards third countries, and produced only a 'patchwork of agreements'. André Rossi also reminded that the Community was the first client and first supplier of the Mediterranean countries. Paradoxically, the United States and Russia had very few business connections but enjoyed considerable political influence.[34]

In this context, the Global Mediterranean Policy, together with the implementation of several other political initiatives in the Arab world, was a turning point in the foreign policy of the Community and especially in its cooperation policy with the Third World. As European Commissioner, Claude Cheysson, asserted 'Les accords conclus aves les pays de la Méditerranée du Sud sont un modèle en matière de conception et de définition des relations entre nations industrialisées et pays en voie de développement'.[35]

It was in this context favourable to global cooperation that the Community suggested that Algeria open negotiations with the aim of concluding a comprehensive global agreement, which would include not only a preferential regime for the exchange of goods, but also other actions concerning economic and financial cooperation. On 10 and 11 July 1972 the first negotiations with Algeria took place.[36] At the same time, the Commission opened discussions with Tunisia and Morocco to re-negotiate the 1969 association agreements. The Commission wanted these first agreements of cooperation, which introduced a global approach in Mediterranean politics, to be ratified in 1974, the last date for the conclusion of new agreements with Morocco and Tunisia.[37]

However, difficulties concerning the negotiation of certain agricultural products (olive oil and wine) and also the question of workers emigrating to the Community would delay ratification of the agreement of cooperation. In 1976 negotiations of the cooperation agreements with the three Maghreb countries were concluded.[38] Negotiations with the Maghreb countries were a benchmark for the other Mediterranean countries, in particular the countries of the Near and Middle East.

Conclusion

Paradoxically, in spite of the attachment of France to the Mediterranean space and its desire to preserve privileged relations with the Maghreb, and Algeria in particular, the numerous tensions with the new independent states, especially Tunisia and Morocco, were important factors in a hesitant French politics. These difficult relations led its former protectorates to demand the European Community to negotiate an agreement of association, in spite of their concerns about the nature of association. The case of Algeria was different. Following a bitter war for independence, the country obtained special treatment from France, de Gaulle having made numerous concessions to the Algerians. Indeed, throughout the 1960s, France supported the preservation of the advantageous status quo in relations between the EEC and Algeria, until questioned by Italy in 1968. This was why Algeria was in no hurry to negotiate a partial agreement, contrary to Morocco and Tunisia.

However, the agreements concluded by the Community with Tunisia and Morocco in March 1969 offer a number of lessons. This was because of the features of the negotiations and the legal peculiarities of the agreements of association compared with previous agreements, and also the essential role played by the Commission in the importance given to these negotiations and their outcome.

The realization of the European policy of cooperation with the Maghreb countries emerged only during the 1970s. It was when Pompidou took power that a real European policy of cooperation with the Mediterranean, and the Maghreb in particular, commenced, supported by the Commission and the European Parliament. Even those member states which were, until then, lukewarm on this question, assumed the opinion of the majority and were convinced by the idea that envisaging real European cooperation with this part of the Mediterranean was necessary, after all.

CHAPTER 14

Turkish Anti-Westernism

Restaging the Euro-Mediterranean World in the Era of Détente

Mehmet Dosemeci

Within superpower politics, détente signalled an easing of tensions and mutual retreat from an unsustainable arms race. For the Mediterranean basin, strait-jacketed into a bi-polar world, détente was about breathing space. It delineated a time when some Mediterranean countries, Turkey among them, were, at least more free to think about who they were and what they were doing. Détente unlocked a whole world of options, of ways of thinking and imagining that had previously been blanketed by geo-strategic necessity. Only in rare instances did the freedom to imagine lead to new alliances or alignments. More often than not, they cleared a space where the Mediterranean world could be re-staged.

For twenty-first-century scholars looking back four decades, détente provides, even insists on, an opportunity to reframe and complicate the Cold War European-Mediterranean order. There is a leitmotif in such an undertaking: it is a desire to search for the seeds of our post-Cold War identifications in the 1970s. The metaphor of the seed, of things that were once planted and have only later sprouted is reinforced by the re-escalation of the Cold War after 1980; when these local homegrown gestures were drowned once again by superpower politics. This paper examines how Turkey made use of the soil provided by détente. It first examines when and why Turkey was passed over by the Cold War and then asks what Turks were doing, saying, and thinking within this new found space.

Turkey in the Cold War

Turkey's importance within the global Cold War follows a sine curve, rising to its height in the first decades after World War II, waning by the mid-1960s to a low point in the years following the 1974 Cyprus crisis, only to rise again with the Soviet invasion of Afghanistan in 1979. Geo-strategic factors account for the majority of these shifts. In the years following the war, the still uncertain boundaries of the European front, Turkish participation in Korea, and the deployment of medium-range Jupiter missiles on Turkish soil all increased Turkey's worth. In contrast, by the mid-1960s, the Cold War shift away from Europe to East Asia, Latin America, and the Middle East, an increased focus on ICBMs, and the secret deal between Kennedy and Khrushchev, struck during the Cuban Missile Crisis to remove nuclear weapons from Turkey, drew attention away from Anatolia.

Turks themselves, at the time, were well aware of these shifts. Turkish leaders and diplomats were constantly playing up Turkey's strategic import in order to secure aid, weapons, and security from the USA and yet, as time went on, found themselves increasingly isolated and expendable – the US embargo in 1974 serving as the painful climax of this trend. By the mid-1960s, it was becoming clear that this uni-dimensional reliance on the USA had cost Turkey dearly. Turkey had lost almost all connections and ties with its neighbours including Greece, the Balkans, and the Middle East, barely noticed the decolonization and Non-Aligned Movement taking place all around it, and found no platform to speak from regarding the Arab–Israeli conflict. As early as 1963, an astute member of Turkey's diplomatic corps remarked on Turkey's peculiar situation among the constellations of global states and peoples:

> In the councils of the West an imperceptible but nonetheless effective curtain separates her [Turkey] from the other members. She is still the newcomer with a different background. As a member of the Afro-Asian group the same psychological barrier affects Turkey in assemblies of non-European nations who regard her more European than Eastern and look upon her presence among themselves as anomalous. With respect to the Muslim group, Turkey, vitally secular in her new instincts, does not regard herself as part of the group, nor is acknowledged as such by that group. She also lacks the instinctive acceptance from which countries belonging to an ethnic grouping such as the Arabs, or the cultural groupings such as the Latin Americans, do benefit. Nor do the anti-colonials, like India, who make a cult of anti-Westernism,

find her a kindred soul. In short Turkey is a lone wolf without instinctive allies or friends.[1]

Feeling abandoned by the USA, and globally isolated, from the late 1960s onwards, Turks turned their attentions to Europe, carrying out a long and drawn-out debate over Turkey's membership bid to the nascent European Economic Community (EEC). I call this conversation, which occurred at the broad intersection of politics and academia, the great Westernization debate. Centred on the Common Market, it involved a wide-ranging discussion of the foundations of the Turkish project and its social, ideological, cultural, and economic relationship with the West.

The first question we have to ask ourselves is why this debate on Turkish Westernization was centred on Europe and not the United States, the new symbol of the West for many. This was by no means a foregone conclusion. Indeed, Turkish–American relations, especially Turkish membership in the Atlantic Alliance, occupied a privileged place in Turkey's post-war project.[2] In the immediate post-war period, the Truman Doctrine, American military power against the perceived Soviet threat, and the simple fascination with a novel and thriving culture, all served to propel the United States as the new symbol of the West. Added to this and compared with the Europeans, the USA had a much greater physical presence within Turkey in the first two decades after the war. American bazaars, American military bases, American nuclear missiles, American technicians, and American-style highway construction funded by American credit, were turning Turkey into what the then Turkish Prime Minister Adnan Menderes gleefully termed a 'little America'.[3]

The United States and NATO also figured prominently in Turkish anti-Western sentiment that began in the mid-1960s and continued on and off through 1980. The 'Yankee Go Home!' mentality manifest in protests against the US Sixth Fleet, the torching of the US ambassador's motorcade, and demands for the closure of US bases certainly echoed throughout broad sectors of Turkish society.[4]

By contrast, Turkey's involvement in the European Common Market came relatively late and progressed much more slowly. Turkey applied to join the EEC in July of 1959, a few months after Greece. While welcomed by the Six, the Turkish economy was by no measure ready to withstand the competition that immediate accession would bring. To solve this dilemma, negotiators on both sides settled upon a gradual process of integration with the aim of full Turkish membership at some future date, drafting a three-stage treaty of association known as the Ankara Agreement.

Despite the much larger material and geo-strategic weight of Turkish–US relations, especially Turkish membership of NATO, their effect on the Turkish social-imaginary paled in comparison with the EEC. There were a number of reasons for this, and a brief outline of the major differences between NATO and the EEC in the Turkish social-imaginary will serve to underscore the centrality of the EEC to Turkey's great Westernization debate.

First, whereas membership of NATO and other post-war organizations such as the Council of Europe and the OECD had been quick or instantaneous, Turkish integration into the EEC was an ongoing and incomplete process. The association agreement between Turkey and the EEC ensured a protracted process, creating a rich grey zone between inclusion and exclusion that Turkey occupied, and continues to occupy, to this day. As long as Turkey remained an associate member of the EEC, the questions of whether Turkey should join, and the merits and costs of membership, remained open.[5]

Second, the instrumental reality of Turkish membership in NATO served to dampen its impact on Turkish self-understandings. Turkey had historically been included in the Western system for strategic reasons. In this sense NATO was the continuation of Turkey's strategic inclusion in the West that began with the Treaty of Paris of 1856. In both instances the threat of Russian influence confirmed Turkish membership into the then European, now transatlantic, system of states. Ironically, membership in NATO actually served to underscore the distinction between inclusion in a strategic orbit, to which Turkey belonged, and being accepted as a member of the European 'club' or 'community', from which Turkey had historically been excluded. By contrast, integration into the EEC, the Turks believed, would mark the end of their historical exclusion.

Third, the East–West discourses of the Cold War were based either on economic distinctions between capitalist or communist modes of production, or on the politico-ideological struggle over the meaning and substance of 'democracy'. Neither had much in common with Turkey's historical understanding of the terms East and West, which was based in the nineteenth-century European dichotomy between an advanced European civilization and its oriental and backward counterpart. By this count, Turkish integration into the EEC resonated much more forcibly with Atatürk's project to transform Turkey from a traditional to a modern society.

Finally, the scope of Turkish membership in NATO was much narrower than Turkish association with the EEC. This difference was especially significant for critics of both organizations. Turkish opposition to NATO was limited to arguments of territorial sovereignty, such as the presence of US bases or the legality of opium production. By contrast, the EEC invoked the very real possibility, welcomed or not, of economic, political, and social union with Europe, resonating with and resurrecting debates over nationalism, modernity, and 'Westernization' that lay at the core of the modern Turkish project.

The Great Westernization Debate

If détente created a space where the direction of the Turkish national project could be openly debated, global isolation, economic crisis, and domestic political paralysis, all worsening throughout the 1970s, lent these debates an existential urgency. The previous section outlined several reasons why the EEC became the central axis of the Great Westernization Debate. This section will first examine the dominant narrative used to frame Turkish understandings of the EEC, and second, summarize the various positions that challenged this narrative.

From the outset, Turks perceived their integration into the EEC in more than economic terms. In fact, the most salient feature of Turkey's long-standing membership bid has been the striking incongruity between the subject matter – i.e. the integration of the Turkish economy into the European common market – and the language used to speak about this integration.

This language, like other national discourses in applicant countries, has been ideological. It has made zealots out of technocrats and statesmen, led to best sellers, theatre productions, and arson. The EEC has been alternately embraced as the crowning symbol of Turkey's accomplishments and disavowed as the re-colonization of the country. Rarely has it been grasped as somewhere, neutrally, in between.

A Civilizational Rhetoric

During the initial period of Turkish–EEC relations between 1959 and 1963, there was near unanimous support for Turkish integration. Nearly all state and civil organizations; the Turkish Foreign Service, members of both political parties, the media, business associations and trade unions approached the EEC with enthusiasm. Cold War considerations to further cement Turkey's place in the Western orbit, the need to secure Western financial aid, or the strategic rationale to not be left out of any organization solicited by Greece were motivations that, to varying degrees, informed Turkish support among different groups.

Yet, remarkably, none of these considerations factored into how Turks vocalized their support for association with the EEC. Instead, Turkish support was, with few exceptions, expressed in *civilizational* terms, as the consummation of Mustafa Kemal Atatürk's vision to 'raise Turkey to the level of contemporary civilisation.' For the Turkish elite, joining the European Common Market was seamlessly incorporated into, and quickly became the benchmark and beacon for, the Turkish project. In explaining the government's decision to apply, Foreign Minister Zorlu stressed how, 'Our application to the EEC was a logical outcome of Turkey's desire to be counted as European,' adding that, 'The formation of the EEC must be seen as another historical opportunity for Ankara to demonstrate Turkey's Europeanness'.[6]

This sentiment was habitually echoed, both within and outside government, during the negotiations of the Ankara Agreement. In September of 1960, a columnist for the daily *Cumhuriyet,* argued that 'For those that wish to see Turkey reach the level of Western Civilisation and the standards of its prosperity, the Common Market must be seen as an opportunity rarely produced by either fortune or history'.[7]

The civilizational rhetoric reached its apex during the signing ceremony of the Ankara Agreement on 12 September 1963. Foreign Minister Feridun Cemal Erkin opened the evening with a moving talk stressing how 'This agreement crowns the fundamental westernisation revolutions of Atatürk by tightly binding Turkey to Western Europe and the highest standards of civilisation that it represents'.[8] Turkish newspapers the following day seemed at pains to outshine each other. *Hurriyet* headlined with, 'Historical Agreement Signed Yesterday. We've Joined the Common Market!' and went on to exclaim how 'This event is the most productive and concrete step in Turkey's 150-year effort to westernize and be considered an equal member of Western Civilization'.[9] *Milliyet* had these words covering half the front page, 'Turkey's Europeanness has been Validated'.[10] *Aksam Gazetesi*, 'Turkey is Inescapably Part of Europe!'[11]

The civilizational language used to understand Turkish–EEC relations formed one side of the great Westernization debate. It tied the dominant way of imagining the modern Turkish project since Atatürk (Westernization) to a concrete and ongoing process (membership of the European Common Market). This had two important consequences. First, it catapulted the social-symbolic significance of the EEC way out of proportion to the EEC's potential economic worth for Turkey, linking, at least for its supporters, the success or failure of the Turkish project to its membership bid. Second, and significantly for the alternate imaginations of Turkey, this coupling provided a concrete target for critics of unabashed Westernization. Opposition to the Common Market challenged not only the merits of Turkey's membership bid, but also the civilizational ideology that supported it. It turned the debate over the EEC into an introspective engagement with Turkey's recent past, one that asked – and sought to redress – how Turkey had come to associate itself with the EEC in the first place. In doing so, anti-EEC groups put forth new ways to understand and orient the Turkish project and its place within the Euro-Mediterranean world.

Turkish Anti-Westernism

Critics of the EEC formed the other side of Turkey's great Westernization debate. Growing in strength and number throughout the 1970s, they included, by the decade's end, all major parties outside of Demirel's Justice Party, all trade unionists and bureaucrats (with the exception of diplomatic corps), as well as many businessmen. Turkish opposition to the EEC cut across the secular/Islamic, Kemalist/populist, and left/right divides of the Cold War era, and saturated university dormitories and state ministries alike. While the rhetoric structure and content of various anti-EEC groups were similar, often employing the same phrases and signifiers, they were internally divided along political-ideological lines that had emerged in the 1960s: namely the left (radical and centre), the radical right, and political Islam. The following will examine how each of these ideologies challenged the civilizational rhetoric and, in the process laid out their own narrative of Turkey's past and vision for its future.

Political Islam

In the late 1960s, well before the European right began defining Europe as a Christian civilization culturally incompatible with Muslim Turkey, Islamic intellectuals and politicians were making these same claims in Turkey. They argued that Turkey's Muslim values would be eroded by membership in the common market – a Western materialist culture based on greed and mass consumerism. As a famous Islamic intellectual Said Nursi noted:

> Before the Muslim Turk only needed three or four things. The present tyrannical Western civilization has encouraged consumption, abuses, wastefulness and the appetites, and, in consequence, has made the nonessential into essential. Now this so-called civil person needs twenty things instead of four. And yet he can only

obtain two of these twenty. He is still in need of eighteen where
before he was in need of a few if that at all. It is in this above all,
that contemporary civilization has impoverished humankind.[12]

Interestingly, the Islamic revival in Turkey did not hark back to a golden
age of Islam but fully embraced the need for Turkish development; not
one that would catch up to the consumerist modernity of the West but
an Islamic modernity that would preserve Muslim values. Turkish development, they believed, should focus on heavy industry, the creation of
distinctively Muslim goods, and interest-free Islamic banking. Needless
to say, none of these policies would be possible for an under-developed
Turkey integrating her economy with those of the West. As the Islamist
economics professor Dr Sabahaddin Zaim wrote in his seminal 1970 study,
The Common Market and Turkey:

> The Common Market and its internal supporters operate on
> principles and perspectives totally at odds with the existence of
> the Turkish people, their national customs [*hars*] and culture.
> Both the long and short term effects of entering into the transi-
> tional stage are incommensurable with our national culture and
> the essential foundations of Turkish-Islamic society, meaning
> Turkish Nationalism, economic development, and our national
> welfare; in short, with all of Turkey's national interests.
> The Turkish people have nothing in common with the
> Common Market states. They are Europeans – we are Asian. We
> are Muslims, they Christian. Our social and cultural institutions
> have been neglected by incompetent leaders – theirs on the other
> hand are cemented, advanced, and strong. If we join the EEC,
> the Turkish people will be infested by the imperialism of Western
> Christian culture. [13]

In the last paragraph, Professor Zaim acknowledged the existence of a hier-
archical scale of development on which Turkey found herself at a relative
level of backwardness vis-à-vis the member states. Yet, he made explicit that
this development was not that of a singular and convergent modernity in
which Turkey's future is that of present-day Europe. Professor Zaim underscored the fundamental incongruity between Turkey's and Europe's social
and cultural institutions, while simultaneously asserting that the European
Common Market states were at a relatively more advanced state of development regarding their own culture and society than Turkey was with hers.

The double move of accepting the epistemological premises of development but arguing for distinct and non-converging developmental paths allowed Professor Zaim to oppose the Common Market on the grounds of cultural imperialism while still claiming the equality if not superiority of Turkish culture.

Turkey's relative economic under-development was often cited by the Islamic right, imparting a specific religious context to anti-imperial rhetoric. In the introduction to the National Order Party's publication, *The Common Market in the Turkish Assembly*, its youth organization leader drew parallels between opposition to Common Market and the Christian–Ottoman wars of the fifteenth century:

> The Independence we fought so valiantly for will be handed back over to the Jews and Christians as they buy out our land, our factories, and colonize our soil [...] Following the words of the great Sultan Fatih Mehmed who said, 'May God, the Great Prophet and I curse anyone who sells one handful of this country,' we will never allow, under the garb of trade, our nation to be abandoned to foreign exploiters.[14]

Necmettin Erbakan, the leader of Turkey's first two Islamic parties in the 1970s was even more direct, casting the EEC as a religiously motivated financial conspiracy: 'The EEC is a three-story building. On the top floor sit the Jews, below them the Americans, and finally on the bottom, the Europeans. They're inviting us into the basement as the building super [*kapıcı*]'.[15]

Rather than remain in this dependent status within the Zionist-Christian world economy, Erbakan proposed an immediate end to relations with the EEC and called on his followers in the State Planning Organization to form a customs union with the Muslim nations of the RCD or the organization for Regional Cooperation and Development set up in 1964 between Pakistan, Iraq, and Turkey.

The Radical and Centre-Left

The ideology of the Turkish left in the 1960s and 70s was conditioned by Turkey's post-war political culture, plagued by the problem of presenting a socialist agenda in a virulently anti-Soviet climate. In these circumstances, the left turned to a re-reading of Atatürk and the birth of the Turkish Republic. Against the dominant narrative, which saw radical Westernization as Atatürk's chief legacy, they resurrected an earlier

Atatürk, seeing Turkey's War of Independence as an anti-imperialist struggle against the West.

This refocus brought a radically new bent to Turkish–EEC relations. The Turkish left viewed contemporary Turkey as sandwiched between two periods of colonization, the first that was overcome through the national struggle after the Great War, the second, the impending recolonization of Turkey by the EEC. Their tactic thus became to resurrect Turkey's past efforts against Western intrusion to galvanize the upcoming struggle. Leftist presses republished old letters sent between Lenin and Atatürk which spoke of Turkey and Russia as initiating the first liberation struggles against European imperialism and leftist leaders called for a 'second – economic – war of independence' against the new imperialists lining up to turn Turkey into their common market.[16]

The Turkish Workers Party (TWP), the first political party to voice opposition to the EEC as early as 1963, set the tone for the radical leftist groups and unions that followed it. In a statement regarding the signing of the Ankara Agreement, TWP made clear the stakes of Turkish membership:

> Whereas, as the writ of this agreement is gradually born out, the livelihood of two million plus peasant families will slowly vanish, those of our craftsmen, even faster. Our infant industry, especially our heavy industry, will disappear in the face of untethered European competition. All this will result in a vast migration of unemployed workers into our towns, whose swelling numbers will fight and claw at the chance to sell, for next to nothing, their labor to a France, a Germany, or a Belgium [...] for all these reasons and more, WE SAY NO![17]

The emergence of Bülent Ecevit and the RPP's turn toward a populist centre-left, dampened the party's earlier enthusiasm for the ECC. In contrast to the TWP and other groups of the radical left who were unequivocal in their condemnation of the Common Market, Ecevit's understanding of Turkish–EEC relations harboured a deep ambivalence. Ecevit believed that Turkey's relationship with Europe was marked by an internal contradiction that had its roots in a crisis of European modernity. He felt that the universal ideals of freedom, social justice, and democracy it birthed had become endangered by the profit-driven imperatives of its 'liberal capitalist' economic system.

Ecevit argued that rather than resolving this contradiction, the West had simply exported the problem through its relations with the developing world. The rise of multinational entities like the Common Market was, for Ecevit, the latest vehicle through which the West's internal crisis was being thrown onto the shoulders of the non-Western world. In 1975 he wrote that: 'It is such that the West, which fosters and takes pride in the functioning of democracy and social justice in their own countries, is, from an economic standpoint, forced to deny these privileges to the developing world'.[18]

For Ecevit, this created an inherent contradiction between the ideological and material relationships the West fostered with the rest of the world. As new multinational entities like the EEC

> largely determined the foreign relations of Western states, the 'natural affinity' between the peoples of the developing world and the Western countries, an affinity derived from 'shared aspirations for freedom and social justice', has been trumped by economic forces that demanded a compliant population.[19]

Yet despite these views, Ecevit never contemplated nullifying Turkey's association agreement with the EEC; moreover, he envisioned membership in the Common Market in Turkey's future. Ecevit felt that if Turkey was to become a free, democratic, and socially just country, it needed to maintain its historic relations with Europe, and a more just and equitable association with the EEC was the only real means of doing so.

The Radical Right

The nationalist radical right was also very much present in the great Westernization debate. Most of Turkey's radical right intellectuals and politicians continued to churn out tired and pedestrian arguments over national sovereignty and territorial integrity that have informed nationalist arguments of many candidate countries. The National Action Party (NAP), the major political centre of the Turkish radical right was exemplary of this. It pointed out how many of Turkey's most important decisions, including her economic development and foreign trade regimes, would have to comply with the EEC, 'eroding our national independence' and 'making Brussels, not Ankara, our capital.'[20]

Yet others on the nationalist right went much further than these staid claims, seeing Turkey's integration efforts as the final instalment of a treasonous Western elite that had ruled Turkey since late Ottoman times. These ideas, as seen in an editorial for the journal *Devlet* [State], entitled the 'Contemporary Civilization Game', turned the tables on the civilizational rhetoric used by the EEC's supporters. Part of a four-week special series of the magazine devoted exclusively to the Common Market, the editorial began with the famous dictum 'Know Thyself' which the author, Mehmet Erdogan, a lawyer from the south-eastern province of Gaziantep, erroneously ascribed to Aristotle. It went on to argue that:

> We've been fooled by the Contemporary Civilization game for the past 150 years. It's nothing but the name of an inferiority complex given to Asians by the Europeans. Europeanization has alienated us from our identity, distanced us from our true surroundings by making us abandon our culture for another culture parading around as civilization. *Real* Contemporary Civilization is to return to oneself, to protect and above all, *understand* and know ourselves.[21]

The underlying claims behind such views are much more radical than they may first appear. Rather than see Atatürk and the modern Turkish Republic as breaking with Turkey's Ottoman past, this strain of the radical rightist thought represented the history of Turkey from the Tanzimat to the present as a single epoch, seeing the continuity, if not the amplification, of Western colonial thought, discourse, and governance between the Ottoman and Turkish periods. Within this context, the ruling elite of the Republic represented intensification, in breadth and scope, of colonial thought *under the guise* of an independent nation-state. This reading maintained that the 'revolutionary reforms' of the Turkish Republic were nothing less than the construction of a colonial state in so far as its social, political, pedagogical, institutional, and above all epistemic structures were based on the precise framework of knowledge correspondent to the structure of Western colonial thought.

At its extreme, the radical right understood the declaration of the Turkish Republic to mark the true colonization of Turkey, which in the Ottoman period had been restricted to procuring certain political and economic concessions. In other words, as the moment wherein colonial thought assumed direct control and administration of the Turkish people.

If, as these radical rightwing authors claimed, the modern Turkish project represented the highest stage of self-colonization, what exactly was this true Turkish nation that had been betrayed? Mehmet Dogan, in his book, *Treasonous Westernization* tried to answer this notoriously difficult question. Following the war of independence, the bureaucrats, Dogan's name for Turkey's Western-oriented intellectual elite, had systematically repressed every custom or local institution that had stood as a competing claim to the national identity and makeup of Turkish society. He pointed out, '[the nation] remains, today, as a silent muted trace of lost customs, language, and traditions of the people.' The only means to recuperate this trace was through a critical subaltern history of the bureaucrats' project, locating the nation in the society they dismissed and dismantled as anachronistic. Without such a historical archaeology, Dogan argued, nationalist arguments against Turkish integration could only be made through the very Western imperial framework that the nationalists sought to reject in the first place.

Restaging Turkey in the World

The above presents a brief summary of the major threads of Turkey's great Westernization debate as it took place around Turkey's membership bid to the EEC. While the Common Market became one of the most discussed and polarizing issues in Turkey between 1963 and 1980, very little was actually accomplished in advancing Turkish integration itself. Despite, or more accurately, because of, this functional paralysis, Turkish–EEC relations during these years held great sway over the Turkish social-imaginary. The impasse in relations created a clearing where the merits of Turkish integration into the Common Market were discussed alongside other possible alignments, enabling Turks to restage the Euro-Mediterranean world and reconceptualize Turkey's place within it.

Within the sphere of foreign relations, this equated to a series of dramatic overtures towards a multi-dimensional policy that reached its apex with the RPP–NSP coalition led by Ecevit and Erbakan in 1974. Both party leaders of the coalition had different conceptions of what a broader foreign policy would entail, as evidenced by their respective international visits during their first year of rule.

Ecevit's initial forays were modest, but in keeping with the new left-of-centre politics of his Party. In March, he travelled to Germany, then led by the SPD's Brandt, and from there to London, where he met with the Labour PM, Harold Wilson. Ecevit soon began to branch out, however, with a visit to Romania in December before embarking on a long Scandinavian tour of Denmark, Sweden, Finland, and Norway. These initially modest departures from Turkey's traditional post-war contacts were followed by more daring state visits to Yugoslavia in May, the USSR in June, and Libya in August. Erbakan, in turn, had his eyes turned firmly toward the Muslim states of the Middle East. Apart from official trips to a number of these countries including Iraq, and later, Iran, he was especially occupied with the Organization of the Islamic Conference (OIC).[22]

The end result of these visits, in material terms, amounted to very little. Most often they concluded with a treaty of friendship and/or agreements of vague promises for economic cooperation. Turkish commentators have all remarked on this fact and stressed that Turkey was in no way unique. They have pointed out how Turkey was just one of many countries taking advantage of the more lenient atmosphere provided by détente to pursue their individual foreign policy agendas, broadening and deepening international contacts which previously had been deemed inappropriate.[23]

Yet what these overtures lacked in terms of their material effect, they more than made up for in symbolic significance. Ecevit and Erbakan's true intentions lay on a different plane. Through these visits, each covered in depth by the press, Ecevit and Erbakan were introducing their countrymen to paths different from the liberal Western model. Each new relationship allowed Turkey to imagine itself within a different constellation of global alignments. Structured around different modes of identification and with differing agendas, Turkey's foreign policy forays toward the non-EEC world broadened its horizons and opened up new ways of imagining the Turkish project.

It is important to note the dialectical relationship of these overtures with the great Westernization debate. On the one hand, they were predicated upon the decentring of the USA and EEC states within the Turkish imagination. This article has examined how Turkish critiques of the Common Market were pivotal in this endeavour. On the other hand, these overtures filled the gap left by disillusion with the EEC with positive alternatives, whether in the socialist states of Scandinavia, the non-aligned bloc, or the Muslim countries of the Middle East. In doing so, these visits allowed Turks to conceive multiple paths to the Turkish project, giving them a sense of choice, stake, and responsibility regarding Turkey's future.

This chapter has argued that the great Westernization debate was made possible by a double clearing: the first, provided by détente which drew Turkey's focus away from the geo-strategic concerns of the Cold War and toward engagement with Europe; the second, provided by the protracted and incomplete structure of Turkish–EEC relations themselves. It argued that the elongated process of Turkish integration into the Common Market allowed a broad swath of Turks to weigh in on the merits of integration, and through this, the place and orientation of Turkey within the world. Generalizing, one could argue that historians and other scholars interested in cultural and intellectual debates would find fertile ground in periods that have been passed over as 'dead zones' within political and diplomatic history. That is to say that lively debate often takes place during times of political or diplomatic paralysis.

CHAPTER 15

The Distant Neighbours

The Cooperation Agreements between the EEC and the Mashreq, 1977

Massimiliano Trentin

The 1970s witnessed a gradual rapprochement between the shores of the Mediterranean and Europe, a process which involved the fields of both economics and politics. This essay focuses on the negotiations and signing of Cooperation Agreements between the European Economic Community and Egypt, Syria and Jordan in 1977. Although it was quite innovative, the new partnership did not, however, challenge the basic asymmetry in power and plenty that divided Europe and the Arab Mediterranean, with *neighbours* remaining *distant*.[1]

Europe and the Eastern Mediterranean

During the 1970s, European politics was heavily conditioned by the social and economic crisis that struck a heavy blow to the development processes of the previous *Trente Glorieuses*. The limits of the combination of Fordism and Keynesism became evident, first in the USA and then in Europe. Politically, the crisis of the 1970s concerned the mismatch between the social changes experienced by industrial societies in Europe after World War II, and the resilience of its political institutions. Although the processes of transformation proved to be less than radical, the European ruling elites nonetheless had to enact some major reforms in order to face the phenomenon of social change.[2] On the whole, the priorities of Western European leaders concerned tackling the domestic crisis, managing their

strategic relationship with the United States, as well as normalizing relations with the socialist camp through 'European' détente. The process of
regional integration also contributed to shaping a continental solution
to changes on the worldwide stage. The EEC extended to include Great
Britain, Ireland and Denmark in 1972–1973 and moved towards Spain,
Portugal and Greece after 1974–1975 following the demise of their fascist
regimes. The 'Monetary Snake' of 1972 and the 1979 introduction of the
European Monetary System would also ostensibly consolidate Western
Europe in the face of transformations in world finance.[3]

Faced with these internal and external challenges, instability affecting
the eastern Mediterranean and the Middle East was an important, but ultimately 'secondary', factor in the European political agenda. The reasons for
paying close attention to the region mainly concerned the issues of stability
of energy supplies, access to local markets, the attraction of capital from
oil-producing countries, and the containment of terrorist acts related to
the unresolved Arab–Israeli conflict. The EEC needed stability in energy
supplies and watched with concern the steady increase in oil prices since
the nationalizations of the mid-1960s. The 'oil shock' in 1973–1974 further
emphasized the vulnerability of Europe in respect to energy supplies. In
parallel, the EEC needed access to the Middle East markets in order to
sell the products and technology that would pay for energy imports and
thus keep the balance of trade on an even keel.[4] The relative and pragmatic
attention paid to the Mediterranean and the Middle East was also part of a
wider context concerning North–South relations. The 1970s saw the peak
and decline of the Third World as a political and organized actor that laid
claim to sovereignty and modern development with the Charter of Algiers
in September 1973 and the declaration of a New International Economic
Order (NIEO) in May 1974.[5]

Reluctant to participate in military intervention, Europe also lacked
a major political power to enforce its needs on the southern partners.
Economic strategies were therefore seen as best suited to dealing with these
challenges. Shortly before, and after the 1973 crisis, the EEC engaged with
the Arab states on projects for a new integrated Mediterranean space. Indeed,
two kinds of programme were elaborated: the Global Mediterranean Policy
(GMP) in 1972 and the Euro-Arab Dialogue in 1974. Western Europe
acted quite swiftly toward changes taking place in the south and eastern
regions, at least compared with the USA. The EEC position on the Arab–
Israeli conflict in 1971, although highly symbolic, marked a significant
step towards a common European stand on the issue. However, it was only
after the 'show of strength' of 1973 that European states were forced to

engage more with the Arab states by setting up the Euro-Arab Dialogue in 1974 and implementing the GMP with the Cooperation Agreements.[6]

The Arab World and Europe

After the shocking military defeat of June 1967, radical and populist Arab nationalism faced a major crisis of legitimacy, which worsened further with the slowdown in profitability and growth affecting their state-led economies. The inward-looking pattern of industrialization was on collision course with the deteriorating balance of payments, and the state experienced difficulty in playing its role as the exclusive engine of growth and modernization. A certain degree of economic liberalization (*infitah*) was initially enforced in order to reverse the decline in productivity and to overcome the obstacles faced by state-owned companies in generating capital and consumer goods. To enable the development of private entrepreneurship and attract foreign investment, the regimes tried to create a more 'business-friendly climate' compared with the more statist policies of the 1960s.[7] In parallel, along with the new oil agreements enforced by Libya in 1969 and the decisions made by OPEC countries in Teheran the following year, the increase in oil revenues changed the balance of power in the Middle East, mostly in favour of the energy-rich states. Contrary to hopes that this might empower projects for unity and independence in the region, the management of oil wealth actually contributed to further fragmentation of the Arab world, with the oil-rich countries moving closer to the West, at least as far as income and consumption were concerned, while the other states struggled to reap the benefit of the flow of capital in financial markets. Having called for a radical restructuring of relations with European and Western powers, these nationalist regimes were now forced to come to better terms with them and their regional allies.[8]

After the autumn of 1970, realpolitik had gained power in Syria under the leadership of Hafez al-Assad, while pro-Western orientations consolidated in Egypt under Anwar al Sadat and in Jordan after the Black September onslaught of the same year.[9] Plans for outward-looking and export-led industrialization, for the world market in the case of Egypt and the regional market for Syria and Jordan, meant that external support was urgently needed: namely, Arab oil production capital and the capital, know-how, technology and markets of the industrial countries, especially those of Western Europe. In particular, Egypt, Syria and Jordan needed access to the EEC market since they were recording increased trade deficits and needed to sell their products to Western Europe in order to balance the trade sheets.[10]

Table 1   Trade Exchanges between the EEC and Egypt, Jordan and Syria in 1976

Millions of UCE (1 UCE= 1.11$)	Egypt	Jordan	Syria	Total
Imports to the EEC from	299.3 (40%)	7.7 (1%)	436.2 (59%)	743.2 (100%)
Exports of the EEC to	1268.6 (63%)	205.5 (10%)	548.8 (10%)	2023 (100%)
Index (1970=100)	383	419	600	–
Surplus of the EEC Trade Balance Sheet	969 (76%)	197 (15%)	112 (9%)	1278 (100%)

Source: CPPE 001458, Parlement européen, Commission des rélations économiques extérieures, *Rapport*, Strasbourg, 11 Mai, 1977, M. J-F. Pintat.

All actors involved had grasped the political consequences of the new setting. Within the region, Egyptian and Syrian leaders put an end to the so-called 'Arab Cold War' against their conservative rivals while at the same time they planned to use European economic support to grant their newly co-opted allies a privileged source of income and rents. The regime enlarged constituencies to include the private sector and conservative forces while diluting, if not completely ending, the phase of Arab socialism. To sum up, the rationales and basic reasons for the Arab leaders to reconcile themselves with Western Europe lay in their need for additional sources of economic growth as well as their need to create more business opportunities for their new constituencies.[11]

Although the ingredients for a convergence in the Mediterranean were already in place, one major obstacle remained. The Arab–Israeli conflict was a disruptive factor in Arab–European relations and also contributed to Soviet involvement in the Middle East. The War of Attrition in the Suez Canal (1969–1970) and the 1973 war marked the highest point of Soviet involvement in the region. However, Arab leaders were already moving towards re-balancing their position in the Cold War.[12] Despite evident rhetoric, the war in October 1973 was intended by Arab leaders to oblige Western powers to intervene and put an end to the unsustainable impasse of the Arab–Israeli conflict. Some kind of settlement was expected to remove a source of tension between the Arab world and the West, thus strengthening the advocates of a fully-fledged partnership. Faced with the failures and difficulties in reaching a negotiated solution with Israel, the Arab leaders decided nonetheless to engage with Western Europe. Leaders, like Hafez al-Assad, retained power and legitimacy despite failing to deliver the Golan Heights to fellow nationalists. They did not fail, however, in providing their business-oriented faithful with privileged access to West European cooperation.[13]

The Global Mediterranean Policy and the Cooperation Agreements of 1977

By 1972, the EEC had already signed preferential trade agreements with the Maghreb states, Israel, Egypt and Lebanon, which would increase the volume of trade and access to the European market. However, given the limited extent of the final deals, the EEC launched the Global Mediterranean Policy during the summit of the Heads of State in Paris held on 6–7 November 1972. It was managed directly by the European Commission and adopted a regional approach that would establish an integrated free-trade zone in the Mediterranean. While including technological and financial coopera-tion, the GMP still relied on the idea that an increased opening-up of trade and international competition would improve the comparative advantages of single countries and 'thus' enhance the respective forces of development.[14] Economic cooperation and trade liberalizations would finally lay the foun-dations of peace and stability in the area. In the aftermath of the fourth Arab–Israeli war, the EEC met some Arab ministers at the Copenhagen summit in December 1973, and established the Euro-Arab Dialogue in 1974. The new partnership also involved the oil-producing monarchies of the Gulf region and enabled a more advanced integration of the 'comple-mentary and balanced forces' of Europe and the Arab world. Accordingly, a type of triangular partnership would support development in the Arab coun-tries where the oil monarchies might lend their poorer neighbours the capital needed to buy EEC products, technology and know-how and thus foster industrialization. Regarding public discourse, a more constructive engage-ment between the north and south-eastern shores of the Mediterranean was justified by the concept of 'interdependence'.[15] In this sense, the GMP was the Mediterranean pillar of the triangular partnership among the EEC and Arab oil and non-oil producers.

The first round of negotiations for the Cooperation Agreements of the GMP started in summer 1973 and involved the states of the Maghreb and Israel. However, it was interrupted and delayed when war erupted in October of that year, and also because of Italian resistance towards granting more concessions on agricultural imports, and the Germans and Dutch who clung to the introduction of the 'most favoured nation' clause in trade opening.[16] Israel signed the Cooperation Agreement in December

1975, although they were again quite dismayed by the limited extent of the deals, while Morocco, Algeria and Tunisia signed in April 1976. In the meantime, on 20 December 1975, the EEC Commission accepted the requests of Egypt, Jordan and Syria to start negotiations, which closed on October 15, 28 and 29, respectively. The related Cooperation Agreements were signed officially in Brussels on 18 January 1977 but took effect only after early 1978.[17]

Negotiations started on January 1976 and are worth noting for the different priorities of the partners. Initially, West Germany, Holland and Great Britain laid down explicit conditions for the granting of any financial aid to the Arabs in order to moderate their stance in the conflict against Israel. Cairo, Damascus and Amman, however, rejected political conditions and focused instead on economic issues. In particular, they refused any deal that did not provide financial cooperation in the belief that mere trade concessions alone would not provide support for their industrial capacities. Other requests concerned the access of agricultural products to the EEC, non-reciprocal reductions in custom tariffs for industrial products, the indexation of prices for export products which would allow a minimum of productive planning, a major contribution towards industrialization through the transfer of technology, scientific licences and professional training. A request for the EEC to adopt a more favourable position in the Arab–Israeli conflict came only as a last issue.[18]

The Assets of the Cooperation Agreements

Both the Global Mediterranean Policy and the Euro-Arab Dialogue expressed the European states' great concern for the problems facing their Arab neighbours, which undoubtedly established a new platform for negotiations. For the EEC itself, the GMP significantly expanded and strengthened its cooperation with the Arab world. This partnership now involved nine out of 20 members of the Arab League, which comprised 68 per cent of the population and nearly 50 per cent of its exports to the Middle East and North Africa. The consolidation of a common, integrated approach to the region was more significant as the Arab world surpassed the USA as the first recipient of EEC exports (13 and 11 per cent, respectively). For the Arab countries themselves, the GMP was the first step towards a more consistent coordination with an economic market absorbing more than 50 per cent of their exports, and representing their first trade partner.[19]

The Cooperation Agreements had indefinite validity that would guarantee long-term access to the EEC market and, in theory, sustain productive investments in the industrial sectors. Access to the market was favoured by a gradual reduction in customs tariffs for certain Arab industrial and agricultural products, such as cotton and lemons, usually at rates between 20 and 50 per cent. European exporters obtained a reduction of between 30 and 40 per cent for their industrial products. This was a clear improvement compared with the previous agreements of 1972.[20] A significant innovation was the inclusion of industrial cooperation, that is, easier terms for transferring patents, the establishment of joint ventures, programmes for professional training of technicians, and medium and top managers. In this regard, the EEC Commission spoke frankly about the fact that industrial and technological cooperation 'should not exclude a well-ordered and gradual re-orientation of certain economic activities of the Community' towards the Arab states, which actually meant the establishment of a new economic specialization across the Mediterranean.[21] However, the most important novelty was the introduction of financial assistance. The European Investment Bank (EIB) granted three different lines of credit, which had five-year renewable terms. The decision to grant loans dated back to 1974 and was aimed at helping Egypt and Syria rebuild some of the infrastructures destroyed during the October 1973 war. However, this ad hoc aid was now enshrined in a framework far more consistent in structure and broader in scope. The EIB granted loans first, according to its statute terms and at market rates, secondly under special conditions, namely a forty-year term and a 1 per cent interest rate, and, finally, according to the non-reimbursable special aid arrangement.[22]

Amongst other sources, the Arab countries of the Mashreq received a total of 300 million ECU while the Maghreb had obtained 339 million ECU in 1976. Egypt was by far the greatest recipient country with 170 million, whereas Syria and Jordan received 60 and 40 million ECU, respectively.[23]

Table 2 Division of the financial aid of the EEC to Egypt, Jordan and Syria

Millions of ECU (1 ECU=$1.11)	*Egypt*	*Jordan*	*Syria*	*Total*
EIB Loans	93	18	34	145
Loans at Special Conditions	14	4	7	25
Non-reimbursable Special Aid	63	18	19	100
Total	170	40	60	270

Source: CPPE 001458, Parlement européen, Commission des relations économiques extérieures, *Rapport,* Strasbourg, 11 Mai, 1977, M. J-F. Pintat.

The GMP was primarily focused on economic issues, but politics also played a part. Both European and Arab capitals wished to detach the issue of the Arab–Israeli conflict from potential economic partnerships, thus preventing different positions from disrupting trade and investments. Indeed, both the Arab and European leaders acknowledged that Europe had neither the key to a solution, nor did they want to engage extensively in the conflict, at least for the time being. The Arabs welcomed the diplomatic stand of European diplomacies in 1971, but after the October 1973 war, they also recognized the USA as the main mediator and power broker.[24] Hence, despite the rhetoric, the political issues advanced by both European and Arab representatives played a role but never prevented both parties from halting negotiations or implementing the Cooperation Agreements even in times of crisis, for example in March 1978 with the Israeli invasion of south Lebanon and the Camp David peace deals during the following September.[25] The promotion of a free-trade zone in the 1970s also meant the EEC giving support to the process of political change in the Arab region. The policies and politics of the *infitah* were based on economic liberalization and the enhancement of private entrepreneurship, of which the EEC Commission was a staunch supporter. Within the Arab context of the 1970s, such strategies effectively helped Arab leaderships to sustain a new class of entrepreneurs and trade intermediaries whose fortunes depended heavily on the privileged positions or monopolies provided by the regime in import–export trade, commercial intermediation, as well as the sub-contracts of foreign investments in production and infrastructures.[26] Control over chains of foreign trade and investment were always a major source of wealth and power in the region, and this was still the case in the late 1970s.

The Limits of the Cooperation Agreements

The significant innovations and high expectations of the GMP should, nonetheless, be further qualified by the actual content of the Cooperation Agreements as well as the broader context in which they were set. In this context, all partners showed their limitations. Despite the ultimate goal of establishing a free-trade area in the Mediterranean, the EEC Commission succeeded in excluding some items produced mainly by Arab countries from reductions in custom tariffs. These items included textiles and most refined oil products. In this regard, Italy staunchly opposed any major concession that might threaten its own production and, ultimately, the agreements did not help the Arab states in developing their agro-industrial and oil-refinement sectors through exports to the EEC.[27]

Industrial cooperation would make a major contribution towards re-balancing this asymmetric relationship. However, this was limited by the few sectors involved and the final amount of funds achieved. The general trend towards granting financial and industrial assistance on the basis of project aid rather than planning aid allowed donor countries to exert major control over their funds, and also to reduce the amount of investments. The EEC financed to a greater extent the purchase of European machinery by Arab partners who would, in turn, produce for local markets or export semi-finished goods back into the EEC. Loans and grants were formally 'untied', however funds were basically intended to finance West European exports and thus support its industrial capacity.[28] Lastly, the limited results of the GMP and Cooperation Agreements were further aggravated by the failure of the Euro-Arab Dialogue. The aim to establish a synergic partnership clashed with the respective priorities and related strategies. The Europeans wanted Arab oil producer investments to be set according to free-market dynamics and rules of the GATT, whereas Arab investors asked for more guarantees and a special focus on industrial projects. The political crises in the Arab world unleashed by the Camp David peace deal in 1978, and the subsequent Arab boycott of Egypt, eventually disrupted the potential of the 'complementary and balanced forces' promoted by the Euro-Arab Dialogue.[29]

The failure of the Cooperation Agreements to support industrial development, however, should be placed in the proper context. Despite the establishment of the first 'Qualified Industrial Zones' or 'Free-Trade Areas' in Egypt, Jordan and Syria, large European corporations did not consider these countries as a privileged area for investment: factors such as mistrust towards the regimes' economic policy and legislation, the resilience of large state monopolies and broader political instability worked against the capacity of Arab states to attract productive investments from Europe and the USA.[30] Moreover, a major divergence over the role of the state in the economy flawed the foundations of the respective projects for international integration. In 1977, Egypt, Jordan and Syria hoped that an economic partnership with the EEC would provide a major incentive for their private sector, but also for the somewhat stagnant public one. At that time, liberalization did not yet involve any strategic shift toward privatization as this might have sparked social instability, inflaming the public anger that already challenged leaders. Public employment and state subsidies were the pillars of popular legitimacy for these regimes, which opted to keep the public institutions afloat and support the growth of a parallel private sector rather than engage in the reform or dismantling of the public one.

By contrast, the EEC sided with the World Bank and the International Monetary Fund and pressured for the privatization of the most profitable activities still under state monopoly, arguing for a fundamental trade-off between integration into the world economy and the permanence of a large state sector.[31]

These factors all contributed towards derailing prospects for development on the southern and eastern shores of the Mediterranean. The pattern of exchange was still based on the Arab countries formally improving their access to the European market with their low value-added products, which also faced the 'market distortion' of the EEC Common Agricultural Policy (CAP). On the contrary, European countries now counted on the 'most favoured nation' clause allowing their high value-added industrial products to enter Arab markets. The net result was the maintenance of an asymmetric pattern of exchange between Europe and the Mashreq and, despite an increase in trade volume excluding oil, the Arab world still recorded another major deficit in the balance of trade with the EEC in 1979. Indeed, it was difficult to combine the promotion of a more balanced partnership with 'the preservation of the exchange balance between the Community and the other countries of the Mediterranean basin'.[32]

Conclusion

Global Mediterranean Policy and the related Cooperation Agreements did not prove to be a landmark contribution to the beginning of a new era across the Mediterranean. However, they do deserve attention as being symptomatic of a new phase in the uneasy relationship between Europe and the Arab world.

The decade spanning from 1956 to 1967 marked the establishment of the Mediterranean as a conflict area between industrial and developing countries. With all due peculiarities, it was part of the wider consolidation of nationalism across the post-colonial world and the parallel fragmentation of the world economy into national or regional spaces. From this perspective, the period sanctioned the integration of Arab societies into the parameters of a modernity based on the nation-state and industrial development.[33] The pursuit of nation-centred development based on direct state intervention in the economy and the latter's transformation into being the main engine for growth were all factors that involved a certain degree of divergence from Western Europe. They implied re-negotiating the relations between the former colonial masters and the newly independent states, rather than enforcing a clear-cut break between them. In fact, at least since the early eighteenth century, the integration of the Middle East into the world economy was mainly conducted along the lines of European colonialism. The impact of this was differentiated across the region but nonetheless enforced patterns of development that were functional more to European than local priorities.[34] The post-colonial nationalist elites tried to eliminate this legacy. One of the most prominent figures of contemporary Arab politics was the Algerian President, Houari Boumedienne. A modernist leader, he embraced the principles of the 'industrial civilisation' of his time and tried to combine integration into the international economy with a staunch defence of national sovereignty.[35]

The inward-looking patterns of development performed quite well for about two decades but soon showed limits in sustaining capital accumulation and production growth, as well as upward social mobility for subaltern groups. The restructuring of the world economy in the 1970s favoured the integration of national markets and both European and Arab elites tried to fit their own domestic interests into this emerging context which was now characterized by development coupled with convergence between the North and South. However, given the existing asymmetry in economic and political power and the growing fragmentation of the Third World, and particularly the Arab world, convergence was to be made mostly along the lines set by the stronger party, namely the industrial powers of North America and Western Europe. This was despite contemporary calls for improving 'South-to-South' partnerships or new international orders.[36] For the Arab elites, convergence was based on access to the markets and capital of the EEC in exchange for protecting European investments from the dangers of nationalization. For the EEC, convergence was based on the stability of energy supplies, and the attraction of 'petrodollars' in exchange for the export of manufactured products and technology. Leaderships in the Mashreq exploited European cooperation to grant business opportunities and rents to their new constituencies while European companies re-established channels that had been previously disrupted during the 1960s and secured a position within the regime-related business community. In this regard, the significance of the Cooperation Agreements was not only limited to its economic effects but was deeply entrenched in the realm of politics.[37]

Arab leaderships finally gained some concessions, which did not however alter the basis of their relationship with Western Europe. Except for the oil monarchies of the Gulf and the tiny ruling elites of the region, the Arab societies as a whole gained little from this process of convergence and interdependence. Unlike the East Asian countries, the Arab states did not profit from integration in the world economy in fostering foreign investments *and* domestic development. None of these states, and particularly Egypt, Syria and Jordan, was to become any sort of 'West Asian Tiger'.[38] Most of the responsibility for this lay on the Arab elites, but neither Europe nor the EEC contributed significantly towards improving their capabilities.

Most EEC attention and resources focused on the European continent, setting a precedent for the Barcelona Process in the 1990s and the European Neighbourhood Policy in 2003. At the same time, the southern and eastern shores of the Mediterranean only entered the political agenda as being functional and subordinate to the solution of the other issues, namely the European integration process and the Cold War or economic restructuring. The GMP and Cooperation Agreements proved to be some sort of palliative to the concerns of the Arab partners and generally did not challenge the century-long asymmetry of power and plenty. In fact, income disparities and deficits in the balance of payments did not diminish. Quite to the contrary, similar to those circumstances prevailing in the rest of the so-called Third World, the patterns of 'growth without development' became firmly entrenched in the Arab Mediterranean and set much of the trend in political and economic dynamics for the coming decades.

CHAPTER 16

Gaddafi's Libya

From Uncertain Alignment with the USSR to Support for Arab Terrorist Movements in the Mediterranean, 1974–1986

Massimiliano Cricco

Support for Arab radical movements was probably one of the reasons behind Gaddafi's decision to purchase a large amount of weapons from the USSR in 1974 and 1975. Libya ordered this equipment, together with a Missile Defence System, for reasons that certainly included the need for better-equipped and greater armed forces. However, these arms seemed to exceed the needs of just the Libyan armed forces.[1] According to a secret British document of June 1975, the level of Soviet arms deliveries to Libya suggests three principal reasons for the Tripoli Government's arms purchases:

> Firstly, Gaddafi may believe that a large Libyan stockpile of weapons would give him considerably more influence in any new Middle East war than he had in October 1973 [Yom Kippur War]. For example, a possible future Libyan tank park of up to three-quarters the present size of Egypt's will undoubtedly be an important factor in assessing the future Arab-Israeli military balance. Secondly, Gaddafi may be planning to give more support to Arab nationalist movements such as the Palestinians [armed groups] and the Eritrean Liberation Front. The equipment here

would be mostly small arms [...] but might include aircraft for a 'Palestinian Airforce in Exile'. Thirdly, Gaddafi may be seeking to improve Libya's relative military position with Egypt [of Sadat] which for various reasons Moscow is glad to do.[2]

Recently declassified documents from British and US archives suggest that Libya wanted to secure greater influence over Arab policy in the second half of the 1970s, particularly against Israel, where Libya took an extreme position, shared only with Iraq and radical Palestinian groups which had split away from the PLO, such as the Abu Nidal terrorist organization,[3] the National Arab Youth Organization for the Liberation of Palestine and the Revolutionary Arab-Palestinian Committees.[4]

When asked by a *Guardian* journalist in 1978 whether Libya was supporting international terrorism, the Libyan leader answered as follows:

Nobody can provide any evidence to support this accusation – It's just propaganda. We stand against Terrorism and we are the largest State in the World which has very strict and harsh laws against terrorism. The aim of this propaganda is to stop us supporting the right causes in the world, like the Palestinian cause. Because they consider the fedayeen to be terrorists and because we support the fedayeen, they consider us to be supporting terrorists – but the truth is that the fedayeen are freedom-fighters.[5]

The close relationship with the most radical Palestinian movements, which were always considered by Gaddafi to be freedom-fighters rather than armed terrorist groups, and the fact that they were being financed by Libya, confirmed the American and British perception of Libya as a 'rogue' state closely involved with international terrorism, especially during the Carter and Reagan administrations in the USA and the second Wilson and the Callaghan governments in Great Britain.

Since the early 1970s, Gaddafi had created terrorist training camps in Libya, offered asylum to wanted terrorists, such as the dangerous terrorist known as Carlos,[6] and began supplying Soviet-made arms to terrorist groups around the world. These also include insurgent rebel groups such as: 'SWAPO, FROLINAT, POLISARIO, the PLO in all their shapes and the Zimbabwe National Front in all of theirs, Moros from the Philippines, Moslems from Thailand, Pushtus'.[7] Weapons included: BM-21 grenade launchers, 122 mm Katyusha rocket launchers, field guns, sub-machine guns, explosive devices and grenades.[8]

According to Geoff Simons, the reason for this strong support to terrorists arose from Gaddafi's stated aim to 'divide the world into imperialists
and freedom fighters' and to help 'national liberation' movements to defeat
the 'imperialist bloc',[9] supporting what the Libyan leader perceived as a
struggle against oppression:

> In November 1976 a Libyan-Algerian agreement was reached to
> arm, finance and train the Basques in Spain, as well the Bretons
> and Corsicans involved in an armed struggle against the French
> Government [...]. [Moreover] Quadhafi supplied money and
> arms to many other groups: the Sandinistas in Nicaragua, factions
> in El Salvador, the Irish Republican Army (IRA) in the United
> Kingdom, Colombian guerrilla groups, the Red Brigade in Italy,
> the Palestinian resistance groups and other terrorist groups in
> Japan, Turkey, Thailand and elsewhere. In mid-1981 Libya sent a
> small number of troops to aid Palestine Liberation Organization
> (PLO) in Lebanon.[10]

A British document entitled: 'Understanding Gaddafi's Foreign Policies'
and signed by Her Majesty's ambassador in Tripoli, Sir Anthony Williams,
states that in foreign affairs Gaddafi was 'still thinking in terms of Nasser's
"three circles" – the Arab, the African and the Islamic' and that 'Libyan
Foreign Policy in the wider context [was] essentially theoretically, rather
than pragmatic, an expression of the dogmas of the "great teacher and
leader" which were attributed to him by the recently created Arab Socialist
Jamahiriya'.[11] In particular, according to Williams:

> Like Nasser, Gaddafi sees the Arab circle as a 'single entity, a
> single region with the same factors and forces, foremost among
> them imperialism [...]'. [This is the starting point for] open-
> ings for Arab Solidarity and interdependence [... and] Gaddafi's
> passionate pan-Arabism. It should be remarked here, however,
> that it is Sadat's betrayal (as Gaddafi sees it) of Nasser's commit-
> ment of Egypt to pan-Arabism which is a main cause of the
> hysterical note [... which found its way] into his relations with
> Sadat. [...] [Concerning Africanism], Gaddafi put his emphasis
> on brotherhood among the people of the Third World, on a global
> interdependence of those threatened by imperialism and neo-
> colonialism [...]. It is often difficult, in his speeches, to disentangle
> his references to the Arabs, the Moslems, the Africans and the

non-aligned [...]. In regard to Nasser's third circle – the Islamic – Gaddafi's intense, fundamentalist, quirkish and simplistic faith leads him into an even stronger commitment than his teacher's to 'the tremendous possibilities [...] through the cooperation of all Moslems'.[12]

At the beginning of the period of antagonism between Washington and Tripoli in the mid-1970s, Secretary of State Kissinger was concerned about the prospective creation of a special relationship between the USSR and Libya, following Cold War logic. By contrast, President Carter, in 1978, after the Camp David Agreement with Egypt and Israel, experienced the more challenging ambiguity of Gaddafi's attitude towards Moscow and the unwillingness of the Tripoli regime to formalize a strong relationship with the Soviet Union. In October 1978, the Libyan leader threatened to join the Warsaw Pact as a protest against the Camp David agreement, but immediately changed his mind, declaring that Libya wished to maintain its non-aligned status.

At the same time, the Soviet leader Leonid Brezhnev was quite sceptical about Gaddafi's uncertain friendship. Nonetheless, the Soviets tried to benefit from it, exploiting the US–Libyan friction in order to achieve propaganda points against American policies in the Middle East. From the USSR's point of view, according to a CIA memorandum:

> Moscow has carefully avoided endorsement of, or identification with, Gaddafi's more controversial actions and theories. President Brezhnev himself underscored Soviet wariness and disapproval when he said in his dinner speech during al-Qadhafi's May 1981 visit there were 'certain differences of an ideological nature between us' and that the two countries [Libya and USSR, ndr] 'differ largely' from one another.[13]

The USSR's misgivings regarding a possible policy of friendship with the eccentric Libyan leader have been evident since the 1970s, in response to Gaddafi's anticommunist statements and 'in December 1980, a Soviet broadcast attacked a Libyan newspaper for alleging that the Soviet "dictatorship" had "deprived the people of the right to power" and transformed its citizens into "slaves"'.[14]

The next tipping-point in American–Libyan relations occurred during the Carter administration with the assault on the US Embassy in Tripoli on 2 December 1979, in support of Iranian militants holding US hostages in

Teheran. Washington immediately protested that the Libyan Government did nothing to protect the American Embassy and accused Gaddafi of collusion with Iran's new fundamentalist regime. According to a secret CIA memorandum dated 7 December 1979, entitled 'US Relations with the Radical Arabs', relations between Washington and Tripoli were predicted to deteriorate in the wake of the US Embassy attack in Tripoli. William L. Eagleton, US chargé d'affaires in Libya, 'recalled the attack had all the earmarks of a planned military event':[15]

> Gaddafi's personal ideological orientation probably precludes any meaningful cooperation on most issues; his behavior will continue to undercut efforts by others in the Libyan government to establish closer ties [with the US]. Libya will continue to regard US military aid to Egypt as directed against itself. Gaddafi will continue to support 'progressive', revolutionary regimes in a way that benefits long-term Soviet, rather than Western interests. Even if Gaddafi cuts back on his support of terrorism – as he currently is – he [...] will continue to fund radical Palestinian groups.[16]

Libyan relations with the West continued to worsen in the wake of a January 1980 attack by Libyan-sponsored guerrillas on the Tunisian town of Gafsa and the subsequent burning of the French embassy in Tripoli.[17] This was followed by several presumed Libyan-backed assassinations during 1980: in April 1980, six influential Libyans were killed in London, Rome and Bonn – among them a former Libyan diplomat, Omar Mehdawi.[18]

From 1981, the Reagan administration aimed to reaffirm American influence in the Middle East and Mediterranean area. The administration's principal concern was the Soviet threat and, in particular, the risk that Soviet-backed radical states such as Libya could endanger American interests in the area, launching terrorist attacks or some form of international aggression in support of the USSR goals. A detailed intelligence report by the CIA Foreign Broadcast Information Service stated that, at the beginning of the 1980s, Gaddafi was supporting almost fifty terror organizations and subversion groups, as well as more than forty radical governments in Africa, Asia, Europe and America.[19]

President Reagan was convinced that Gaddafi was a destabilizing actor, and that he should be restrained, if not removed. Accordingly, the USA devised a new strategy to deliberately increase diplomatic, military, and economic pressure on Libya, as can be seen from a National

Security Council document focusing on US policy toward Libya, dated 22 May 1981:

> Libya under Gaddafi is a major threat to U.S. interests throughout the Middle East/African region and [...] to our concept of an international order. Gaddafi's support for international terrorism, his dreams of empire (now becoming a reality in Chad[20]), his arrogation of the right to murder Libyan dissidents abroad, his hatred for and potential violence against Israel and key Arab moderates, and his potential for developing nuclear weapons require a concerted program of counteraction. Libya poses a threat to the long Mediterranean lifeline of our capability to project power into the Persian Gulf area as well as directly threatening the survival of friendly regimes in the area. This could endanger our entire strategy in that region. Our ultimate objective, therefore, must be no less than a basic reorientation of those Libyan policies and attitudes which are now harmful to our interests.[21]

The new US foreign policy toward Libya was immediately launched with the closing of the Libyan People's Bureau – equivalent to an Embassy – in Washington D.C. on 5 May 1981.[22] The NSC meeting on US policy toward Libya, held on 4 June 1981, approved a series of follow-up actions designed to reinforce the attitude of Reagan against Libya. According to the NSC meeting memorandum, these actions included:

> A media campaign to focus world attention on Libyan misdeeds; an approach to European and regional governments to both inform them of our policy and enlist maximum cooperation; an approach to countries which have provided military sales or training to Libya with the aim of eliminating or cutting back this activity; Sixth Fleet naval manoeuvres for August in international waters now illegally claimed by Libya; a commitment in principle to more tangible measures such as increased FMS levels (some already approved), training, and joint manoeuvres with countries most threatened by Libya (such as Tunisia and Sudan); contingency studies for evacuation and other emergencies and proposals for coping with Soviet initiatives to support Libya in some new aggressive actions; an action plan designed to prevent Libya from obtaining nuclear weapons; additional steps for dealing with the long-term security threat posed by Libya.[23]

The first direct US challenge to Gaddafi's regime was the Sixth Fleet naval and air exercises in the Gulf of Sidra (August 1981), in the international waters that Libya claimed in contravention of international law. The exercise was prepared with scrupulous attention to detail to prevent all possible responses from Libya, as can be seen in an Interagency Intelligence Assessment dated 10 August 1981:

> The Libyan Government is likely to view the exercise as a conspiracy directed against it [...], the Libyan Government may view the penetration of its claimed waters and air space as 'an incident'; there are several non military reaction options open to Tripoli, notably a petroleum boycott, nationalization of petroleum facilities, and harassment of US nationals [...]; Libya's adoption of a clandestine terrorist reprisal policy is also possible; [...]; the Soviets will be able to speed the pace and broaden the scope of their military cooperation with Libya.[24]

Nonetheless, the US Government decided to take military action off the Libyan coast. During the exercise, on 19 August, two USAF F-14 Tomcats downed two Libyan Sukoi 22 attack planes. The naval exercise was a test for American policy in the Mediterranean: if the Soviet reaction had been stronger, Reagan's aggressive approach towards Libya would probably have been curtailed somewhat. Therefore, the vulnerability demonstrated by Libya, together with the 'cautious' response by the USSR, encouraged the US Government to carry on with its policy of pressure on the Tripoli regime, culminating in the bombing of Tripoli and Benghazi in 1986.[25]

The US bombing of the main Libyan cities was officially in retaliation to the latest terrorist incident in Western Europe – a bomb explosion at 'La Belle discotheque' in West Berlin on 5 April 1986 – viewed by the Americans as the last straw in the already strained relations with Libya. It was decided on 9 April 1986, during an NSC extraordinary meeting, to 'use this opportunity to deal decisively with Gaddafi [...] in escalating conventional American strikes [against] Libyan terrorism'.[26]

The Berlin attack had been preceded by terrorist attacks just four months beforehand, on 27 December 1985 on Vienna and Rome international airports. These were ascribed to the Abu Nidal organization with Libyan support, about which President Reagan asserted 'irrefutable evidence of Libyan connection to Berlin terrorist bombing [...] that was planned and executed under the direct orders of Libyan regime'.[27]

The Reagan administration was persuaded that the impact of the April 1986 raids on Libya would be shocking, causing Gaddafi's regime to be forced to modify its foreign policy hostile to the USA and the West, potentially diminishing his opportunity for political survival.[28] After a short period of voluntary isolation, however, Gaddafi came back on the world scene with his forces intact. From the point of view of internal policy, the American air strike rallied revolutionary elements behind Gaddafi and strengthened the influence and authority of his regime. Concerning Libyan foreign policy, the Colonel became even more convinced that the USA wanted to dominate the Arab world, while his personal fears of US plots and provocations increased.

The Libyan leader's approach to terrorism, although more circumspect, remained adamantly opposed to the international order and he was determined to make use of all of Libya's military and intelligence resources to destabilize this order. This is highlighted by the accusation that he planned, with the help of Libyan 'terror masterminds', the Lockerbie and Niger airline bombings in 1988 and 1989.

Notes

1 Fault Lines in the Post-War Mediterranean and the 'Birth of Southern Europe', 1945–1979

1 Gaddis, John L., *Strategies of Containment: A Critical Appraisal of American National Security Policy during the Cold War* (Oxford, 2005); Stephanson Anders, *Kennan and the Art of Foreign Policy* (Cambridge, Mass., 1989).

2 Calandri, Elena and Varsori, Antonio (eds), *The Failure of Peace in Europe, 1943–48* (London, 2002); Pedaliu, Effie G. H., *Britain, Italy and the Origins of the Cold War* (London, 2003); Pons Silvio, *Obiettivo mediterraneo: la politica Americana in Europa meridionale e le origini di guerra fredda, 1944–1946*, http://dspace.uniroma2.it/dspace/bitstream/2108/1379/1/OBIETTIVO+MEDITERRANEO.pdf.

3 Agosti, Aldo, 'Il PCI e la svolta di 1947', *Studi Storici*, n.31 (1990), pp.53–88; Aga Rossi, Elena and Zaslavsky, Victor, *Stalin e Togliatti: Il PCI e la politica estera staliniana negli archivi di Mosca* (Bologna, 1997); Pons, Silvio, 'Stalin, Togliatti, and the Origins of the Cold War in Europe', *Journal of Cold War Studies*, Vol.3/2 (2001), pp.3–27.

4 Elwood, David W., *Italy, 1943–45* (Leicester, 1985), pp.23–5; Miller, James E., *The United States and Italy, 1940–1950* (Chapel Hill, 1986).

5 Creswell, Michael, *A Question of Balance: How France and the United States Created Cold War Europe* (Cambridge, Mass., 2006); Wall, Michael, *The United States and the Making of Postwar France, 1945–1954* (New York, 1991); Hitchcock, William I., *France Restored: Cold War Diplomacy and the Quest for Leadership in Europe, 1944–1954* (Chapel Hill, 1998).

6 Iatrides, John O. (ed.), *Greece in the 1940s: A Nation in Crisis* (Hanover, 1981), p.237; Clogg, Richard, *Greece, 1940–1949: Occupation, Resistance, Civil War: a Documentary History* (New York, 2003); Close, David (ed.), *The Greek Civil War 1943–1950: Studies of Polarization* (London, 1993); Kuniholm, Bruce R., *The Origins of the Cold War in the Near East: Great Power Conflict and Diplomacy in Iran, Turkey and Greece* (Princeton, 1980), pp.383–431.

7 *Foreign Relations of the United States* (*FRUS*), 1944, *The Near East, South Asia, and Africa, the Far East*, Volume V, pp.17–20, 27–34; Gendzier, Irene, *Notes from the Minefield: United States Intervention in Lebanon and the Middle East, 1945–1958* (New York, 1998).

8 Arcidiacono, Bruno, 'La Gran Bretagna e il "pericolo communista" in Italia: gestazione, nascita e primo sviluppo di una percezione, 1943–44', *Storia delle Relazioni Internazionali*, Vol.3 (1985), pp.239–66; Ross, G., 'Foreign Office

Attitudes to the Soviet Union, 1941–45', *Journal of Contemporary History*, Vol.16 (1981), pp.521–40; Rothwell, Victor H., *Britain and the Cold War, 1941–47* (London, 1982), pp.74–290; Watt, Donald C., 'Britain the United States and the Opening of the Cold War', in Richie Ovendale (ed.), *The Foreign Policy of the British Labour Governments, 1945–51* (Leicester, 1984), pp.50–9.

9   Greenwood, Sean, *Britain and European Cooperation since 1945* (Oxford, 1992), pp.7–17; Young, John W., *Britain and the World in the Twentieth Century* (London, 1997), pp.142–56; Warner, Geoffrey G., 'Britain and Europe in 1948: the View from the Cabinet', in J. Becker, and F. Knipping (eds), *Power in Europe? Great Britain, France, Italy and Germany in a Postwar World, 1945–50* (Berlin, 1986), pp.28–37; Pedaliu: *Britain, Italy*, pp.128–56.

10   Kent, John, 'The Foreign Office and Defence of the Empire', in G. Kennedy (ed.), *Imperial Defence: the Old World Order, 1856–1956* (London, 2008), pp.50–70; Hennessy, Peter, *Never Again: Britain, 1945–1951* (London, 1992), pp.238–44.

11   Miller: *The United States and Italy*, pp.191–2, 203, 215, 230; Pedaliu: *Britain, Italy*, p.48.

12   Digital National Security Archive (Digital Collections published by Chadwyck-Healey from Pro-Quest Information and Learning Group, hereafter DNSA): doc., 00011, NSC 5/2, 12/2/1948; doc. 00175, NSC 67/3, 5/1/1951; Pedaliu, Effie G. H., 'Truman, Eisenhower and the Mediterranean Cold War, 1945–57', *The Maghreb Review*, Vol.31/1–2, (2006), pp.2–20; Iatrides: *Greece in the 1940s*, pp.239–57, 220–8; Varsori, Antonio, 'La Gran Bretagna e le elezioni politiche italiane del 18 aprile 1948', *Storia Contemporanea*, Vol.13/1 (1982), pp.5–71; Miller, James E., 'Taking Off the Gloves: The United States and the Italian Election of 1948', *Diplomatic History*, Vol.VII (1983), pp.35–55; Brogi, Alessandro, *A Question of Self-Esteem: The United States and the Cold War Choices – France and Italy, 1944–1958* (Westport, 2001); Pedaliu: *Britain, Italy*, pp.58–95.

13   Malanima, Paolo and Zamagni, Vera, '150 Years of the Italian Economy, 1861–2010', *Journal of Modern Italian Studies*, Vol.15/1, (2010), pp.1–20.

14   Leontidou, Lila, *The Mediterranean City in Transition. Social Change and Urban Development* (Cambridge, 1990), pp.89–100.

15   Asselain, Jean-Charles, *Histoire économique de la France du XVIIIe siècle à nos jours* (Paris, 1984).

16   Ellwood, David W., *Rebuilding Europe: America and West European Reconstruction* (London, 1992); Hogan, Michael J., 'American Marshall Planners and the Search for a European Neocapitalism', *The American Historical Review*, Vol.90/1 (1985), pp.44–72; Kipping, Matthias and Bjarnar, Ove (eds), *The Americanisation of European Business* (London, 1998); Leffler, Melvyn P., 'The United States and the Strategic Dimensions of the Marshall Plan', *Diplomatic History*, Vol.12/3 (1998), pp.277–306.

17   *FRUS*, 1952–1954, *Western European Security*, Vol.5/1–1, pp.199–401; Leitz, Christian and Dunthorn, David J. (eds), *Spain in an International Context, 1936–1959* (New York, 1999), pp.265–74; Pedaliu, E. G. H. 'Truman, Eisenhower and the Mediterranean Cold War, 1945–57', *The Maghreb Review*, Vol.31/1–2 (2006), p.14; Hatzivassiliou, Evanthis, *Greece and the Cold War: Front Line State, 1952–1967* (London, 2006).

18   Athanassopoulou, Ekavi, *Turkey: Anglo-American Security Interests, 1945–1952: The First Enlargement of NATO* (London, 1999); Smith, Mark, *NATO Enlargement during the Cold War: Strategy and System in the Western Alliance* (Basingstoke, 2000).

19   Khalidi, Rashid, *Sowing Crisis: The Cold War and American Dominance in the Middle East* (Boston, MA, 2009); Fawaz, Gerges A., *The Superpowers and the Middle East, 1955–1967* (Boulder, CO, 1994;) Lesch, David W. (ed.), *The Middle East and the United States: A Historical and Political Reassessment* (Boulder, CO, 1999); Brown, L. Carl, *International Politics and the Middle East: Old Rules, Dangerous Game* (Princeton, 1984).

20   Onozawa, Toru, 'Formation of American Regional Policy for the Middle East, 1950–1952: The Middle East Command Concept and Its Legacy', *Diplomatic History*, Vol.29/1 (2005), pp.117–48.

21   Popp, Roland, 'Accommodating to a Working Relationship: Arab Nationalism and U.S. Cold War Policies in the Middle East, 1958–60', *Cold War History*, Vol.10/3 (2010), pp.397–427.

22   Dockrill, Saki, *Eisenhower's New Look National Security Policy, 1953–61* (London, 1996); Ashton, Nigel J., *Eisenhower, Macmillan, and the Problem of Nasser: Anglo-American Relations and the Arab Nationalism, 1955–1959* (Basingstoke, 1996).

23   DNSA, National Security Council Memorandum, NSC 5436/1, 'US Policy towards French North Africa', 18/10/1954.

24   Nogee, L. and Donaldson, R. H., 'Soviet Foreign Policy since World War II' in R.A. Melanson and D. Mayers (eds), *Re-evaluating Eisenhower: American Foreign Policy in the Fifties* (Urbana, 1987), pp.7–8; Dawisha, Adeed and Dawisha, K., *The Soviet Union and the Middle East: Policies and Perspectives* (London, 1982), pp.8, 10–11, 46.

25   *FRUS*, 1969–1976, Volume XII, *Soviet Union*, January 1969–October 1970, Document 138; Pedaliu: 'Truman, Eisenhower', pp.15–18; Yaqub, Salim, *Containing Arab Nationalism: The Eisenhower Doctrine and the Middle East* (Chapel Hill, 2004); Takeyh, Ray, *The Origins of the Eisenhower Doctrine: The United States, Britain and Nasser's Egypt, 1953–7* (New York, 2000); Zubok, Vladimir and Pleshakov, Konstantin, *Inside the Kremlin's Cold War from Stalin to Khrushchev* (Cambridge, Mass., 1996); Zubok, Vladimir, *A Failed Empire: The Soviet Union in the Cold War from Stalin to Gorbachev* (Chapel Hill, 2007), pp.109–10; Brands Jr., H.W., *The Specter of Neutralism: The United States and the Emergence of the Third World, 1947–1960* (New York, 1989); Pedaliu: 'A Sea of Confusion', p.741.

26   Kitroeff, Alexandros, *The Greeks in Egypt, 1919–1937: Ethnicity and Class* (London, 1989); Karanasou, Floresca, 'The Greeks in Egypt from Mohammed Ali to Nasser' in R. Clogg (ed.), *The Greek Diaspora in the 20th Century* (London, 1999).

27   De Grazia, Victoria, *Irresistible Empire: America's Advance Through 20th-Century Europe* (Cambridge, MA, 2005); Stephan, Alexander, *The Americanization of Europe: Culture, Diplomacy, and Anti-Americanism after 1945* (New York, 2006).

28   Varsori, Antonio (ed.), *Alle origini del presente: L'Europa occidentale nella crisi degli anni Settanta* (Milano, 2007); Simpson, Alfred W. Brian, *Human Rights and the End of Empire: Britain and the Genesis of the European Convention* (Oxford, 2001); Garton Ash, Timothy, *Free World: America, Europe, and the Surprising Future of the West* (New York, 2004); Checkel, Jeffrey T. and Katzenstein, Peter J. (eds), *European Identity* (Cambridge, 2009); Judt, Tony, 'The Past is Another Country: Myth and Memory in Post-War Europe', in Jan-Werner Muller (ed.), *Memory and Power in Post-War Europe* (Cambridge, 2004); Larat, Fabrice, *Presenting the Past: Political Narratives on European History and the Justification of EU Integration* (Cambridge, 2004); Gfeller, Aurélie E., 'Imagining European

244   Détente in Cold War Europe

Identity: French Elites and the American Challenge in the Pompidou–Nixon Era', *Contemporary European History*, Vol.19/2, (2010), pp.133–149; Pedaliu, Effie G. H. '"A Discordant Note": NATO and the Greek Junta, 1967–74', *Diplomacy and Statecraft*, Vol.22/1 (2011), pp.101–20; Pedaliu, Effie G. H., 'Human Rights and Foreign Policy: Wilson and the Greek Dictators, 1967–1970', *Diplomacy and Statecraft*, Vol.18/1 (2007), pp.185–214.

29   Bass, Warren, *Support Any Friend: Kennedy's Middle East and the Making of the U.S.–Israel Alliance* (Oxford, 2003); Summitt, April R., *John F. Kennedy and U.S.–Middle East Relations: A History of American Foreign Policy in the 1960s* (Lewiston, N.Y., 2008); Patterson, Thomas, G. (ed.), *Kennedy's Quest for Victory: American Foreign Policy, 1961– 1963* (Oxford, 1989).

30   *FRUS*, 1969–1976, Volume E-5, Part 2, *Documents on North Africa, 1969–1972*, document 11. Martin.

31   Calandri, Elena, *Il Mediterraneo e la difesa dell'Occidente: eredità imperiali e logiche di guerra fredda* (Firenze, 1997); Brogi, Alessandro, '"Competing Missions": France, Italy and the Rise of American Hegemony in the Mediterranean', *Diplomatic History*, Vol.30, n.4 (2006), p.748; Calandri, Elena, 'Italy's Foreign Assistance policy, 1959–69', *Contemporary European History*, Vol.12/4 (2003), pp.509–25; Pedaliu, Effie G. H., 'A Sea of Confusion: The Mediterranean and Détente, 1969–1974', *Diplomatic History*, Vol.23/4 (2009), pp.739–40.

32   *FRUS*, 1969–1976, Volume XXIX, *Eastern Europe; Eastern Mediterranean*, 1969–1972, document 220.

33   http://www.nato.int/acad/fellow/97–99/schwartz.pdf, Schwartz, Thomas A., *NATO, Europe, and the Johnson Administration: Alliance Politics, Political Economy, and the Beginning of Detente, 1963–1969*, pp.1–53; Ellison, J., *The United States, Britain and the Transatlantic Crisis: Rising to the Gaullist Challenge, 1963–86* (London, 2007).

34   Segev, Tom, *1967: Israel, the War and the Year that Transformed the Middle East* (London, 2007); Lesch: *The Middle East and the United States*, p.191.

35   *FRUS*, 1969–1976, XII, document 138; DNSA, 00445, 5/3/1970.

36   National Archives and Records Administration (hereafter NARA), RG 59, Central Files 1967–69, POL 27 ARAB-ISR; *FRUS*, 1964–1968, Volume XIX, *Arab–Israeli Crisis and War*, 1967, Document 268.

37   Kolodziej, E., *French International Policy under de Gaulle and Pompidou* (Ithaca, 1974).

38   Fromkin, David, 'The Strategy of Terrorism', *Foreign Affairs*, July 1975.

39   *FRUS*, 1969–1976; Volume E-1, *Documents on Global Issues*, 1969–1972, document 431.

40   *FRUS*, 1969–76, E-5/2, document 31; *FRUS*, 1964–1968, Volume XXIV, *Africa*, document 186.

41   *FRUS*, 1969–1976, XII, document 138.

42   *FRUS*, 1969–1976, Volume I, *Foundations of Foreign Policy*, 1969–1972, I, Document 71.

43   *The White House Years* 1979.

44   Pedaliu: 'A Sea of Confusion', pp.744–48.

45   *FRUS*, 1969–76, I, document 41.

46   *Ibid.*, document 71.

47   *FRUS*, 1969–76, XII, document 138.

48   *FRUS*, 1969–76, E-5/2, document 11; *FRUS*, 1969–76, XII, document 138.

49   NARA, Nixon Presidential Materials, NSC files, 109; *Ibid.*, Italy, 694; *Ibid.*, NSDM67, 296; *Ibid.*, White House, Subject files, Italy, 41; DNSA, 00085,

14/11/69; 00109, 25/6/1970; 00565, 24/3/1970; DBPO, III, V, Documents 13 and 14; Gualtieri, Roberto, 'The Italian Political System and Détente', *Journal of Modern Italian Studies*, Vol.9/4 (2004), pp.428–49.

50   *FRUS*, 1969–76, I, document 59.

51   Pedaliu: 'A Discordant Note', pp.102, 114.

52   *FRUS*, 1969–1976, Volume XVIII, *China*, 1973–1976, Documents 87, 121,123.

53   The National Archives, UK (hereafter TNA) FCO 9/2401, 15/10/1976.

54   NARA, Nixon Presidential Materials, NSC files, 28 and 169; DNSA, 00553, 24/3/1970; 01006, 17/2/1970.

55   TNA/FCO 9/2309, 2/9/75, 1/9/75; Hamilton, Keith and Salmon, Patrick (eds), *Documents on British Policy Overseas Series III, Volume V, The Southern Flank in Crisis, 1973–76* (London, 2006); Del Pero, Mario, 'A European Solution for a European Crisis: The International Implications of Portugal's Revolution', *Journal of European Integration History*, Vol.15 (2009), pp.15–34; Fonseca, Ana M., 'The Federal Republic of Germany and the Portuguese Transition to Democracy, 1974–1976', *Journal of European Integration History*, Vol.15 (2009), pp.35–56; Hamilton, Keith, 'Régime Change and Détente: Britain and the Transition from Dictatorship to Democracy in Spain and Portugal, 1974–76', *The Maghreb Review*, Vol.31/1–2 (2006), pp.21–41; MacQueen, Norrie, '"Butcher Meets Grocer": Marcello Caetano's London visit of 1973 and the end of Portugal's *Estado Novo*', *Cold War History* 10/1 (2010), pp.29–50.

56   Varsori, Antonio, 'The EEC and Greece from the Military Coup to the Transition to Democracy, 1967–1975' in Svolopoulos, Konstantinos, Botsiou, Konstantina E. and Hatzivassiliou, Evantis (eds), *Konstantinos Karamanlis in the Twentieth Century, vol.: I* (Athens, 2008), pp.317–38.

57   Calandri, Elena, 'A Special Relationship under Strain: Turkey and the EEC, 1963–1976', *Journal of European Integration History*, Vol.15 (2009), pp.57–76; Ahmad, Feroz, *The Turkish Experiment in Democracy, 1950–1975*. (Boulder, CO, 1977); Campany, Richard, *Turkey and the United States: The Arms Embargo Period* (New York, 1986).

58   Wall, Irwin, 'L'amministrazione Carter e l'eurocomunismo', *Ricerche di storia politica*, n.2 (2006), pp.181–96; Njølstad, Olav, 'The Carter Administration and Italy: Keeping the Communists Out of Power Without Interfering', *Journal of Cold War Studies*, Vol.4/3, pp.56–94; Bernardini, Giovanni, 'Stability and Socialist Autonomy: The SPD, the PSI and the Italian Political Crisis of the 1970s', *Journal of European Integration History*, Vol.15 (2009), pp.95–114.

59   *FRUS*, 1969–76, I, documents 39, 41, 71, 73; Bennett, G. and Hamilton, K. (eds), *Documents on British Policy Overseas Series III, Volume III, Détente in Europe, 1972–1976* (London, 2001), documents 4 and 6.

60   Nuti, Leopoldo (ed.), *The Crisis of Détente in Europe: From Helsinki to Gorbachev, 1975–1991* (Routledge, 2009); Loth, Wilfried, *Overcoming the Cold War: A History of Détente, 1950–91* (Basingstoke, 2002).

61   Mockli, Daniel, *European Foreign Policy during the Cold War: Heath, Brandt, Pompidou and the Dream of Political Unity* (London, 2009); Van der Harst, Jan (eds), *Beyond the Custom Union: the European Community Quest for Deepening, Widening and Completion, 1969–1975* (Bruxelles/Paris/Baden-Baden, 2007); Guasconi, Maria E., *L'Europa tra continuità e cambiamento: Il vertice dell'Aja del 1969 e il rilancio della costruzione europea* (Firenze, 2004).

62   TNA/ PREM 15/1281, 8/5/1972; Romano, Angela, *From Détente in Europe to European Détente: How the West Shaped the Helsinki CSCE*, (Bruxelles/Bern,

2009); Snyder, Sarah B., 'The US, Western Europe, and the CSCE, 1972-1975', in M. Schulz and T. A. Schwartz (eds) *The Strained Alliance: U.S.-European Relations from Nixon to Carter* (Cambridge, 2009).

63   *FRUS*, 1973-1976, Volume XXX, *Greece; Cyprus; Turkey, 1973-1976*, document 28.

64   Tsoukalis, Loukas, 'The EEC and the Mediterranean: Is 'Global' Policy a Misnomer?', *International Affairs (RIIA)*, Vol.53/3 (1977), pp.422-38.

65   Jawad, Haaifa A., *Euro-Arab Relations: A Study in Collective Diplomacy* (Reading, 1992), pp.21-80; Al-Mani, Saleh A., *The Euro-Arab Dialogue. A Study in Associative Diplomacy* (London, 1983).

66   Varsori, Antonio, 'Crisis and Stabilization in Southern Europe during the 1970s: Western Strategy, European Instruments', *Journal of European Integration History*, Vol.15/1 (2009), pp.5-14.

67   TNA/FCO 17/1168, 12/12/70.

68   Del Pero, Mario, Gavín, Victor, Guirao, Fernando and Varsori, Antonio (eds), *Democrazie: L'Europa meridionale e la fine delle dittature* (Firenze, 2010); Bicchi, Federica, *European Foreign Policy Making toward the Mediterranean* (Basingstoke, 2007); Featherstone, Kevin and Kazamias, Gerasimos (eds) *Europeanisation and the Southern Periphery* (London, 2001).

2 The United States, the EEC and the Mediterranean

1   This was mirrored in the NATO command structure in the area, where the US Commander in Chief CINCSOUTH depended on SHAPE, and national commands for Italy, Greece and Turkey were subordinated to CINCSOUTH.

2   Calandri, Elena, 'Strategic thinking, military cooperation and political interests in France, Britain and United States' Nato policies in the Mediterranean: from cooperation to crisis 1948-1951', in Dockrill, S. et al. (eds), *L'Europe de l'Est et de l'Ouest dans la guerre froide 1948-1953* (Paris, 2002), pp.45-60. De Gaulle's 1959 decision to withdraw the French Mediterranean Fleet from NATO's military structure was only the continuation of a quarrel about NATO's Mediterranean commands started as early as 1951. See Calandri, Elena, *L'Occidente e la difesa del Mediterraneo. Eredità coloniali e logiche di guerra fredda* (Firenze, 1997).

3   Calandri, Elena, 'Unsuccessful Attempts to Stabilize the Mediterranean: The Western Powers and the Mediterranean Pact (1948-1958)', in Varsori, A. (ed.), *Europe 1945-1990s: The End of an Era?* (London, 1994), pp.275-96.

4   Calandri, Elena, 'Stratégie de développement, option identitaire: la Turquie et l'Europe occidentale, de l'aide multilatérale à l'association à la CEE', in Petricioli, M. (ed.), *L'Europe méditerranéenne Mediterranean Europe*, (Bruxelles, 2008), pp.267-9, 278-9.

5   Calandri, Elena, 'La CEE et les relations extérieures 1958-1960', in Varsori, A. (ed.), *Inside the European Community. Actors and Policies in the European Integration 1957-1972* (Baden-Baden/Brussels, 2006), pp.399-432.

6   Calandri, Elena, 'Italy's Foreign Assistance Policy, 1959-1969', *Contemporary European History*, Vol.12/4 (2003).

7   See Migani, Guia, 'La politique de coopération européenne: une politique étrangère *ante litteram*? Le rôle de la CEE au DAC pendant les années soixante', in Rasmussen, M., Knudsen, A-C.L. (eds), *The Road to a United Europe. Interpretations of the Process of European Integration* (Bruxelles, 2009), pp.189-204.

8   For example, RG 59 Bureau of European Affairs Oecd, EC and Atlantic
    Political-Economic Affairs (Eur/Rpr) Records relating to European Integration
    1962–1966, Lot File 67D33, 5303 box 8, Nara, *Visit of EEC Commisioners* March
    5–6, 1964. *Position Paper EEC External Relations*: see Calandri, Elena 'L'eterna
    incompiuta. La politica mediterranea fra sviluppo e sicurezza', in Calandri, E.
    (ed.), *Il primato sfuggente. L'Europa e l'intervento per lo sviluppo 1957–2007*
    (Milano, 2009), pp.89–117.

9   RG 59 Bureau of European Affairs Oecd, EC and Atlantic Political-Economic
    Affairs (Eur/Rpe) Records relating to European Integration 1962–1966, Lot
    File 67D33, 5303 box 10, Nara. 'First, we tend to agree with the Six that
    for political reasons the Turkish desire for some tie with the EEC should be
    satisfied. The Turks have an increasingly uncomfortable feeling of isolation,
    which was emphasized by the special way in which they became involved in
    the Cuban crisis. Second, the Turkish Government has apparently gone way
    out on a limb at home in promising association, and its domestic stabilization
    program could be seriously hurt if association were refused. Third, our special
    bilateral arrangements with Turkey could also be hurt if [...] the Turks ended
    up with the feeling that we were the one responsible for a refusal. Last, if an
    EEC–Turkey arrangement is inevitable, a more positive attitude on our part
    [...] will give us a better chance to see that the arrangement does a minimum
    of harm to our interests [...]': *Joel W.Biller (Rpe) to C.Hoyt Price (US Mission
    Brussels)*, 21–12–1962 Confid, See Calandri, Elena, 'A Special Relationship
    Under Strain: The EEC and Turkey 1963–1976', *Journal of European Integration
    History*, n.1 (2009), pp.57–76.

10 Belgium 13 million, FRG and France 58.5, Italy 32 million, Luxembourg 0.3
    million, Netherlands 12.7 million.

11 See Vaïsse, Maurice, *La puissance ou l'influence? La France dans le monde depuis
    1958* (Paris, 2009), pp.360–76.

12 For example, the Association Europe-Proche Orient created in June 1967 at the
    European Parliament proposed Israel's association as a precondition for Arab
    countries' association and European financial aid for countries that recognized
    Israel.

13 Vaïsse: *La puissance*, pp.365–70.

14 *Avis de la Commission au Conseil concernant les demandes d'adhésion du
    Royaume-Uni, de l'Irlande, du Danemark et de la Norvège*, 29–9–1967, Supplement
    to *Bulletin des Communautés Européennes*, Paris, n.10, 1967, p.16.

15 The envisaged negotiations on agricultural products and manpower circulation
    were suspended and the remaining $56million of the first financial protocol were
    frozen.

16 Trouvé, Mathieu, *L'Espagne et l'Europe. De la dictature de Franco à l'Union euro-
    péenne* (Bruxelles, 2009), pp.78, 80–1.

17 Papacosma: 'Greece', p.363.

18 In 1963, for example, the PPS stated: 'U.S. objectives are to preserve the North
    African ties which presently exist with the West, to try to strengthen them when
    and where they need strengthening and to rebuild them where they have been
    damaged; to utilize our influence wherever feasible to provide a strong economic
    base for this cooperation through strengthened North African–EEC ties; to
    present the image of the U.S.A. as responsively enthusiastic toward helping the
    new independent nations so that the alternative of turning toward the Soviet
    Bloc will become less and less attractive': *FRUS*, 1961–1963, Vol.XXI, Africa,

Doc. 5 Report Prepared by the Policy Planning Council, September 23, 1963, North Africa in the Mediterranean Littoral.

19 RG 59 Bureau of European Affairs Oecd, EC and Atlantic Political-Economic Affairs (Eur/Rpr) Records relating to European Integration 1962–1966, Lot File 67D33, 5303 box 8, NARA, *Visit of EEC Commissioners* March 5–6, 1964, documents by Joel Biller, John Tuthill, H.Bell,

20 RG 59 Bureau of European Affairs Oecd, EC and Atlantic Political-Economic Affairs (Eur/Rpr) Records relating to European Integration 1962–1966, Lot File 67D33, 5303 box 23, NARA, *Discussion Paper on Formulating a General U.S. Policy on EEC Associations* 22–11–1966.

21 *FRUS*, 1969–1976, Vol.XXIV, Middle East Region and Arabian Peninsula, 1969–1972; Jordan, September 1970, Doc. 26 Minutes of a National Security Council Meeting, June 17, 1970, Mediterranean, Greece, Italy: NSSM 90.

22 Archivio centrale dello Stato, Rome, Aldo Moro Personal Papers (hereafter Moro), Mae 2, folder Visita in Italia del Presidente della Commissione delle Comunità europee Jean Rey, 11 April 1970, MAE, DGAE CEE, *Appunto*, 9 April 1970.

23 *FRUS*, 1969–1976, Vol.IV, Foreign Assistance, International Development, Trade Policies, 1969–1972, Doc. 241, Telegram from the Embassy in Germany to the Department of State Bonn, August 3, 1970, Subj: US Trade Policy.

24 HAEU, Fond Carlo Maria Malfatti, 12, Communication de la Commission au Conseil, 15 May 1970.

25 Moro, MAE 15 CEE, folder 43 'CEE Riunioni del Consiglio dei ministri e dei ministri degli Esteri 1970', *Consiglio dei ministri dell'8–9 giugno 1970 e dell'11–12 maggio 1970, progetti di intervento del ministro Moro.

26 See for example Moro, MAE 2 folder 'Riunione dei capi missione in Medio Oriente, Istanbul 30 aprile-1 maggio 1970'.

27 As in the Moro–Scheel meetings in April, the Moro–Schumann in May, the visits to the UAR and Turkey.

28 Meneguzzi Rostagni, Carla, 'La politica estera italiana e la distensione: una proposta di lettura', in F. Romero, A. Varsori (eds), *Nazione, interdipendenza, integrazione, Le relazioni internazionali dell'Italia (1917–1989)* (Roma, 2005).

29 Moro, MAE 5, folder 'Visita in Italia del Presidente della Commissione delle Comunità economiche europee Franco Maria Malfatti 13–14 Novembre 1970, Politica comunitaria nei riguardi di alcuni paesi del Nord Africa e del Medio Oriente'; however, the Italian Ministry spent many more words asking for an EEC initiative toward Latin America.

30 Archive du Ministère des Relations Extérieures, Paris (hereafter AMRE) Europe 1971–76, Communautés européennes, boite 3801, Direction des affaires politiques Europe, *Note*, 12 May 1971.

31 See for example, AMRE, Europe 1971–76 Communautées européennes, boite 3801, Amb France en Italie, 25 May 1971, a.s. Coopération des Six en Méditerranée, n.16 DA/EU.

32 Moro, MAE, folder Visita in Francia del ministro degli Affari Esteri On.Aldo Moro, 19–20 May 1970.

33 AMRE, Europe 1971–76 Communautées européennes, boite 3801, tel. Roma 28 May 1971, no. 1361–78, reservé secret Coopération communautaire ou coopération franco–italienne en Méditerranée.

34 To prevent this, only months before France had opposed that the WEU discuss a Mediterranean initiative.

35 AMRE, Série Europe, Communauté européennes, boite 3772, Note, 24 April 1972.

36 Financed by the United States, Italy, Germany, Netherlands and Belgium: Moro, 124, folder *Visita a Roma di Anthony Mamo, Presidente di Malta*, 5–1975.

37 Moro, MAE 11, folder 'Visita del Ministero degli affari esteri on. Aldo Moro a Malta 22–23 maggio 1972', *Relazioni Cee-Malta*.

38 On Mansholt as Commission President, see van der Harst, Jan, 'Sicco Mansholt', in M. Dumoulin (ed.), *The European Commission 1958–72: history and memories* (Brussels, 2007).

39 Moro, MAE 16 Cee folder 4, Consiglio dei ministri Cee 5–6 giugno 1972, 31 May 1972.

40 Historical Archives of the European Union, Fiesole, Fond Emile Noël, EN 000126, Cee, Cabinet J.F. Deniau, *Note. Les relations avec les pays en voie de développement à la Conférence au Sommet de Paris*, 24–9–1972 and *Propositions d'amendement présentées par la délégation française à l'occasione de la réunion du Groupe ad hoc des 374 oct 1972*, 5 October 1972.

41 AMRE, Série Europe 1971–76, Communautées européennes 3801, DAEF, Service de coopération économique, Circulaire n.446, 10 October 1972.

42 For example, in November, the Quai noted that 'les pressions exercées par les Étas Unis sur nos partenaires n'ont pas, pour le moment, réussi à arrêter un processus qui va donc pouvoir continuer à se développer': AMRE, Série Europe 1971–76, Communautées européennes 3801, Telegram Delfra Bruxelles, 7 November 1072, n.3461–3482.

43 In the agreements signed with the Maghreb (1976) and Mashreq (1977), the inverse preferences were dropped and France also had to renounce them in the Lomé Convention.

44 For Britain, this was the case for Turkey in particular. Britain had helped Turkey to gain a place in the EPC: see Calandri: 'A special relationship'.

45 But see Mökli, Daniel, *European Foreign Policy during the Cold War: Heath, Brandt, Pompidou and the dream of political unity*, (London, 2009).

46 Vaïsse: *La puissance*, pp.370–79.

47 Mélandri, Pierre, 'La France et l'Alliance Atlantique sous Georges Pompidou et Valéry Giscard d'Estaing', in M. Vaïsse et al., *La France et l'Otan* (Paris, 1996), pp.519–58, 532–5, and Mélandri, Pierre, 'Une relation très spéciale: La France, les États-Unis et l'Année de l'Europe, 1973–1974', in *Georges Pompidou et l'Europe* (Paris, 1995), pp.89–132.

48 Hanhimäki, Jussi, *The Flawed Architect. Henry Kissinger and American Foreign Policy* (Oxford, 2004), pp.275–7, 348–52.

3 Rediscovering the Mediterranean

1 Pedaliu, Effie G.H., 'Truman, Eisenhower and the Mediterranean Cold War, 1945–57', *Maghreb Review*, vol.31, n.1–2 (2006), pp.2–20. Calandri, Elena, *Il Mediterraneo e la difesa dell'occidente. Eredità imperiali e logiche di guerra fredda* (Firenze, 1997); Brogi, Alessandro, *L'Italia e l'egemonia americana nel Mediterraneo* (Firenze, 1996).

2 Di Nolfo, Ennio, 'The Cold War and the transformations of the Mediterranean 1960–75', in Leffler, M.P. and Westad, O.A. (eds) *The Cambridge History of the Cold War*, Vol.2 (Cambridge, 2010), pp.244–7.

3 However, we need to keep in mind that in July 1972 Sadat expelled the Soviet advisors from Egypt. On the Cold War in the Mediterranean cf. Pedaliu, Effie G.H., '"A sea of confusion": The Mediterranean and détente, 1969–1974',

Diplomatic History, vol.33 n.4 (September 2009), pp.740–1. On the Soviet fleet see Kurth, Ronald J., 'Gorshkov's gambit' and Cernâvskij, Sergej, 'The era of Gorshkov: triumph and contradictions', both in *Journal of Strategic Studies* (2005–04) vol.28, n.2, pp.261–80 and 281–308. Cf. also Herrick, Robert W., *Soviet Naval Doctrine and Policy, 1956–1986* (Lewiston NY, 2003).

4 Vego, Milan N. 'Yugoslavia and the Soviet Policy of Force in the Mediterranean since 1961', Professional Paper 318, Alexandria (Virginia, US), Institute of Naval Studies/Center for Naval Analyses, August 1981.

5 'En dépit d'une certaine stabilisation à la suite du conflit israélo-arabe, la flotte de l'URSS continue de s'accroitre en quantité et en qualité. Il arrive, à certaines époques, que le total des navires soviétiques effectivement présents (plus d'une cinquantaine) soit supérieur à celui de la VIème flotte américaine. Celle-ci conserve toutefois avec les navires des pays occidentaux une supériorité stratégique manifeste, notamment en raison de la faible de la couverture aérienne soviétique.' French Archives of the Foreign Affairs Ministry (AMAEF), Europe 1971–76, 3828, Note sur 'L'URSS et la Méditerranée', 10 March 1972.

6 Bicchi, Federica, *European Foreign Policy Making Towards the Mediterranean* (New York, 2007), pp.68–73. On terrorism see also: Laurens, Henry and Delmas-Marty, Mireille (eds), *Terrorismes: histoire et droit* (Paris, 2009).

7 Greece 1961, Turkey 1963, Israel 1964, Lebanon 1965, Morocco and Tunisia 1969, Israel II, Spain and Malta 1970, Lebanon II, Cyprus and Egypt 1972. Cf. Bicchi: *European Foreign Policy*, pp.52–60 and more in general, Petit-Laurent Philippe, *Les fondements politiques des engagements de la Communauté européenne en Méditerranée* (Paris, 1976); Pierros, Filippos, Meunier, Jacob, Abrams, Stan, *Bridges and Barriers. The European Union's Mediterranean policy, 1961–1988* (Aldershot, 1999).

8 Gomez, Ramon, "The EU's Mediterranean Policy: Common Foreign Policy by the Back Door?" in J. Peterson, H. Sjursen (eds), *A Common Foreign Policy for Europe? Competing visions of the CFSP* (London/New York, 1998), p.134. See also Bicchi: *European Foreign Policy*, pp.43–61.

9 On Aldo Moro's foreign policy see Caviglia, Daniele, De Luca, Daniele, *Aldo Moro nell'Italia contemporanea* (Roma, 2011). On French foreign policy among others see Vaïsse, Maurice, *La puissance ou l'influence? La France dans le monde depuis 1958* (Paris, 2009). Laurens, Henry, 'La France, l'Angleterre et les États Unis dans la Méditerranée et le monde arabe', *Relations internationales*, 1996, n.87, pp.277–92. On the European political cooperation, among others, see Möckli, Daniel, *European Foreign Policy during the Cold War: Heath, Brandt, Pompidou and the Dream of Political Unity* (London, 2009).

10 For a summary of consultations among Spain, France and Italy on the Mediterranean: AMAEF, Europe 1971–76, 3828, Note sur 'Entretiens franco–italo–espagnols sur la Méditerranée', 19 January 1972.

11 Cricco, Massimiliano, Caviglia, Daniele, *La diplomazia italiana e gli equilibri mediterranei* (Soveria Mannelli, 2006); Calandri, Elena, 'Il Mediterraneo nella politica estera italiana', in A. Giovagnoli, S. Pons, (eds), *L'Italia repubblicana nella crisi degli anni settanta* (Soveria Mannelli, 2003), pp.351–82. De Leonardis, Massimo (ed.) *Il Mediterraneo nella politica estera italiana del secondo dopoguerra* (Bologna, 2002); Brogi: *L'Italia e l'egemonia americana*.

12 Varsori, Antonio, *La Cenerentola d'Europa. L'Italia e l'integrazione European dal 1947 a oggi* (Soveria Mannelli, 2010).

13 AMAEF, Europe 1971–76, 3801, Télégramme de Rome, 13 December 1971.

14 Bicchi, *European Foreign Policy*, p.48.
15 On the links between *Ostpolitik* and development policy see Lorenzini, Sara, 'Ostpolitik e aiuti allo sviluppo. Continuità e discontinuità nella Entwicklungspolitik dela Republica Federale Tedesca', in A. Varsori, D. Caviglia (eds), *Dollari, petrolio e aiuti allo sviluppo. Il confronto Nord-Sud negli anni '60–'70* (Milano, 2008) pp.171–86.
16 AMAEF, Europe 1971–76, 3801, 'Thèses susceptibles de faciliter la discussion sur le thème "L'Europe et la situation dans la Méditerranée"', undated (May 1971).
17 AMAEF, Europe 1971–76, 3801, dépêche de l'ambassade de France à Rome, 25 May 1971.
18 *Ibid.* The French Ambassador also wrote in the same letter: 'Tout récemment encore, la nécessité de coordonner les politiques des pays consommateurs de pétrole devant les nationalisations opérées en Libye et en Algérie ont d'autre part renforcé les Italiens dans la conviction que ce genre de questions devrait faire l'objet en premier lieu d'une action concertée des six pays.'
19 AMAEF, Europe 1971–76, 3828, Note sur la 'Méditerranée comme sujet de coopération politique européenne', 3 November 1971.
20 AMAEF, Europe 1971–76, 3801, télégramme de Paris (Maurice Schumann) à Rome, 8 June 1971.
21 AMAEF, Europe 1971–76, 3801, Note de la présidence, 27 January 1972
22 'Il ne peut y avoir de véritable action politique en Méditerranée qui ne soit basée sur une action économique visant au développement des pays riverains non membres de la Communauté. Les pays membres de la CEE et la Communauté elle-même devraient s'efforcer de mener dans cette région une politique de coopération économique et technique conforme à leurs moyens et adaptée aux circonstances.' AMAEF, Europe 1971–76, 3801, Rapport du Groupe de travail sur la Méditerranée, 8 February 1972.
23 Historical Archives of the European Union (HAEU), BAC 28/1980, 768, Rapport sur la politique commerciale de la Communauté dans le bassin méditerranéen. Rapporteur: M. Rossi, 1 February 1971.
24 HAEU, BAC 86/2005, 412, Bruxelles le 27 mars 1972, Note de la délégation de la Commission sur les négociations sur l'élargissement.
25 Cf. Berdat, Christophe, 'L'avènement de la politique méditerranéenne globale de la CEE', *Relations internationales,* n.130, (2007/2), pp.87–109. See also Migani, Guia, 'La politique globale méditerranéenne de la CEE, 1970–1972' in A.Varsori, G. Migani (eds), *Europe in the international arena during the 1970s: entering a different world* (Brussels, 2011); Pierros, Meunier, Abrams: *Bridges and barriers*, pp.82–125. For a long-term vision on the EEC Mediterranean policy see Calandri, Elena, 'L'eterna incompiuta: la politica mediterranea tra sviluppo e sicurezza' in E. Calandri (ed.), *Il primato sfuggente. L'Europa e l'intervento per lo sviluppo 1957–2007* (Milano, 2009), pp.89–117.
26 United Kingdom National Archives (UKNA), FCO 30/1258, letter of Mason (EID) to Bullard (EESD), 'EEC political consultations: Mediterranean', 23 February 1972.
27 'L'influence politique de l'URSS reste considérable en Egypte et en Syrie mais subit quelques fluctuations. Ces deux pays cherchent manifestement à s'y soustraire mais dépendent quasi entièrement des fournitures d'armes soviétiques. L'idéologie communiste ne semble pas pénétrer en profondeur dans ces deux pays, malgré leur régime socialiste.' UKNA, FCO 30/1258, relations des pays

de la Communauté avec les pays du Levant (document rédigé par les Pays Bas), undated.

28   'So long as the Soviet leaders maintain their interest in détente in Europe, it is realistic to assume that they will make no great efforts to undermine Yugoslavia's independence, even though she will continue to be a source of irritation to the Soviet Union for political, ideological and strategic reasons. But when Tito goes, the temptation for the Soviet Union to exploit the opportunities of the new situation will be strong.' UKNA, FCO 30/1258, United Kingdom paper for the Mediterranean working group. Yugoslavia, undated.

29   On the Soviet strategy in Malta and Cyprus, AMAEF, Europe 1971–76, 3828, Note sur 'l'URSS et la Méditerrannée', 5 October 1971. As an exsmple of Western suspicions and fears, cf. *ibid.*, télégramme de Moscou sur 'relations entre Malte et l'Union soviétique', 14 March 1972.

30   UKNA, FCO 30/1258, Comité politique européen – groupe de travail sur la Méditerranée (Malte) – undated.

31   UKNA, FCO 30/1258, United Kingdom paper for the Mediterranean working group. Yugoslavia, undated.

32   UKNA, FCO 30/1258, Contribution néerlandaise au rapport du groupe de travail du Comité politique de la Communauté européenne sur la Méditerrané (Libye), undated.

33   AMAEF, Europe 1971–76, 3801, La péninsule ibérique, Bonn, 1 May 1972.

34   UKNA, FCO 30/1259, Note sur l'Algérie (MAEF), 12 April 1972.

35   UKNA, FCO 30/1259, Eléments proposés par la délégation italienne pour le prochain rapport du G.d.T, 24 April 1972.

36   UKNA, FCO 30/1259, EEC political consultations: Mediterranean working group (Meeting of 24–25 April 1972). 1 May 1972.

37   UKNA, FCO 30/1259, Telegram n.169 from Luxembourg, 19 May 1972.

38   *Ibid.*

39   AMAEF, Europe 1971–76, 3801, compte-rendu de la réunion du groupe de travail sur la Méditerranée, Luxembourg 15 June 1972.

40   UKNA, FCO 30/1259 Telegram from Luxembourg to FCO 19 May 1972.

41   *Ibid.*

42   AMAEF, Europe 1971–76, 3828, Rapport du Comité politique, Luxembourg le 18 mai 1972.

43   See Nicolas Badalassi's chapter in this book.

44   UKNA, FCO 30/1260, Annexe C, note pour le groupe de travail sur la Méditerranée, 4 September 1972.

45   Statement from the Paris Summit (19 to 21 October 1972), www.ena.lu.

46   Cf. for example the Political Directors' report of 18 May 1972. AMAEF, Europe 1971–76, 3828, Rapport du Comité politique, Luxembourg le 18 mai 1972. For a long-term vision on the relations between Europe and the Mediterranean see Petricioli, Marta (ed.), *Mediterranean Europe* (Brussels, 2008); Dumoulin, Michel, Duchenne, Geneviève (eds), *L'Europe et la Méditerranée* (Brussels, 2001).

47   The Common Foreign and Security Policy was introduced only in 1992 with the Maastricht Treaty. What we mean here by common foreign policy is the adoption of common positions on matters related to the foreign policy and the international relations, such as was the case for the CSCE.

4 Sea and Détente in Helsinki

1   Note de la sous-direction d'Europe méridionale, 26 June 1972. Archives of the French Foreign Minister (AMAE), CSCE, vol.25.

2   According to the young Foreign Minister Abdelaziz Bouteflika in August 1975. Note CSCE, 26 August 1975. AMAE, Europe 1971–76, URSS, vol.3689.

3   Circulaire n°327, Puaux, 4 July 1972. AMAE, Europe 1971–76, Organismes, vol.2924.

4   Document of the French delegation to the sous-comité CSCE, 1973. AMAE, CSCE, vol.24.

5   Compte rendu of the Franco–Italo–Spanish meeting, 29 June 1972. AMAE, CSCE, vol.25.

6   Finally, Algeria did not manage to organize this conference, whose goal was to improve peace and security in the Mediterranean. France refused to join because most of its allies were not invited.

7   Note de la sous-direction d'Europe méridionale, 26 June 1972. AMAE, CSCE, vol.25.

8   Note du directeur d'Europe, 5 March 1973. AMAE, CSCE, vol.25.

9   Télégramme n°622/625, Soutou, 14 March 1973. AMAE, CSCE, vol.31. Bouteflika moderated these comments by saying that the Algerian government 'would not use the hearing which would possibly be granted to it to raise the Near East question in itself'. Cf. télégramme n°708–710, Soutou, 24 March 1973. AMAE, CSCE, vol.31.

10 Télégramme n°2712/15, André, 4 June 1973. AMAE, CSCE, vol.32.

11 Department of State, Briefing Paper, July 1975, folder 'July 26 – August 4, 1975 – Europe – Briefing Book – CSCE Bilateral Book – Volume II (1)', Box 11, National Security Adviser, Trip Briefing Books and Cables for Gerald Ford, Gerald R. Ford Library.

12 Document CSCE/CC/44, delegation of Malta, 11 September 1974. CSCE Archives (Prague), Book 5.

13 Télégramme n°3548/59, Fernand-Laurent, 19 September 1974. AMAE, CSCE, vol.14.

14 Cable, from Sherer to Sonnenfeldt, 7/12/1975, folder 'July 9–12, 1975 – Europe – TOSEC (8)', Box 17, NSA. Trip Briefing Books and Cables of Henry Kissinger. Gerald R. Ford Library.

15 Document CSCE/CC/44, delegation of Malta, 11 September 1974. CSCE Archives, Book 5.

16 The talks on MBFR (Mutual and Balanced Forces Reductions), which started in Vienna in 1973, brought together the countries of the Warsaw Pact and NATO, except France which did not want to take part in a 'bloc à bloc' negotiation and thought political détente had to precede military détente.

17 Note CSCE n°74, 3 January 1973. AMAE, CSCE, vol.28.

18 Cf. Möckli, Daniel, *European Foreign Policy during the Cold War. Heath, Brandt and Pompidou and the Dream of Political Unity* (New York, 2009), pp.68–78.

19 Note de la sous-direction d'Europe méridionale, 7 December 1972. AMAE, CSCE, vol.25.

20 Télégramme n°219–239, André, 22 January 1973. AMAE, CSCE, vol.31.

21 Télégramme n°66, André, 17 January 1973. AMAE, CSCE, vol.31.

22 Télégramme au départ n°314–315, Alphand, towards Helsinki, 27 November 1972. AMAE, Europe 1971–76, Organismes, vol.2925.

23 Relations were particularly tense between France and Algeria in the late 1960s and early 1970s. In 1968, Algiers reappraised the French exploitation of its oilfields and decided to nationalize them in 1971, aggravating bilateral relations between both states. In addition, the Arabian countries suspected France of not respecting its embargo on weapons to Israel, by turning a blind eye to the departure of five battleships – the 'vedettes' – which was organized by Mossad in Cherbourg harbour on Christmas night of 1969. Cf. Wauthier, Claude, *Quatre présidents et l'Afrique* (Paris, 1995), pp.192–202.

24 Cherigui, Hayète, *La politique méditerranéenne de la France. Entre diplomatie collective et leadership* (Paris, 1997), p.49.

25 Document WG/P/50, delegation of France, 23 May 1973. CSCE Archives, Book 1, Working Group proposals.

26 Circulaire NR 147, de Courcel, 6 March 1973. AMAE, CSCE, vol.25.

27 Department of State, Briefing Paper, July 1975, folder 'July 26 – August 4, 1975 – Europe – Briefing Book – CSCE Bilateral Book – Volume I (6)', Box 10, NSA, Trip Briefing Books and Cables for Gerald Ford, Gerald R. Ford Library.

28 Document CSCE (73) 22F, January 1973. AMAE, CSCE, vol.28.

29 Télégramme n°1796/1802, André, 4 May 1973. AMAE, CSCE, vol.32.

30 Note pour le président de la République, 8 November 1973. French National Archives, 5 AG 2 1015. Grande-Bretagne. 1973.

31 Télégramme n°2808/12, André, 6 June 1973. AMAE, CSCE, vol.32.

32 Hanhimäki, Jussi M., '"They can write in Swahili": Kissinger, the Soviets, and the Helsinki Accords, 1973–75', *Journal of Transatlantic Studies*, Vol.1/1 (2003), pp.40–2.

33 Memorandum from Henry Kissinger to President Ford, December 1974, folder 'Martinique. General (1)', Box 6, NSA. Trip briefing Books and Cables of Gerald Ford. Gerald R. Ford Library.

34 Franco-Italian EPC document, 1st quarter 1975. AMAE, CSCE, vol.14.

35 Télégramme n°3894/96, Fernand-Laurent, 6 November 1974. AMAE, CSCE, vol.14.

36 Report from the president of the sous-comité CSCE (EPC), 23 May 1975. AMAE, CSCE, vol.18.

37 Cable, from Sherer to Sonnenfeldt, 7/12/1975, folder 'July 9–12, 1975 – Europe – TOSEC (8)', Box 17, NSA. Trip Briefing Books and Cables of Henry Kissinger. Gerald R. Ford Library.

38 US intelligence analysts suggested the following reasons for this build-up: an impending large-scale exercise in the Mediterranean; a Soviet decision to establish a new level of Soviet naval commitment in the Mediterranean; a Soviet desire to have a force available for rapid deployment through the Suez Canal to the Indian Ocean should circumstances require it. Memorandum for Secretary Kissinger, 6/30/1975, folder 'June 27 – July 4, 1975 – Caneel Bay, Virgin Islands – TOHAK (2)', Box 15, NSA. Trip Briefing Books and Cables of Henry Kissinger. Gerald R. Ford Library.

39 Cable, from Secretary Kissinger to General Scowcroft, July 1975, folder 'July 9–12, 1975 – Europe – HAKTO', Box 16, NSA. Trip Briefing Books and Cables of Henry Kissinger. Gerald R. Ford Library.

40 Kissinger/Gromyko discussion, July 10, 1975, Geneva, folder 'July 10–11, 1975 – Kissinger/Gromyko Meetings in Geneva (1)', Box 1, NSA. Kissinger Reports on USSR, China, and Middle East discussions. Gerald R. Ford Library.

41   Cable, from Sherer to Sonnenfeldt, 7/12/1975, folder 'July 9–12, 1975 – Europe – TOSEC (8)', Box 17, NSA. Trip Briefing Books and Cables of Henry Kissinger. Gerald R. Ford Library.

42   Note CSCE n°220, 2 December 1975. AMAE, Europe 1971–76, Malte, vol.3412.

43   Comments to the press, August 1975. Note CSCE, 26 August 1975. AMAE, Europe 1971–76, URSS, vol.3689.

44   Dumas, Marie-Lucy, *Méditerranée occidentale. Sécurité et coopération* (Paris, 1992), pp.235–6.

5 Regional Détente or a New International Order?

1   Fondazione Istituto Gramsci, Archivio del partito comunista italiano (APC), Fondo Mosca, 1947, Comitato centrale, riunione 1–4 luglio, microfilm (mf.) 276–7.

2   Togliatti, Palmiro, *Discorsi parlamentari*, II, 1952–1964, Camera dei deputati (Chamber of Deputies), (1984), Seduta 13 June 1956, p.928.

3   Togliatti, Palmiro, L'intervista a *Nuovi Argomenti*, in Id., *Opere*, 6, 1956–1964 (Rome, 1984); Id., 'La via italiana al socialismo rapporto al Comitato centrale del Partito comunista italiano' (24 June 1956), pp.157–8

4   Zubok, Vladimir, *A Failed Empire: The Soviet Union in the Cold War from Stalin to Gorbachev* (Chapel Hill, 2009), pp.101ff.

5   Galeazzi, Marco, *Togliatti e Tito Tra identità nazionale e internazionalismo* (Rome, 2005), pp.147–52.

6   Ferro, Marc, *1956, Suez Naissance d'un Tiers-Monde* (Brussels, 2006).

7   APC, 1958, Direzione, riunione 25 luglio, mf.22, p.318.

8   APC, 1959, Estero, Cina, Incontro con Liu Sciao Ci, Peng Chen, Wang Gio Giang, Tang Chiang Kung, Liung Wing Yi, mf. 464, p.2877.

9   Togliatti, Palmiro, Rapporto all'VIII Congresso del Pci, in Id., *Opere*, 6, pp.153–4.

10 'L'Assemblea del Cairo', *l'Unità*, 17 December 1957. See 'Crepuscolo del colonialismo', *Rinascita* A. XV., nn.11–12, November–December 1958.

11 State Archives of the Republic of Serbia (AJ), Centralnog Komiteta Saveza Komunista Jugoslavije (CK SKJ), Record group 507 (507), IX-48/I, Bundle (b.) 5, File (f.) 129, About the conversation at Mieli's dinner see 19 October 1955, p.3.

12 APC, 1959, Estero, Movimento anticoloniale, Nota sulla III Conferenza anticoloniale del Mediterraneo and M.O., Belgrado, 2–5 dicembre 1959, mf. 465, pp.2191–sgg.

13 This hypothesis is confirmed in the documents of the Home Office on the activities of PCI representative in the Maghreb and Somalia (see Galeazzi: *Togliatti e Tito*, pp.206–7), a line adopted explicitly by Ambassador Betteroni in his talks with the Italian delegation in Algiers in January 1964 (APC, 1964, Estero, Algeria Informazione della compagna Maria Antonietta Macciocchi sul viaggio della delegazione del PCI in Algeria, mf. 520, p.151).

14 APC, 1961, Estero, Algeria, Appunti sui precedenti storici, mf. 483, p.2389.

15 APC, 1958, Direzione, riunione del 3 ottobre, mf. 22, p.3.

16 'I paesi non allineati e la coesistenza. Intervista di Tito al nostro giornale' (Tortorella, A. ed.), *l'Unità*, 12 September 1961.

17 Togliatti, Palmiro, *Discorsi parlamentari*, II, seduta del 27 settembre 1961, p.1216.

18 APC, 1962, Direzione, riunione del 31 ottobre, mf. 26, pp.523–31.

19 Togliatti, Palmiro, *Discorsi parlamentari*, II, seduta del 24 gennaio 1963, p.1267.

20 Cf. Spagnolo, Carlo, *Sul Memoriale di Yalta Togliatti e la crisi del movimento comunista internazionale* (Roma, 2007), pp.41–5; Galeazzi: *Togliatti e Tito*, pp.259–64.

21 APC, 1964, Estero, Algeria, Informazione della compagna Maria Antonietta Macciocchi sul viaggio della delegazione del PCI in Algeria, mf. 520.

22 Pappagallo, O., *Il Pci e la rivoluzione cubana La via 'latino americana' al socialismo (1959–1965)* (Roma, 2009) pp.200–11.

23 AJ CK SKJ, 507, IX-48/I, b.5, ff. 270–94, Materials on the PCI delegation visit (15–21 January 1964), Minutes from the meeting between the LCJ and the PCI. Cf. Galeazzi: *Togliatti e Tito*.

24 APC, Informazione della compagna Maria Antonietta Macciocchi, mf. 520, pp.124–5.

25 Comunicato sugli incontri fra i dirigenti del FLN algerino e la delegazione del PCI (10 gennaio 1964), in *Documenti politici dal X all'XI Congresso del Pci* (Roma, 1966), p.220.

26 AJ CK SKJ, 507, Materials on the PCI delegation visit, pp.25–9.

27 Ivi, pp.34–7.

28 APC, 1964, Estero, Jugoslavia, Sull'incontro tra le delegazioni dei Comitati centrali del Pci e della LCJ svoltisi a belgrado (15–21 gennaio 1964), mf. 520, p.1404; AJ CK SKJ, 507, Materials on the PCI delegation visit, pp.62–3.

29 AJ CK SKJ, Materials on the PCI delegation visit [...] cit., p.78.

30 *Ibid.*

31 AJ CK SKJ, Materials on the PCI delegation visit, p.78.

32 Per l'unità del movimento operaio e comunista internazionale rapporto al Comitato centrale e alla Commissione centrale di controllo del Pci 21–23 aprile 1964, in Togliatti: *Opere*, 6, pp.804–5.

33 Cfr. Spagnolo: *Memoriale*; Galeazzi: *Togliatti e Tito*.

34 APC, 1964, Estero, Algeria, Viaggio in Algeria in occasione delle celebrazioni del 1° novembre, mf. 520, p.225.

35 Ivi, p.228.

36 Galeazzi: *Togliatti e Tito*, pp.262–3.

37 APC, 1964, Direzione, riunione del 7 settembre, mf.28, p.859.

38 Ledda, Romano, 'Dal Cairo un ruolo attivo per il mondo non allineato', *Rinascita*, a.XXI, n.41, 17 ottobre 1964.

39 *Ibid.*

40 APC, 1965, Estero, Egitto, Rapporto delegazione PCI nella RAU (10–22 febbraio 1965), mf. 527.

41 Archivio Centrale dello Stato, Fondo Aldo Moro,5, Serie Ministero degli Esteri (1963–1968), Visita di una delegazione del Pci al Cairo, 23 febbraio 1965, p.2.

42 APC, 1965, Direzione, riunione del 2 marzo, mf. 29, p.605.

43 Galluzzi, Carlo, *La svolta Gli anni cruciali del partito comunista italiano* (Milano 1983), pp.52–3.

44 APC, 1965, Direzione, riunione del 12 febbraio, mf. 29, p.570.

45 APC, 1965, Estero Incontri internazionali Discorso di Berlinguer all'incontro di Mosca marzo 1965, mf. 528, pp.859–64.

46 APC, 1965 Estero, Algeria, mf. 527, pp.1603–12.

47 Calchi Novati, Gianpaolo,'I paesi non allineati dalla conferenza di Bandung a oggi', in Rainero, R.H. (ed.), *I problemi del mondo attuale dalla seconda guerra mondiale a oggi*, I (Milano, 1985).

48 APC, 1965, Direzione. II semestre, riunione del 23 dicembre, mf. 29, p.1142.

49 APC, 1965, Estero, Francia, Incontro Longo-Waldeck Rochet (Ginevra 24 May 1965), mf. 527.

50 APC, 1966, Estero, Francia, Waldeck-Rochet-Longo (1.4.1966), mf. 536, p.1860; APC, 1966, Direzione, riunione del 13 maggio, Informazione sull'incontro di Sanremo con i compagni francesi (3–4 May 1966), mf. 18, pp.647–8.

51 APC, 1966, Estero, Jugoslavia, Incontro tra le delegazioni della LCJ e del PCI 9 novembre 1966, mf. 536, p.2453.

52 *XI Congresso del Partito comunista italiano Atti e risoluzioni* (Rome, 1966).

53 AJ CK SKJ IX-48/I, Nota sui colloqui tra Tito e Luigi Longo nella Villa Bianca a Brioni 20 gennaio 1967. Ivi, On the second part of the meetings, pp.6–17.

54 APC, Fondo Enrico Berlinguer (FEB), Movimento operaio internazionale (Moi), b.120, Unità Archivistica (UA) 48/2, pp.25–33.

55 APC, 1967, Estero, Jugoslavia, Riunione a Belgrado tra partiti mediterranei (19–20.12.1967), mf. 545, pp.2152–3.

56 APC, 1969, Sezione esteri (21 aprile 1969), mf.305, pp.188–sgg. Cfr. Nota sulla situazione del Terzo Mondo, FEB, Moi, b.120, UA 45, p.14.

57 APC, 1969 I Commissione, riunione del 1° luglio, mf. 305.

58 Berlinguer, Enrico, 'Unità e autonomia nel movimento comunista internazionale', in Id., *La questione comunista (1969–1975)* I (Roma, 1975), pp.42ff.

59 APC, 1969 Direzione, riunione del 20 giugno, mf.6. Sul dibattito nel Pci e sulla posizione di Berlinguer cf: Pons, Silvio, *Berlinguer e la fine del comunismo* (Torino, 2006); Guerra, Antonio, *La solitudine di Berlinguer Governo etica e politica Dal 'no' a Mosca alla 'questione morale'* (Rome, 2009).

60 APC, 1973 Comitato centrale Relazione di Berlinguer al Comitato centrale (7–9 febbraio 1973), mf. 41, p.110.

61 Rubbi, Antonio, *Con Arafat in Palestina la sinistra italiana e la questione mediorientale* (Roma, 1996), p.36.

62 APC, 1971 Estero Algeria Nota sulla situazione in Algeria, (13 febbraio and 3 aprile 1971), mf. 162, pp.18–sgg.

63 APC, FEB Moi Incontro con la delegazione del FLN algerino (13 ottobre 1971), b. 126, UA 100.

64 APC, 1971 Sezione esteri Uno sguardo sull'Egitto paese chiave del Maschreq (sic) arabo (4 novembre 1971), mf. 158, pp.1154–1157; Nota sull'Egitto, settembre 1971, mf. 162– 1151–sgg; Informazione sul viaggio a Beyrut (sic) del compagno R.Ledda, settembre 1971, mf. 162, pp.1160–sgg.

65 AJ CK SKJ, 507, b.11, f.454, 19–20 maggio 1970.

66 APC, 1972, Direzione, riunione del 2 febbraio, mf. 32, pp.448–50.

67 APC, 1971 sezione esteri Relazione di Enrico Berlinguer al Comitato centrale e alla Commissione centrale di controllo (11 novembre 1971), mf.159. See also: E. Berlinguer, la nostra lotta per l'affermazione di una alternativa democratica (Dalla relazione al CC e alla CCC, 11–13 novembre 1971), in Id., *La questione comunista*, I (Roma, 1975).

68 Berlinguer, Enrico, 'Una sola via per uscire dalla crisi: cambiare il meccanismo di sviluppo' (Dall'intervento svolto nel corso della sessione del CC e del CCC, 17–18 dicembre 1973), in Id., *La questione comunista*, II, p.681.

69 Berlinguer, Enrico, 'Per uscire dalla crisi per costruire un'Italia nuova' (rapporto e conclusioni al CC e alla CCC in preparazione del XIV Congresso del Pci, 10–12 dicembre 1974), in Id., *La questione comunista*, II, p.830.

70 Westad, O. Arne, *The Global Cold War: Third World Interventions and the Making of Our Times* (Cambridge, 2005), pp.158ff.

71 Berlinguer, Enrico, 'Più dura la nostra opposizione per le gravi scelte della DC (Discorso alla Camera sulla fiducia al governo pronunciato il 22 marzo 1974)', in Id., *La questione comunista*, II, p.696.

72 Berlinguer: 'Per uscire dalla crisi', pp.829–30.

73 APC, 1974 Direzione V bimestre, riunione del 16 ottobre, mf. 81, p.89.

74 Migliardi, G., 'Confronto di ipotesi ad Algeri sul ruolo del non-allineamento', *l'Unità*, 8 settembre 1973; Id., 'I non-allineati si sforzano di dare continuità a una loro azione comune', *l'Unità* 9 settembre 1973. Jacoviello, A. 'A Copenhagen i ministri arabi si sono incontrati con i «Nove»', *l'Unità*, 18 dicembre 1973. On the relations between Europe and the Third World, see Garavini, Giuliano, *Dopo gli imperi L'integrazione europea nello scontro Nord-Sud* (Milano, 2009).

75 APC, 1973 Direzione IV trimestre, riunione del 24 ottobre, mf. 57, p.65.

76 Berlinguer, Enrico, 'Costruire un sistema di pacifica coesistenza e di cooperazione fra tutti i paesi', Rapporto al XIV Congresso del partito comunista italiano, in Id., *La politica internazionale dei comunisti italiani 1975–76* (Roma, 1976) p.12.

77 Pons, *Berlinguer e la fine del comunismo*, p.22.

78 Varsori, Antonio, 'Puerto Rico (1976): le potenze occidentali e il problema comunista in Italia', *Ventunesimo secolo*, n.16, 2008, pp.89–121.

79 APC, 1975, Direzione, II bimestre, Incontro del compagno Berlinguer con Tito, mf. 204, pp.420–7.

80 APC, 1978, Direzione, riunione del 19 ottobre, Nota di Rubbi (non corretta) Verbale degli incontri di Berlinguer con il Pcf (4–5 ottobre 1978), con il Pcus (6–9 ottobre) e con la Lega dei comunisti jugoslavi (10–11 ottobre) mf. 7812, pp.83–92.

81 Berlinguer, Enrico, 'Per una Carta della pace e dello sviluppo', in Id., *Idee e lotta per la pace* (Napoli, 1986), pp.61–70.

82 Ivi, pp.66–7.

83 APC, FEB, Moi, b.130, UA 174.2, Incontro 12 ottobre 1981.

84 'Per una Carta della pace', p.68.

85 Pons: *Berlinguer e la fine del comunismo*.

6 A Window of Opportunity?

1 For a comparative perspective: Del Pero, Mario, Gavín, Victor, Guirao, Fernando, Varsori, Antonio, *Democrazie. L'Europa meridionale e la fine delle dittature* (Firenze, 2011).

2 Please note that détente and peaceful coexistence are used as synonyms.

3 Valenta, Jíri, 'Eurocommunism and Eastern Europe', *Problems of communism*, March–April 1978, p.46.

4 Even among domestic adversaries, opinion of Eurocommunism differed drastically. See for example, two Italian Christian Democrat leaders: Forlani, Arnaldo, *Potere discreto* (Venezia, 2009), p.185; Cossiga, Francesco, *La versione di K. Sessant'anni di contro storia* (Milano, 2009), pp.80–1.

5   Kapur, Harish, 'L'eurocommunisme – une introduction historique', in H. Kapur
    and M. Molnar (eds), *Le nouveau communisme. Etude sur l'eurocommunisme et
    l'Europe de l'Est* (Geneva, 1978), p.33.
6   Valenta: 'Eurocommunism and Eastern Europe', pp.42–4; 50–52. Different
    view in Zubok, Vladislav, *Zhivago's Children. The last Russian intelligentsia*
    (Cambridge, 2009), pp.295–6.
7   Höbel, Alexander, 'Il PCI, il '68 cecoslovacco e il rapporto col PCUS', *Studi
    storici*, n.4 (2001), p.1147. For the PCF, Pelikán, Jíri, 'Les répercussions du
    Printemps de Prague sur le monde communiste et la gauche occidentale', in F.
    Fejtö and J. Rupnik, *Le Printemps Tchécoslovaque 1968* (Paris, 2008), pp.214–15.
8   Bracke, Maud, *Which Socialism, Whose Détente? West European Communism and
    the 1968 Czechoslovakian Crisis* (Budapest–New York, 2007), pp.197–8, p.44;
    Kapur: 'L'eurocommunisme – une introduction historique', p.19.
9   Valenta: 'Eurocommunism and Eastern Europe', p.50.
10 Kapur: 'L'eurocommunisme – une introduction historique', pp.27–8.
11 Speech by Marchais during the PCI–PCF meeting, 19 March 1973, Fondazione
    Istituto Gramsci (hereafter FIG), MF 046, pp.352–65.
12 Enrico Berlinguer, Giancarlo Pajetta, Minutes, 24 October 1973, FIG, MF
    057, p.44. Internationalism is intended as the special relationship which existed
    between communist parties as part of the international communist movement.
13 Minutes, 23 October 1975, FIG, MF 208, pp.0377–0401. Pons: *Enrico Berlinguer
    e la fine del comunismo*, pp.70–2; minutes by Antonio Rubbi, 15 January 1975,
    FIG, MF 201, pp.779–83.
14 Del Pero, Mario, 'I limiti della distensione: gli Stati Uniti e l'implosione del
    regime portoghese', in A. Varsori (ed.), *Alle origini del presente. L'Europa occiden-
    tale nella crisi degli anni Settanta* (Milano, 2007) pp.39–66.
15 'L'alignement de M. Marchais', *L'Express*, 18 August 1975; Pons: *Berlinguer*,
    pp.52–5. See: statement of René Piquet, Archives Départementales de la Seine
    Saint-Denis (hereafter ADSSD), Comité Central, 18–19 janvier 1974; minutes
    by Pancaldi, 30 June 1975, FIG, MF 207, pp.830–9.
16 'Déclaration conjointe des parties communistes italien et espagnol', in *Les PC
    espagnol, français et italien face au pouvoir* (Paris, 1976), pp.25–9.
17 'Déclaration commune du Parti Communiste Italien et du Parti Communiste
    Français', 15 November 1977, in *Les PC espagnol*, pp.30–6.
18 Pons: *Berlinguer*, p.88.
19 'Per la pace, la sicurezza, la cooperazione e il progresso sociale in Europa', *L'Unità*,
    12 July 1976, pp.12–13.
20 'Dichiarazione congiunta di PCI, PCF e PCE', *L'Unità*, 4 March 1977, p.1.
21 Lomellini, Valentine, *L'appuntamento mancato. La sinistra italiana e il dissenso nei
    regimi comunisti, 1968–1989* (Firenze, 2010), pp.83–96; 102–12.
22 Minutes, 7–8 May 1969, FIG, MF 006, pp.1524 ss.
23 According to Bracke, the difference between the understanding of the PCI and
    the CPSU became clear on occasion of the Czechoslovakian crisis. Bracke: *Which
    Socialism*, p.213.
24 Panvini, Guido, *Ordine nero, guerriglia rossa: la violenza politica nell'Italia degli
    anni Sessanta e Settanta, 1966–1975* (Torino, 2009).
25 Santone, Alessandro, *Il PCI e i giorni del Cile. Alle origini di un mito politico* (Roma,
    2008), pp.175–182. After the coup d'état in Chile, in September 1973, Enrico
    Berlinguer proposed the idea of a 'historical compromise' between the two main
    political parties of Italy – the Christian Democrats and the Italian Communist

Party. This dialogue would have allowed governments to cope with a particular difficult domestic situation (economic crisis; government instability; terrorism).

26   Minutes, 30 June 1975, FIG, MF 205, pp.121–88.

27   Minutes, 26 September 1975, FIG, MF 208, pp.0152 ss; minutes, 24 July 1975, FIG, MF 207, pp.64–116.

28   Natta: minutes, 26 September 1975, FIG, MF 208, pp.152 ss.

29   Letter to the PCI by the CPSU, 7 March 1977, FIG, MF 0297, pp.1496–1497; statement by Natta, minutes, 12 December 1975, FIG, MF 209, pp.49–102.

30   Meeting with Ponomarëv, 20 January 1976, FIG, MF 212, pp.376–81; letter of the PCI to the CPSU, 7 November 1976, FIG, MF 243, pp.553–554.

31   Pajetta's final remarks, minutes, 18 July 1977, FIG, MF 299, pp.111 ss.

32   Statement by Bufalini, ivi.

33   Meeting between Zagladin and delegation of 'L'Unità', 27 January 1977, FIG, Documentazione non classificata, fasc. 106, pp.542–8. It must be added that there was a tough private confrontation between the PCI and Moscow about political trials in 1978: FIG, MF 0365, fasc. 7812, 0057/0082.

34   Minutes by Valori, 6 January 1979, FIG, fasc.7901, pp.107–9.

35   Letter of the CPSU to the PCI, January 1979, FIG, fasc.7901, pp.83–91.

36   'Forte preoccupazione', L'Unità, 29 December 1979, p.1.

37   Lazar, Marc, Maisons rouges. Les Partis communistes français et italien de la Libération à nos jours (Paris, 1992); Robrieux, Philippe, Histoire intérieure du Parti Communiste, 1972–1982. Du programme commun à l'échec historique de Georges Marchais (Paris, 1981).

38   Bracke: Which Socialism, pp.222–3.

39   Marchais, Georges, Le Défi Démocratique (Paris, 1973), pp.228–30.

40   Etienne Fajon and Jean Kanapa, CC of the PCF, ADSSD, CC January 1974, plage 2 et 3. See also: Jean Kanapa, 'Communiqué au Comité Central', Cahiers du Communisme, June 1977, pp.11–22.

41   Minutes, 24 October 1973, FIG, MF 057, pp.44ff; 'L'alignement de M. Marchais', L'Express, 18 August 1975. Interview with Sergio Segre, Rome, 26 November 2009; interview with Antonio Rubbi, Rome, 25 November 2009.

42   Minutes, April 1975, 23rd, FIG, Direzione, pp.346–87.

43   Statement by Pajetta, minutes, 24 July 1975, FIG, MF 207, pp.64–116.

44   Minutes, 21 November 1975, FIG, MF 209, p.32.

45   Cohen, Samy and Smouts, Marie Claude (eds), La politique extérieure de Valery Giscard d'Estaing (Paris, 1985).

46   Meeting with Marchais and Kanapa, 29 September 1975, FIG, MF 0208, pp.1810–18.

47   'Pour la libération de six intellectuels meeting ce soir à la Mutualité à l'appel du comite des mathématiciens', L'Humanité, 21 October 1976, p.5; Juquin, Pierre, De battre mon cœur n'a jamais cessé (Paris, 2006), pp.468–9.

48   Meeting between Sergio Segre, Jean Kanapa and Jacques Denis, 14 October 1976, FIG, MF 0243, pp.1771–5.

49   Letter from the CPSU to the PCF, 18 October 1976, ADSSD, Correspondence PCF–PCUS, 317 J 13.

50   Meeting between Segre, Rubbi, Kanapa, Denis and Streiff, 6 April 1976, FIG, MF 0228, pp.565–7.

51   Elleinstein, Jean, 'The Skein of History Unrolled Backwards', in G.R. Urban (ed.), Euro-communism. Its Roots and Future in Italy and Elsewhere (London, 1978), p.94.

52 VIII Congreso del PCE, 15 August 1972; Fundación de Investigaciones Marxistas (FIM), 1972, agosto: octavo congreso del PCE.

53 This statement was in fact followed by criticism of Nixon's policy towards Vietnam; ivi.

54 Aniversario de la Revolucion de Octubre, 'Ganar a las masas, hacer la revolucion', Saludo al P.C. de la Union sovietica, 14 November 1972; FMI, Carpeta 26 M.O. n.19.

55 'Manuel Azcárate's report to the Eighth Congress of the PCE', 1972, P. Lange and M. Vannicelli (eds), *The Communist Parties of Italy, France and Spain. Postwar changes and continuity* (London, 1981), p.345.

56 'Declaracion del Comité Ejecutivo del PCE', *Nuestra Bandera*, no. 71 (April–June 1973), pp.77–8.

57 'Discurso de Manuel Azcárate', *Nuestra Bandera*, no. 72 (October–December 1973), pp.18–21.

58 Del Pero, Gavín, Guirao, Varsori: *Democrazie*, pp.205–6.

59 Program of the PCE, 4 September 1975; FIM, 1975, septiembre: manifiesto-programa del PCE, II conferencia del PCE, carpeta 56.

60 Declaracion del Comité Ejecutivo del PCE, 1975, FIM, 1975, septiembre: manifiesto-programa del PCE, II conferencia del PCE, carpeta 56.

61 'Intervista di Carrillo sulla Conferenza dei PC europei', *L'Unità*, 1 May 1975; FIG; MF 206, p.323; 'Intervista di Carrillo sulle elezioni in Italia', *L'Unità*, 22 June 1975, ivi, p.327.

62 Valenta: 'Eurocommunism and Eastern Europe', p.51.

63 Zamorski, 'Polish Criticism of Carrillo's Book; Soviet Version of Trybuna Ludu Article', 12 August 1977; Open Society Archives (OSA), Country: Poland, 44–6–162.

64 Carrillo: *L'eurocomunismo e lo stato*, pp.129–34.

65 Carrillo's speech, press conference, 3 March 1977, FIG, MF 0297, fasc.1425.

66 Carrillo's statement, IX Congreso del PCE, PCE official document, 1978, pp.22–3.

67 Azcárate, Manuel, 'What is Eurocommunism?', in Urban, G.R.: *Eurocommunism*, pp.27–8.

68 Tannahill, R. Neal, *The Communist Parties of Western Europe. A Comparative Study* (Westport, Conn., 1978), pp.77–8.

7 The American–Israeli 'Special Relationship'

1 Ben-Zvi, Abraham, *The United States and Israel: The Limits of the Special Relationship* (New York, 1993). An excellent analysis of Washington's Middle East policy during the Eisenhower and Kennedy Administrations is in Barrett, Roby C., *The Greater Middle East and the Cold War: US Foreign Policy under Eisenhower and Kennedy* (London–New York, 2007).

2 Gardner, Lloyd C., *Three Kings: The Rise of an American Empire in the Middle East after World War II* (New York and London, 2009), p.205.

3 Rusk, Dean, *As I Saw It, as Told to Richard Rusk*, D. S. Papp (ed.) (New York–London, 1990), p.381.

4 Ben-Zvi, Abraham, *Decade of Transition: Eisenhower, Kennedy, and the Origins of the American–Israeli Alliance* (New York, 1998).

5 Ben-Zvi, Abraham, *John F. Kennedy and the Politics of Arms Sales to Israel* (Portland, OR, 2002).

6   Ben-Zvi, Abraham, *Lyndon B. Johnson and the Politics of Arms Sales to Israel: In the Shadow of the Hawk* (London–Portland, OR, 2004).
7   Kerr, Malcolm H., *The Middle East Conflict* (New York, 1968), p.54.
8   Aron, Raymond, 'Richard Nixon and the Future of American Foreign Policy', *Daedalus*, vol.101/4 (Fall, 1972), p.23.
9   *Memorandum from Kissinger to the President*, 13 February 1969, in US National Archives and Records Administration [thereafter NARA], College Park, MD, Nixon Presidential Materials Project [thereafter NPMP], National Security Council Files [thereafter NSC], Country File Israel, Vol.I, Box 604, Folder 1.
10 Kerr: *The Middle East Conflict*, p.57.
11 *Memorandum of Conversation*, 17 March 1969, in NARA, NPMP, NSC Files, Country File: Israel, Vol.I, Box 604, Folder 1.
12 Lewis, Bernard, 'The Great Powers, the Arabs and the Israelis', in W. Laqueur (ed.), *The Israel–Arab Reader: A Documentary History of the Middle East Conflict* (Harmondsworth, 1969), p.561. The article was originally published in *Foreign Affairs*, July 1969.
13 Hahn, Peter L., *Crisis and Crossfire: The United States and the Middle East since 1945* (Washington, DC, 2005), p.56.
14 *Memorandum from Rogers to the President*, 12 March 1969, in NARA, NPMP, NSC Files, Country File Israel, Vol.I, Box 604, Folder 1.
15 *Memorandum from Kissinger to the President*, 13 March 1969, in NARA, NPMP, NSC Files, Country File Israel, Vol.I, Box 604, Folder 1.
16 Nixon, Richard, *The Memoirs of Richard Nixon* (London, 1978), p.479.
17 Kerr, Malcolm H., Introduction to M. H. Kerr, (ed.), *The Elusive Peace in the Middle East* (Albany, N.Y., 1975), p.12.
18 *Memorandum of Conversation*, 13 May, 1969, in NARA, NPMP, NSC Files, Country File Israel, Vol.I, Box 604, Folder 1.
19 Kerr, Malcolm H., 'Nixon's Second Term: Policy Prospects in the Middle East', *Journal of Palestine Studies*, vol.2/3 (Spring, 1973), p.16.
20 *Memorandum from the Secretary of Defence (Melvin R. Laird) to Kissinger*, 22 August 1969, in NARA, NPMP, NSC Files, Country File Israel, Vol.II, Box 604, Folder 2.
21 *Memorandum from Kissinger to the President*, 25 September 1969, in NARA, NPMP, NSC Files, Country File Israel, Vol.II, Box 604, Folder 2; Meir, Golda, *My Life*, (London, 1975), pp.386–94.
22 National Security Council, *Discussion Paper on Israel's Assistance Requests*, 5 January 1970, in NARA, NPMP, NSC Files, Country File Israel, Vol.III, Box 605, Folder 2.
23 Nixon: *The Memoirs of Richard Nixon*, p.480.
24 Stephens, Elizabeth, *US Policy towards Israel: The Role of Political Culture in Defining the 'Special Relationship'* (Brighton–Portland, OR, 2006), p.122.
25 Nixon: *The Memoirs of Richard Nixon*, p.481.
26 Reich, Bernard, 'Israeli Foreign Policy', in C.L. Brown (ed.), *Diplomacy in the Middle East: The International Relations of Regional and Outside Powers* (London–New York, 2004), p.127.
27 *Memorandum of Conversation*, 17 November 1969, in NARA, NPMP, NSC Files, Country File Israel, Vol.III, Part I, Box 605, Folder 1.
28 *Memorandum for the President*, 18 December 1969, in NARA, NPMP, NSC Files, Country File Israel, Vol.III, Part I, Box 605, Folder 1. Meeting between Kissinger and Rabin.

29 *Memorandum for the President*, 23 December 1969, in NARA, NPMP, NSC Files, Country File Israel, Vol.III, Part I, Box 605, Folder 1.

30 Kissinger, Henry A., *The White House Years* (Boston, MA–Toronto, 1979), pp.378–9.

31 *Further Action on Israel's Assistance Requests: NSSMs 81 and 82*, 2 January 1970, in NARA, NPMP, NSC Files, Country File Israel, Vol.III, Part I, Box 608, Folder 2; *Discussion Paper on Israel's Assistance Requests*, 5 January 1970, in NARA, NPMP, NSC.

32 Nixon: *The Memoirs of Richard Nixon*, p.481.

33 Yaqub, Salim, 'The Politics of Stalemate: The Nixon Administration and the Arab–Israeli Conflict, 1969–73', in Ashton, Nigel (ed.), *The Cold War in the Middle East: Regional Conflict and the Superpowers, 1967–73* (London and New York, 2007), p.41.

34 *Memorandum from Rogers to the President*, 3 March 1970, in NARA, NPMP, NSC Files, Country File Israel, Vol.IV, Box 606, Folder 1.

35 *Memorandum from Kissinger to the President*, 3 March 1970, in NARA, NPMP, NSC Files, Country File Israel, Vol.IV, Box 606, Folder 1.

36 *Letter from Meir to Nixon*, 12 March 1970, in NARA, NPMP, NSC Files, Country File Israel, Vol.IV, Box 606, Folder 1.

37 *Memorandum of Conversation*, 12 March 1970, in NARA, NPMP, NSC Files, Country File Israel, Vol.IV, Box 606, Folder 1.

38 Kissinger: *The White House Years*, p.571; Nixon: *The Memoirs of Richard Nixon*, pp.480–1; Rabin, Yitzhak, *The Rabin Memoirs* (Boston and Toronto, 1979), pp.167–9; Eban, Abba, *An Autobiography* (New York, 1977), p.465.

39 Ginor, Isabella and Remez, Gideon, 'The Tyranny of Vested-Interest Sources: Shaping the Record of Soviet Intervention in the Egyptian–Israeli Conflict, 1967–1973', *The Journal of the Middle East and Africa*, vol.1/1 (2010), pp.43–66.

40 Rabin: *The Rabin Memoirs*, p.171; Stephens: *US Policy towards Israel*, p.134; Spiegel, Steven L., *The Other Arab–Israeli Conflict: Making America's Middle East Policy, from Truman to Reagan* (Chicago and London, 1985), p.191.

41 Bureau of Intelligence and Research, *Israel–UAR–USSR: When is a Lull a Lull?*, 13 March 1970, in NARA, NPMP, NSC Files, Country File Israel, Vol.IV, Box 606, Folder 1.

42 Kissinger: *The White House Years*, p.571; Little, Douglas, *American Orientalism: The United States and the Middle East since 1945* (Chapel Hill, N.C., 2002), pp.104–5.

43 *Memorandum from Kissinger to the President*, 2 July 1970, in NARA, NPMP, NSC Files, Country File Israel, Vol.V, Box 607, Folder 1. Meir's letter to Nixon is annexed to the memorandum.

44 Embassy of Israel at Washington, *Russian Military Intervention. The Third Phase: Soviet-Manned Sam-III's Move into Suez Canal Battle Zone*, 7 July 1970, in NARA, NPMP, NSC Files, Country File Israel, Vol.V, Box 607, Folder 1; Rabin: *The Rabin Memoirs*, p.178; Kissinger: *The White House Years*, pp.580–1.

45 Kissinger: *The White House Years*, pp.575–9; Rabin: *The Rabin Memoirs*, p.177; Meir: *My Life*, p.385; Spiegel: *The Other Arab–Israeli Conflict*, p.193.

46 *Memorandum of Conversation*, 29 July 1970, in NARA, NPMP, NSC Files, Country File Israel, Vol.V, Box 607, Folder 1.

47 *Memorandum from Kissinger to the President*, not dated, in NARA, NPMP, NSC Files, Country File Israel, Vol.V, Box 607, Folder 1.

48 'Memorandum of Conversation (U.S.)', New York, 23 October 1970, in *Soviet–American Relations: The Detente Years, 1969–1972*, Washington, D.C., U.S. Government Printing Office, 2008, p.230.
49 Quandt, William B., *Peace Process: American Diplomacy and the Arab–Israeli Conflict since 1967* (Washington, D.C.–Berkeley and Los Angeles, CA, 1993), pp.94–115.
50 Little: *American Orientalism*, p.106.
51 Lasensky, Scott, 'Dollarizing Peace: Nixon, Kissinger and the Creation of the U.S.–Israeli Alliance', *Israel Affairs*, vol.13/1 (2007), pp.164–86.
52 Kochavi, Noam, *Nixon and Israel: Forging a Conservative Partnership* (Albany, N.Y., 2009), pp.7–28.
53 Siniver, Asaf, *Nixon, Kissinger, and U.S. Foreign Policy Making: The Machinery of Crisis* (Cambridge, 2008), p.122.

8 'The Gods of War were Inspecting their Armaments'

1   Kissinger, Henry, *The White House Years* (London, 1979), p.558.
2   *Airgram from the Department of State to the Embassy in the Soviet Union* ('Soviet Policy toward the Middle East'), December 17, 1969, in U.S. National Archives and Records Administration (hereafter NARA), Record Group 59 (hereafter RG 59), Central Files 1967–69, POL NEAR E-USSR, College Park, MD.
3   Kissinger: *The White House Years*, pp.558–9.
4   Quandt, William B., *Decade of Transition: American Policy toward the Arab–Israeli conflict, 1967–1976* (Berkeley, CA: 1977), p.104. See also Quandt, W.B., 'The Middle East Conflict in US Strategy, 1970–71', *Journal of Palestine Studies*, vol.1/1 (Autumn 1971), pp.45–6.
5   Garfinkle, A.M., 'U.S. Decision Making in the Jordan Crisis: Correcting the Record', *Political Science Quarterly*, vol.100/1 (Spring 1985), pp.117–18.
6   Kerr, M.H., *The Arab Cold War: Gamal Adb al-Nasir and His Rivals, 1958–1970* (London, 1971), p.142.
7   Shlaim, A., *Lion of Jordan: The Life of King Hussein in War and Peace* (London, 2007), p.313.
8   Zak, M. 'Israeli–Jordan Negotiations', *Washington Quarterly*, vol.8/1 (Winter 1985), pp.167–76.
9   Quoted in Shlaim: *Lion of Jordan*, p.315.
10 *Memorandum for the Record* ('Aircraft Hijackings'), September 6, 1970, in NARA, Nixon Presidential Materials (hereafter NPM), NSC Files, Box 330, Subjects Files, Hijackings.
11 *Memorandum from the President's Deputy Assistant for National Security Affairs (Haig) to President* Nixon ('Middle East Developments'), September 6, 1970, in NARA, NPM, NSC Files, Box 646, Country Files, Middle East.
12 *Intelligence Information Cable* ('Iraqi Complicity in Multi-Hijackings'), September 12, 1970, in NARA, NPM, NSC Files, Box 330, Subjects Files, Hijackings.
13 Shlaim: *Lion of Jordan*, p.324. For a detailed account of the hijackings see Raab, David, *Terror in Black September: The First Eyewitness Account of the Infamous 1970 Hijackings* (New York, 2007).
14 *Memorandum from the President's Assistant for National Security Affairs (Kissinger) to President Nixon* ('Options in Jordan'), September 16, 1970, in NARA, NPM, NSC Files, Box 615, Country Files, Middle East, Jordan.

15 Kissinger: *The White House Years*, p.612.

16 *Memorandum from the President's Assistant for National Security Affairs (Kissinger) to President's Chief of Staff (Haldeman)*, September 16, 1970, in NARA, NPM, NSC Files, NSC Institutional Files (H-Files), Box H-077, WSAG Meetings, WSAG Meeting Jordan 9/15/70.

17 *Minutes of a Washington Special Actions Group Meeting*, September 17, 1970, NARA, NPM, NSC Files, NSC Institutional Files (H-Files), Box H-114, WSAG, WSAG Minutes (Original) 1969 and 1970.

18 *Transcript of a Telephone Conversation between President Nixon and President's Assistant for National Security Affairs (Kissinger)*, September 17, 1970, NARA, NPM, Kissinger Telephone Conversations, Box 30, Chronological Files.

19 *Memorandum from the President's Assistant for National Security Affairs (Kissinger) to President Nixon*, September 20, 1970, NARA, NPM, NSC Files, Box 615, Country Files, Middle East, Jordan.

20 *Telegram from the Department of State to Embassy in Jordan*, September 20, 1970, RG 59, Central Files 1970–73, POL 23–9 Jordan.

21 *Memorandum from the President's Assistant for National Security Affairs (Kissinger) to President Nixon*, September 20, 1970, NARA, NPM, NSC Files, NSC Institutional Files, Box H-77, WSAG Meetings, WSAG Meeting Middle East 9/20/70.

22 *Minutes of a Washington Special Actions Group Meeting*, September 20, 1970, NARA, NPM, NSC Files, NSC Institutional Files (H-Files), Box H-114, WSAG, WSAG Minutes (Original) 1969 and 1970.

23 *Telegram from the Embassy in Jordan to the Department of State*, September 21, 1970, in NARA, RG 59, Central Files 1970–73, POL Jordan–US.

24 Nixon, Richard, *The Memoirs of Richard Nixon* (New York, 1978), p.483.

25 *Meeting between Presidential Assistant Kissinger and Ambassador Dobrynin*, December 22, 1970, in NARA, NPM, NSC Files, Box 490, President's Trip Files, Dobrynin/Kissinger, 1970, Vol.3.

26 *Transcript of a Telephone Conversation between the President's Assistant for National Security Affairs (Kissinger) and the Israeli Ambassador (Rabin)*, September 20, 1970, NARA, NPM, Kissinger Telephone Conversations, Box 30, Chronological Files.

27 *Minutes of a Washington Special Actions Group Meeting*, September 20–21, 1970, NARA, NPM, NSC Files, NSC Institutional Files (H-Files), Box H-114, WSAG, WSAG Minutes (Original) 1969 and 1970.

28 Kissinger: *The White House Years*, p.622. See also *Memorandum of Conversation (USSR)*, September 25, 1970, in U.S. Department of State, *Soviet–American Relations: The Détente Years, 1969–1972* (Washington, DC: 2007), p.194.

29 Astorino-Courtois, A. 'Clarifying Decisions: Assessing the Impact of Decision Structures on Foreign Policy Choices during the 1970 Jordanian Civil War', *International Studies Quarterly*, vol.42/4 (December 1998), pp.733–4.

9 The Middle Eastern Test of Détente

1 http://otkpblto.ru/index.php?s=af48d7fbb2abd6bb4c04b5dcdde729c1&showtopic=2892, responding to an article by Yuliya Latynina, 'Armiya, kotoraya proigryvaet i zhaluetsya na zhenshchin,' which describes the Egyptian–Syrian surprise attack of 6 October 1973 as 'one of the most brilliant operations conceived by Soviet military advisers and their Arab friends', http://www.novay-agazeta.ru/data/2004/79/02.html.

2   'The origins of a misnomer: the "expulsion of Soviet advisers" from Egypt in
     1972', in Ashton, Nigel (ed.), *The Cold War in the Middle East: Regional Conflict
     and the Superpowers 1967–73* (London, 2007), pp.136–63; 'The Tyranny of
     Vested-Interest Sources: Shaping the Record of Soviet Intervention in the
     Egyptian–Israeli Conflict, 1967–1973', *Journal of the Middle East and Africa* i/1
     (2010), pp.43–66.

3   Lavrov, Sergei et al. (eds), *Soveskot–amerikanskie otnosheniyas: gody razryadki
     1969–1976* (Moscow, 2007); Keefer, Edward C. et al. (eds), *Soviet–American
     Relations: The Détente Years, 1969–1972* (Washington, 2007).

4   Felgenhauer, Pavel, 'Medvedev Forms a Commission to Protect Russian History'
     Eurasia Daily Monitor vol. vi, n.98, 21 May 2009,http://www.jamestown.org/
     single/?no_cache=1&tx_ttnews[tt_news]=35018&tx_ttnews[backPid]=13&cHa
     sh=6729b2258e.

5   Zubok, Vladislav M., *A Failed Empire: The Soviet Union in the Cold War from
     Stalin to Gorbachev* (Chapel Hill, NC, 2007), p.238.

6   E.g. Markovsky, Viktor Yu., 'My gotovili voynu', first published in *Aerohobby*
     magazine, reproduced at www.foxbat.ru/article/mig25/mig25_1.htm.

7   Yena, Andrei Vasil'evich, 'Zashchishchaya nebo nad Egiptom', in Meyer, M.S.
     et al. (eds), *Togda v Egipte... Kniga o pomoshchi SSSR Egiptu v Voennom protivo-
     stoyanii s Izrailem* (Moscow, 2001), p.136.

8   Agafonov, Vladimir, *Vremya Novostey*. #198, 22 October 2003. Other sources put
     the delivery of the Scud system earlier, e.g. Egyptian Lt.-Gen.Bassam Kakish,
     who dates it at the beginning of the year. Parker, Robert B. (eds), *The October
     War: A Retrospective* (Gainesville, FL, 2001), p.92.

9   Akopov, Pavel transcript of 1997 interview for *The 50 Years War: Israel and the
     Arabs*, a six part television documentary made by Brian Lapping Associates,
     1998, p.28. The authors thank Brook Lapping Productions and the Trustees
     of the Liddell Hart Centre for Military Archives, King's College London, for
     granting of access to, and permission to quote from, this material.

10   Parker: *October War*, p.141.

11   Memorandum of Conversation, 7 May 1973, Munteanu, Mircea et al. (eds),
     The Rise of Detente: Document Reader (Washington and Florence, 2002), Vol.1,
     section III, doc. 13, p.18.

12   Golan, Galia, *Soviet Policies in the Middle East: From World War II to Gorbachev*
     (Cambridge, 1990), p.86.

13   Zolotaryov, Maj.-Gen.V.A. et al. (eds), *Rossiya (SSSR) v lokal'nykh voynakh i voen-
     nykh konfliktakh vtoroy poloviny XX veka* (Moscow, 2000), p.199.

14   Protocol of the meeting of the Supreme Council of Syrian and Egyptian forces
     #6198, 29 August 1973, file #1, in G. Pernavsky (ed.), *Arabo–Izrail'skie voynu;
     arabsky vzglyad* (Moscow, 2008), pp.105–7. The book is 'composed of testimonies
     by Arab officers and generals who studied at Soviet military academies.... They
     were required to provide detailed descriptions of their combat experience', p.4.

15   Bregman, Ahron and El-Tahri, Jihan, *The Fifty Years War* (London, 1998),
     pp.116–17.

16   Parker: *October War*, p.130.

17   Ginor and Remez, *Foxbats over Dimona; The Soviets' Nuclear Gamble in the
     Six-Day War* (New Haven, 2007), pp.79–81.

18   Total of surface warships, submarines and auxiliaries. Zaborsky, V.V., 'Sovetskaya
     srednomorskaya eskadra' in Filonik, A.O. (eds), *Blizhny Vostok: komandirovka na
     voynu* (Moscow, 2009), pp.67–8 (originally published in *Nezavisimoe Voennoe*

Obozrenie, 13 October 2006, p.68). He puts the Sixth Fleet's strength at the time at 140 units. Previous estimates, apparently counting only combat ships, placed the Soviet strength at 58 units (Watson, Bruce W., *Red Navy at Sea: Soviet Naval Operations on the High Seas, 1956–1980* (Boulder, CO, 1982), p.87) as against the Sixth Fleet's 48 warships (Bouchard, Joseph F., *Command in Crisis* (New York, 1991), pp.106–7.

19 Zaborsky: 'Srednomorskaya eskadra', pp.67–8.

20 Ben-Porat, Yeshayahu et al., *Ha-Mehdal* (Tel Aviv, 1973–4), p.16.

21 Mallin, Col. (ret.) Valery B., 'Boevye sluzhby: god za godom', http://belostokskaya.ru/BS/f_service/.

22 Rozin, Aleksandr, 'Voyna "sudnogo dny" 1973g.: protivostoyanie SSSR-SShA na more', http://alerozin.narod.ru/oktovr.htm; Zaborsky, 'Srednomorskaya eskadra', p.69.

23 Sadat, Anwar al, *In Search of Identity* (London, 1978), p.246.

24 Vinogradov, Vladimir, M., *Diplomatiya: lyudi i sobytiya, iz zapisok poslya.* (Moscow, 1998), p.239.

25 Akopov, interview, p.32.

26 Sadat: *In Search of Identity*, p.246.

27 Israelyan, Victor, *Inside the Kremlin during the Yom Kippur War* (University Park, PA, 1997), pp.10–11.

28 Israelyan: *Inside*, pp.4, 16.

29 Zolotaryov: *Lokal'nykh voynakh*, p.199; Parker: *October War,* p.49.

30 Israelyan: *Inside*, p.2; p.3 clarifies that this level was the Politburo.

31 Israelyan: *Inside*, p.2.

32 Akopov, interview, pp.31–2; Israelyan: *Inside*, p.4.

33 Goldstein, Lyle J. and Zhukov, Yuri M., 'A Tale of Two Fleets: A Russian Perspective on the 1973 Naval Standoff in the Mediterranean', *Naval War College Review* 57/2 (2004), p.44, http://www.dtic.mil/cgi-bin/GetTRDoc?Location=U2&doc=GetTRDoc.pdf&AD=ADA422490.

34 Personal communication from Dr Yon Degen, Ramat-Gan, Israel, June 2003.

35 Heikal, Mohamed,*The Road to Ramadan* (New York, 1975), pp.6, 18.

36 Herzog, Chaim, *The War of Atonement* (London, 1998; originally published 1975), p. 37–8.

37 Israelyan: *Inside*, p.5.

38 Pavlovich Kutsenko, Major-General (ret.) Viktor, 'Pyl' nad Suetskim Kanalom', *Literaturnaya Rossiya*, 4 May 2001, http://www.litrossia.ru/archive/38/soul/900.html.

39 Gross Stein, Janice, 'The Failures of Deterrence and Intelligence', in Parker: *October War*, p.80; Ben-Porat: *Ha-Mehdal*, p.50.

40 'TV Profiles, Shows Lifetime Work of Top Russian Missile Designer', Moscow Channel One TV, 23 May 2003, Russian Military and Security Media Coverage 2326 (17 June 2003), http://groups.yahoo.com/group/RMSMC/message/2351.

41 Pochtaryov, Andrei, 'Orden za "amerikantsa"', *Krasnaya Zvezda*, 28 February 2002, www.redstar.ru/2002/02/28_02/2_02.html.

42 Prokopenko, Sergei and Baranets, Viktor, 'Pokhishchenie "Tsenturiona"', *Komsomolsakaya Pravda*, 27 May 1999, http://www.rol.ru/misc/news/99/05/27_095.htm; Ginor: 'Hasifat ha-tzariah', *Ha'aretz*, 10 June 1999.

43 Rozin, 'Voyna "sudnogo dnya"'; 'Sergei' (surname withheld), 'Blizhnevostoshnyi konflikt 1973 goda', thesis submitted at Moscow State University, undated (before 2001), p.37. http://www.btvt.by.ru/73.htm.

44 Golan: *Soviet Policies*, p.87; Zolotaryov: *Lokal'nykh voynakh*, p.201.
45 Markovsky, 'Idite v zemlyu Egipetskuyu', http://mig-25inegipt.narod.ru/index1. htm.
46 Minayev, Aleksandr, 'Polet nad Tel'–Avivom', *Nezavisimaya Gazeta* military supplement, 24 October 2008, http://nvo.ng.ru/printed/217663. Minayev quotes a book by the senior government aviation specialist Yevgeny Fedosov, *50 let v aviatsi: zapiski akademika*.
47 Minayev, 'Polet nad Tel'–Avivom', quoting *Ilya Mikhailovich Livshits: uchenyy i chelovek* (Kharkov, Ukraine, 2008).
48 Markovsky, 'Idite v zemlyu Egipetskuyu'.
49 Talov, B. L., 'Yadernye raketonostsy-khraniteli mira', *Russky Dom* #11, http:// rd.rusk.ru/98/rd11/home11_15.htm.
50 Blechman, Barry M. and Hart, Douglas M., 'Nuclear Weapons and the 1973 Middle East Crisis', in R. J. Art, and K. Waltz (eds), *The Use of Force: Military Power and International Politics*, Fifth Edition (Lanham, MD, 1999), p.243. At the time, Kissinger cited mainly Soviet threats to intervene unilaterally if the US did not agree to a joint ceasefire supervision force; Documents 8A-D: DEFCON 3 During the October War, in William Burr (ed), 'More Dubious Secrets', National Security Archive, http://www.gwu.edu/~nsarchiv/nukevault/ ebb281/index.htm.
51 Israelyan: *Inside,* p.143.

10 Conflict and Détente in the Eastern Mediterranean

1   I would like to thank Professor John Iatrides for his most useful comments on an earlier draft of this paper. Fouskas, Vassilis, 'Uncomfortable questions: Cyprus, October 1973–August 1974', *Contemporary European History* 14/1 (2005), pp.46, 55.
2   Maull, Hanns, *Oil and Influence: The Oil Weapon Examined*, Adelphi Paper, n.117 (London, 1975), p.6.
3   Campbell, John C., *Defense of the Middle East: Problems of American Policy* (New York, 1958), pp.4–5.
4   In May 1953, US Secretary of State John Foster Dulles, during his trip to the Middle East, referred for the first time to the 'northern tier' consisting of Greece, Turkey, Iran and Afghanistan as a political–military concept aimed at a collective security region on the southern borders of the Soviet Union. Kuniholm, Bruce, *The Origins of the Cold War in the Near East: Great Power Conflict and Diplomacy in Iran, Turkey and Greece* (Princeton, 1980).
5   Kissinger, Henry, *Years of Renewal* (New York, 1999), p.225.
6   *FRUS*, vol.30, *Greece, Cyprus, Turkey 1973–76*, Cyprus, memorandum of conversation, 13 August 1974.
7   In 1967, the annual aid provided to Israel amounted to just $13 million.In the following years aid began to increase sharply, with the United States providing $76 million in 1968 and $600 million in 1971. Lieber, Robert, 'US–Israeli relations since 1948', *MERIA (Middle East Review of International Affairs)*, 2/3 (September 1998), http://meria.idc.ac.il, p.3.
8   FCO 82/304, despatch UK embassy Washington to Douglas-Home, 'the Middle East and US/UK relations', 9 January 1974.
9   FCO 93/250, 'Western interests in the Middle East over the next fifteen years', 7 June 1973 and letter Heath to Nixon, 31 October 1973, PREM 15/1981.

10 Kissinger, Henry, *Years of Upheaval* (Boston, 1982), pp.711–12, 715, 723, and especially 730.

11 Kissinger: *Years of Upheaval*, p.718.

12 FCO 41/1154, conversation, Secretary of Defense Peter Carrington with Schlesinger in The Hague on 7 November 1973; Kissinger: *Years of Upheaval*, 720–1. See also Hughes, Geraint, 'Britain, the transatlantic alliance, and the Arab–Israeli war of 1973', *Journal of Cold War Studies* 10/2 (2008), pp.3–40.

13 Kissinger: *Years of Upheaval*, p.708.

14 Sakkas, John, 'The Greek dictatorship, the USA and the Arabs, 1967–74, *Journal of Southern Europe and the Balkans* 6/3 (December 2004), p.225.

15 On 21 March 1974, a British defence review was announced by the newly elected Wilson government involving considerable cuts in defence spending overseas, including Cyprus. Cmnd 5976, Statement on the Defence Estimates 1975, London, HMSO, March 1975, pp.1, 7, 14–15.

16 O'Malley, Brendan and Craig, Ian, *The Cyprus Conspiracy: America, Espionage and the Turkish Invasion* (London, 1999), p.144.

17 *FRUS*, Memorandum of conversation, 15 August 1974.

18 Levey, Zach, 'Israel's entry into Cyprus, 1959–1963: Diplomacy and strategy in the eastern Mediterranean', 7/3 (September 2003), *MERIA (Middle East Review of International Affairs)*, http://meria.idc.ac.il.

19 Bolukbasi, Suha, 'Behind the Turkish–Israeli alliance: A Turkish view', *Journal of Palestine Studies*, 29/1 (autumn 1999), p.26.

20 Beit-Hallahmi, Benjamin, *The Israeli Connection: Who Israel Arms and Why* (New York, 1987), p.89. On 19 August 1974, *Der Spiegel* revealed that 'hiding behind this issue (i.e. the Turkish invasion of Cyprus) was Israel' and that 'the telephone line between Nicosia – Tel Aviv had been connected two days before the coup and only the embassy of Israel or Israeli journalists could use it'. This probably means that Israel and its embassy in Nicosia were aware of the coup against pro-Arab Makarios.

21 Kissinger: *Years of Renewal*, p.206.

22 Boyatt's attitude during the Cyprus crisis has been described in detail in Costas Venizelos and Michalis Ignatiou, *Kissinger's Secret Archives: The Decision to Partition* (in Greek), (Athens, 2002). See also Kissinger, *Years of Renewal*: p.205. Among the six contingency scenarios outlined in the paper prepared by State Department officials, Thomas Boyatt and Richard Erdman, on 6 May 1974, were a) an attempted coup by pro-*enosis* forces in Cyprus and b) a mainland Greek putsch against Makarios. *FRUS*, Study prepared by the interdepartmental group for Near East and South Asia, 6 May 1974.

23 The telegram from Henry Tasca, US ambassador to Athens (24 June, number 3936), to the State Department shows that the American Embassy in Greece was aware of the danger of a coup against Makarios.

24 In telegram 1224 from Nicosia, 27 June, the Embassy agreed with Tasca about the gravity of the Greece/Cyprus situation and recommended that the USA, in approaching Ioannides, stress that after Makarios', 'Athens could have trouble with Soviets and Third World if it went after Makarios'. *FRUS*, Telegram from the Department of State to the Embassies in Greece and Cyprus, footnote 3, 29 June 1974.

25 *FRUS*, Telegram from the Embassy in Turkey to the Department of State, 17 July 1974 ('if intervention necessary, it will be "bloodier" the longer it is put off. Therefore, Government of Turkey not prepared to delay intervention beyond "few days"').

26 *FRUS*, Telegram from the Department of State to the Embassies in Greece and Cyprus, 29 June 1974 ('from various reports, it is evident that Ioannides is seriously considering way to topple Makarios from power').

27 Stern, Laurence, *The Wrong Horse: The Politics of Intervention and the Failure of American Diplomacy* (New York, 1977), p.94.

28 Attalides, Michael, *Cyprus. Nationalism and International Politics* (Edinburgh, 1979), p.166. The American involvement in the Nicosia coup is still being debated. The CIA had been actively involved both with the Greek junta and in funding anti-Makarios extremist groups.

29 Kissinger: *The Years of Renewal*, pp.210–12.

30 Asmussen, Ian, *Cyprus at War. Diplomacy and Conflict during the 1974 Crisis* (London and New York, 2008), p.292.

31 Bolukbasi, Suha, *The Superpowers and the Third World: Turkish–American Relations and Cyprus* (London and New York, 1988), pp.188–9.

32 Kissinger: *The Years of Renewal*, p.208.

33 Kissinger: *The Years of Renewal*, p.218.

34 A Turkish demand since 1957, which provided for the union of each of the two parts of the island with its motherland.

35 *FRUS*, transcript of telephone conversation between Kissinger and Schlesinger, 19 July 1974.

36 *FRUS*, transcript of telephone conversation between Kissinger and Colby, 19 July 1974.

37 Kissinger: *Years of Renewal*, p.229.

38 Venizelos and Ignatiou: *The Secret Archives of Kissinger*, pp.236–7.

39 Kazamias, George, *From Pragmatism to Idealism to Failure: Britain in the Cyprus Crisis of 1974*, GreeSE paper no. 42, Hellenic Observatory Papers on Greece and Southeast Europe (London, 2010), pp.13–14.

40 *FRUS*, Minutes of Meeting of the Washington Special Action Group, 21 July 1974.

41 Kissinger: *The Years of Renewal*, p.213.

42 Kissinger: *The Years of Renewal*, p.222.

43 For more on American – and British – policy toward the amount of territory that should be controlled by Turkey in Cyprus and on Kissinger's concept of the 'balance of forces' in the island see Kazamias, *From Pragmatism to Idealism*.

44 Audin, Mustafa, 'Determinants of Turkish Foreign Policy: Changing Patterns and Conjunctures during the Cold War', *Middle Eastern Studies* 36/1 (January 2000), p.124.

45 Bolukbasi: *The Superpowers*, p.119.

46 Bolukbasi: *The Superpowers*, pp.118–19.

47 Kazamias: *From Pragmatism to Idealism*, p.11.

48 *FRUS*, Minutes of meeting of Washington Special Actions Group, Washington, 22 July 1974. It should be noted that Kissinger had reached an 'understanding' with the Soviet leadership during his trip to Moscow in October 1973 and the successful negotiations on ending the 1973 Arab–Israeli war. See Israelyan, Victor, 'The October 1973 war: Kissinger in Moscow', *The Middle East Journal* 49/2 (1995), p.248–68.

49 *FRUS*, Minutes of meeting of Washington Special Actions Group, Washington, 14 August 1974.

50 *FRUS*, Memorandum of Conversation, 15 August 1974.

51 *FRUS*, Paper prepared in the Department of State, undated.

52 Stergiou, Andreas, 'Soviet Policy towards Cyprus', *The Cyprus Review* 19/2 (fall 2007), pp.96–8.

53 Venizelos and Ignatiou: *Kissinger's Secret Archives*; O'Malley and Craig: *The Cyprus Conspiracy*; Drousiotis, Makarios, *Cyprus 1974. Greek Coup and Turkish Invasion*, Peleus, vol.32 (Mannheim, 2006); Hitchens, Christopher, *The Trial of Henry Kissinger* (London and New York, 2002).

54 *FRUS*, memorandum of Conversation between Ford and Kissinger, 13 August 1974.

11 The Post-Cold War Legacies of US Realism

1 O'Malley, Brendan and Craig, Ian, *The Cyprus Conspiracy. America, Espionage and the Turkish Invasion* (London/New York, 1999), p.x. Another major work arguing for an American-led conspiracy is: Christopher Hitchens, *Hostage to History. Cyprus from the Ottomans to Kissinger* (London/New York, 1997).

2 The House of Commons, *Report from the Select Committee on Cyprus, together with the proceedings of the Committee, minutes of evidence and appendices, Session 1975–7* (London, 8 April 1976), p.ix.

3 NSC Interdepartmental Group for Near East and South Asia., Contingency Study for Cyprus, April 1974. Nixon Presidential Materials Staff, National Security Council Institutional ('H') Files, Meeting Files (1969–1974), Washington Special Action Group Meetings, WSAG Meetings Cyprus 18 July 1974 to WSAG [Cyprus] 23 July 1974, Box H-097.

4 See Asmussen, Jan, *Cyprus at War: Diplomacy and Conflict During the 1974 Crisis* (London, 2008); Asmussen, Jan, 'Poppies, Pistols and Intelligence: United States Policy towards Turkey in the 1970s', in P. McGreevy (ed.), *Liberty and Justice: America and the Middle East, Proceedings of the Second International Conference sponsored by the Center for American Studies and Research at American University of Beirut* (Beirut, 2008), pp.226–40.

5 Kalb, Martin and Kalb, Bernard, *Kissinger* (London, 1974), p.21.

6 Evans, Roland and Novak, Robert D., *Nixon in the White House, The Frustration of Power* (New York, 1971), p.11.

7 Hacke, Christian, *Zur Weltmacht verdammt. Die amerikanische Außenpolitik von Kennedy bis Clinton* (Berlin, 1997), p.120.

8 Bell, Coral, *The Diplomacy of Detente, The Kissinger Era* (London, 1977), p.38.

9 Hacke: *Zur Weltmacht verdammt*, p.121.

10 Hacke: *Zur Weltmacht verdammt*, p.124.

11 Kissinger, Henry A., 'Central Issues of American Foreign Policy' in K. Gordon (ed.), *Agenda for the Nation* (New York, 1969), p.611.

12 Schwabe, Klaus, *Weltmacht und Weltordnung. Amerikanische Außenpolitik von 1898 bis zur Gegenwart. Eine Jahrhundertgeschichte* (Paderborn, 2006), p.356.

13 Hacke: *Zur Weltmacht verdammt*, p.120.

14 Hacke: *Zur Weltmacht verdammt*, p.161.

15 Hacke: *Zur Weltmacht verdammt*, p.135.

16 Litwak, Robert S., *Détente and the Nixon Doctrine. American Policy and the Pursuit of Stability, 1969–1976* (Cambridge, 1984), p.1.

17 'Statement to Senate Committee on Foreign Relations 1975' quoted in Garthoff, Raymond L., *Détente and Confrontation, American Soviet Relations from Nixon to Reagan* (Washington, 1985), p.30.

18 Litwak: *Détente and the Nixon Doctrine*, p.153.

19 Kissinger speech titled 'Pragmatism and Moral Force in American Foreign Policy' delivered at the US Naval Academy on 5 June 1974, *Department of State Bulletin* LXXI, No. 1827.

20 Litwak: *Détente and the Nixon Doctrine*, p.3.

21 Asmussen: *Cyprus At War*, pp.3, 87, 177, 291.

22 Nixon, Richard M., *The Memoirs of Richard Nixon* (New York, 1978), p.654 passim, 790 passim, 1072 passim.

23 Hacke: *Zur Weltmacht verdammt*, p.163. See Woodward, Bob and Bernstein, Carl: *All the President's Men* (New York, 2005).

24 Hacke: *Zur Weltmacht verdammt*, p.162.

25 Garthoff, Raymont L., *Détente and Confrontation. American Soviet Relations from Nixon to Reagan* (Washington, 1985), p.409.

26 Kalb and Kalb: *Kissinger*, pp.506–7.

27 Kissinger, *Years of Upheaval* (London, 1982), pp.1111–23.

28 Garthoff: *Détente and Confrontation*, pp.410–11.

29 Bell: *The Diplomacy of Detente*, p.48.

30 Schmitz, David, *The United States and Right-Wing Dictatorships, 1965–1989* (Cambridge, 2006), p.121.

31 Schmitz: *The United States and Right-Wing Dictatorships*, p.142.

32 Interview with Oriana Fallaci in 1972 quoted in Bell: *The Diplomacy of Detente*, p.47.

33 Bell: *The Diplomacy of Detente*, p.47.

34 Bell: *The Diplomacy of Detente*, p.44–5.

35 Bell: *The Diplomacy of Detente*, p.45.

36 Kissinger: *Years of Upheaval*, pp.246–55, 979–98.

37 Litwak: *Détente and the Nixon Doctrine*, p.153.

38 Schwabe: *Weltmacht und Weltordnung*, p.378.

39 Szulc, Tad, *The Illusion of Peace, Foreign Policy in the Nixon Years* (New York, 1978), p.797.

40 Schmitz: *The United States and Right-Wing Dictatorships*, p.78.

41 Memorandum of Conversation, 11 April 1969, NSC, White House Central Files, Box 593, Nixon Presidential Materials Staff, National Archives at College Park, Maryland.

42 Schmitz: *The United States and Right-Wing Dictatorships*, p.80.

43 Presidential Determination 72–11, 17 February 1972, NSC, Presidential Determinations, Box 370, Nixon Materials.

44 Stoessinger, John G., *Henry Kissinger, The Anguish of Power* (New York, 1976), p.139.

45 Stoessinger: *Kissinger*, 143.

46 See Asmussen, Jan, 'Poppies, Pistols and Intelligence', pp.226–40.

47 Theodor Draper, for example, charged that Kissinger's warning to the Soviet Union vis-à-vis the Angolan crisis during his 23 December 1975 press conference was 'to détente what Prime Minister Chamberlain's reaction after 15 March 1939 had been to appeasement.' See Draper, Theodor, 'Appeasement and Détente,' in R. Conquest et al., *Defending America, Toward a New Role in the Post-Detente World* (New York, 1977), p.19.

48 Quoted in Bell: *The Diplomacy of Detente*, p.51.

49 Bell: *The Diplomacy of Detente*, p.32.

50 Litwak: *Détente and the Nixon Doctrine*, p.189.

51 Bell: *The Diplomacy of Detente*, p.32.

52   Kissinger, Henry, *A World Restored, The Politics of Conservatism in a Revolutionary Age* (New York, 1964), p.1.

53   Kissinger speech, Washington, 2 August 1973 quoted in *The Times*, 25 August 1973.

54   Statement to the Senate Foreign Relations Committee, Department of State Bulletin, 19 September 1974.

55   Kissinger, Henry A., *A World Restored, The Politics of Conservatism in a Revolutionary Era* (London, 1977), p.213.

56   Kissinger: *A World Restored*, p.325.

57   Schmitz: *The United States and Right-Wing Dictatorships*, p.73.

58   Johnson, Loch K., *A Season of Inquiry, The Senate Intelligence Investigation* (Lexington, 1985). pp.5–15.

59   Schmitz: *The United States and Right-Wing Dictatorships*, p.131.

60   US Government Printing Office, *Congressional Quarterly Almanac 32* (Washington, 1975), pp.304–307.

61   Schmitz: *The United States and Right-Wing Dictatorships*, p.134.

62   Schmitz: *The United States and Right-Wing Dictatorships*, pp.135–7.

63   Litwak: *Détente and the Nixon Doctrine*, p.194.

64   Burt, Richard, 'New Weapons Technologies, Debate and Direction', *Adelphi Papers*, N. 126, IISS (London, Summer 1976), pp.26–9.

65   Litwak: *Détente and the Nixon Doctrine*, p.148.

66   Litwak: *Détente and the Nixon Doctrine*, p.149.

67   Bell: *The Diplomacy of Detente*, p.23.

68   Fukuyama, Francis, *After the Neocons, America at the Crossroads* (London, 2006), p.34.

69   http://www.newamericancentury.org/statementofprinciples.htm.

70   Fukuyama: *After the Neocons*, p.ix.

71   Fukuyama: *After the Neocons*, p.8.

72   Fukuyama: *After the Neocons*, p.9.

73   Falk, Richard A., *The Declining World Order, America's Imperial Geopolitics* (New York, 2004), p.7.

74   Falk: *The Declining World Order*, p.15.

75   Falk: *The Declining World Order*, p.12.

76   Falk: *The Declining World Order*, pp.22–6.

77   Falk: *The Declining World Order*, p.40.

78   Kissinger, Henry, *Does America Need a Foreign Policy? Toward a Diplomacy for the 21st Century* (London, 2002), p.17.

79   Kissinger: *Does America Need a Foreign Policy?*, p.18.

80   Kissinger: *Does America Need a Foreign Policy?*, p.18.

81   Kissinger: *Does America Need a Foreign Policy?*, p.19.

12 The Fact-finding Missions of the Socialist International in the Middle East, 1974–1976

1   This article is an extended and revised version of Oliver Rathkolb, 'Brandt, Palme and Kreisky as Political Entrepreneurs: Social Democratic Networks in Europe's Policy towards the Middle East', in W. Kaiser, B. Leucht and M. Gehler (eds), *Transnational Networks in Regional Integration.Governing Europe 1945–83* (Basingstoke) pp.152–75.

2   For a biography of Brandt see Merseburger, Peter, *Willy Brandt, 1913–1992. Visionär und Realist* (Stuttgart, 2002); Schöllgen, Gregor, *Willy Brandt. Die*

Biographie (Berlin, 2001); Wein, Martin, *Willy Brandt. Das Werden eines Staatsmannes* (Berlin, 2001).

3   See also Sassoon, Donald, *One Hundred Years of Socialism. The West European Left in the Twentieth Century* (London, 2006) p.470; Günsche, Karl-Ludwig and Lantermann, Klaus, *Kleine Geschichte der Sozialistischen Internationale* (Bonn, 1997), p.143.

4   See also the annotated English edition of an abridged version of Kreisky's memoirs: Berg, Matthew Paul, Lewis, Jill and Rathkolb, Oliver (eds), *The Struggle for a Democratic Austria. Bruno Kreisky on Peace and Social Justice* (New York – Oxford, 2002), p.218 and p.435.

5   Lappenküper, Ulrich, 'Willy Brandt, Frankreich und die Ost-West-Beziehungen (1974–1990)', in H. Möller and M. Vaïsse (eds), *Willy Brandt und Frankreich* (Munich, 2005), p.239.

6   Brandt, Willy, *Bruno Kreisky und Olof Palme, Briefe und Gespräche 1972 bis 1975* (Frankfurt am Main – Cologne, 1975).

7   Roberts, Nancy and King, Paula, 'Policy Entrepreneurs: Their Activity, Structure and Function in the Policy Process', *Journal of Public Administration Research and Theory* vol.1/2 (1991), p.48.

8   Montville, Joseph V. and Davidson, W.D., 'Foreign Policy According to Freud', *Foreign Policy* no. 45 (Winter 1981–82), pp.145–57; Montville, Joseph V., *Transnationalism and the role of track-two diplomacy* (Washington D.C., 1991); McDonald, John W. and Bendahmane, Diane B. (eds), *Conflict resolution.Track two diplomacy* (Washington D.C., 1995).

9   For an overview see Wolleh, Oliver, *Die Teilung überwinden. Eine Fallstudie zur Friedensbildung in Zypern* (Berlin, 2002) p.24.

10 Thakur, Ramesh, Cooper, Andrew F. and English, John (eds), *International commissions and the power of ideas* (Tokyo, 2005).

11 Faulenbach, Bernd, 'Die Siebzigerjahre – ein Sozialdemokratisches Jahrzehnt?', *Archiv für Sozialgeschichte* vol.44 (2004), pp.1–37.

12 Rathkolb, Oliver, 'The Cancún Charade 1981: Lessons of History – A Pioneering Attempt at Global Management that Failed', in W. Hoppenstedt, R. Pruessen and O. Rathkolb (eds), *Global management* (Münster – Vienna, 2005), pp.61–70.

13 Silver, Arnold M., 'The New Face of the Socialist International', *Institutional Analysis* (The Heritage Foundation) 16, 19 October 1981, http://www.heritage. org/Research/PoliticalPhilosophy/IA16.cfm?renderforprint=1.

14 Salinger, Pierre, *Iran hostage crisis 1979–1981* (New York, 1981), p.250.

15 Johansson, Karl Magnus, *Transnational party alliances. Analysing the hard-won alliance between Conservatives and Christian Democrats in the European Parliament* (Lund, 1997). See also Kaiser, Wolfram, *Christian democracy and the origins of European Union* (Cambridge, 2007), Chapter 8.

16 Misgeld, Klaus, *Die 'Internationale Gruppe demokratischer Sozialisten' in Stockholm 1942–1945. Zu sozialistischen Friedensdiskussion während des Zweiten Weltkrieges* (Uppsala, Bonn-Bad Godesberg, 1976).

17 http://www.vidc.org/index.php?id=44.

18 For Palme's political objectives and assessments see O. Palme and F. Duve (eds), *Olof Palme. Er rührte an die Herzen der Menschen. Reden und Texte* (Reinbek, 1986). See also http://www.olofpalme.org/litteratur/.

19 http://www.time.com/time/magazine/article/0,9171,920549,00.html?promoid= googlep. Cf. also the memoirs of peace activists: http://www.kreisky.org/kreisky-forum/pdfs/2007/2007_02_27.pdf and, regarding these individuals, the highly

personal memoirs by Taufar, Barbara, *Die Rose von Jericho. Autobiographie* (Vienna, 1994).

20 Nonneman, Gerd, 'The Three Environments of Middle East Foreign Policy Making and Relations with Europe', in G. Nonneman (ed.), *Analyzing Middle East foreign policies and the relationship with Europe* (London, 2005), p.32.

21 Weingardt, Markus A., *Deutsche Israel- und Nahostpolitik. Die Geschichte einer Gratwanderung seit 1949* (Frankfurt am Main, 2001), p.231.

22 See *Akten zur Auswärtigen Politik der Bundesrepublik Deutschland 1975*, hrsg. im Auftrag des Auswärtigen Amts vom Institut für Zeitgeschichte. Bearbeitet von Michael Kieninger, Mechthild Lindemann und Daniela Taschler unter der wissenschaftlichen Leitung von Ilse Dorothee Pautsch, Munich: xx, 2006, footnote 3.

23 Besuch Rabin, 7 July 1975, 8. Archiv der sozialen Demokratie der Friedrich Ebert-Stiftung (AdsD), Bestand Helmut Schmidt Bundeskanzler, HSAA 007089.

24 Wolffsohn, Michael and Bokovoy, Douglas, *Israel. Grundwissen–Länderkunde. Geschichte–Politik–Gesellschaft–Wirtschaft* (Opladen, 1984), p.269.

25 See also Richardson, John P., 'Europe and the Arabs. A developing relationship', *The Link* vol.14/1 (1981): http://www.ameu.org/page.asp?iid=181&aid=226&pg=108.

26 *Ibid.*, p.272.

27 http://www.zeit.de/1981/06/Offener-Brief-von-Willy-Brandt-an-Lew-Kopelew.

28 Védrine, Hubert, *Les mondes de François Mitterrand* (Paris, 1996), pp.390–91.

29 See also the chapter entitled 'Kreisky, Israel und der Nahe Osten', in Gehler, Michael, *Österreichs Außenpolitik der Zweiten Republik. Von der alliierten Besatzung bis zum Europa des 21. Jahrhunderts*, vol.1 (Innsbruck – Vienna – Bozen, 2005), pp.388–402.

30 Raider, Mark A. (ed.), *Nahum Goldmann: Statesman Without a State* (Albany, 2010); Goldmann, Nahum, *Mein Leben als Deutscher Jude*, 1. Band der Autobiographie (München–Wien, 1980).

31 Patai, Raphael and Goldmann, Nahum, *His Missions to the Gentiles* (Tuscaloosa, 1987), pp.169–201.

32 Patai, Goldmann, pp.202–67.

33 See the summary in the historical Austria Presseagentur dossier: http://www.historisch.apa.at/cms/apa-historisch/dossier.html?dossierID=AHD_19700301_AHD0002; Thalberg, Hans, 'Die Nahostpolitik', in Bielka, E., Jankowitsch, P. and Thalberg, H. (eds), *Die Ära Kreisky. Schwerpunkte der österreichischen Außenpolitik* (Vienna – Munich – Zurich, 1983), pp.302–4.

34 First Mission, March 8–16, 1974, 6. Stiftung Bruno Kreisky Archiv (SBKA), Vienna, Reports of the Socialist International fact-finding missions to the Middle East.

35 Memorandum of conversation, Nixon, Kissinger, Scowcroft, Kreisky, Kirchschläger, 11 June 1974, http://www.fordlibrarymuseum.gov/library/document/memcons/1552720.pdf.

36 Spandauer Volksblatt, 10–11 December 1977, SBKA, Länderbox Bundesrepublik Deutschland 1.

37 Besuch 1978, Rede Kreisky, 13. SBKA, Länderbox Großbritannien.

38 Press conference 4 July 1978, 1, *ibid.*

39 See the relevant dossier entitled Nahostpolitik, SBKA.

40 Shafir, Shlomo, 'Nahum Goldmann and Germany', in Raider, Mark A. (ed.) *Nahum Goldmann: Statesman Without a State* (Albany NY, 2009), p.222.

41 Goldmann to Kreisky, 1 June 1977, in: SBKA, correspondence Goldmann-Kreisky.

42 Willy Brandt, Bonn, 4 November 1977, Archiv der sozialen Demokratie der Friedrich-Ebert-Stiftung in Bonn, Willy Brandt Archiv, A19, Folder 43. Additional material on this conference is in Folder 41.

43 Quoted after Röhrlich, Elisabeth, *Kreiskys Außenpolitik. Zwischen österreichischer Identität und internationalem Programm* (Göttingen, 2009) p.324.

44 *Ibid.*, p.309.

45 See his public statements, e.g. Goldmann, Nahum, 'True Neutrality for Israel', *Foreign Policy* vol.37 (1979/1980), pp.133–41.

46 *Der Spiegel*, 27 January 1975.

47 http://larouchepub.com/eiw/public/1979/eirv06n35–19790911/eirv06n35–19790911_033–camp_david_with_a_balkan_face.pdf.

48 Avnery, Uri, *My Friend, the Enemy* (Westport, Conn, 1986), p.148.

49 Goldmann, Nahum, *Mein Leben. USA–Europa–Israel.* 2. Band der Autobiographie (München–Wien, 1986), p.310.

50 Brandt, Willy, *Über Europa hinaus: Dritte Welt und Sozialistische Internationale,* Bernd, Rother and Wolfgang, Schmidt (eds), (Bonn, 1986), pp.9, 276–9.

51 *Ibid.*, p.548.

52 Goldmann: *Mein Leben*, p.306.

53 *Time Magazine*, 24 July 1978, http://www.time.com/time/printout/0,8816, 946860,00.html.

54 Ziv, Guy, *Hawk-to-dove foreign policy change. The case of Shimon Peres*, Paper, April 9, 2007, University of Maryland, http://www.bsos.umd.edu/gvpt/irworkshop/ziv.pdf.

55 Garfinkle, A.M., 'West European Peace Diplomacy in the Levant: But Will They Come?' in Beling, Willard A. (eds), *Middle East Peace Plans* (London, 1986), p.136.

56 Report by the Austrian ambassador to Kairo, Zl. 219 – Res/1980, 1 September 1980. SBKA, Prominentenkorrespondenz Thorn.

57 Richardson: *Europe and the Arabs*, p.4.

58 *Ibid.*, p.9.

59 *Ibid.*

60 *Akten zur auswärtigen Politik der Bundesrepublik Deutschland 1975*, p.899.

61 Bippes, Thomas, *Die europäische Nahostpolitik* (Frankfurt am Main – Vienna, 1987), pp.88, 185–6; Nouschi, André, *La France et le monde Arabe depuis 1962* (Paris, 1994), p.113.

62 Coghe, Samuël, *Die französische Nahostpolitik: Sprengstoff für die GASP?*, http://www.weltpolitik.net/texte/policy/israel/nahost_fr_gasp.pdf.

63 Richardson: *Europe and the Arabs*, p.9.

64 Conversation Schmidt-Khadam, 12 May 1975, AdsD, HSAA 007044.

65 See Kohl, Helmut, *Erinnerungen 1982–1990* (Munich, 2005), p.310.

66 Kreisky to Mitterrand, 6 July 1981, Mitterrand to Kreisky, 7 August 1981, SBKA, Länderbox Frankreich 2.

67 Weingardt: *Deutsche Israelpolitik*, p.309.

68 Minning, Silke M., *Der Dialog zwischen der israelischen Friedensbewegung und den palästinensischen Friedenskräften: Divergenzen und Konvergenzen 1973 – 1993* (Münster, 2005), p.28.

69 Brandt: *Erinnerungen*, p.448.

70 For further information on his multiple activities and contacts see http://israeli-palestinianpeace.org/issues/66toi.htm.

71 Sartawi to Kreisky, 7 April 1977, 2, SBKA, Sartawi-Korrespondenz.
72 *Ibid.*, to Kreisky, 14 December 1978, 4, *ibid.*
73 *Ibid.*, to Sartawi, 1 October 1980.
74 http://www.middleeast.org/mab.htm. Cf. the excerpts from the original decla-
     ration and Sartawi's reply: http://www.lyceepmf.com/pgs/pmf/pages/txts/txts6.
     htm.
75 Nasr, Kameel B., *Arab and Israeli terrorism. The causes and effects of political
     violence, 1936–1993* (Jefferson, NC, 1997), p.134.
76 http://www.kreisky.org/human.rights/deutsch/preisverleihungen.htm.
77 Henriksen Waage, Hilde, *Norwegians? Who needs Norwegians? Explaining the
     Oslo back channel: Norway's political past in the Middle East* (Oslo, 2006), foot-
     note 229.
78 Rabie, Mohamed, *US–PLO dialogue. Secret diplomacy and conflict resolution*
     (Jacksonville, 1995), pp.66–8.
79 Rabie: *US–PLO Dialogue*, reviewed by Saunders, Harold H., *Foreign
     Affairs*, vol.74/6 (November/December 1995), http://www.foreignaffairs.
     org/19951101fabook4716/mohamed-rabie/u-s-plo-dialogue-secret-diplomacy-
     and-conflict-resolution.html.
80 Richmond, Oliver P. and Carey, Henry F., *Subcontracting peace: the challenges of
     the NGO peacebuilding* (Aldershot, 2005), p.76.
81 http://www.zeit.de/1979/36/Arafats-Mann-in-Bonn.
82 Allen, David and Pijpers, Alfred (eds), *European foreign policy-making and the
     Arab–Israeli conflict* (Den Haag, 1994), p.236.

13 France, the European Community and the Maghreb, 1963–1976

1 Archive du Ministère des affaires étrangères et européennes, Paris, (ACMF),
    Papiers Wormser, dossier 31, Déclaration d'intention en vue de l'association à la
    CEE des pays indépendants appartenant à la zone franc. Conférence intergouver-
    nementale pour le Marché commun et l'Euratom-Acte final.
2 Archive of the European Commission (AEC), Bac 25/ 1980 N: 426/1, associa-
    tion de la CEE–Tunisie: rapport du Groupe de travail sur les questions appli-
    cables et aide-mémoire sur la situation économique de la Tunisie. Note sur le
    courrier de Bourguiba.
3 Archive of the Council of Ministers (ACM), CM2 1960 138, réunion restreinte
    du Comité des représentants permanents, Bruxelles.
4 AEC, fond CECA Haute Autorité, CEAB 5 N: 2173/2, association des pays
    et territoires d'outre-mer (PTOM) à la CEE: considération sur le futur régime
    d'association.
5 El Machat, Samya, *Les États-Unis et la Tunisie, de l'ambiguïté à l'entente, 1945–
    1959* (Paris, 1996), p.213; El Machat, Samya, *Les relations franco–tunisiennes,
    histoire d'une souveraineté arrachée 1955–1964* (Paris, 2005), p.254.
6 ACM, CM2 1963 899, demande d'ouverture de conversations exploratoires
    avec la CEE présentée par le Maroc, 14 décembre 1963. ACM, CM2 1963 900,
    demande du gouvernement tunisien, du 8 octobre 1963, d'ouverture des conver-
    sations exploratrices avec la CEE. ACM, CM2 1964 1347, lettre du gouverne-
    ment algérien du 18 décembre 1963 demandant l'ouverture de conversations sur
    les relations futures entre la CEE et l'Algérie et réponse du Conseil.
7 AEC, CEAB 5 – 1544/4, relation de la CEE avec les pays du Maghreb (1963–
    1966); conversations exploratoires au sujet des possibilités de conclusion d'un

accord entre la CEE et les pays du Maghreb et leurs incidences éventuel, le 14 décembre 1966.

8 AEC, BAC 144 1992–259, mandat en vue de l'ouverture des négociations avec la Tunisie et le Maroc, régime pour les produits agricoles, le 16 avril 1965.

9 *Ibid.*

10 AEC, G(65) 153, réunion du 18 mars 1965 du Comité des Représentants permanents.

11 AEC, BAC 7/1973 17, conclusion d'un accord d'association avec le Maroc et la Tunisie; réunions et rapports du Groupe de travail 'Maroc-Tunisie'; BAC 25/1980 400, association de la Tunisie aux Communautés européennes: texte et signature de l'accord d'association à Tunis, 28 mars 1969 avec les annexes et l'acte final.

12 Article 238: The Community can conclude with a third State, a union of States or an international organization, agreements creating an association character-ized by mutual rights and duties, actions in common and particular procedures. These agreements are concluded by the Council acting unanimously and after consultation of the Assembly. When these agreements imply amendments to the present Treaty, these last ones must be beforehand adopted according to the procedure planned in the article 236.

13 Grimaud, Nicole, *La Tunisie à la recherche de sa sécurité*, PUF (Paris, 1995). See also El Machat, *Etats Unis*, p.254.

14 Vaïsse, Maurice, *La Grandeur, politique étrangère de De Gaulle, 1958–1969* (Paris, 1998), p.727.

15 Archives of the National Foundation of the Political sciences (ANFP), Fonds Debré, 2 DE 21, lettre au ministre des Affaires étrangères, 3 mars 1960; see also Migani, Guia, *La France et l'Afrique sub-saharienne, 1957–1963. Histoire d'une décolonisation entre idéaux eurafricains et politique de puissance* (Bruxelles, 2008), p.196.

16 AEC, BAC 7/1973 N18/1, relations entre la CEE et l'Algérie, rapport au sujet des conversations exploratoires engagées avec l'Algérie (communication de M. Rey).

17 *Ibid.*

18 AEC, BAC 7/1973 N18/2, rapport au sujet des conversations exploratoires enga-gées avec l'Algérie, le 25 août 1964: 'La délégation française expose les relations entre la France et l'Algérie, à la demande de la Commission, le 24 juin 1964, p.42; AEC BAC 144/1922 948, travail du Groupe 'Algérie–Maroc–Tunisie' et ses délibérations concernant certains produits: fruits, légumes, vins, pommes de terre, figues, le 16 février 1966.

19 AEC, CEAB 1 N/402, communication de la Commission au Conseil sur les rela-tions entre la CEE et la Tunisie et le Maroc, le 9 février 1968.

20 AEC, BAC 144/1922 948, *ibid.*

21 AEC, BAC 12/1972 N2/1, compte rendu sur la visite à la Commission effec-tuée par une délégation algérienne, le 8 janvier 1968; communication de la Commission au Conseil.

22 AEC, BAC 38/1984 47, conversations exploratoires entre la CEE- le Maroc, la Tunisie et l'Algérie, le 12–14 juillet 1965; statistiques et régime des importations de vins en Italie et en République fédérale d'Allemagne.

23 AEC, BAC 7/1973 N/18.3, compte rendu sur la visite à la Commission effec-tuée par une délégation algérienne, le 8 janvier 1968 et communication de la Commission au Conseil, le 19 janvier 1968.

24 *Ibid.*

25 Historical Archives of the European Union (AHEU), EN 1510, compte-rendu sur les relations avec l'Algérie, sans date.

26 AHEU, EN 1510, idem.

27 Chneguir, Abdelaziz, *La politique extérieure de la Tunisie, 1956 à 1987* (Paris, 2004).

28 AEC, CEAB 5 N1545/2, réunion du Comité des Représentants Permanents du 5 juillet 1967 – Relations de la CEE avec les pays du Maghreb.

29 ACMF, direction Europe, 3828, note, 26 juin 1972.

30 AEC, BAC 86/2005 426: Négociations d'adhésion du Royaume-Uni, de l'Irlande, du Danemark et de la Norvège: relations entre la Communauté et l'Algérie, 1972.

31 Berstein, Serge, Milza, Pierre *Histoire de la France au XXe siècle (1958–1974)* (Bruxelles, 1999), pp.338–48.

32 *Ibid.*

33 Parlement européen, Rapport intérimaire fait au nom de la Commission des relations économiques extérieures sur la proposition de résolution présentée au nom du Groupe socialiste, sur la politique de la Communauté à l'égard des pays du Bassin méditerranéen, rapporteur: M. Westerterp, Bruxelles, 20 février 1969, Document de séance 221, PE 455/def, p.3 /BDT 173/1995, Dossier 1075 (boite 408). See also Berdat, Christophe, 'L'avènement de la politique méditerranéenne globale de la CEE', *Relations internationales*, n.130/2007, p.94.

34 AEC, BAC 28/1980–768, Rapport sur la politique commerciale de la Communauté dans le bassin méditerranéen. Rapporteur: M. Rossi, le 1er février 1971.

35 Berstein, Milza, *Histoire de la France au XXe siècle.*

36 AEC, dossier 906, Relations commerciales de l'Algérie: négociations d'un accord intérimaire CEE – Algérie; projet de texte, acte final (1970–1976).

37 AEC, dossier 906, Relations commerciales de l'Algérie, idem.

38 AEC, dossier 885, Relations commerciales des pays du Maghreb (Maroc, Tunisie, Algérie): communication de la Commission sur les relations de la CEE avec les pays du Maghreb; documents de référence de la Commission, aide-mémoire sur la situation économique desdits pays; propositions de règlements du Conseil et application de dispositions des Accords intérimaires avec les pays du Maghreb et leur prorogation (1971–1978).

14 Turkish Anti-Westernism

1 Eren, Nuri, *Turkey Today and Tomorrow: An Experiment in Westernization* (New York, 1963), p.246.

2 See Athanassopoulou, Ekavi, *Turkey. Anglo–American Security Interests 1945–1952: The First Enlargement of NATO* (London, 1999) and Harris, George S., *Troubled Alliance: Turkish American Problems in Historical Perspective, 1945–71* (Washington D.C., 1972).

3 Erogul, Cem, *Demokrat Parti* (Ankara, 1970), p.57 and Abou-El-Fadl, Reem, 'Turkey's Accession to NATO: Building a "Little America"' LSE Contemporary Turkish Studies 2nd Doctoral Dissertation Conference (1 May 2009), www2.lse.ac.uk/europeanInstitute/research/.../Paper%20RA.pdf.

4 İTÜÖB, *6. Filo Bekledigin Ekonomik Düzen Yurdumuzdan Kovulacaktır* (Istanbul, 1969).

5   In much the same way that incomplete and protracted assimilation of the German Jewry kept the debate among Jews open for centuries. See Sorkin, David, *The Transformation of German Jewry, 1780–1840* (Detroit, 1999).

6   Çalis, Saban, *Türkiye – Avrupa Birligi iliskileri* (Ankara, 2001), p.41.

7   Ergin, Feridun, *Cumhuriyet*, 24 September 1960.

8   Türkiye Ticaret Odası, *Discours Tenus a l'Occasion de la Signature de l'Accord Créant une Association Entre la Communauté Economique Européenne et la Turquie. 1963* (Ankara, 1963), p.11.

9   *Hürriyet*, 13 September 1963.

10 *Milliyet*, 13 September 1963.

11 *Aksam*, 13 September 1963.

12 Nursi, Said, *Emirdag Lahikası* (Istanbul, 1959) p.98. as quoted in Atatsoy, Yıldız, 'Islamic Revivalism and the Nation-State Project: Competing Claims for Modernity', *Social Compass* 44(1) 1997, pp.83–99.

13 Zaim, Sabahaddin, *Müsterek Pazar ve Türkiye* (Istanbul, 1970), p.17.

14 Milli Nizam Partisi, *Mecliste Ortak Pazar* (Izmir, 1971), p.55.

15 Birand, Mehmet Ali, *Türkiye'nin Büyük Avrupa Kavgası 1959–2004* (Istanbul, 2005), p.203. In Turkey, the *kapıcı* is a lower-class superintendent (usually a recent migrant from Eastern Anatolia) of the building who attends to the small tasks of the apartment (cleaning, trash collection, market shopping, etc.).

16 Aybar, Mehmet Ali, *Atatürk'ün Ölümünün 26ıncı Yıl Döneminde Verilen Konusma* (Ankara, 1964).

17 Aren, Sadun, *TIP Olaylari, 1961–1971* (Istanbul, 1993), pp.64–6.

18 Ecevit, Bülent, *Batının Bunalımı* (Ankara, 1975), p.29.

19 *Ibid.*, p.33.

20 Ülkü Ocaklar Birligi, *Ortak Pazara Hayir* (Ankara, 1970).

21 Erdogan, Mehmet, 'Muasır Medeniyet Oyunu', *Devlet*, 22 December 1969.

22 The OIC was set up in Rabat, Morocco, on September 25, 1969 in reaction to an arson attack against the Al-Aqsa Mosque on August 21, 1969. The primary goal of the OIC is, according to its Status, 'to consult together with a view to promoting close cooperation and mutual assistance in the economic, scientific, cultural and spiritual fields, inspired by teachings of Islam.' While Turkey was present at the initial meeting and has participated in every OIC gathering since its inception, it has never ratified any of the provisions of these meetings citing that these would contravene Turkey's constitutional requirement of secularism. For more information on Turkey and the OIC see Divanlıoglu, I., 'Islam Konferansları ve Türkiye', *Disisleri Bakanligi Disisleri Akademisi Dergisi*, (April 1972), pp.97–105 and Alpkaya, Gökçen, 'Türkiye Cumhuriyeti, Islam Konferanslı Örgütü ve Laiklik' *Siyasal Bilgiler Fakültesi Dergisi*, vol. 46/1–2, 1999, pp.55–68.

23 See Ahmad, Feroz, *The Turkish Experiment in Democracy: 1950–1975* (London, 1977), pp.421–3, Çalis, *Türkiye – Avrupa Birligii Iliskileri*, p.173; Aryeh, Shmuelevitz, *Republican Turkey: Aspects of Internal and External Affairs* (Istanbul, 1999), p.68–71. *The Economist* also seemed to support this view: 'In Search of Friends', *The Economist*, 5 June 1978.

15 The Distant Neighbours

1   Ayubi, Nazih (ed.), *Distant Neighbours: The Political Economy of Relations between Europe and the Middle East/North Africa* (Reading, 1995), pp.23–6.

2   Berend, Ivan T., *Storia economica dell'Europa nel XX secolo* (Milano, 2008)
     pp.300–5; Maier, Charles S., 'Malaise: The Crisis of Capitalism in the 1970s', in
     N. Ferguson, C.S. Maier, E. Manela (eds), *The Shock of the Global: The 1970s in
     Perspective* (Cambridge, 2010), p.25.

3   See Varsori, Antonio (ed.), *Alle origini del presente*. *L'Europa occidentale nella crisi
     degli anni Settanta* (Milano, 2007); Romano, Angela, *From Détente in Europe to
     European Détente: How the West Shaped the Helsinki CSCE* (Bern, 2009).

4   Historical Archives of the European Union (HAEU), EN-1928, Commission,
     Direction générale des relations extérieures, *Actions que pourrait entreprendre la
     Communauté pour contribuer à la solution des problèmes économiques du Moyen-Orient*,
     July 16, 1969; Vassiliou, George, 'Trade Agreements between the EEC and the Arab
     Countries of the Eastern Mediterranean and Cyprus' in Shlaim, A., Yannopoulos,
     G.N. (eds), *The EEC and the Mediterranean Countries* (Cambridge, 1976) p.205.

5   Both of these are the basic features of European-based *modernity*, namely, the
     nation-state and industrial capitalism. See, Berger, Marc T., *The Battle for Asia:
     From Decolonization to Globalization* (London, 2004). See also note 33.

6   HAEU, KM-39, Commission, Dossier, *Dialogue euro-arabe*, Bruxelles, July 12,
     1974, Klaus Meyer. See Calandri, Elena, 'L'eterna incompiuta: la politica medi-
     terranea tra sviluppo e sicurezza', in Calandri, Elena (ed.), *Il primato sfuggente:
     L'Europa e l'intervento per lo sviluppo (1957–2007)* (Milano, 2009), pp.89–117.

7   See Richards, Alain, Waterbury, John, *A Political Economy of the Middle East*
     (Boulder, 1998), p.212.

8   Regarding diplomacy, a major watershed took place during the Arab League
     conference in Khartoum in August 1967 where pro-Western conservative states,
     like Saudi Arabia, set out the basics of the Arab compromise: '*No to Israel, Yes to
     the West*', the latter being the mediator and main partner at the expense of the
     socialist bloc. See Corm, Georges, *Le Proche-Orient éclaté, 1956–2006* (Paris,
     2006), pp.302–7; Hinnebush, Raymond, *The International Politics of the Middle
     East* (Manchester, 2003), pp.29–32.

9   Cleveland, William L., *A History of the Modern Middle East* (Boulder, 2000),
     pp.322, 363, 386.

10   HAEU, BAC 28/1980, n.886, Comité économique et social, Dossier n.30/
     RKT, *Annexe au Rapport de la séction des rélations extérieures sur la 'politique
     de la Communauté dans le bassin méditerranéen'*, Bruxelles, January 16, 1975;
     The inward-looking development strategy focused on the domestic market as a
     source of accumulation and growth whereas the outward-looking one focused
     on production for export in order to enhance capital accumulation and develop-
     ment. The latter was successful among the so-called *Asian tigers* and banked on
     the growing delocalization of production processes from the First World to the
     developing countries. For the single countries, see Owen, Roger, Pamuk, Sevket,
     The Middle East Economies in the Twentieth Century (London, 1998).

11   Beinin, Joel, *Workers and Peasants in the Modern Middle East* (Cambridge, 2001),
     p.142; Rivier, François, 'Rente pétrolière et politiques industrielles des États non
     pétroliers: Egypte, Jordanie, Liban, Syrie' in A. Bourgey (ed.), *Industrialisation et
     changements sociaux dans l'Orient arabe* (Beirut, 1982), pp.71–8.

12   For Egypt and Syria see Adamsky, Dima P, 'Zero-Hour for the Bears: Inquiring
     into the Soviet Decision to Intervene in the Egyptian–Israeli War of Attrition,
     1969–70', *Journal of Cold War Studies*, vol.6/1 (2006), pp.113–36; Trentin,
     Massimiliano, 'Modernization as State-Building. The Two Germanys in Syria,
     1963–1972', *Diplomatic History*, vol.33/3, (2009).

13   Shlaim, Avi, *The Iron Wall: Israel and the Arab World* (New York, 2000), pp.283–6. See also Perthes, Volker, *The Political Economy of Syria Under Assad* (London, 1997), pp.118, 224.

14   HAEU, BAC 28/1980, n.886, Comité économique et social, dossier n.30/ RKT, *Annexe au Rapport de la séction des relations extérieures sur la politique de la Communauté dans le bassin méditerranéen*, Bruxelles, 16 janvier 1975.

15   HAEU, KM-39, Commission, DGVIII, *Relation de la CEE avec les pays du bassin méditerranéen et du Moyen-Orient*, January 27, 1974. See Calandri: 'L'eterna incompiuta', pp.106–7.

16   HAEU, BAC28/1980, n.886, Conseil, aide-mémoire, *Approche globale méditerranéenne. Adoption des mesures d'organisation de marché auxquelles se trouvent subordonnées les concessions agricoles*, April 21, 1975; Vassiliou, George: 'Trade Agreements' p.209.

17   HAEU, BAC28/1980, n.886, Le Conseil, *Décision*, Annexe I, Bruxelles, December 20, 1975. As for the texts of the Agreements, see http://ec.europa.eu/ world/agreements.

18   HAEU, CPPE 001458, Parlement européen, Commission des rélations économiques extérieures, *Rapport sur des projets de règlement du Conseil (doc. 89/77) portant conclusion des accords de coopération entre la Communauté économique européenne et la République Arabe d'Egypte, la Royaume Hachémite de Jordanie, la République Arabe de Syrie*, Strasbourg, 11 Mai, 1977, M. J-F. Pintat. Regarding the establishment of *joint-ventures*, the European proposals did not differ from those of the Socialist camp: Trentin, Massimiliano, *Engineers of Modern Development: East German Experts in Ba'thist Syria, 1965–1972* (Padua, 2010) pp.37, 45.

19   HAEU, CPPE 001458, Parlement européen, Commission des relations économiques extérieures, *Rapport, Avis de la Commission du développement et de la coopération*, Strasbourg, 11 Mai, 1977, M. M. Fioret.

20   See note 18.

21   However, some European countries supported this option while others, such as West Germany and Italy, resisted, respectively HAEU, KM-40, HAEU, KM-39, Communautés européennes, Commission, *Note à l'attention de M. de Sedoui*, Bruxelles, January 15, 1975, Klaus Meyer; and BAC28/1980, n.886, Comité économique et social, dossier n.30/RKT, *Avis de la séction des relations extérieures sur la politique de la Communauté dans le bassin méditerranéen*, January 16, 1975.

22   HAEU, BEI-19, *Rapport annuel, 1976*, Luxembourg, 1 Avril, 1977; BEI-20, *Rapport annual 1977*, Luxembourg, April 21, 1977.

23   HAEU, BEI, 'The role of the Bank in the Community's Mediterranean Policy', *BEI Information*, n.9, 1977, pp.6–8.

24   For the interplay among the Cold War, the Mediterranean and the Middle East, see Khalidi, Rashid, *Sowing Crisis: The Cold War and American Dominance in the Middle East* (Boston, 2009), pp.1–39; Di Nolfo, Ennio, 'The Cold War and the Transformations of the Mediterranean' in Leffler, Melvyn, Westad O. Arne (eds), *The Cambridge History of the Cold War*, Vol.II (Cambridge, 2010), pp.238–57.

25   The EEC even departed from the provision of non-discrimination among contracting parties because the Arab states wished to maintain their boycott of companies dealing with Israel. However, in this case, the EEC Commission accepted the Arab demand as it was widely known that the boycott was not implemented even in the states advocating it, see reference in note 19 and HAEU, KM-39, Commission, *Note à l'attention de Monsieur M.B. Krohn*,

Directeur général pour Développement et Coopération, 'Visite de M. Cheysson en Jordanie, le 31 Mai, 1975. Accord à conclure entre la CEE et la Jordanie', Bruxelles, June 3, 1975. See also, Fischer, Stanley, Rodrik, Dani and Tuma, Elias (eds), *The Economics of Middle East Peace: Views from the Region* (Cambridge Mass., 1993), pp.14–9.

26 See Batatu, Hanna *The Egyptian, Syrian, and Iraqi Revolutions: Some Observations on Their Underlying Causes and Social Character* (London, 1984); Rivier: 'Rente pétrolière', pp.118–23.

27 HAEU, BAC28/1980, n.886, Council, Décision, annexe, liste n.1, 20 décembre 1975; CPPE 001458, Parlement européen, Commission des relations économiques extérieures, 'Rapport, Avis de la Commission de l'Agriculture', May 11, 1977. See also the archives of the UN Economic and Social Commission for Western Asia (ECSWA), E/ECWA/NR/SEM/1.12, Kubursi, Ahmad, 'Induced Innovation and the Role of Agriculture in Economic Development. A Case Study of Egypt and Syria', October 10–14, 1977.

28 HAEU, BAC28/1980, n.884, Council, *Rapports des conseillers commerciaux des pays de la CEE en République arabe d'Egypte (32ème rapport)*, Bruxelles, May 26, 1977. See Balcet, Giovanni, *Industrializzazione, multinazionali e dipendenza tecnologica. L'esperienza dei Paesi arabi esportatori di petrolio* (Torino, 1980), pp.73–6.

29 HAEU, KM-43, Commission, Note à l'attention M. Marekamp, M. Cheysson, M. Davignon, *Dialogue euro–arabe. Convention euro–arabe sue la promotion et la protéction des investissements*, Bruxelles, February 14, 1977, Klaus Meyer; HAEU, Commission, Document interne, *Interruption et relance du Dialogue euro–arabe*, Bruxelles, December 18, 1980; Calandri, 'L'eterna incompiuta', pp.109–10.

30 HAEU, BAC28/1980, n.884, Council, *Rapports des conseillers commerciaux des pays de la CEE en République arabe d'Egypte (31ème rapport)*, Bruxelles, January 6, 1977; ECSWA, EN/ECWA/NR/SEN.1/25, *Development of Industrial Technology through Specialized Centres*, October 10, 1977, p.15.

31 Contention over this issue was temporarily frozen as soon as the 'bread revolts' threatened the Egyptian and Jordanian regimes in late 1977–8, see Harrigan, Jane, El-Said, Jane R. *Aid and Power in the Arab World: World Bank and IMF Policy-Based Lending in the Middle East and North Africa* (Basingstoke, 2006), pp.10–2; Pioppi, Daniela, 'Il legame tra liberalizzazione economica e liberalizzazione politica nel mondo arabo', in F. Bicchi, L. Guazzone and D. Pioppi (eds) *La questione della democrazia nel Mondo Arabo: Stati, società e conflitti* (Milano, 2004), pp.101–19.

32 HAEU, EN-120, Commission, DGVIII, *Rapport annuel sur la situation économique de la Commuanuté: Proposition de la Commission au Conseil*, Bruxelles, October 20, 1977. Also Khader, Bikhara, 'Euro–Arab Trade Relations', in N. Ayubi, *Distant Neighbours*, pp.23–6; Hershlag, Z.-Y. 'Industrialisation in Arab Countries' in R. Aliboni (ed.), *Arab Industrialisation and Economic Integration* (London, 1979), p.73.

33 Gelvin, James L., *The Modern Middle East: A History* (Oxford, 2005), pp.69–88, 231; Tibi, Bassam, *Arab Nationalism: Between Islam and the Nation-State* (London, 1997), pp.21–3.

34 Thobie, Jacques, *Ali et les 40 voleurs* (Paris, 1985), pp.12–18; Owen, Roger, *The Middle East in the World Economy 1800–1914* (London, 2002), pp.83, 287.

35 Corm: *Le Proche-Orient éclaté*, p.303; Rist, Gilbert, *Le développement: Histoire d'une croyance occidentale* (Paris, 1996), p.234.

36   Gilpin, Robert, *The Challenge of Global Capitalism: The World Economy in the 21st Century* (Princeton, 2000), pp.218–20; Glyn, Andrew, *Capitalism Unleashed: Finance, Globalization, and Welfare* (Oxford, 2006), pp.53–4.

37   Amin, Samir, El Kenz, 'Ali, *Le monde arabe. Enjeux sociaux et perspectives méditerranéennes* (Paris, 2003), pp.6–12, 80, 124.

38   Arrighi, Giovanni, Zhang, Lu, 'Dopo il neoliberismo. Il nuovo ruolo del Sud del mondo', in G. Cesarale, M. Pianta (eds), *Capitalismo e (Dis)ordine mondiale* (Roma, 2010), pp.182–9.

16 Alignment and Terrorism in Gaddafi's Libya

1   Cricco, Massimiliano and Cresti, Federico, *Gheddafi. I volti del potere* (Roma, 2011), pp.79–81.

2   The National Archives, London (hereafter, TNA), FCO 93/605, 'Report from Ministry of Defence to R. L. Bucknell: "Libya: Arms purchases from Soviet Bloc"', London, June 1975.

3   International terrorist organization (ANO) founded by Sabri al-Banna (alias Abu Nidal). Split from PLO in 1974. With the complicity of Libyan intelligence, Abu Nidal carried out his most infamous operation: the simultaneous attacks on Israel's El Al ticket counter at Leonardo Da Vinci International Airport in Rome and on passengers in Vienna International Airport waiting to check in to a flight to Tel Aviv (December 27, 1985). See: Seale, Patrick, *Abu Nidal: A Gun for Hire: The Secret Life of the World's Most Notorious Arab Terrorist* (New York, 1992).

4   Simons, Geoff, *Libya and the West: From Independence to Lockerbie* (London, 2003), p.125.

5   Declassified Documents Reference System, Gale Group, 2009 (hereafter, DDRS), CIA, FBIS Special Memorandum, *Quotations from Qadhafi on Terrorism*, Washington D.C., December 9, 1981.

6   Ilich Ramírez Sánchez, alias 'Carlos the Jackal', Venezuelan terrorist who, in the early 1970s became a member of the Popular Front for the Liberation of Palestine. He obtained asylum in Libya after the attack on the OPEC headquarters in Vienna, on December 20, 1975. See Yallop, David A., *Tracking the Jackal: The Search for Carlos, the World's Most Wanted Man* (New York, 1993).

7   TNA, FCO 93/1384, HM Ambassador at Tripoli, Williams, to the Secretary of State for Foreign and Commonwealth Affairs: *Understanding Qadhafi's Foreign Policies*, Tripoli, November 13, 1978, conf.

8   Simons: *Libya and the West*, pp.123–4.

9   *Ibid.*, p.124.

10   *Ibid.*, pp.124–5.

11   The Jamahiriya or 'Libyan Arab Jamahiriya' (Arabic, meaning 'State of the masses') was the new kind of statehood of Libya from 1977, inspired by the political philosophy of Gaddafi, according to which the Libyan leader no longer holds public office, but retains the honorific title of *Qa'id*, meaning the 'Guide of the September 1st Great Revolution of the Socialist People's Libyan Arab Jamahiriya'. See Cricco, Cresti: *Gheddafi*, pp.65–75.

12   TNA, FCO 93/1384, HM Ambassador at Tripoli, Williams, to the Secretary of State for Foreign and Commonwealth Affairs: *Understanding Qadhafi's Foreign Policies*, Tripoli, November 13, 1978, conf.

13   DDRS, CIA, FBIS Special Memorandum, *Quotations from Qadhafi on Relations with the Soviet Union*, Washington D.C., December 16, 1981, secr.

14   *Ibid.*

15   St John, Ronald Bruce, 'Redefining the Libyan revolution: the changing ideology of Muammar al-Qaddafi', *The Journal of North African Studies*, vol.13/1 (2008), p.96.

16   Carter Library, NLC-6-51-7-9-3, Central Intelligence Agency, National Foreign Assessment Center Memorandum: *US Relations with the Radical Arabs*, Washington D.C., December 7, 1979, secr.

17   St John: 'Redefining the Libyan revolution', pp.96–7.

18   Simons: *Libya and the West*, p.126.

19   DDRS, CIA, FBIS Special Memorandum, *Quotations from Qadhafi on Relations with the Soviet Union*, Washington D.C., December 16, 1981, secr.

20   The Libya–Chad war (1978–1987) was an unconventional conflict between Libyan and Chadian forces. The conflict was marked by a series of Libyan interventions in Chad, in 1978, 1979, 1980–1981 and 1983–1987. On all these occasions, Gaddafi supported some factions participating in the civil war, while Libya's opponents obtained French support. The main reason behind Gaddafi's involvement in Chad was his intention to annex the Aouzou Strip, the northern part of Chad, in the Sahara and rich in uranium deposits. See Azevedo, Mario J., *The Roots of Violence: A History of War in Chad* (London, 1998).

21   DDRS, *NSC Meeting to discuss US policy toward Libya*, Washington, May 22, 1981, secr./sens.

22   *Ibid.*

23   DDRS, NSC *Memorandum for the Vice-President on US policy toward Libya*, Washington, June 5, 1981, secr.

24   DDRS, Interagency Intelligence Assessment: *Ramifications of US Naval exercise in the Gulf of Sidra*, Washington, August 10, 1981, top-secr. umbra.

25   Cricco, Massimiliano, *The United States and the Soviet Union: From the Rise of Qadhafi to Ronald Reagan's Policy of Pressure*, in Massimiliano Guderzo and Bruna Bagnato (eds), *The Globalization of the Cold War: Diplomacy and Local Confrontation, 1975–85* (London, 2009), pp.55–70.

26   DDRS, *NSC Memorandum for John M. Poindexter: Oval Office Discussion of Libya*, Washington, April 10, 1986.

27   Simons: *Libya and the West*, p.127.

28   DDRS, *CIA, Intelligence analysis of Libyan Head of State Muammar al Qadhafi's political position following the US air strike against that country*, Washington, July 17, 1986. secr.

Index